THE SURVIVAL OF THE
HESSIAN NOBILITY,

1770–1870

GREGORY W. PEDLOW

The Survival of the
Hessian Nobility
1770–1870

PRINCETON UNIVERSITY PRESS

Copyright © 1988 by Princeton University Press
Published by Princeton University Press, 41 William Street,
Princeton, New Jersey 08540
In the United Kingdom: Princeton University Press, Guilford, Surrey

Library of Congress Cataloging in Publication Data will be
found on the last printed page of this book

ISBN 0–691–05503–3

Publication of this book has been aided by the Whitney Darrow
Fund of Princeton University Press
This book has been composed in Janson Linotron

Clothbound editions of Princeton University Press books
are printed on acid-free paper, and binding materials are
chosen for strength and durability. Paperbacks, although satisfactory
for personal collections, are not usually suitable for library rebinding

Printed in the United States of America by Princeton University Press,
Princeton, New Jersey

To J. Watson Pedlow
and the Memory of
Marion Wick Pedlow

CONTENTS

LIST OF ILLUSTRATIONS

ix

LIST OF TABLES

ACKNOWLEDGMENTS

The original research on the social and economic history of the Hessian nobility was made possible by a grant from the German Academic Exchange Service in the years 1975–77. Support for additional research to add material not contained in the dissertation, in particular on the political activities of the nobility, was provided by the Institut für Europäische Geschichte in Mainz, the German Academic Exchange Service, and the Research Council of the University of Nebraska. This research was conducted in 1980 and the summers of 1981, 1982, 1983, and 1985.

For assistance rendered at various stages in the creation of this book I would like to thank Professors Vernon Lidtke, Mack Walker, and Robert Forster of the Johns Hopkins University; Professor Helmut Berding of the University of Giessen and his former colleague Professor Volker Press, now at the University of Tübingen; Professor Karl Otmar Freiherr von Aretin and Dr. Ralph Melville of the Institut für Europäische Geschichte; Professor Helmut Seier and his doctoral students at the University of Marburg; Professor Charles Ingrao of Purdue University; Professor Gerald Soliday of the University of Texas at Dallas; and the staff of the Hessian State Archive in Marburg, in particular Dr. Uta Löwenstein. I would also like to mention the cooperation of many present-day members of the Hessian nobility, in particular Dr. Raban von der Malsburg-Escheberg, Frau Friederike Elsner von Gronow, Herr Sigismund Freiherr Waitz von Eschen, Herr Friedrich von Löwenstein, and the late Dr. Alexander Freiherr von Dörnberg. I am very grateful to Sue Joyce for help in preparing the illustrations, and to the staff of Princeton University Press for editorial assistance.

Finally I would like to thank my wife, Gabriele, for all her support during the many years that went into this book. Our marriage and our children, Christopher and Stephanie—not this book—are the most important result of my years in Germany.

ABBREVIATIONS

ADB   *Allgemeine deutsche Biographie*
ARSK   Archiv des ritterschaftlichen Stiftes Kaufungen
HLO   Hessische Landes-Ordnungen (*Sammlung fürstlich hessischen Landes-Ordnungen*)
LTV   Landtags-Verhandlungen (*Verhandlungen des kurhessischen Landtags*)
StAM   Staatsarchiv Marburg

THE SURVIVAL OF THE
HESSIAN NOBILITY,
1770–1870

INTRODUCTION

Long after the end of the ancien régime in Germany the leading social order of that era, the nobility, continued to play a vital role in German social, economic, and political life. Throughout the nineteenth century most top officials of the army and bureaucracy came from the nobility, and many members of the German bourgeoisie tried to emulate what they saw as the "aristocratic" way of life by buying estates, joining student fraternities, or becoming reserve officers. Furthermore, noble land-owners remained a powerful economic force and exercised considerable political power through the Conservative party and pressure groups such as the Agrarian League.

If German society had undergone little change during the nineteenth century, the nobility's continued importance would easily be under-standable. But the nineteenth century had actually witnessed the con-stant erosion of the foundations for the nobility's dominant position dur-ing the ancien régime. In a series of reforms that began during the Napoleonic era and continued throughout the nineteenth century, no-bles lost virtually all of their legal and financial privileges. An even more important change was the end of the traditional agrarian system. The entire economic base of many noble families was placed in jeopardy when landlords lost the right to collect seigneurial dues and services from peasants. Nobles' traditional predominance in government offices also came under fire in the nineteenth century as qualifications, not so-cial origins, began to determine who was hired and promoted. Further-more, nobles faced increased competition for positions in government service as more and more members of the bourgeoisie sought to enter the bureaucracy and officer corps. Finally, in many German states the po-litical power of the nobility was weakened by liberal reforms that ended or reduced nobles' traditional rights of representation.

To understand how the leading social order of the ancien régime con-tinued to play such a prominent role in Germany throughout the nine-teenth century despite tremendous social, economic, and political change, historians must study the ways in which nobles reacted to change in all of these areas. Such studies are best conducted on a re-gional basis in order to examine in detail changes in demographic struc-ture, landownership, income, occupation, and political power. Fur-thermore, the size, wealth, and traditions of nobilities fluctuated considerably from state to state within Germany, so regional studies are

3

necessary to understand the variations within the nobility and thus avoid problems of oversimplification.

Regional studies of the nobilities of western and southern Germany are particularly valuable because, until recently, historians who have studied the German nobility in the nineteenth century have tended to focus on Prussia, the largest and most prosperous state.[1] As a result the East Elbian Junker has become virtually a stereotype for the German noble in the nineteenth century, even though much of Germany had economic and social systems that differed considerably from those of Prussia. The continued strength of the Prussian nobility in the nineteenth century is well documented, but what about the nobilities of western and southern Germany? As owners of estates much smaller than those in Prussia, which made them heavily dependent on peasant dues and services, were these nobles devastated by the reforms of the nineteenth century, as some historians have suggested?[2]

Studying the nobility is important not only to determine the reasons for the survival or decline of that elite; the history of the nobility is

[1] All surveys of the European nobility in the eighteenth and nineteenth centuries deal only with Prussia in their discussion of the German nobility: Albert Goodwin, ed., *The European Nobility in the Eighteenth Century* (London, 1953); Rudolf Vierhaus, ed., *Der Adel vor der Revolution: Zur sozialen und politischen Funktion des Adels im vorrevolutionären Europa* (Göttingen, 1971); Jean Meyer, *Noblesses et pouvoirs dans l'europe d'ancien régime* (Paris, 1973); David Spring, ed., *European Landed Elites in the Nineteenth Century* (Baltimore, 1977). Many works on the German nobility also focus solely on the Prussian Junker: Walter Görlitz, *Die Junker: Adel und Bauer im deutschen Osten*, 3d ed. (Limburg, 1964); Friedrich Wilhelm von Oertzen, *Junker: Preußischer Adel im Jahrhundert des Liberalismus* (Oldenburg, 1939); Lysbeth Walker Muncy, *The Junker in the Prussian Administration under William II, 1889–1914* (Providence, 1944); Hans Rosenberg, *Bureaucracy, Aristocracy, and Autocracy: The Prussian Experience, 1660–1815* (Cambridge, Mass., 1958); Ernest K. Bramsted, *Aristocracy and the Middle Classes in Germany: Social Types in German Literature, 1830–1900*, 2d ed. (Chicago, 1964); Fritz Martiny, *Die Adelsfrage in Preußen vor 1806 als politisches und soziales Problem, erläutert am Beispiele des kurmärkischen Adels* (Stuttgart, 1938); Nikolaus von Preradovich, *Die Führungsschichten in Österreich und Preußen (1804–1918)* (Wiesbaden, 1955); Robert M. Berdahl, "Prussian Aristocracy and Conservative Ideology: A Methodological Examination," *Social Science Information* 15 (1976): 583–99; idem., "Conservative Politics and Aristocratic Landholders in Bismarckian Germany," *Journal of Modern History* 44 (1972): 1–20. In recent decades there have been a number of important studies of noble groups outside the Prussian Junkers, in particular the imperial knights in the eighteenth century and the mediatized princes in the nineteenth (see below, chapter 2, notes 7 and 18). The most important new work on a non-Junker nobility is Heinz Reif's massive study of the Catholic nobility of Westphalia, *Westfälischer Adel, 1770–1860: Vom Herrschaftsstand zur regionalen Elite* (Göttingen, 1979).

[2] Werner Wittich, "Epochen der deutschen Agrargeschichte," *Grundriß der Sozialökonomik* 7 (1922): 21–22; Friedrich Luetge, *Geschichte der deutschen Agrarverfassung vom frühen Mittelalter bis zum 19. Jahrhundert* (Stuttgart, 1963), 226.

closely related to many significant problems in German social and economic history. The effects of the agrarian reforms of the nineteenth century are particularly important, because large amounts of capital came into the hands of former landlords at a time when Germany was beginning to industrialize. How did landlords utilize this capital? Did any of it contribute to the process of industrialization? Even less is known about the extent of direct participation by nobles in industry as entrepreneurs.[3]

Research on the nobility can also provide important information about demographic changes and the history of the family. Many important developments in these areas started in the upper classes before becoming common in the population as a whole, but demographic studies in Germany have virtually ignored the nobility.[4] Analysis of demographic changes within the nobility can not only provide useful comparisons with other European elites and with the lower classes but also reveal important characteristics of the nobility itself, such as attempts to limit population growth by placing restraints upon marriage or family size. The amount of growth within the nobility is in turn closely related to matters such as landownership, family settlements, and occupations.

The political activities of the nobility are also an important area for study. Nobles are generally assumed to have been strongly conservative, but in reality they often held a wide range of political views. How did nobles react to the loss of traditional rights and privileges and the pressure for even more liberal reforms in the nineteenth century? Was there any cooperation between noble and bourgeois deputies in the legislature? How much of its former privileged position was the nobility able to retain?

The present study of Hesse-Kassel attempts to answer all of these questions for a region that combines elements of both western and southern Germany, thanks to its central location. The small and not particularly prosperous Hessian nobility seemed likely to be highly vulnerable to massive social, economic, and political change, and when I began

---

[3] Contacts between German nobles and industrialists are discussed in Wolfgang Zorn, "Unternehmer und Aristokratie in Deutschland," *Tradition* 8 (1963): 241–54. For the industrial activities of other European nobilities see Guy Richard, *Noblesse d'affaires au XVIIIe siècle* (Paris, 1974); Fritz Redlich, "Europäische Aristokratie und wirtschaftliche Entwicklung," in *Der Unternehmer: Wirtschafts- und sozialgeschichtlichen Studien* (Göttingen, 1964), 280–98.

[4] Reif's *Westfälischer Adel* provides considerable insight into the history of the noble family, but the book's demographic information is presented in a format that makes comparison with other elites difficult.

the research on this study, I suspected that I would be chronicling the "decline and fall" of the Hessian nobility. But as the chapters that follow will show, Hessian nobles demonstrated a mixture of flexibility and conservatism that enabled them to survive the turmoil of the nineteenth century surprisingly well.

· 1 ·

HESSE-KASSEL:
LAND AND POLITICS

If you place your finger right in the middle of a map of the present-day Federal Republic of Germany, you will discover the location of the Electorate of Hesse-Kassel, a medium-sized German state that disappeared from the map of Europe over a century ago. Although Hesse-Kassel became the center of attention in Germany on at least two occasions—during the late eighteenth century as the source for mercenaries used by Britain in the American Revolution and during the mid-nineteenth century as the scene of a major confrontation between Prussia and Austria—the general outline of Hessian history is not widely known. To provide a background for the discussion of the survival of the Hessian nobility, this chapter will briefly summarize the main economic, social, and political developments in Hesse-Kassel during the eighteenth and nineteenth centuries.

Hesse-Kassel's central location gave it considerable strategic importance—particularly to Prussia, because Hesse-Kassel lay across the main lines of communication to Prussia's territories in western Germany. Hesse-Kassel itself was a curious amalgamation of territories. The oldest portion of the state consisted of the Landgraviate of Hesse-Kassel, which was divided into Lower Hesse, centered on Kassel, and Upper Hesse, centered on Marburg. The landgraviate also included two small principalities outside its borders: Schaumburg inside Hanover and Schmalkalden in Thuringia. In 1736 Hesse-Kassel gained the territory of Hanau, northeast of Frankfurt, and the reforms of Napoleon and the Congress of Vienna led to the acquisition of most of the former Bishopric of Fulda and the territories of a number of mediatized princes and former imperial knights.

At first the newly acquired territories were not integrated into the Hessian legal and administrative systems; each retained its own laws, bureaucracy, and special privileges. Finally in 1821 the entire legal and administrative system was reformed. All regional differences were abolished, and the state was divided into the four provinces—Upper Hesse, Lower Hesse, Hanau, and Fulda—shown in figure 1.1. Each of the provinces was further divided into counties (*Kreise*).

Although agriculture dominated the Hessian economy, the country did not possess particularly good soil for farming. Much of the area was

7

Figure 1.1 Hesse-Kassel, 1815–1866.

hilly and heavily forested; in the nineteenth century forests covered more than 40 percent of the total territory. The state was the largest owner of wooded land with 55 percent of the total forest area; communities owned another 19 percent, nobles 15 percent, and foundations 3 percent; and the remaining 7 percent was owned jointly by communities and the state.[1]

In contrast to the forests, most of the agriculturally useful land (fields, pastures, and gardens) was owned by the peasantry. In the eighteenth and nineteenth centuries, peasants held over 90 percent of the nonforest land, while the rest was owned by nobles, bourgeois, churches, communities, and the state.[2] Thus the structure of landownership in Hesse-Kassel, as in the rest of western and southern Germany where *Grundherrschaft*[3] was the rule, contrasted sharply to that of eighteenth-century France, where peasants owned only about 35 percent of the land, the rest being held by the nobility, the bourgeoisie, and the church.[4]

Although the Hessian peasantry controlled nine-tenths of the arable land, most peasants were far from wealthy, and few owned even enough land to be self-sufficient, which required at least three to five hectares. The others had to supplement their landed income by working as day laborers or by practicing a trade. Over one-half of the peasants owned less than one hectare in the nineteenth century.[5] Small as the peasants' individual holdings were, most were further divided into tiny parcels

---

[1] Otto Bähr, *Der hessische Wald: Eine Darstellung der in dem vormaligen Kurfürstenthum Hessen am Walde bestehenden Rechtsverhältnisse* (Kassel, 1879), 5.

[2] Prior to 1848 most of the peasant land lay under the *Obereigentum* (overlordship) of various landlords (generally the state or nobles), who collected a variety of dues and services from the peasant owners, but the peasants were considered to be the actual owners of their land and generally could dispose of it as they wished. See below, chapter 5.

[3] The system of *Grundherrschaft* (landlordship) common in western and southern Germany consisted of landlords who collected dues and services from peasants but did not generally possess large landholdings of their own. As a result, these landlords were normally not involved in running estates and were often absentee landlords. Landlords also did not usually have sole jurisdiction over an area, so individual villages were often subject to a number of different landlords. In contrast, under the system of *Gutsherrschaft* (estate lordship) prevalent in eastern Germany, nobles had larger demesne holdings and were often directly involved in the day-to-day affairs of their estates. Most of these nobles also had sole control over the lands under their jurisdiction, so villages in eastern Germany generally did not have more than one landlord.

[4] Eberhard Weiss, "Ergebnisse eines Vergleichs der grundherrschaftlichen Strukturen Deutschlands und Frankreichs vom 13. bis zum Ausgang des 18. Jahrhunderts," *Vierteljahrschrift für Sozial- und Wirtschaftsgeschichte* 57 (1970): 1–14.

[5] Arnold von Baumbach, "Die bäuerlichen Verhältnisse im Regierungs-Bezirk Kassel," *Schriften des Vereins für Sozialpolitik* 22 (1881): 118–22.

scattered over the countryside as a result of generations of division of peasant landholdings through inheritance. These parcels averaged about one-quarter *Kasseler Acker* (one-sixteenth hectare) each,[6] so even a relatively large peasant holding of ten hectares might have consisted of over one hundred widely scattered strips of land. Although some large peasant farms (*Hufengüter*) had remained intact because Hessian law prohibited their division, the general picture was one of numerous tiny plots of land.

The shortage of land was aggravated by increasing population pressure. As in the rest of Germany, the population of Hesse-Kassel grew substantially during the first half of the nineteenth century. The number of inhabitants was 555,084 in 1812 but by 1834 had already topped 700,000. The population continued to grow until 1849, when it reached a peak of 759,816, but the rate of increase had already slowed during the 1840s, owing to poor harvests and a growing economic crisis. In the 1850s the population declined substantially as tens of thousands of Hessians sought to escape their country's economic misery by emigrating. Thus by 1858 Hesse-Kassel contained only 726,739 inhabitants, a decline of 4 percent from the peak in 1849. The population began to climb again in the early 1860s but at a much slower rate than in the first half of the century.[7]

In many areas of Germany the most significant form of population movement was not the emigration of many inhabitants to other parts of Germany or overseas but rather the tremendous migration of individuals from the countryside to the cities. This was not the case in Hesse-Kassel, which remained primarily an agricultural state throughout the nineteenth century. In 1818, 75 percent of the population lived outside the cities and towns, and fifty years later the proportion of the population living in rural areas had declined only 2 percent.[8] Industrialization had thus made little headway in Hesse-Kassel. Most of the towns dif-

[6] Eihachiro Sakai, *Der kurhessische Bauer im 19. Jahrhundert und die Grundlastenablösung* (Melsungen, 1967), 14.

[7] Wolfgang Köllmann, ed., *Quellen zur Bevölkerungs-, Sozial- und Wirtschaftsstatistik Deutschlands, 1815–1875*, vol. 1, *Quellen zur Bevölkerungsstatistik Deutschlands, 1815–1875* (Boppard, 1980), 129–34; Kurfürstliche Statistische Kommission, "Die Bevölkerung Kurhessens und deren Bewegung," *Zeitschrift für Hessische Geschichte* 8 (1860): 328–76. For changes in the rate of population growth in the provinces of Upper and Lower Hesse see Ulrich Möker, *Nordhessen im Zeitalter der Industriellen Revolution* (Cologne, 1977), 23. The rate of growth varied from a peak of 1.6 percent annual increase in the years 1833–34 to an annual decline of 0.87 percent in 1853–55.

[8] Bruno Hildebrand, *Statistische Mittheilungen über die volkswirtschaftlichen Zustände Kurhessens* (Berlin, 1853), 62; Ludwig Metz, *Statistische Beschreibung des Regierungsbezirks Kassel* (Kassel, 1871), 22.

fered little from large villages, where agriculture still predominated. Of the cities only Hanau, neighbor to Frankfurt, and the capital city of Kassel contained any substantial amount of industry.

Given the lack of industrial development in Hesse-Kassel, it is not surprising that the Hessian bourgeoisie was weak in comparison to those of the other German states.[9] The most numerous and prosperous element of the Hessian bourgeoisie was not the economic bourgeoisie (*Besitzbürgertum*) of merchants and entrepreneurs but the more traditional educated bourgeoisie (*Bildungsbürgertum*), composed primarily of jurists, academics, and other members of the bureaucracy. These bourgeois civil servants and the bourgeois army officers enjoyed high status in Hesse-Kassel, and it was they, along with bourgeois leaseholders and estate administrators, who were most active in the land market, not the economic bourgeoisie.

Hesse-Kassel's lack of progress in the economic sphere was more than matched by the slow pace of its political development. Until the mid-sixteenth century the Landgraviate of Hesse had often played an important role in German politics, but Hesse's influence was dissipated in 1567 by the will of Landgrave Philip the Magnanimous, which divided the country among his four sons. Two of the lines soon died out, leaving the remaining two states, Hesse-Kassel and Hesse-Darmstadt, to squabble and fight over the spoils until a final settlement was reached in 1648.

The rulers of Hesse-Kassel felt themselves to be the true heirs of Hesse's former glory and often embarked upon programs that would have been appropriate to a much larger state. The landgraves continually sought to enlarge their territory and spent much of the eighteenth century attempting to gain the prestigious title of elector (*Kurfürst*), so that they could join the small group of German princes who selected the Holy Roman Emperor. At home the landgraves maintained a huge standing army, which was out of all proportion to the size of the population and could only be supported by renting it to larger powers. At times the search for subsidies from foreign powers was carried to unusual extremes, as in 1743, when Hessian troops found themselves fighting on both sides during the War of the Austrian Succession.[10] The

---

[9] Information about the bourgeoisie of Hesse-Kassel in the nineteenth century is extremely sparse. Manfred Bullik's *Staat und Gesellschaft im hessischen Vormärz: Wahlrecht, Wahlen und öffentliche Meinung in Kurhessen, 1830–1848* (Cologne, 1972) provides information only on the political activities of the bourgeoisie (pp. 47–48, 77–86) and does not describe its composition.

[10] Although Hessian troops fought on both sides during this war, the rental contracts specified that the two different Hessian contingents could not be used against each other. Karl Demandt, *Geschichte des Landes Hessen*, 2d ed. (Kassel, 1972), 275.

11

rental of portions of the Hessian army became a major source of income for the Hessian state, but little of this wealth trickled down to benefit the populace.

During the Seven Years' War Hessian troops fought on the side of England and Prussia in return for English subsidies, and Hesse-Kassel became the site of numerous campaigns because of its central location, as French and Hessian-Hanoverian armies maneuvered back and forth across the land. Kassel, the capital city, changed hands five times during the war.[11] Damage from the fighting and the requisitions of friendly and enemy troops left the country in desolate condition at the end of the war.

The Seven Years' War strongly influenced the thinking of Landgrave Frederick II (1760–85), who had spent part of the war in Prussia before succeeding his father. During this period Frederick became a great admirer of Frederick the Great, and once the war ended, the new landgrave began to remodel many Hessian institutions along Prussian lines. However, most of these changes, such as the creation of a War and Domains Board and the office of *Landrat* (county councilor), did not survive long after his death. Landgrave Frederick II is best known as the ruler who rented his army to England during the American Revolution. The income from this transaction made Frederick one of the wealthiest rulers in Europe, and he soon became an important source of credit for other European princes as well as for Hessian officials and nobles. Frederick also spent considerable sums of money enlarging the court and improving cultural life in Kassel.[12]

The vast wealth accumulated from the English subsidy treaties made Frederick II and his son, William IX (1785–1821), virtually independent of the Hessian diet, whose control over finances had become little more than a formality. During William IX's long reign the diet met only twice, in 1797 and in 1815.[13]

William did not inherit his father's extravagant tastes. Although most of the vast family fortune was still intact, he slashed government expenses by shrinking the size of the court and eliminating his father's imitations of Prussian bureaucratic institutions. William was a staunch foe of the French Revolution, and his armies participated in the campaigns against France in the early 1790s (again in return for English payments). However, when Prussia made a separate peace with France in 1795, Hesse-Kassel immediately followed suit. In the negotiations conducted

[11] Hugo Brunner, *Geschichte der Residenzstadt Kassel* (Kassel, 1913), 258–84.

[12] The best biography of Frederick II is Wolf von Both and Hans Vogel, *Landgraf Friedrich II von Hessen-Kassel: Ein Fürst der Zopfzeit* (Munich, 1973).

[13] F. L. Carsten, *Princes and Parliaments in Germany: From the Fifteenth to the Eighteenth Century* (Oxford, 1969), 185–90.

to regulate the territorial changes caused by the wars, Hesse-Kassel gained little territory, allegedly because the landgrave was too stingy to give out bribes as large as those of other states, but in 1803 he finally received the title of elector of the Holy Roman Empire, long a goal of Hessian diplomacy. This triumph soon became meaningless when the empire itself was dissolved in 1806. Nevertheless, Hesse-Kassel retained the title of electorate until the end of its existence as an independent state in 1866.[14]

Despite his long-standing ties with Prussia, Elector William I (the new title of Landgrave William IX) declared Hesse-Kassel neutral when war broke out between France and Prussia in 1806, but this declaration did not prevent Napoleon from occupying the land in October of that year. The elector fled to Prague, and the following year his country ceased to exist when it was incorporated into the newly created Kingdom of Westphalia, ruled by Napoleon's brother Jerome.[15]

The new kingdom carried out extensive reforms in the fields of law and administration, but many planned social reforms foundered on the realities of Westphalia's lack of true independence from France and the requirements of the Napoleonic Wars. Thus laws enabling peasants to free themselves from seigneurial dues and services remained ineffective because no adequate means of carrying out these laws were ever created.[16]

Most of the population remained loyal to their exiled ruler, and several groups staged revolts that were put down by French troops. But Westphalia's fate was sealed by Napoleon's defeat at Leipzig in October 1813. Jerome fled to France, and the following month the elector returned from exile, greeted by jubilant crowds. William immediately set about abolishing all traces of the Kingdom of Westphalia's existence and restored almost all of the laws that had been in effect in 1806, although he did retain several new taxes and advantageous financial reforms.

The Congress of Vienna made important alterations in the size of

[14] Demandt, *Geschichte des Landes Hessen*, 544–45. For a biography of the first Hessian elector see Philipp Losch, *Kurfürst Wilhelm I, Landgraf von Hessen* (Marburg, 1923).

[15] The short-lived Kingdom of Westphalia, created by Napoleon out of Hesse-Kassel, Hanover, Brunswick, and West Elbian Prussia, should not be confused with the eighteenth-century principalities annexed by Prussia in 1803, which became the province of Westphalia.

[16] Part of the French administration actively defended the old system of seigneurial dues against the Westphalian reforms because such dues were an important source of income for the Hessian royal demesnes, which had become French, not Westphalian, property in 1808. Napoleon granted many of these estates to his new service aristocracy and did not want to see their value diminished. Helmut Berding, *Napoleonische Herrschafts- und Gesellschaftspolitik im Königreich Westfalen, 1807–1813* (Göttingen, 1973), 108–11.

Electoral Hesse. Several smaller Hessian exclaves were given to Prussia, Hanover, and Saxony, but Hesse-Kassel received the lion's share of the former Bishopric of Fulda and several previously independent principalities, whose rulers became *Standesherren* (mediatized princes with special privileges).[17]

The Hessian Estates met in 1815 and 1816 to try to create a constitution, but all efforts to reach an agreement with the elector failed because he refused to separate his own wealth from that of the state and also because the estates themselves were divided over issues such as taxation and noble privileges.[18] The aging elector finally died in 1821, and his son William II completely reorganized and modernized the administrative and legal systems, but he too took no steps toward granting a constitution. The new elector's reluctance to allow political reforms created tension that was greatly aggravated by his scandalous personal life. William lived with his mistress Emilie Ortlöpp, upon whom he bestowed the title of Countess Reichenbach, and had no contact with his wife, a Prussian princess who enjoyed widespread popularity. Mistresses and illegitimate children were nothing new for the rulers of Hesse-Kassel, but William II was less circumspect than his predecessors, and public tolerance for marital scandals by monarchs had declined by the nineteenth century.[19]

With public opinion so alienated from the elector, the unrest that swept through Europe after the July 1830 revolution in Paris found fertile soil in Hesse-Kassel. Riots in Hanau and Kassel forced the elector to give in to popular demand and call for an assembly to draft a constitution. The estates, led by University of Marburg professor Sylvester Jordan, quickly drew up Hesse-Kassel's first constitution, which was proclaimed on 8 January 1831.

The populace's continued hatred of the Countess Reichenbach soon forced the elector to choose between his throne and his mistress, and in March 1831 he chose the latter, following her to Hanau where she had been forced to flee by riots protesting her presence in Kassel. William declared his son Frederick William to be co-ruler, but in reality the government was now in the hands of the crown prince.

The early years of Frederick William's rule brought several important

---

[17] Although the *Standesherren* were no longer independent rulers after 1815, they were given special privileges and exemptions in the states that had absorbed their territories, and they also were accorded social status equal to that of the ruling families.

[18] See below, pp. 208–16.

[19] Much of the anger against the countess resulted from the way she used her influence with the elector to benefit herself, her relatives, and her friends. Philipp Losch, *Geschichte des Kurfürstentums Hessen, 1803–1866* (Marburg, 1922), 127–29.

reforms that had been promised by the constitution. Peasants were allowed to rid themselves of the burden of many of their dues and services to landlords, and a new lending institution, the *Landeskreditkasse* (State Credit Bank), was established to provide peasants with low-interest loans for the purpose of converting their annual obligations into lump-sum payments. However, Frederick William was no friend of the constitution; he longed to return to the absolutism of his predecessors. His reactionary chief minister, Ludwig Hassenpflug, worked to undermine the constitution and break the power of the liberals, and in 1839 he had their leader, Sylvester Jordan, arrested on trumped-up charges.

As had been the case with William II, Frederick William's unpopularity was increased by his personal life. His morganatic marriage to Gertrude Lehmann, née Falkenstein, who had divorced her husband (a Prussian officer) in order to be free to marry Frederick William, was looked upon with widespread disfavor both inside and outside Hesse-Kassel.[20]

The Hessian economy faced a severe crisis in the late 1840s, when the rural population was plagued by bad harvests.[21] A further source of tension in the countryside was the continued existence of the system of seigneurial dues and services. Despite the reforms of the early 1830s, many unpopular exactions had not yet been abolished, and the redemption of others was proceeding too slowly to satisfy the peasants. Furthermore, large numbers of artisans were having great difficulty making a living, especially in the areas of wool and linen making. These traditional centers of Hessian manufacture had been hit hard by the competition of British machine-produced goods. The combination of economic, social, and political tension made the country a tinderbox that burst into flame in March 1848 once news of the uprising in Paris reached Hesse-Kassel. Riots immediately broke out in Hanau, and unrest soon swept other cities and the countryside. The elector capitulated before the tumult, naming new liberal ministers and promising freedom of the press and religion.[22]

Liberal rule did not last long in Hesse-Kassel, as was also the case in the rest of Germany. Within two years a new political crisis engulfed the state after the elector replaced the liberal "March Ministry" with a

[20] Ibid., 149–227. For a biography of Frederick William see Philipp Losch, *Der letzte deutsche Kurfürst: Friedrich Wilhelm I von Hessen* (Marburg, 1937).

[21] Jürgen Bohmbach, "Die Hungersjahre 1846/47 in Oberhessen, eine Darstellung aus den Akten der Regierung Marburg," *Hessisches Jahrbuch für Landesgeschichte* 23 (1973): 333–65.

[22] Demandt, *Geschichte des Landes Hessen*, 557; Losch, *Geschichte des Kurfürstentums*, 232–42.

highly conservative government headed by Ludwig Hassenpflug. Hassenpflug encountered such strong resistance from the legislature and the bureaucracy that he declared martial law, but this step led to the threatened resignation of almost nine-tenths of the officer corps, who refused to violate their oath to the constitution. The elector then sought assistance from the diet of the German Confederation, which dispatched Bavarian troops to restore order in Hesse-Kassel. This move was initially opposed by Prussia, leading to a confrontation between Austria and Prussia, but the Prussians soon backed down and signed the Olmütz agreement in November 1850. The occupation of Hesse-Kassel by Confederation troops lasted only one year, but for the next fifteen years Hessian politics saw a sharp division between the elector and his conservative government on the one hand and the liberal-dominated legislature on the other. The division even extended to Hesse-Kassel's foreign policy, with most legislators favoring Prussia while the elector supported Austria.

Frederick William's pro-Austrian policy had disastrous results in 1866, when he ordered mobilization in support of Austria despite the legislature's vote in favor of accepting Prussia's demand for neutrality. Prussian troops quickly overran the country and captured the elector, who continued to refuse to make an agreement with Prussia, thus sealing the fate of his country and his dynasty. Later that year Prussia formally annexed Hesse-Kassel, making it part of the new Prussian province of Hesse-Nassau, which consisted of two administrative districts: *Regierungsbezirk* Kassel (formerly Electoral Hesse) and *Regierungsbezirk* Wiesbaden (formerly the Duchy of Nassau).[23]

---

[23] Losch, *Geschichte des Kurfürstentums*, 258–82; Hans A. Schmitt, "Prussia's Last Fling: The Annexation of Hanover, Hesse, Frankfurt, and Nassau, June 15–October 8, 1866," *Central European History* 8 (1975): 316–47.

· 2 ·

THE HESSIAN NOBILITY

The size of the nobilities of Europe varied tremendously at the end of the eighteenth century. The percentage of nobles in the total population ranged from approximately 0.5 percent in Sweden to between 10 and 15 percent in Poland, although the most common size of the nobility was approximately 1 to 2 percent, as was the case in France, Italy, and Russia.[1] Few statistics on the size of the nobility in the German states are available, but nobles in these states probably constituted less than 1 percent of the total population. Among the German states the largest percentage of nobles (approximately 1 percent) could be found in Prussia, whose nobility had grown substantially in size during the eighteenth century as the result of population growth among older families, increased ennoblement, and immigration of nobles from other countries.[2] In the lesser German states the nobility was numerically quite small by European standards. The nobility of the ecclesiastical state Münster, for example, constituted less than 0.4 percent of the population in the eighteenth century, and nobles in Bavaria made up approximately 0.3 percent of the population in 1815.[3] Similarly small was the nobility of Hesse-Kassel. A government survey of nobles residing within the country in 1835 listed only 465 adult males, which would make the nobility as a whole (including women and children) approximately 0.3 percent of the total population.[4]

---

[1] Meyer, *Noblesses et pouvoirs*, 30–31.

[2] Martiny, *Adelsfrage in Preußen*, 72–80.

[3] Reif, *Westfälischer Adel*, 37, 58; Walter Deml, "Der Adel im Königreich Bayern, 1808–1817," paper presented to the conference "Der Adel im bürgerlichen Zeitalter 1780–1860," held at Bad Homburg, Germany, 30 September–2 October 1982.

[4] It is not possible to calculate this percentage precisely, because the 1835 *Adelsmatrikel* (roll of nobles) includes only nobles aged eighteen and above whereas the available population statistics group together all males over age fourteen (202,244 in the census of 1827; Hildebrand, *Statistische Mittheilungen*, 40). The only surviving copy of the *Adelsmatrikel* is located in the Hessian State Archive at Marburg (Staatsarchiv Marburg, hereafter cited as "StAM"), Bestand 300 (Hessen-Rumpenheim), Abt. 11 (Geheimes Kabinett), C 32, Nr. 6. Future citations to this archive will consist of the abbreviation StAM, followed by the number of the holding (*Bestand*) and then any further subdivisions such as the accession or box number. The name of a *Bestand* will be included in the first reference; subsequent references to the *Bestand* will include only the number. If the material cited comes from a

The 1835 survey did not include the members of the upper nobility because this group was generally considered to be a different *Stand* (social order) from the lower nobility.[5] In many respects there was a greater gap between the upper and lower nobilities than between the lower nobility and the bourgeoisie, as can be seen by the almost complete absence of intermarriage between the families of the upper and lower nobilities in Hesse-Kassel. In contrast, lower nobles married bourgeois fairly often.[6] There were very few members of the upper nobility in Hesse-Kassel, just several cadet lines of the ruling family and five families of *Standesherren* (former ruling princes whose territories had been incorporated into Hesse-Kassel and other German states in 1815). The landholdings of these mediatized princes were located in the province of Hanau and in neighboring states. Since the upper nobility was small and quite distinct from the lower nobles, it will not be a major area of emphasis in this study of the Hessian nobility, particularly because the *Standesherren* have already been the subject of considerable research.[7]

The lower nobility can be subdivided into those noble families which were part of a *Ritterschaft* (knighthood)[8] and those which were not. Generally the families in the corporate bodies of knights had enjoyed noble status much longer and owned much more land than did other lower nobles. Within the borders of nineteenth-century Hesse-Kassel there were three different knighthoods: the *Althessische Ritterschaft* (Old Hessian

---

section of the archive other than the documents (*Akten*), it will be identified by the appropriate term (*Kataster, Urkunden, Handschriften, Rechnungen, Materialsammlungen*, or *Zeitungen*) rather than a *Bestand* number.

[5] Upper nobles were ruling families with a seat and vote in the imperial diet. The lower nobility consisted of the imperial knights, who were subject only to the emperor, and the territorial nobles, who were under the sovereignty of another ruler. One late-eighteenth-century work devoted over five hundred pages to the distinctions between these two groups: Johannes Stephan Pütter, *Über den Unterschied der Stände, besonders des hohen und niederen Adels in Teutschland* (Göttingen, 1795).

[6] See below, p. 45.

[7] Some recent works dealing with the *Standesherren* include Heinz Gollwitzer, *Die Standesherren: Die politische und gesellschaftliche Stellung der Mediatisierten, 1815–1918*, 2d ed. (Stuttgart, 1964); Ulrich Neth, *Standesherren und liberalen Bewegung: Der Kampf des württembergischen standesherrlichen Adels um seine Rechtsstellung in der zweiten Hälfte des 19. Jahrhunderts* (Stuttgart, 1970); Hartmut Weber, *Die Fürsten von Hohenlohe im Vormärz: Politische und soziale Verhaltensweise württembergischer Standesherren in der ersten Hälfte des 19. Jahrhunderts* (Schwäbisch Hall, 1977); Erwein H. Eltz, *Die Modernisierung einer Standesherrschaft: Karl Egon III und das Haus Fürstenberg in den Jahren nach 1848/49* (Sigmaringen, 1980); Harald Winkel, *Die Ablösungskapitalien aus der Bauernbefreiung in West- und Süddeutschland: Höhe und Verwendung bei Standes- und Grundherren* (Stuttgart, 1968).

[8] The term *knighthood* is not used in this book in the British sense, that is to say an honor granted to certain individuals, but rather to mean a corporate body of landed nobles with specific requirements for membership based upon ancestry and estate ownership.

Knighthood), the Schaumburg Ritterschaft, and members of the former *Reichsritterschaft* (imperial knighthood). Each of these three corporate bodies will be described in turn.

The most prominent group within the Hessian lower nobility was the *Althessische Ritterschaft*, which originally consisted of all the noble families represented at the Landtag of 1532, when Landgrave Philip the Magnanimous presented two secularized cloisters (Kaufungen and Wetter) to the Hessian knighthood in return for its acceptance of a new tax. In the sixteenth century the terms *nobility* and *knighthood* were virtually synonymous, but in the centuries that followed, the composition of the nobility changed as new families became nobles and members of non-Hessian noble families came to Hesse. As a result, the Ritterschaft gradually became a special group within the nobility. By the eighteenth century a leading Hessian jurist could state, "Not every noble who lives in Hesse is a member of the Hessian Ritterschaft, no matter how many noble ancestors he has or how much land he owns."[9]

The Hessian Ritterschaft originally numbered approximately 175 families, but within a hundred years this number had declined to 94. For the next two centuries the Ritterschaft continued to shrink in size as old families died out or left Hesse and were not replaced.[10] Finally in the mid-eighteenth century the Ritterschaft began to take steps to replace its losses. In 1763 the knighthood drew up a definitive list of its members and then established requirements for the admission of new members. Candidates for membership in the Hessian Ritterschaft needed eight quarterings of noble ancestry (all eight great-grandparents had to have been born noble) and had to possess a noble estate in Hesse-Kassel and reside within the country. Upon acceptance, new members were required to pay one thousand *Kammergulden* (eight hundred *Reichstaler*) to the knighthood's foundation (*Stift*) at Kaufungen. In addition, newly admitted families had to be Protestant, although some of the older families in the Ritterschaft were Catholic.[11] Candidates also needed the approval of the landgraves of both Hesse-Kassel and Hesse-Darmstadt as well as that of the majority of the members of the Ritterschaft. Using these new rules, the knighthood admitted a total of ten new families in the eighteenth and nineteenth centuries, but its shrinkage continued nevertheless, as twenty-five old families died out during the same period.[12]

---

[9] Conrad Wilhelm Ledderhose, *Kleine Schriften*, 5 vols. (Marburg, 1787–89; Eisenach, 1792–95), 1: 29.

[10] Carl Knetsch, "Von der hessischen Ritterschaft," *Hessische Chronik* 7 (1918): 65–67; Bruno Jacob, "Die hessische Ritterschaft," *Deutsches Adelsblatt* 52 (1934): 352–54.

[11] Ledderhose, *Kleine Schriften*, 1: 29–31.

[12] Knetsch, "Ritterschaft," 66–67. One of the new families, von Lindau (admitted in

The requirement for new members of the Ritterschaft to be fifth-generation nobles (even the great-grandparents were supposed to have been noble by birth rather than by ennoblement) meant that it was not drawing upon rising members of the middle class to replace its losses. This is quite evident in the composition of the membership in the mid-nineteenth century. Thirty-one of the forty families[13] were *Uradel* (ancient nobility: noble before 1400) and had been in the Ritterschaft for centuries. Another four families were *Uradel* from other states who had settled in Hesse, bought land, and later joined the Ritterschaft (von Canstein in 1776, von Hesberg in 1820, von Osterhausen in 1830, and von Amelunxen in 1842). Two families were offspring of the ruling family: the Cornbergs (admitted in 1777) were descended from an illegitimate son (ennobled in 1582) of Landgrave William IV, while the Princes of Hanau were the sons of Elector Frederick William's morganatic marriage and were admitted to the knighthood in 1835. Another two families were relatively new nobles by the knighthood's standards. The Heydwolffs were ennobled in 1530 and admitted into the Ritterschaft in 1741, and the Verschuers were ennobled in 1696 and admitted in 1820.[14]

Only once did the Ritterschaft accept a candidate without requiring the traditional test for noble ancestry (*Ahnenprobe*). In 1804 Minister of State Friedrich Freiherr Waitz von Eschen, whose father had been ennobled in 1768 after being adopted by his father-in-law (whose nobility was also by patent rather than by birth), was enthusiastically accepted by the members of the Ritterschaft despite his lack of sufficient noble ancestry.[15] Waitz was very popular owing to his success in negotiating an end to the war with France in 1795.

A number of other applications by nobles to join the official body of Hessian knights in the late eighteenth and early nineteenth centuries were rejected, so the Ritterschaft does not seem to have been interested

---

1760), also died out in the nineteenth century. For a complete list of the families in the Ritterschaft during the eighteenth and nineteenth centuries see appendix A.

[13] The term *family* is used here to mean individuals descended from a common ancestor. Some of these families were quite large, having up to ten different branches, each with several nuclear families.

[14] Knetsch, "Ritterschaft," 66–67.

[15] Waitz seems to have been approved unanimously by the knights, many of whom signed their ballots "with pleasure." Archiv des Ritterschaftlichen Stiftes Kaufungen, 3504 Oberkaufungen (hereafter cited as ARSK), Rep. VI, Gef. 12–14, Nr. 25. Ironically, just eleven years earlier the Ritterschaft had asked the landgrave to ensure that the use of the ancestry test be retained for all prospective members so that the knighthood would remain "ancient nobility." StAM 5 (Hessischer Geheim Rat), Nr. 54, Ritterschaft to Landgrave William IX, 20 July 1793.

in expanding its numbers or even in replacing all of its losses. One rather extreme viewpoint on accepting new members was expressed by Wilhelm von Baumbach-Sontra[16] in 1820 as he voted against the admission of the von Hesberg family: "In my humble opinion the only advantage derived from membership in the Hessian Ritterschaft is the eligibility for the benefits of the noble foundations, and thus without any reflection on the qualifications of the present candidate, I find in general that it is disadvantageous for the existing members if their number is increased."[17]

The Hessian Ritterschaft was based entirely on the sixteenth-century Landgraviate of Hesse, so when new territories were added in later centuries, their nobilities were not incorporated into the Hessian Ritterschaft. Thus the old landed nobility of the tiny Hessian exclave Schaumburg formed its own Ritterschaft. In 1835 this group numbered twenty-six adult males. Since this small knighthood was located far from the main portion of Hesse-Kassel and often had closer ties to Hanover than Hesse, it will not receive detailed coverage in the chapters that follow. Therefore the term *Ritterschaft*, if used alone, refers only to the Hessian Ritterschaft, which was by far the largest type of knighthood, with 181 adult males in the 1835 survey.

Hesse-Kassel also contained a third group of knights in the nineteenth century, the former *Reichsritter* (imperial knights). This portion of the lower nobility had previously not been subject to the Hessian landgraves but had owed allegiance directly to the emperor. Along with the *Standesherren*, the imperial knights lost their independence at the start of the nineteenth century when their tiny principalities were incorporated into the surrounding states. Unlike the states of southwestern Germany, Hesse-Kassel contained few former imperial knights. None had resided within the borders of the old landgraviate; the estates of the eighteen former imperial knights listed in the 1835 survey of nobles were all located in the provinces of Hanau and Fulda.[18]

[16] Nobles' names often included the name of their estate following a hyphen; this was particularly necessary in huge families with numerous branches such as the Baumbachs. In some families the name of the main estate had in the course of centuries become incorporated into the family name. Thus a member of the von Trott zu Solz family did not necessarily belong to the branch residing at Solz; one of the owners of the estate Imshausen would be called "von Trott zu Solz-Imshausen." The term *von und zu* indicated that the family owned the estate from which the surname had been derived. The von und zu Gilsa family resided at Gilsa, for example.

[17] ARSK, Rep. VI, Gef. 12–14, Nr. 26.

[18] Like the *Standesherren*, the imperial knights in Germany have been the subject of considerable study. See Gerd Kollmer, *Die schwäbische Reichsritterschaft zwischen Westfälischen Frieden und Reichsdeputationshauptschluß: Untersuchung zur wirtschaftlichen und sozialen Lage der*

In addition to the nobles who belonged to one of the three corporate bodies of knights, a large number of other nobles resided in Hesse-Kassel in 1835 (245 out of the total of 465 adult males). The composition of this portion of the nobility was never steady, for it was constantly being increased by ennoblement and by the entry of nobles from other states into Hesse and decreased by noble families leaving the country or dying out. This part of the nobility was therefore quite diverse, with extreme ranges of both age of nobility and landownership.

One-half of the 130 noble families who did not belong to a knighthood in 1835 had been ennobled since 1700 (see table 2.1).[19] In contrast, three-quarters of the families of the Hessian Ritterschaft had been noble since time immemorial or at least prior to 1400, so age of nobility was an important difference between the knights and many other nobles. Although thirty-six families of other nobles had noble pedigrees just as distinguished as those of the Ritterschaft, most of these families actually consisted of only one or two individuals from a noble family located outside of Hesse who had taken service in the Hessian bureaucracy, court, or officer corps.

The members of non-Hessian nobilities who had taken service in Hesse were generally younger sons or members of cadet lines who had inherited little or no land and were forced to seek employment in government service. It is therefore not surprising that most of these non-Hessian nobles as well as many of the new nobles possessed little land other than a house and garden. In the 1860s members of the three types of knighthoods owned a total of almost fifty thousand hectares of land

---

Reichsritterschaft in den Ritterkantonen Neckar-Schwarzwald und Kocher (Stuttgart, 1979); Dieter Hellstern, *Der Ritterkanton Neckar-Schwarzwald, 1560–1805: Untersuchungen über die Korporationsverfassung, die Funktionen des Ritterkantons und die Mitgliedsfamilien* (Tübingen, 1971); Hartmann von Bechtolsheim, *Des Heiligen Römischen Reiches unmittelbar-freie Ritterschaft zu Franken, Ort Steigerwald, im 17. und 18. Jahrhundert: Ein Beitrag zur Verfassungs- und Gesellschaftsgeschichte des reichsunmittelbaren Adels* (Würzburg, 1972); Wolfgang von Stetten, *Die Rechtsstellung der unmittelbaren freien Reichsritterschaft, ihre Mediatisierung und ihre Stellung in den neuen Landen: Dargestellt am fränkischen Kanton Odenwald* (Schwäbisch Hall, 1973); Thomas Glas-Hochstettler, "The Imperial Knights in Post-Westphalian Mainz: A Case Study of Corporatism in the Old Reich," *Central European History* 11 (1978): 131–49.

[19] Information on the age of nobility was compiled from the statements made by the nobles themselves in the *Adelsmatrikel* of 1835 and from E. H. Kneschke, *Neues allgemeines deutsches Adelslexikon*, 9 vols. (Leipzig, 1859–70); Deutsches Adelsarchiv, *Genealogisches Handbuch des Adels*, 87 vols. to date (Limburg, 1951–); *Gothaisches Genealogisches Taschenbuch der Gräflichen Häuser*, 115 vols. (Gotha, 1825–1942); *Gothaisches Genealogisches Taschenbuch der Freiherrlichen Häuser*, 92 vols. (Gotha, 1848–1942); *Gothaisches Genealogisches Taschenbuch der Uradeligen Häuser*, 41 vols. (Gotha, 1900–1942); *Gothaisches Genealogisches Taschenbuch der Briefadeligen Häuser*, 34 vols. (Gotha, 1907–1942).

TABLE 2.1.
Age of Nobility for Nobles
Not in a Ritterschaft (1835)

When Ennobled	Number of Families
19th century	21
18th century	44
17th century	14
16th century	5
15th century	2
Ancient nobility	36
Cannot be determined	8
Total	130

while the more numerous other nobles owned less than six thousand hectares.[20]

Because the Hessian Ritterschaft was by far the dominant landowning group within the lower nobility and because its composition did not vary as greatly as did that of the mass of nobles not in a knighthood, it will be the main focus of the chapters on the noble family and on noble landownership. However, information on the other groups within the lower nobility will be included wherever possible, and all nobles are studied in the chapters on officeholding and politics.

The size of the lower nobility was not being substantially increased by ennoblement. Prior to 1806 most new nobles in Hesse-Kassel had been ennobled by the emperor. On numerous occasions during the eighteenth century, the Hessian landgraves requested that the emperor grant noble status to distinguished members of the Hessian bureaucracy and, to a lesser degree, the officer corps. In this manner bourgeois families such as Motz and Schmerfeld, which had produced many civil servants over several generations, advanced into the nobility. But overall the number of such ennoblements was small. Between 1750 and 1806 only approximately twenty Hessian families were ennobled by the emperor (see appendix B).[21]

[20] See below, p. 97.

[21] For ennoblement by the emperor see Karl F. von Frank, *Standeserhebungen und Gnadenakte für das deutsche Reich und die österreichischen Erblande bis 1806*, 5 vols. (Schloß Senftenegg, Austria, 1967–74).

The dissolution of the Holy Roman Empire permanently blocked this route to noble status for members of the Hessian bourgeoisie. They were now dependent upon the rulers of Hesse-Kassel, who were very parsimonious in their elevations to the nobility. Landgrave Frederick II made only two ennoblements, both cases involving illegitimate offspring of his son, the crown prince.[22] Landgrave William IX (Elector William I) made a total of nine ennoblements in addition to two cases in which nobles without heirs were allowed to adopt non-nobles (one a son-in-law, the other a sister's son) and transmit their names and coats of arms. Five of the nine ennoblements involved higher civil servants, two of whom had already been ennobled by King Jerome of Westphalia (such elevations were not recognized by William after his return from exile). The other four were army officers.

During the last years of his reign, William I became very romantic in his choices of names for new nobles. In 1818 he drew up a list filled with such fanciful names as Eisenherz (Heart of Iron), Fürstentreu (True to the Prince), Stahlheld (Hero of Steel), and Mauerbrecher (Wall Breaker). Fortunately for the nobility, the elector gave out only three of the names on this list before his death in 1821, and his son did not continue the process of creating names for new nobles.[23]

Under Elector William II many ennoblements were connected with his highly controversial relationship with Emilie Ortlöpp, his mistress. Shortly after his ascension to the throne in 1821, he named her the Countess Reichenbach, and he ennobled her brother Ferdinand in 1830. The countess's gray eminence at court, Geheimer Kabinettsrat Carl Rivalier, also became a noble in 1825. In order to give these two controversial new noblemen more respectability, the elector abandoned his father's practice of inventing new names and instead gave both men the names and coats of arms of ancient and distinguished noble families that had died out. The elector also made six less controversial ennoblements: two army officers (one a diplomat, the other the elector's adjutant), a high-ranking civil servant, a general from Baden who had saved the city of Hersfeld from destruction during the Napoleonic Wars, and two individuals whose background is unknown.[24]

Little change in ennoblement occurred under the new ruler, Frederick William (crown prince and co-regent, 1831-47; elector, 1847-66). He

[22] The families were von Heimrod and von Haynau. Maximilian Gritzner, *Standes-Erhebungen und Gnadenakte deutscher Landesfürsten während der letzten drei Jahrhunderte* (Görlitz, 1881), 535.

[23] StAM 300, Abt. 11, C 32, Standeserhöhungen, Nr. 5. The three names that the elector did give out were Helmschwerdt, Ritterholm, and Sturmfeder.

[24] Gritzner, *Standes-Erhebungen*, 538–40.

also made few ennoblements, and, as had been the case under his father, several of these were involved with a controversial relationship. Shortly after his morganatic marriage to the divorcée Gertrude Lehmann, he named her the Countess of Schaumburg. All offspring of this marriage were also to bear this rank (the marriage was morganatic, so these children could not inherit the throne). In 1853 the countess and her sons by the elector were raised to princely rank under the names Princess and Princes of Hanau. In addition, her two sons by her first marriage were ennobled under the name von Hertingshausen in 1835. Two years later their name was changed to von Scholley, after an old noble family that had just become extinct in the male line, and in 1847 they became barons. Frederick William ennobled only two other families: the three Rieß brothers (as Rieß von Scheuernschloss), who had all attained high civil and military offices, and Georg Andrée (as von Hohenfels), the elector's adjutant.[25]

Overall the level of ennoblement was quite low in the nineteenth century (only twenty instances between 1814 and 1866). Elector William I had ennobled a number of officers and civil servants in the years following his return from exile, but after his death in 1821, his successors seldom used ennoblement to reward faithful servants of the state. Under the last two electors ennoblement was used most frequently in attempts to bolster the social standing of a mistress or morganatic wife and their offspring. In keeping with this policy of infrequent ennoblement, the electors did not sell titles of nobility. Thus the request of a Viennese wholesale merchant in 1829 to be ennobled (presumably in return for payment) and the offer of an Englishman to donate five hundred pounds sterling to any institution in return for a patent of nobility were both rejected.[26]

The Hessian rulers were also far from generous in their bestowal of elevations in rank to families that were already noble. Frederick II and William I made no such elevations, while William II and Frederick William raised only three older noble families to the rank of *Freiherr* (baron). However, these last two electors showered elevations on their controversial partners and their offspring, as has already been detailed. In ad-

[25] Ibid., 540–45.

[26] Hessian files relating to ennoblement were later transferred to the Prussian heraldry office (*Heroldsamt*) in Berlin, where they were destroyed during World War II. Only the indexes remain in StAM 165 (Preußische Regierung Kassel, Abteilung des Innern), Nr. 888. Other German states such as Bavaria and Saxe-Coburg were more willing to sell titles of nobility during the nineteenth century, and Emperors William I and William II ennobled individuals who made large gifts to charities. Lamar Cecil, "The Creation of Nobles in Prussia, 1871–1918," *American Historical Review* 75 (1970): 781–84.

dition, Ferdinand Graf zu Ysenburg-Büdingen, a *Standesherr* who married a daughter of Frederick William's morganatic marriage, was later raised to the rank of prince.[27]

Besides being reluctant themselves to grant elevations in rank, the rulers of Hesse-Kassel refused to recognize any such promotions of Hessian nobles made by other German monarchs, except of course the emperor, and this source of elevation was cut off in 1806. During the Westphalian period three members of the Hessian Ritterschaft in Westphalian service were named counts and several others barons, but these promotions were not recognized after 1813.[28] As a result, virtually all Hessian noblemen were equal in rank. They were simply nobles with the prefix *von*. Only eleven families were confirmed in their right to bear the title *Freiherr* when an official list was drawn up in 1845.[29]

Older noble families, especially those in the Ritterschaft, felt entitled to call themselves barons and often used the title in their correspondence, but the Hessian and later also the Prussian governments refused to extend blanket recognition of baronial status to members of the Ritterschaft and ordered knights who could not show proof of their rank as barons not to use the title.[30] In the late nineteenth century the Prussian government raised a number of knights serving in the Prussian army and bureaucracy to the rank of baron, but only after first investigating their political views to see if they held the proper national rather than particularist sentiments.[31]

PRIVILEGES

Noble status alone brought with it few formal privileges in eighteenth-century Hesse-Kassel. Nobles possessed a privileged trial status (cases involving them or their estates were not tried before the lower courts but

[27] Gritzner, *Standes-Erhebungen*, 545.

[28] A list of all Westphalian ennoblements and elevations is contained in StAM, Materialsammlung 45a (Deutsches Adelsgenossenschaft), Nr. 23, 43.

[29] Only four of these families belonged to the Ritterschaft: von Dörnberg, von Riedesel zu Eisenbach, von Verschuer, and Waitz von Eschen. StAM 300, Abt. 11, C 32, Nr. 10, Kurhessische Freiherrn-Matrikel.

[30] Government orders asking nobles to cease using the title of baron are found in ARSK, Rep. VI, Gef. 11, Nr. 2 and StAM 150 (Oberpräsidium der Provinz Hessen-Nassau), Nr. 458–62; 180 (Landratsämter) Wolfhagen, Nr. 1877. In neighboring Hesse-Darmstadt, all members of the Hessian Ritterschaft were entitled to use the title *Freiherr*. Staatsarchiv Darmstadt, E 12 (Adel), Konv. 1, Fasc. 2.

[31] For example, in 1890 the Prussian interior minister, Count Eulenburg, asked the head of the provincial government in Hesse to check the political sentiments of Arthur von Bodenhausen, who had requested permission to use the title *Freiherr*. StAM 150, Nr. 462.

only in higher courts such as the *Regierungen*),[32] and nobles also enjoyed a number of religious privileges such as the right to be married in their homes, exemption from the requirement to announce three times their intention to marry, and the right of Lutheran nobles to receive communion in their homes.[33] But the most important noble privileges were associated with either membership in the Ritterschaft or ownership of a noble estate (*Rittergut*).[34]

In addition to the above religious and legal privileges, members of the Ritterschaft held the exclusive right to serve in certain government offices such as the eleven *Landräte* (county councilors) and the four *Rittersteuerobereinnehmer*, who supervised the collection of taxes from the Ritterschaft and its subjects. Knights also had the right to send their letters sealed, and all communications to them from the government had to contain special honorific salutations.[35]

Most of the knights' privileges were connected with their ownership of noble estates. First and foremost of these privileges was the right of seigneurial justice held by all the families of the knighthood in the eighteenth century. Using seigneurial courts, noble landlords could obtain swift judgments against peasants who were in arrears. Fees and penalties from seigneurial courts also supplemented nobles' landed income. Furthermore, seigneurial justice reinforced the high status of the Ritterschaft.

Most *Gerichtsherren* (landlords with seigneurial jurisdiction) were also patrons of one or more churches in the territory under their jurisdiction. A *Kirchenpatron* possessed the right to approve or even nominate candidates for vacant pastorates, although the candidates had to be qualified for the positions. However, a patron could not suspend a pastor or interfere with the administration of the church. Patronage over a church brought with it a number of symbolic honors: the patron was included in the church's prayers, bells were rung in mourning for extended pe-

---

[32] Ledderhose, *Kleine Schriften*, 4: 81. In the eighteenth century the lowest level of justice was administered by the town courts, the rural *Amtsgerichte*, and the seigneurial courts. The *Kriminalgerichte* in Kassel, Marburg, and Schmalkalden had jurisdiction over criminal cases. The next level of appeal consisted of the provincial *Regierungen*, which were both judicial and administrative bodies in the eighteenth century. At the highest level of the judicial system came the *Oberappellationsgericht* (supreme court). Both and Vogel, *Landgraf Friedrich II*, 39–40.

[33] Conrad Wilhelm Ledderhose, *Versuch einer Anleitung zum Hessen-Casselischen Kirchenrecht* (Kassel, 1785), pp. 44, 141, 188, 200–201.

[34] For a European-wide survey of noble privileges during this period see Michael Bush, *Noble Privilege* (New York, 1983).

[35] Ulrich Friedrich Kopp and Carl Friedrich Wittich, *Handbuch zur Kenntnis der Hessen-Casselschen Landes-Verfassung und Rechte*, 7 vols. (Kassel, 1796–1808), 1: 100–102, 104, 109.

riods of time when he or members of his family died, there was no music in the church for six months following the death of the patron himself or six weeks for his wife and children, and the patron and his family had the right to be buried in the church.[36]

Another right possessed by many members of the Ritterschaft was that of *Judenaufnahme*. Jews who wished to settle in villages under the jurisdiction of these nobles had to obtain permission and pay an annual "protection" fee (*Judenschutzgeld*).[37] Noble landlords with seigneurial jurisdiction could also collect fees from peasants who moved into or out of their territories (*Einzugs- und Auszugsgelder*).

Owners of noble estates enjoyed a wide range of financial benefits in the eighteenth century. *Rittergüter* were exempt from the heavy burden of the contribution, a land tax used primarily to defray military expenditures. Instead, such estates were subject only to the much lower *Rittersteuer* (knights' tax), also known as the *Petri- und Martinisteuer* because it was collected twice a year on the days of Saints Peter and Martin. Furthermore, members of the Ritterschaft who owned noble estates possessed the right of *Tafelfreiheit* (exemption for the table), under which a large portion of the income of a noble estate was exempt even from the knights' tax if the owner resided on his estate and was thus considered to consume the products of the estate himself. Finally, owners and leaseholders of noble estates did not have to pay excise taxes on alcoholic beverages produced on the estates for their own consumption. With the exception of *Tafelfreiheit*, all of these financial privileges depended upon the noble status of the estate, not its owner, and thus could be exercised by non-noble as well as noble owners of *Rittergüter*.[38]

Along with the bourgeoisie, the nobility was not liable to compulsory military service in the eighteenth century. This exemption also included

---

[36] Ledderhose, *Kirchenrecht*, pp. 281–86. Even after the members of the Ritterschaft lost their patrimonial jurisdiction in the nineteenth century, they retained their rights as *Kirchenpatrone*. Thus when the head of the von der Malsburg-Escheberg family died in 1821, the family's steward ordered the church bells rung. A local government official objected, stating that the family was no longer *Gerichtsherr* for the village, but the *Regierung* ruled that the family still retained the right to the mourning bells (*Trauergelaut*). StAM 17d (Regierung Kassel, Familienrepositur), Generalia, Paket 8. Other examples of conflicts over the rights of *Kirchenpatrone* are found in Paket 11. To this day many members of the Hessian Ritterschaft are still the patrons of their local churches, although with considerably fewer privileges than in the nineteenth century.

[37] Kopp and Wittich, *Landes-Verfassung und Rechte*, 4: 490–91. In all other areas Jews had to make these payments to the state.

[38] Endemann, "Versuch einer Geschichte der Veranlagung der direkten Steuern in Hessen-Kassel," 2 vols. (manuscript in StAM, Handschriften 107), 1: 192, 221–22, 237, 415–17; Kopp and Wittich, *Landes-Verfassung*, 1: 69.

servants on nobles' estates. But to prevent the loss of too many able-bodied men for the army, nobles were instructed not to hire as a servant any man over five feet, four inches tall.[39]

The Ritterschaft's many financial privileges had originally been granted in return for its obligation to provide military service. Although personal service by vassals had last been required in Hesse-Kassel in the sixteenth century, Landgrave William IX attempted to revive the custom in 1794. He called upon the knights and other vassals either to serve personally as officers in the army or each to furnish a horseman with mount and a hunter on foot so that a cavalry and a *Jaeger* (light infantry) corps could be formed to protect against a possible French invasion. This proposed revival of the feudal knights' service known as the *Ritterpferde* caused consternation within the ranks of the Ritterschaft, and its chief official, Erbmarschall Ludwig Freiherr von Riedesel,[40] immediately searched his records for precedents. Riedesel determined that the *Ritterpferde* had last been requested in the years 1654 and 1672 and both times the Ritterschaft had not served personally but had made a cash payment to the landgrave after debating the issue in the diet.[41]

Opposition to the landgrave's request was virtually universal in the Ritterschaft as its members raised the following objections: the *Ritterpferde* had last been requested more than one hundred years before, and conditions had changed in the meantime; the Ritterschaft now paid the knights' tax in place of its obligation to serve personally; the Ritterschaft no longer possessed serfs and thus could not order any of its subjects to serve; and the whole question should be decided by a meeting of the estates, which was already two years overdue.

After hearing the knights' objections, the landgrave informed the Ritterschaft that he had "graciously decided to dispense with the requirement for personal service" and would accept a suitable sum of money in its place. Riedesel replied that the Ritterschaft was willing to help but felt that the matter should be regulated by the estates. Since the landgrave was unwilling to summon the diet at that time, he dropped the matter, expressing his disappointment in the Ritterschaft's lack of support.[42]

[39] Kopp and Wittich, *Landes-Verfassung und Rechte*, 1: 105, 7: 243.

[40] The *Erbmarschall* (hereditary marshal) served as the chief official of the Ritterschaft and also presided over the Hessian diet. This position was always held by the senior male member of the Freiherren von Riedesel zu Eisenbach family.

[41] ARSK, Rep. VI, Gef. 15, Nr. 10, Decree of 19 April 1794; Erbmarschall to the deputies of the Ritterschaft, 23 June 1794.

[42] Ibid., William IX to Erbmarschall Riedesel, 16 October 1794; Riedesel to William IX, 31 December 1794. The landgrave never actually expected the vassals to serve in per-

29

The Ritterschaft's representation in the diet (*Landtag* or *Landstände*) was one of its most important rights. Only members of the Ritterschaft who owned noble estates were entitled to vote for or serve as delegates from the nobility. Thus in contrast to the diets of many other German states, non-nobles or even nobles who did not belong to the Ritterschaft could not represent the nobility in the Hessian diet, even if they owned a *Rittergut*. Furthermore, members of the Ritterschaft itself were not eligible to vote or serve if they were not owners or co-owners of noble estates.

In the eighteenth century the knighthood elected five delegates to the diet, one from each of the five *Strombezirke* (regions named after the five rivers that flowed through Hesse-Kassel: Fulda, Diemel, Schwalm, Werra, and Lahn). But the nobility's representation was not confined to the knights' estate. The so-called *Prälatenstand* (prelates' estate) no longer had any connection to the church and was composed almost entirely of nobles. The "prelates" consisted of three nobles—the head of the Marburg chapter of the Teutonic Order, the director of the state hospitals, and one of the directors of the noble Stift (foundation) at Kaufungen— and one bourgeois academic, who represented the University of Marburg. By the eighteenth century the prelates and knights no longer met separately but had been combined into a single estate, the *Prälaten- und Ritterstand*. The Hessian diet contained one additional member of the Ritterschaft; the senior member of the Freiherren von Riedesel zu Eisenbach family served as the diet's hereditary presiding official (the *Erbmarschall*).[43]

In addition to the nine nobles and one bourgeois in the prelates' and knights' estate, the diet contained eight members of the bourgeoisie, representing the towns. Beginning in 1815 the number of non-nobles increased by five when a third estate, the peasantry, was created. But the two non-noble estates could not combine to outvote the nobility because decisions of the diet required the approval of all three estates (until the constitution was passed in 1831).[44]

In the course of the nineteenth century the nobility saw virtually all of its former prerogatives either abolished outright or greatly dimin-

---

son; he just wanted to scare them into making a cash payment. The government was not even in a position to call upon the vassals for service, for it had no current lists of the knight service owed by each vassal. StAM, 17d Generalia, Pak. 6.

[43] For information on the Hessian diet in the early modern period see Carsten, *Princes and Parliaments*, 183–89; Adolf Lichtner, *Landesherr und Stände in Hesse-Cassel, 1797–1821* (Göttingen, 1913); Karl E. Demandt, "Die hessischen Landstände im Zeitalter des Frühabsolutismus," *Hessisches Jahrbuch für Landesgeschichte* 15 (1965).

[44] Lichtner, *Landesherr und Stände*, 3, 84; Carsten, *Princes and Parliaments*, 184.

ished. The process started with the French occupation of Hesse-Kassel and its incorporation into the new "model state," the Kingdom of Westphalia, in 1808. During this period nobles lost all of their financial and judicial advantages, but their dominant position as landlords was not seriously affected because the peasantry's dues to landlords were not abolished outright. Peasants were simply given the opportunity to free themselves of their burdens by paying a lump sum of cash, something that few peasants were in a position to do.

The nobility's hopes that the return of the elector from exile in December 1813 would bring about a complete return to the old order of things were not fulfilled. The key right of seigneurial justice, which had been abolished by the Westphalian constitution, was not restored by the elector in 1814, despite considerable protest by the Ritterschaft.[45] The end of patrimonial jurisdiction also meant the loss of several other fees that had been connected with local police powers: the annual "protection" payments (*Judenschutzgelder*) from Jews and the *Einzugs- und Auszugsgelder* from subjects moving into or out of a *Gerichtsherr*'s territory.

A second major disappointment for the knighthood in 1814 was the elector's refusal to abolish completely the Westphalian system of equal taxation in favor of the pre-1806 taxes. Instead, William I declared that the Ritterschaft would remain subject to the contribution (land tax) but would pay only two-thirds the normal rate rather than the full amount as it had under the Westphalian government. Furthermore, the Westphalian *Personalsteuer*, a tax to which all individuals were liable, was continued under the name *Landesschuldentilgungssteuer* (tax to pay off the national debt), replacing the previous knights' tax, which had been much more favorable to the nobility. The government's actions prompted a short-lived "taxpayers' revolt" by a number of knights who refused to pay their taxes as a protest against the loss of their financial privileges.[46]

By 1815 the Ritterschaft had also lost its exclusive right to hold certain

[45] The government never seriously considered going back to the old system of seigneurial justice because of its many disadvantages, some of which were listed in a memorandum of 12 January 1814 by a bourgeois member of the *Regierung* in Kassel, Johannes Hassenpflug (father of the notorious interior and justice minister of the 1830s and 1850s): "The rights of jurisdiction of the holders of patrimonial justice are not consistent. Some had both high and low justice and large areas of jurisdiction consisting of several villages. For others the jurisdiction was limited to the peasants who owed them dues and services; thus it was not uncommon to find three or more different *Gerichtsherren* for the same village." StAM, 17d Generalia, Paket 8. The abolition of seigneurial justice also benefited the state, which now collected the fees and penalties previously given to noble landlords and also no longer had to share this portion of its sovereignty with the nobility.

[46] StAM 5, Nr. 6886, Steuer Collegium to Elector Wilhelm I, 27 September and 3 November 1814.

government offices. The office of *Landrat* had been abolished in the 1790s, and when a similar office (*Kreisrat*, later also called *Landrat*) was created in the 1820s, none of its holders was noble. The four positions as *Rittersteuerobereinnehmer* also disappeared when the tax that they were supposed to collect was abolished in 1806.

The erosion of the nobility's privileges continued after the ratification of Hesse-Kassel's first constitution in 1831. Nobles no longer received special consideration in legal matters; they were now subject to the lower courts like all other citizens. Nobles were also no longer exempt from military service. Furthermore, the end of the nobility's rights as landlords was signaled by the constitution's declaration that all dues and services owed to landlords could be abolished in return for compensation. Laws to this effect were enacted the following year (1832) and in 1848.

The only important right that remained in the hands of the Ritterschaft after the 1830s was its right to representation in the Landtag. As in the eighteenth century, the knighthood elected five deputies to the diet. However, even though these delegates were joined by a number of other noble delegates (the *Erbmarschall*, representatives of the royal family and the *Standesherren*, a director of the Stift Kaufungen, and one representative each from the Schaumburg Ritterschaft, the former imperial knights, and the nobles in the province of Hanau), the nobility's relative strength in the Landtag was far less than in 1815, because the number of non-noble delegates had more than doubled and now included sixteen delegates from the cities and towns and sixteen delegates from the countryside. Furthermore, voting was conducted by head, not by estate, so the nobility could no longer block unfavorable legislation.[47]

The constitution guaranteed the remaining rights of the Ritterschaft, which were set forth in a bill presented to the legislature in 1836, the "Statuten der althessischen Ritterschaft."[48] The statutes reaffirmed the existing requirements for admission to the Ritterschaft, including the knights' right to select new members without interference, a right that had been violated several times in the previous decade by Elector William II.

[47] The composition of the Landtag was set forth in article 63 of the constitution of 1831, which is contained in *Sammlung von Gesetzen, Verordnungen, Ausschreiben und sonstigen allgemeinen Verfügungen für die Kurhessischen Staaten*, 18 vols. (Kassel, 1813–1866), 6: 10–11 (hereafter cited as *Sammlung von Gesetzen*).

[48] *Verhandlungen des kurhessischen Landtages* (Kassel, 1831–66), Landtag of 1836–37, 3. Periode, 1. Versammlung, Beilage 34 (hereafter cited as *LTV*). Although accepted by the elector, the statutes were never confirmed in their entirety by the Landtag. See below, pp. 227–28.

The statutes also made some changes in the Ritterschaft's traditional organizational structure. The *Erbmarschall*, always a member of the Freiherren von Riedesel family, remained the leader of the Ritterschaft, but if he resided outside Hesse-Kassel or was otherwise incapacitated, his duties were assumed by the *Vize-Marschall*, who was elected for life by the members of the knighthood. The knights also elected the three directors (*Obervorsteher*) of the Stift Kaufungen for life and five deputies (*Stroms-Deputierten*) along with five alternates who served five-year terms representing the knighthood in the Landtag and their districts at the annual conference of the Ritterschaft at the Stift Kaufungen. All major decisions required the approval of the majority of the members of the Ritterschaft, whose opinions were gathered by the deputies before the annual conference and for special issues.

The Ritterschaft as a corporate body owned a valuable piece of property, the Stift Kaufungen (along with a smaller Stift at Wetter). Because Landgrave Philip the Magnanimous's donation of the Stift had in part been compensation for the loss of church positions for noble daughters, the income from the Stift's landholdings was set aside to provide dowries for eight daughters from the Ritterschaft each year. The amount of each woman's dowry (*Ehesteuer*) was originally set at 80 *Reichstaler* but by the mid-eighteenth century had risen to 243 talers, with no limit on the number of individuals who could receive dowries (although the number of recipients rarely exceeded eight per year, averaging between four and five in the years 1738-57).[49] Thereafter the size of the dowry remained constant until 1803, when it rose to 406 talers. Further increases followed in 1822 (500 talers) and in 1860 (800 talers), and finally in 1870 dowries from the Stift were fixed at 1,200 talers and did not rise for the rest of the century.[50]

The Stift Kaufungen also provided support other than dowries. Beginning in 1735 the Stift began granting an annual allowance to widows and daughters of deceased knights, for in most cases women were not entitled to inherit much if any of their families' holdings. This so-called *ordentliche Stiftssteuer* originally amounted to thirty talers per person, gradually rose to one hundred talers by 1802, and reached two hundred talers in 1856. Only widows and daughters without personal wealth were eligible for this support. In addition the Stift granted an extraor-

---

[49] Lists of annual payments of all types of support given by the Stift Kaufungen are contained in StAM 304 (Stift Kaufangen), Rep. II, Gef. 1, Nr. 19.

[50] Wilhelm Wolff, *Die Säkularisierung und Verwendung der Stifts- und Klostergüter in Hessen-Kassel unter Philipp dem Grossmütigen und Wilhelm IV* (Gotha, 1913), 162–74; Otto von und zu Gilsa, *Studien über die wirtschaftliche Entwicklung des ritterschaftlichen Stiftes Kaufungen, besonders im 18. und 19. Jahrhundert* (Marburg, 1927), 43–45.

dinary payment (*ausserordentliche Stiftssteuer*) to needy noblewomen who did not meet the requirements for the other grants. Thus daughters who married outside the nobility received a small extraordinary payment instead of the normal dowry. The Stift also gave extraordinary support to some needy daughters whose fathers were still alive, which made the women ineligible for the normal yearly support payments. However, in such cases the father had to provide proof that his income was too small for him to give his daughters a proper education. During the nineteenth century applicants for extraordinary assistance for their daughters had to have less than one thousand talers in income from all sources. The recipients of the yearly extraordinary payments thus belonged to the poorest families of the Ritterschaft.[51]

Although the Ritterschaft had retained its corporate property (the Stift Kaufungen), its political representation, and the right to elect its own officers and select new members without outside interference, the knights, along with the other nobles in Hesse-Kassel, had lost virtually all of their other legal and financial privileges in the course of the nineteenth century. The economic effect of these losses is examined in chapter 5, but the resultant loss of status for the nobility is something that cannot be easily measured.

[51] In each of the following families, three or more nobles requested extraordinary assistance in supporting their daughters in the nineteenth century: von Löwenstein, von Baumbach-Freudenthal, von Baumbach-Gilserhof, von Schenk zu Schweinsberg-Fronhausen, von Dalwigk, Treusch von Buttlar, von Schutzbar genannt Milchling, and von Biedenfeld. Applications to the Stift Kaufungen for extraordinary payments are found in StAM 304, Rep. II, Gef. 11–13.

· 3 ·

THE NOBLE FAMILY

MARRIAGE

The nobilities of early modern Europe faced a constant dilemma: how to ensure the continuation of noble lineages without endangering the preservation of their landholdings. Large numbers of children would eliminate the danger of families' becoming extinct, but too many children could prove a threat to the economic stability of noble families. Most European nobilities chose to emphasize the preservation of noble property and therefore adopted inheritance systems based on primogeniture to keep holdings intact. The question then arose as to what was to be done with the younger sons and daughters, who were precluded from inheriting. The solution to this problem varied from country to country, but many nobilities attempted to reduce the severity of the problem by limiting both the number of marriages and the size of families.[1]

In French noble families the eldest son generally inherited the bulk of his father's holdings, but in return he had to pay substantial cash settlements to his brothers and sisters. To prevent too great a strain on the family fortune, many nobles placed some of their children in church positions, thereby removing the need to provide them with settlements. A large proportion of the younger sons never married, and when they died, their portions frequently reverted to their families.[2]

A similar but even more rigid system of family control was practiced by the Catholic *Stiftsadel* (nobles belonging to a cathedral chapter that elected the ruler of an ecclesiastical state) of Westphalia. Generally only eldest sons could marry and inherit estates. To compensate younger sons for their celibacy and lack of inheritance rights, Westphalian families provided them with a good education and then a secure office in the cathedral chapter, army, or bureaucracy. The Westphalian nobility's control over the marriages of its children was not limited to the number of marriages; even more important was the kind of marriages contracted,

[1] For a detailed survey of noble inheritance patterns see J. P. Cooper, "Patterns of Inheritance and Settlement by Great Landowners from the Fifteenth to the Eighteenth Centuries," in *Family and Inheritance: Rural Society in Western Europe*, ed. Jack Goody, Joan Thirsk, and E. P. Thompson (Cambridge, 1976), 192–327.

[2] Cooper, "Patterns of Inheritance," 268–76; Robert Forster, *The Nobility of Toulouse in the Eighteenth Century: A Social and Economic Study* (Baltimore, 1960), 120–30; Jean Meyer, *La noblesse bretonne au XVIIIe siècle*, 2 vols. (Paris, 1966), 1: 121–27.

35

because offices in the cathedral chapter and positions in the institutions for unmarried noble daughters required proof that all sixteen great-great-grandparents of an applicant had been nobles. As a result, marriage to a non-noble was out of the question for most members of the Westphalian nobility; even many nobles were unacceptable marriage partners owing to a "blemish" somewhere in their noble pedigree. Catholic nobles in Westphalia therefore tended to marry within a very limited circle of families, and few of the daughters or younger sons were able to marry at all.[3]

Family control was not limited to nobilities practicing primogeniture. The Venetian nobility had no strict system of inheritance but instead developed an informal system of controls under which only one son per family married. Since it was often the youngest son who married, the Venetian nobility declined steadily in size because if the youngest son failed to produce an heir, his older brothers were often already dead or too set in their ways to marry and father children. At times none of a family's sons married, thus accelerating the Venetian nobility's shrinkage even more.[4]

The landed nobility of Hesse-Kassel adopted a far different approach to the problems of inheritance and marriage. Primogeniture never took hold within the nobility, which is perhaps not surprising in a country whose most famous ruler, Philip the Magnanimous, thought nothing of dividing his territory among his four sons in the sixteenth century. Hessian feudal law specified that all sons were equally entitled to inherit a fief, and because the bulk of the nobility's land was held in this form, primogeniture and its accompanying concepts of "eldest" and "younger" sons never gained acceptance among Hessian nobles. But in contrast to that of Venice, the Hessian nobility's system of equal inheritance rights was not accompanied by an attempt to limit the number of marriages.

The lack of strict family controls upon marriage enabled a large proportion of both the sons and daughters of the Hessian Ritterschaft to marry, and this high rate of marriage remained unchanged from the seventeenth through the nineteenth centuries (see table 3.1).[5] More than

[3] Reif, *Westfälischer Adel*, 78–88, 240–42; idem., " 'Erhaltung adligen Stamms und Namens': Adelsfamilie und Statussicherung im Münsterland, 1770–1914," in *Studien zur Geschichte der Familie in Deutschland und Frankreich vom 16. bis zum 20. Jahrhundert*, ed. Neithard Bulst, Joseph Goy, and Jochen Hoock (Göttingen, 1981), 277–78.

[4] James C. Davis, *The Decline of the Venetian Nobility as a Ruling Class* (Baltimore, 1962), 62, 72.

[5] The data for this study of the marriages and fertility of the Hessian Ritterschaft has

two-thirds of all males reaching the age of twenty or above married, and the percentage who married is even higher when males dying in their twenties are excluded, because the average age at marriage for men almost always exceeded thirty (see table 3.2). Noble daughters generally married in their early twenties. Like that of noble sons, the percentage

TABLE 3.1.
Frequency of Marriage

	Men				Women	
Year of Parents' Marriage	Total Men Age 20+	Number Who Married	Total Men Age 30+	Number Who Married	Total Women Age 20+	Number Who Married
1650–99	330	208 (63%)	267	196 (73%)	278	206 (74%)
1700–49	298	185 (62%)	256	174 (68%)	258	186 (72%)
1750–99	317	207 (65%)	277	204 (74%)	318	222 (70%)
1800–49	388	282 (73%)	356	279 (78%)	375	242 (65%)
1850–99	370	255 (69%)	322	250 (78%)	337	225 (67%)

been compiled primarily from a comprehensive nineteenth-century collection of noble genealogies—Rudolf von Buttlar-Elberberg, *Stammbuch der althessischen Ritterschaft* (Wolfhagen, 1888)—supplemented by material from noble family archives deposited in the Hessian State Archive at Marburg. Three later works have continued the genealogies to the present day: Karl von Baumbach-Nassenerfurth, *Stammtafeln der althessischen Ritterschaft aus neueren Zeit* (Rudolstadt, 1932); Siegfried Freiherr von Dörnberg, *Stammtafeln der althessichen Ritterschaft* (Bad Hersfeld, 1958); and Winfried von Schutzbar genannt Milchling, *Stammtafeln der althessischen Ritterschaft* (Göttingen, 1977). The available data included approximately 3,300 adult men and women of the Ritterschaft from the seventeenth through the nineteenth century. Detailed analysis was made of 1,046 marriages contracted by noblemen between 1650 and 1899 (although marriages from the 1880s and 1890s were not included in the analysis of marital fertility and child mortality because the three twentieth-century sets of genealogies are not as comprehensive as that of Buttlar, frequently omitting children who died young or entire branches that died out). Owing to missing data, not every marriage was usable for all questions asked, particularly in the earlier cohorts. There is of course a slight amount of bias in the available data because the genealogies include only families that were still in existence in the nineteenth century and thus ignore a number of families that became extinct during the preceding two centuries. However, the degree of bias is probably not too great, since the genealogies encompass all members of a given lineage, including branches that died out centuries earlier, rather than just the families directly in the line of descent to the nineteenth- or twentieth-century members, as is the case in most handbooks of noble families.

TABLE 3.2.
Age at First Marriage

Year Married	Men				Their Wives				Age Difference:	
	Mean	Median	Range	N	Mean	Median	Range	N	Means	Medians
1650–99	31.4	30.6	20–52	92	23.2	22.8	13–34	64	8.2	7.8
1700–49	33.1	32.0	18–55	137	22.4	22.1	14–34	93	10.7	9.9
1750–99	31.5	30.2	18–56	131	23.1	22.7	14–40	102	8.4	7.5
1800–49	30.3	29.8	19–51	213	23.8	23.2	15–39	198	6.5	6.6
1850–99	32.5	32.0	22–57	249	24.0	23.1	17–47	244	8.5	8.9

of daughters who married was quite high, remaining above 70 percent until the nineteenth century.

Although it is difficult to speak of a "typical" age at marriage for European noblemen, the men of the Hessian Ritterschaft do seem to have married later than most other nobles. Even as early as the seventeenth century, the average Hessian noble did not marry until after he had reached the age of thirty, whereas the average age at marriage for the males of British ducal families and the Westphalian and Austrian nobilities did not exceed thirty until the nineteenth century.[6] The opposite extreme, early marriage, was found among the French dukes and peers. Their average age at marriage, already low in the seventeenth century, proceeded to decline even further during the following century. By the second half of the eighteenth century, the median age at marriage was below twenty.[7] However, the low marriage age of the dukes and peers was probably caused by economic considerations[8] and is probably not typical of the French nobility as a whole during the period.[9] As table 3.3

[6] T. H. Hollingsworth, "A Demographic Study of the British Ducal Families," in *Population in History*, ed. D. V. Glass and D.E.C. Eversly (London, 1965), 365; Reif, *Westfälischer Adel*, 243, 247; Michael Mitterauer, "Zur Frage des Heiratsverhaltens im österreichischen Adel," in *Beiträge zur neueren Geschichte Österreichs: Festschrift für Adam Wandruszka*, ed. Heinrich Fichtenau and Erich Zöllner (Vienna, 1974), 179.

[7] Claude Lévy and Louis Henry, "Ducs et pairs sous l'Ancien Régime: Caractéristiques démographiques d'une caste," *Population* 15: 813.

[8] The early marriages of the sons of the ducal family Saulx-Tavanes resulted from the need to acquire large dowries as soon as possible in order to improve the family's finances. Robert Forster, *The House of Saulx-Tavanes: Versailles and Burgundy, 1700–1830* (Baltimore, 1971), 50.

[9] The demographic characteristics of the French nobility are still virtually unstudied,

illustrates, the average age at marriage of European upper classes varied widely, with two non-noble elites, the bourgeoisies of Geneva and Lower Saxony,[10] exhibiting an average marriage age similar to that of the Hessian Ritterschaft.

Why did so many Hessian noblemen delay marriage until they were in their thirties or even forties? The answer lies in part in the participation of the vast majority of nobles in some form of government service. Both the Hessian army and the Hessian bureaucracy placed restrictions upon the marriage of young, lower-ranking officers and civil servants. Furthermore, the meager salaries of the former and the small or even nonexistent salaries of the latter made it nearly impossible for a young lieutenant or junior civil servant to support a family without considerable outside income.[11] In most cases, however, a noble could not count on much income from his estates until after the death of his father. But late marriage did not result solely from economic considerations, for it was also common among wealthy nobles who were not involved in government service. Late marriage had thus become an accepted practice for most noblemen in Hesse-Kassel.

Once nobles did marry, they generally chose wives much younger than themselves, so marriages in which the difference in ages amounted to fifteen or more years occurred frequently, although the average difference ranged between six and eleven years. Occasionally such differences were quite extreme, as in 1772 when the eighteen-year-old Josine von Schenck zu Schweinsberg married Heinrich von Knoblauch, age fifty-six. This thirty-eight-year gap in ages was, however, quite unusual; the next most extreme cases were the marriages of Ludwig von Eschwege (fifty-one) to Friederike von Selchow (twenty-two) in 1803 and

---

but a recent examination of noble officials in Brittany reveals a much higher marriage age than that of the dukes and peers:

	Présidents	Conseillers	Greffiers en chef
16th century	32.0	31.5	30.8
17th century	27.9	28.5	28.6
18th century	28.2	31.1	30.1

Jean Meyer, "La noblesse parlementaire bretonne," in *Vom Ancien Régime zur Französischen Revolution*, ed. Ernst Hinrichs, Eberhard Schmidt, and Rudolf Vierhaus (Göttingen, 1978), 316.

[10] Louis Henry, *Anciennes familles genevoises: Étude démographique, XVIe–XXe siècle* (Paris, 1956), 55; Adelheid von Nell, "Die Entwicklung der generativen Strukturen bürgerlicher und bäuerlicher Familien von 1750 bis zur Gegenwart" (Ph.D. diss., University of Bochum, 1973), 72.

[11] See below, chapter 6.

39

Table 3.3.
Marriage Age of European Elites: Husbands

Year Married	Hessian Ritterschaft		British Ducal Families	Austrian Nobility		Westphalian *Stiftsadel*		French Dukes and Peers		Genevan Bourgeoisie		Lower Saxon Bourgeoisie
	Mean	Median	Mean	1st Son Mean	Ygr. Sons Mean	1st Son Mean	Ygr. Sons Mean	Mean	Median	Mean	Median	Mean
1650–99	31.4	30.6	—	26.6	29.7	—	—	25.5	23.8	32.6	30.9	—
1700–49	33.1	32.0	28.6	28.2	29.5	26	—	23.6	21.7	31.9	30.5	30.9
1750–99	31.5	30.2	28.6	28.3	36.5	28	30	21.3	19.8	31.5	29.7	32.2
1800–49	30.3	29.8	30.5	32.0	34.5	32	37	—	—	29.4	28.2	31.9
1850–99	32.5	32.0	30.0	29.3	33.1	—	—	—	—	29.2	27.6	32.8

SOURCES: Hollingsworth, *British Ducal Families*, 365; Mitterauer, "Frage des Heiratsverhaltens," 179; Reif, *Westfälischer Adel*, 243, 247; Lévy and Henry, "Ducs et pairs," 813; Henry, *Anciennes familles genevoises*, 55; Nell, "Entwicklung der generativen Strukturen," 72.

NOTE: Some of the studies did not use the above dating system, but data from such groups has been placed in the most appropriate time period to facilitate comparison. Averages from the British ducal families are based upon the husband's year of birth in the following periods: 1680–1729, 1730–79, 1780–1829, and 1830–79. Therefore the marriages occurred approximately ten years later than the periods listed in the table. The data for the Westphalian nobility is based upon the year of marriage, but the periods studied were twenty years later than those in the table: 1720–69, 1770–1819, and 1820–69. The marriages of the Genevan bourgeoisie are listed under the husband's year of birth, not the year of marriage, so the marriages occurred approximately thirty years later than the dates in the table.

Melchior von Bodenhausen (forty) to Sophia von Reisewitz (thirteen) in 1693. Despite her young age, Sophia bore her first child the following year, and other nobles' wives who married in their early teens also had children within a year or two, so Hessian nobles did not follow the example of many seventeenth-century English aristocrats, who often did not consummate marriages to young girls until several years after the wedding or limited themselves to a token consummation followed by several years of separation.[12] Instances of Hessian nobles marrying women older than themselves were rare; even marriages between partners of the same age were not common.

Noblemen's preference for young wives remained unchanged from the seventeenth through the nineteenth century, so they had obviously not attempted to limit family size through the simple expedient of marrying women in their late twenties and early thirties. This method of reducing the number of potential childbearing years was often practiced by European peasants[13] and may also have been used by nobles in Westphalia. The mean age at marriage for the wives of the eldest sons (*Stammherren*) of Westphalian noble families rose from nineteen in the mid-eighteenth century to twenty-six in the nineteenth century.[14] With the exception of these Westphalian nobles' wives and the wives of the French dukes and peers (who like their husbands married quite early), the wives of European elites, both noble and bourgeois, married at approximately the same age, as can be seen in table 3.4.

The high frequency of marriage by Hessian nobles demonstrates that no attempt was made to limit the number of children who married, but the question remains whether or not the kind of persons married was regulated, either by law, by the Ritterschaft itself, or by parents. Unlike some German states such as Prussia, where marriages between noblemen and non-noble women (except for members of the upper bourgeoisie) were forbidden until the 1860s,[15] Hesse-Kassel placed no restrictions upon marriages between nobles and commoners. The Ritterschaft also had no rules forbidding such marriages. Although candidates for admission to the corporate body of Hessian knights had to show proof of four generations of nobility in both their paternal and their maternal line-

[12] Lawrence Stone, *The Crisis of the Aristocracy, 1558–1641* (London, 1965), 656–59.

[13] E. A. Wrigley, "Family Limitation in Pre-Industrial England," *Economic History Review* 19 (1966): 86–87; Arthur E. Imhof, "Ländliche Familienstrukturen an einem hessischen Beispiel: Heuchelheim 1690–1900," in *Sozialgeschichte der Familie in der Neuzeit Europas*, ed. Werner Conze (Stuttgart, 1976), 207.

[14] Reif, *Westfälischer Adel*, 243–44.

[15] Reinhard Koselleck, *Preußen zwischen Reform und Revolution: Allgemeines Landrecht, Verwaltung und soziale Bewegung von 1791 bis 1848* (Stuttgart, 1975), 105.

TABLE 3.4. Marriage Age of European Elites: Wives

Year Married	Hessian Ritterschaft		British Ducal Families	Austrian Nobility	Westphalian (*Stiftsadel*) (Eldest Sons)	French Dukes and Peers		Genevan Bourgeoisie		Lower Saxon Bourgeoisie
	Mean	Median	Mean	Mean	Mean	Mean	Median	Mean	Median	Mean
1650–99	23.2	22.8	—	22.4	—	20.0	18.6	26.2	23.2	—
1700–49	22.4	22.1	22.4	22.5	19	19.4	18.4	25.5	24.0	22.4
1750–99	23.1	22.7	23.4	22.8	23	18.3	17.7	23.5	22.1	22.1
1800–49	23.8	23.2	24.5	22.9	26	—	—	22.7	21.4	24.4
1850–99	24.0	23.1	24.3	23.7	—	—	—	24.7	23.0	25.3

Sources: Hollingsworth, *British Ducal Families*, 366; Mitterauer, "Frage des Heiratsverhaltens," 179; Reif, *Westfälischer Adel*, 243; Lévy and Henry, "Ducs et pairs," 813; Henry, *Anciennes familles genevoises*, 55; Nell, "Entwicklung der generativen Strukturen," 74.
Note: The variations in dating systems listed under table 3.3 also apply to this table.

ages, existing members were free to marry as they saw fit. Only the daughters of the Ritterschaft faced any limitation in their choice of marriage partners, and this restriction consisted solely of a financial loss, not outright prohibition. The Ritterschaft's foundation at Kaufungen would not make its normal marriage payment to a daughter who married outside the nobility unless her husband was at least a major in the army or a privy councilor (*Geheimer Rat*) in the bureaucracy, offices that were in the fourth class of the government's *Rangordnung* (a table of ranks used to determine the order of precedence at court; for details, see appendix C).[16] Although this restriction represented an improvement over the sixteenth-century practice of limiting the marriage gifts solely to those daughters who married within the nobility, only a small proportion of the women who married bourgeois were eligible to receive the marriage payment. Most of the bourgeois marriage partners had not yet attained such high rank, owing to the torpid pace of advancement in both the Hessian army and bureaucracy.[17]

Marriages between noble daughters and young bourgeois lieutenants or assessors (offices only in the sixth class of the table of ranks) were not uncommon, and during the early nineteenth century sentiment within the Ritterschaft grew strong for a modification of the marriage rules. In 1838 the directors (*Obervorsteher*) of the Stift Kaufungen debated whether or not to change the requirements. Obervorsteher Friedrich von Trott zu Solz argued that it was simply a matter of time before a junior officer or civil servant advanced in rank, so the marriage rules should be loosened. His more conservative colleague, Obervorsteher Carl von Eschwege, replied, "A line must be drawn somewhere, and if we make the individuals who are presently in the sixth class of the table of ranks equal to the nobility, we thereby cheapen nobility." Eschwege also noted that after a short period of time there would again arise a clamor to lower the marriage requirements, a development that "in the end will drag the nobility down to the level of the lowest orders."[18] Trott's views finally prevailed in 1848, when the delegates to the annual conference of the Ritterschaft voted to lower the limit for acceptable marriage partners from individuals in the fourth class to those in the sixth class of the table of ranks.[19]

The delegates' action in approving a wider range of individuals as ac-

[16] Kopp and Wittich, *Landes-Verfassung und Rechte*, 6: 522–23.

[17] Between 1800 and 1870 only four of the forty-six women who asked the Stift Kaufungen for a dowry after marrying outside the nobility had married bourgeois in the rank of at least major or *Geheimer Rat*. StAM 304, D Rep. II, Gef. 2–5.

[18] StAM 304, D Rep. II, Gef. 2–5. Nr. 119.

[19] Kaufungen Archive, Rep. VI, Gef. 2, Nr. 6, 8.

ceptable marriage partners was part of a gradual change in attitude among many Hessian nobles during the nineteenth century. Less than fifty years earlier the directors of the Stift Kaufungen had denied a request for the marriage payment by a noblewoman married to a bourgeois lieutenant, stating, "There has never been an exception made to the rule and it would thus be very dangerous to make one for the applicant, for this would lead to a large number of similar requests and would undermine the goal of hindering misalliances [*unstandesmäßige Heiraten*]."[20] By the 1840s the officials of the Stift Kaufungen were willing to loosen but not completely eliminate the restrictions upon marriages, but one prominent Hessian noble went much further and argued that the entire concept of misalliances was no longer valid: "No reasonable member of the nobility sees a good match with an educated girl from the upper bourgeoisie as a misalliance any more, and if this is true for a good match, then there is certainly no reason to regard a poor match, that is to say one with a girl of no means, as a misalliance."[21]

The absence of legal restrictions upon marriages outside the nobility, the lack of significant disadvantages resulting from such marriages for both the individuals involved and their offspring, and the changed attitude of many nobles toward "misalliances" all contributed to a steady increase in the number of marriages between noblemen and non-noble women. By the early twentieth century such marriages had become just as common as those by noblemen with women of their own class. For noblewomen the situation was somewhat different, because marriage to a commoner in effect resulted in the loss of noble status. Therefore noblewomen continued to marry within the nobility to a greater extent than did noblemen. Nevertheless the percentage of marriages by noblewomen to commoners increased steadily (see table 3.5).

What sort of commoners did noblemen marry? It is natural to assume that nobles sought whenever possible to marry bourgeois heiresses in order to bolster their sagging fortunes, but such marriages were the exception rather than the rule for the Hessian Ritterschaft.[22] Generally nobles married into the bourgeois families with which they had the most con-

---

[20] StAM 304, D Rep. II, Gef. 2–5, Nr. 4.

[21] Wilhelm von Schenck zu Schweinsberg, *Über den niederen Adel und dessen politischen Stellung in Deutschland* (Stuttgart, 1842), 22. Schenck was appointed foreign minister during the revolution of 1848, but his liberal views quickly alienated the elector, who fired him in early 1849.

[22] One member of the Ritterschaft who did marry a bourgeois heiress was Lieutenant Ernst von Hesberg. His 1773 marriage to Marie Wilhelmine Goeddaeus brought him the estates Laar and Betzigerode. After her death in 1788, he married her sister, Marie Amalie, perhaps to further cement his claim to the estates.

TABLE 3.5. Marriage Partners of the Ritterschaft

Cohort Born	Men Married:		Women Married:	
	Nobles	Non-nobles	Nobles	Non-nobles
1650–99	196 (97%)	7 (3%)	199 (92%)	17 (8%)
1700–49	155 (88%)	22 (12%)	185 (96%)	8 (4%)
1750–99	155 (76%)	48 (24%)	175 (83%)	36 (17%)
1800–49	174 (64%)	100 (36%)	174 (70%)	73 (30%)
1850–99	132 (51%)	129 (49%)	152 (64%)	87 (36%)

tact, namely those involved in the same career. Thus noble civil servants and their children frequently married members of bourgeois civil servant families, and marriages between the families of noble and bourgeois army officers were also commonplace. As a result, most non-noble wives of members of the Ritterschaft came from the families of civil servants, army officers, and landowners.[23]

Like their brothers, noblewomen frequently married into bourgeois families involved in the same careers as their fathers, but in addition a number of noblewomen married pastors, who were often the only educated men with whom daughters on isolated rural estates came into contact. In the nineteenth century the occupations for fifty-eight non-noble husbands of women from the Ritterschaft are known: sixteen pastors and church officials, fifteen civil servants, ten army officers, six doctors, three professors, three estate owners, one pharmacist, one court employee, one official of the Stift Kaufungen, and one leaseholder of a noble estate.

Marriages by noblewomen to non-nobles were most common among the poorer families of the Ritterschaft, possibly because they could provide their daughters little or no dowry with which to snare a nobleman and because these families were declining in status. Thus in 1829 Amalia von Baumbach-Gilserhof wrote to the Stift Kaufungen, "Some time ago I became engaged to a worthy young man, the tenant Dippel on Gilserhof, a man who deserves public admiration and is also in the position to assure me a proper existence. I did so because I recognized

---

[23] In thirty-four nineteenth-century marriages for which the occupation of a non-noble wife's father is known, the following occupations were represented: fifteen civil servants, six army officers, five estate owners, two professors, two leaseholders of noble estates, one physician, one pharmacist, one pastor, and one innkeeper.

the danger that as a poor girl I would never be able to marry a noble-man."[24] But impoverished nobles were not always willing to sanction their daughters' misalliances. Amalia's father, Major Carl von Baum-bach, whose indebtedness led to the loss of all his holdings in the 1830s, bitterly opposed his daughter's loss of noble status through marriage to a commoner, perhaps because he did not want his already low social standing to decline even more. Amalia was forced to sue her father to obtain his consent for the marriage. Baumbach's desire to avoid a mis-alliance was not confined solely to his daughter, for he also attempted to block the marriage of his son into the same family. Friedrich von Baum-bach joined in his sister's lawsuit, complaining that his father opposed his proposed marriage to Gertrude Dippel because "my fiancée is not wealthy enough." Friedrich rejected his father's demand that he break his engagement, stating, "We love each other too deeply to ever consider breaking our vow. We would both be extremely unhappy, especially be-cause my fiancée is expecting a baby in five months." The superior court (*Obergericht*) ruled against the father in both cases, and the marriages took place.[25]

Unlike many European nobles, members of the Hessian Ritterschaft seldom were able to enlarge their holdings by marrying heiresses. Few Hessian bourgeois families owned estates, and heiresses were very rare among the families of the nobility, since daughters generally could not inherit land and received small dowries. As a result, nobles seeking wives with large cash dowries or even entire estates usually had to look outside the borders of Hesse-Kassel. Occasionally a noble's attempt to marry well was based upon a miscalculation. In 1762 Wilhelm von Butt-lar-Elberberg (aged thirty) married the fifteen-year-old Friederike von Voss, heiress of a supposedly wealthy Westphalian family. Afterward he discovered that the family was hopelessly in debt. Despite this finan-cial disappointment, the couple proved to be congenial and produced thirteen children, but often such marriages of convenience did not turn out so well. Buttlar's son Georg also married a wealthy daughter of a non-Hessian family, Marianne Gräfin von der Schulenberg, who

[24] StAM 304, Rep. II, Gef. 11–13, Nr. 4, Amalia von Baumbach to Stift Kaufungen, 21 June 1829.

[25] StAM 270f (Obergericht Kassel), Verz. 2, B-4. Baumbach threw his daughter out of his house, and she married Martin Dippel in 1830. Unfortunately he proved unsuccessful as a leaseholder, and Amalia later found it necessary to write to other families of the Rit-terschaft begging for assistance for herself and her ten children (one such letter from 1848 is found in StAM 340 (Familienarchive und Nachlässe) v. Bodenhausen, Paket 216). As for her brother Friedrich, he worked for the railroad after his family lost its landholdings, and then in 1856 he emigrated to the United States. August von Baumbach, *Geschichte der zur althessischen Ritterschaft gehörenden Familie von Baumbach* (Marburg, 1886), 55–56.

brought a dowry of ten thousand talers into their marriage in 1801. The union was not a happy one, and Marianne deserted her husband for an English diplomat five years later.[26]

Marriages to the daughters of non-Hessian noble families were often motivated by financial considerations. For example, Carl von Baumbach-Nassenerfurth, whose family's estate stood under sequestration in the 1790s, first saw Amalie von Hendrich at the Leipzig Trade Fair in 1798 but did not speak to her at the time. After learning that she came from a wealthy family, he asked a friend living near her parents to see if a marriage could be arranged. His friend's approach was successful, and in January 1799 Baumbach set off for her home in Meiningen. As he later noted, his actions were "rather frivolous, for I scarcely knew Amalie, but I was blinded by the Hendrich wealth."[27] This marriage based upon wealth also proved unsuccessful; Amalie left Baumbach for another man in 1806.

The use of an intermediary to sound out a woman's family about the prospect of marriage was common even in marriages that were not motivated by financial considerations. Thus in 1795, when Wilhelm von Dörnberg decided to marry Julie Gräfin von Münster-Meinhövel, whom he had known since childhood, he first had a friend approach her parents to see if they considered him acceptable as a son-in-law.[28]

Although parents generally retained the right of approval of marriage partners, the actual selection of a partner was almost always in the hands of the son or daughter. Quite often fathers were no longer alive by the time their sons chose brides, because of the large gaps between generations resulting from late marriage by men. The daughters of the Ritterschaft were also generally free to choose their own husbands in the nineteenth century. Feelings typical of many noblewomen were expressed by Sophie von Verschuer in a letter to Wilhelm von Baumbach-Sontra in 1832 in which she thanked him for his attempt to arrange a marriage for her but added, "I regret very much that I cannot make use of your thoughtfulness, as it has always been my unshakable resolve *never* to marry without true inner conviction and *never* to contract a marriage as

[26] Friedrich Hueck, "Geschichte der Familie von Buttlar-Elberberg" (typescript, 1950), no. 48/52, p. 2; no. 24, p. 4. I would like to thank Walrab von Buttlar-Elberberg for loaning a copy of this manuscript to me. Some of the letters from Marianne von Buttlar to the Englishman are printed in Ralph Heathcote, *Letters of a Young Diplomat and Soldier during the Time of Napoleon, Giving an Account of the Dispute between the Emperor and the Elector of Hesse* (London, 1907), 62–73.

[27] Reinhold von Baumbach, *Carl Ludwig Friedrich August von Baumbach: Ein Lebensbild* (Rudolstadt, 1910), 21.

[28] Hugo von Dörnberg-Hausen, *Wilhelm von Dörnberg: Ein Kämpfer für Deutschlands Freiheit* (Marburg, 1936), 18.

if it were a commercial transaction."[29] Baumbach of all people should have recognized the determination of noblewomen to choose their own marriage partners, for just seven years earlier Catharine von Berlichingen had written to him saying, "I am marrying you of my own free will and in doing so I am following an inner voice that has made me decide so quickly and firmly."[30]

Marriages were major social occasions for the Hessian nobility, with friends and relatives coming from near and far to participate in the festivities. One such wedding in 1799, that of Sophie von Baumbach-Ropperhausen to Heinrich von der Malsburg-Elmarshausen, may well have been typical of others in this period, although descriptions of weddings are scarce. The ceremony was described in detail in a letter written by the bride's cousin, Friederike von Baumbach (1779-1847):

> Around noon, as we returned from a walk, we found Geheimrat Baumbach and Carl, who had come for the wedding. Then we went up to our room (I was staying together with Sophie) and got dressed. Sophie fixed my hair first and then I did hers; she then dressed all in white, from her head to her feet, with a myrtle wreath in her hair, and looked very pretty. Ernestine and I as bridesmaids were also dressed in white with fresh roses in our hair. We then went to eat, where I sat on one side of the groom, Sophie on the other. After the meal, around three o'clock, the wedding took place, up in the general's wife's room, where a table covered in white stood in place of an altar. Ernestine and I stood behind the bride. She was so nervous that she shivered and shook. The pastor kept the ceremony short and then we were done. Next we had coffee and then warm punch, and most of the guests departed. We all changed our clothes, went for a walk, drank tea outside, and returned to the house around suppertime. As we came into the dining room we saw a small altar on the table on which a candle was burning; this was surrounded by garlands of flowers, and Florenz had written a few nice poems, which he gave to the bridal pair. We were very merry at the table, drank to everyone's health, even sang; all at once we all ran to the window to see why the courtyard was so bright. The entire courtyard was illuminated by a large *S* and *H* burning in the orchard. Everything was lit up, and this was the beginning of a real fireworks display. After all these events we went back into the house, where the married women—the general's wife and the old cook—brought the bridal cap in, took the wreath out of

[29] StAM 340 v. Baumbach-Kirchheim, Paket 105, Nr. 5, letter of 8 March 1832.
[30] Ibid., letter of 18 September 1825.

the bride's hair, and put on her cap; then her eyes were bound tightly shut and all of us unmarried men and women danced around the wreath—and I got it! Then Kammerherr von der Malsburg came and took off Sophie's garter, from which I have enclosed a piece for you. In the meantime Florenz had changed into women's clothing and had offered his services as a chambermaid. Then we all brought Sophie up into my room, undressed her, and put on a pretty piqué negligee with a pink trim, and Ernestine and I led her into the bridal chamber, where the groom in his white nightshirt was waiting for her, along with the Kammerherr; then we tucked Sophie into bed and the groom lay down next to her. We kissed them both heartily and then left them alone.[31]

FAMILY SIZE

Given the high rate of marriage by the members of the Hessian Ritterschaft, it is natural to ask whether this led to the early adoption of some form of family limitation in order to prevent families from expanding too rapidly. We have just seen that nobles made no attempt to limit the size of families by marrying women who were already past many of their most fertile years, but other methods of birth control were known in this period. In both France and England contraceptive practices had become widespread among the upper classes by the early eighteenth century.[32]

One fairly simple method of checking for the use of birth control is to compare the size of completed families (families in which the marriage remained intact at least until the wife reached age forty-five, thus virtually exhausting all possible fertility). The changes in completed-family size within the Ritterschaft shown in table 3.6 suggest that birth control was not practiced to any substantial degree before the early nineteenth century.[33]

The largest completed family in the Ritterschaft was that of Georg Treusch von Buttlar. His wife, Sophie von Buttlar-Ziegenberg, married

[31] Otto von der Malsburg, "Aufzeichnungen aus der Familiengeschichte derer 'von der Malsburg' " (typescript, n.d.), 14–16. I would like to thank Dr. Raban von der Malsburg-Escheberg for loaning this manuscript to me.

[32] Lévy and Henry, "Ducs et pairs," 815–20; Forster, *Nobility of Toulouse*, 130; Lawrence Stone, *The Family, Sex and Marriage in England, 1500–1800* (London, 1965), 415–23.

[33] The decline in the average size of completed families in the early eighteenth century may have been caused more by the large number of childless marriages than by birth control among fertile couples. Because of missing data, which makes it impossible to determine whether or not many childless marriages were completed, the frequency of childless marriages among completed families in the 1650–99 cohort is probably underrepresented.

TABLE 3.6.
Completed Family Size

Year Married	Number of Families with x Children:														Total Families	Total Children	Average Size
	0	1	2	3	4	5	6	7	8	9	10	11	12+			
1650–99	2	0	0	1	2	6	2	3	5	5	5	3	5	39	306	7.8
1700–49	7	2	2	2	4	6	3	8	6	4	4	1	2	51	299	5.9
1750–99	5	3	4	1	7	6	4	3	7	3	0	6	4	56	360	6.4
1800–49	10	5	14	12	25	11	13	11	8	7	1	2	1	121	563	4.7
1850–79	7	6	8	15	14	14	10	2	5	2	0	0	1	84	338	4.0

him in 1715 at the age of seventeen and bore a total of seventeen children. All were born within the space of twenty-one years, so she gave
birth almost once a year. Even in the mid-nineteenth century a few nobles' wives were still bearing children at intervals of approximately
eighteen months. Thus Marie von Eschwege, who married Rudolf von
Keudell in 1853, gave birth to a total of thirteen children, the first when
she was twenty-two, the last at age forty.

Comparing the size of completed families is not the most desirable
method of determining changes in fertility because many families are
not included, particularly in the earlier generations, when marriages
that were cut short by the death of one of the partners greatly outnumbered completed marriages. Another measure of fertility, the age-specific fertility rate, avoids this problem because it includes data from families of both completed and incomplete fertility. Age-specific fertility is
determined by comparing the number of births to the number of years
lived by married women at specific ages, and the rate is expressed in
births per year for women in five-year age groups. In groups that do not
attempt to limit fertility, the reduced ability of women to bear children
as they grow older is reflected in the gradual decline of births per year
from the younger to the older age groups. In groups where family limitation is practiced, the number of births per year may be large in the
younger groups of women but declines sharply at older ages because
couples begin practicing fertility control once the desired number of
children has been attained. The fertility curves from the age-specific fertility rates of the Hessian Ritterschaft shown in figure 3.1 indicate no
appreciable drop in marital fertility until the nineteenth century. (The
precise figures are found in appendix D.)

Age-specific fertility rates cannot be easily used to compare fertility
rates among different populations, but they can be used to generate several other measures of fertility that are more suitable for this purpose.
The technical details of these measures are contained in appendix D, and
they reveal that the Hessian Ritterschaft began limiting family size
much later than other European elites that have been studied and also
did so to a lesser degree.

As has already been shown, a large percentage of the members of the
Ritterschaft married, and very few of them used birth control before the
nineteenth century. What effect did this basically unrestricted system of
marriages and births have on the overall size of the nobility (and therefore upon the inheritance and landownership systems)? Table 3.6,
which listed average completed family sizes of six or more children prior
to the nineteenth century, gave the impression that the nobility must
have been expanding at a fantastic rate each generation, but it should be

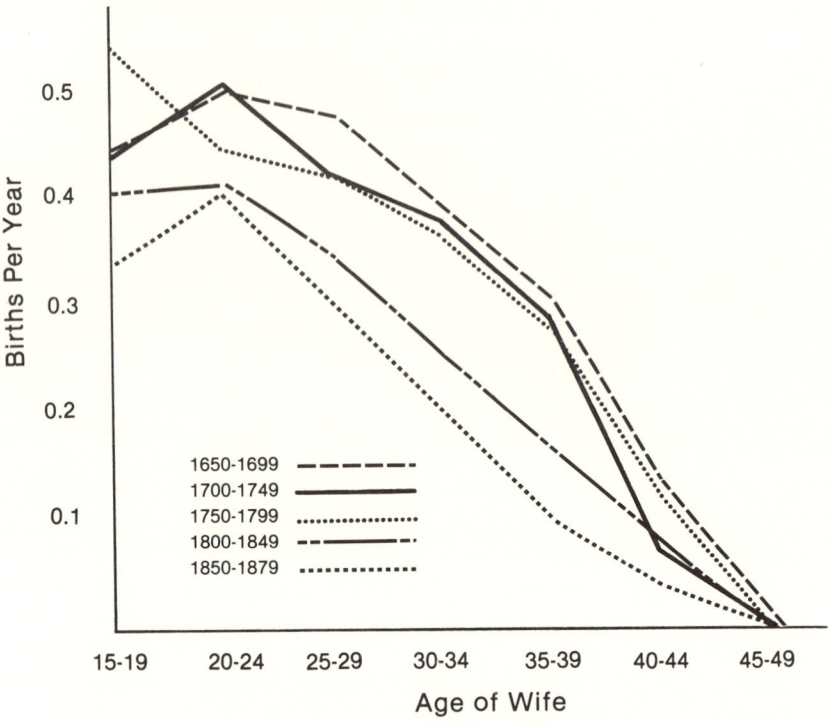

Figure 3.1. Age-Specific Marital Fertility.

recalled that this table included only completed families. Marriages that lasted until the wife had almost no more chance of bearing children were in the minority until the nineteenth century for two reasons: the high marriage age for men meant that many marriages were ended by the husband's death before the wife reached age forty-five, and the large number of births was a constant source of risk for wives, many of whom died in childbirth or shortly thereafter. It was not until the early nineteenth century that completed marriages outnumbered incomplete ones.

The end of a nobleman's marriage through divorce or the death of his wife did not usually set the ultimate limit on the size of his family, because in over two-thirds of such cases the husband remarried, either to have more children (especially if the first marriage had not produced an heir) or to provide his children with a new mother. As a result, any measure of the total increase in size of the nobility must take second marriages into account. Between 1650 and 1899, 219 marriages of Hessian noblemen were cut short by the wife's death or by divorce before the wife had reached age forty-five. The husband remarried in 147 of these cases (67 percent). In contrast, wives seldom remarried after the husband's death unless the marriage had not produced any children. Widows frequently became the guardians of minor children and administered the family's finances (often along with a male relative) until the children came of age.

An additional key factor in determining the rate of increase in size of the nobility is infant and child mortality. During the seventeenth century almost four out of every ten children of Hessian nobles did not live to see their twentieth birthday. The greatest number of deaths occurred among infants under one year of age, followed by children between one and five years, but substantial numbers of children died at older ages, even in their late teens. Child mortality did not begin to decline substantially until the mid-eighteenth century and thereafter sank steadily for the next hundred years.[34] The decline in mortality among the children of Hessian nobles is similar to that of other elites, although comparison of the extent of child mortality is made difficult by variations in the definition of child mortality. Some studies have included only deaths before the age of fifteen, others age twenty (see table 3.7).

When child mortality is taken into account, the completed family size

TABLE 3.7. Child Mortality among European Elites

	Hessian Ritterschaft (To Age 20)	Genevan Bourgeoisie (To Age 20)	British Peerage (To Age 15)	Lower Saxon Bourgeoisie (To Age 15)
1650–99	36.9%	44.6%	34.8%	——%
1700–49	34.4%	33.4%	32.6%	30.0%
1750–99	26.8%	24.9%	21.3%	22.4%
1800–49	18.8%	18.0%	15.8%	16.9%
1850–99	13.9%[a]	9.4%	10.7%	13.5%

SOURCES: Henry, *Anciennes familles genevoises*; Hollingsworth, "British Peerage," 66; Nell, "Entwicklung der generativen Strukturen," 63–64.

[a] Includes only the years 1850–79.

[34] The level of mortality among children born 1650–99 was probably even higher than listed. Girls appear to have been underenumerated, which suggests that some girls who died in infancy or childhood were not included in the genealogies during this period.

of the Hessian Ritterschaft shows much less change than depicted in table 3.6, which included all births, because the reduction in family size brought about by birth control was counterbalanced to a great degree by the decline in child mortality. The average number of children surviving to age twenty in each completed family was 4.8 in families in which the parents married in 1650–99, 3.6 in 1700–49, 4.9 in 1750–99, 3.8 in 1800–49, and 3.4 in 1850–79.

A final factor in determining the growth of the nobility is childless marriages. Infertility or the untimely death of one of the partners caused a number of marriages to end without issue. Since a nobleman generally remarried after the death of his wife, most childless marriages were caused by the early death of the husband or by infertility. Between 1650 and 1899 approximately 12 percent of all married noblemen produced no offspring in any of their marriages.

In order to determine the rate at which the nobility was changing in size, it is necessary to combine the following previously mentioned factors: remarriage, childlessness, child mortality, and the frequency of marriage of adult sons. Only sons could continue the family name and inherit estates, so an examination of the rate of increase in size of the nobility must be confined to that of males. Table 3.8 compares the number of married noblemen to the number of their adult sons from all (first and subsequent) marriages who in turn married (and thus could potentially carry on the family name). The ratio of increase is therefore the average number of married sons produced by each married nobleman.

Table 3.8 demonstrates that the Hessian Ritterschaft was not increasing in size very rapidly. The rate of increase of less than 20 percent found in the years 1650–99 and 1750–99 meant that the nobility would take approximately five generations to double in size, and the interval between generations was quite lengthy owing to the late marriage age

TABLE 3.8. Rate of Increase in Size of the Ritterschaft

Year of 1st Marriage	Married Males	Sons Aged 20+	Number Who Married	Ratio of Increase
1650–99	176	326	206	1.17:1
1700–49	209	302	189	0.90:1
1750–99	177	319	208	1.18:1
1800–49	231	400	292	1.26:1
1850–99	253	357	242	0.96:1

for males. Furthermore, the nobility did not even always increase at this modest rate. Nobles who married between 1700 and 1749 did not succeed in replacing themselves with an equal number of sons who married and were thus potentially capable of continuing their lines. Only once did the nobility experience a rapid rate of growth. In the first half of the nineteenth century fewer children died, fewer marriages were cut short by the premature death of one of the partners, and more adult males married, giving the Ritterschaft a 26 percent rate of increase. But in the second half of the century this rate declined sharply as family limitation became widespread and fewer noblemen married.

INHERITANCE

With marriages and births virtually uncontrolled until the early nineteenth century, how did the Hessian Ritterschaft solve the problems of land transmission and inheritance? Primogeniture, the method most commonly used by nobilities to transmit their landholdings, was ruled out by Hessian feudal law and custom, which gave all sons equal inheritance rights while excluding daughters from the right to inherit fiefs. Did the lack of primogeniture lead to the division of estates and a resultant impoverishment of the nobility?

Quite frequently it was not necessary to divide a family's landholdings, because only one son survived to inherit his family's estates. As table 3.9 demonstrates, approximately one-half of all noble families did not have to face the problem of multiple heirs because no son or only one son survived to adulthood. Even some families with two or more adult sons had only one son left alive to inherit when the time came, since wars and disease continually thinned the ranks of adult sons. In the seven-

TABLE 3.9. Adult Sons per Family

											Percentage with:			
Year of Marriage	Families with x Sons Ages 20%:										No Sons	One Son	Two+ Sons	Total
	0	1	2	3	4	5	6	7	8	Total				
1650–99	41	41	43	24	14	8	4	1	0	176	23.3	23.3	53.4	100.0
1700–49	76	50	34	28	11	5	4	1	0	209	36.4	23.9	39.7	100.0
1750–99	55	34	33	23	19	7	4	1	1	177	31.1	19.2	49.7	100.0
1800–49	51	60	60	36	16	3	3	1	1	231	22.1	26.0	51.9	100.0
1850–99	75	74	53	34	12	2	3	0	0	253	29.6	29.2	41.1	99.9

teenth century approximately 19 percent of all sons who reached the age of twenty did not live to see their thirtieth birthday; in the eighteenth century, 13 percent.

If a family did have more than one heir, the most common form of settlement prior to the late eighteenth century was to give each son an equal share of the family's wealth. The most important part of a family's holdings was its landed estates, each of which consisted of a manor house, various farm buildings, fields, pastures, and occasionally forests.[35] In addition a noble estate served as a collecting point for a wide variety of dues and services owed by the surrounding peasants. As a rule, individual estates were not subdivided by family settlements; instead parcels of land and peasant dues not associated with a particular estate or even outstanding loans were used to compensate for differences in the value of estates so that each heir's share was equal.

The exact terms of the family settlement were set forth either by the father's testament or, more frequently, by an agreement drawn up by the sons after their father's death. Once the composition of the various shares had been established, the question of which property went to which brother was often settled by lot.[36]

The division of a family's landholdings among several sons did not necessarily lead to a permanent splintering of the family's property, because many nobles failed to continue their lines. Such failures occurred when sons either remained single or married but did not produce any sons who survived to adulthood. The frequency of nobles' dying without heirs can be estimated by combining data from tables 3.1 and 3.9. In the years 1650–99, 63 percent of men aged twenty and above married, and 77 percent of the married noblemen produced at least one son who reached adulthood. Thus approximately 49 percent of the noblemen had one or more heirs.[37] The first half of the eighteenth century saw a sharp decline in the number of noblemen with heirs, as 62 percent of the male

[35] Generally the lands of a noble estate were in one or more large tracts separate from the holdings of the local villagers, but some *Rittergüter* consisted of many small parcels of land intermixed with those of the peasants. Hessian estates were small in comparison to those of other nobilities. In 1865 over two-thirds of the estates owned by nobles in Hesse-Kassel were less than two hundred hectares in size (see below, figure 4.3).

[36] Some examples of family settlements providing for the division of the family's estates are found in StAM: Urkunden, X 5, v. Baumbach-Nassenerfurth, 12 February 1707, v. Milchling zu Schönstadt, 1 June 1728, v. Dörnberg, 29 August 1745; StAM 340 v. Baumbach-Kirchheim, Nr. 99, 100; 340 v. Buttlar-Elberberg, Nr. 13; 340 v. Bodenhausen, Nr. 165; 340 v. Stockhausen, Nr. 4.

[37] The actual percentage of nobles with male heirs would be somewhat lower, because some of the individuals listed in table 3.9 as reaching adulthood died before they could inherit.

nobles married but only 64 percent of the married nobles had adult sons. Therefore only approximately forty out of every hundred members of the Ritterschaft continued their lines. This figure rose to 45 percent in 1750–99, reached 57 percent in 1800–49, and then dropped back to 52 percent in 1850–79.

When a noble died without male heirs, his estate automatically fell to his closest male relative if it was a fief and in most cases did so even if allodial, owing to custom or to provisions in a previous family settlement requiring that the estate remain in the family. The process of inheritance did not always run smoothly, for relatives often filed lawsuits claiming that they should have been the ones to inherit. The records of the Hessian law courts are full of lawsuits between different families, different branches of the same family, and individuals within the same branch of a family. Some nobles with a smattering of legal knowledge and lots of free time engaged in constant suits against relatives over inheritances and real or imagined grievances.[38] Such lawsuits were rarely successful, but they often did succeed in delaying the transfer of holdings from one family to another.

Despite legal challenges from disgruntled distant relatives, the process of inheritance sometimes reunited estates that had been divided by a family settlement several generations earlier. In the von Buttlar-Ziegenberg family, for example, three estates that had been divided among three brothers in 1690 finally came together again in one hand 120 years later through the complicated inheritance process depicted in figure 3.2.

Although this example of the reunification of formerly divided estates is not unique, many families that were increasing in size gradually divided their holdings until each branch had only one or two estates, making a simple division of estates impractical or even impossible. As a result, a second form of family settlement—joint ownership—became increasingly common. Under this system no attempt was made to divide the family's property among the heirs; instead each received an equal share of the annual profits from all the estates and other incomes. As part of this process, the main estate or estates were leased to bourgeois tenant farmers, and the family hired an administrator to collect the rents as well as the various peasant dues. The administrator kept the account books for the estates and either made payments to the co-owners throughout the year or distributed the profits from the holdings at the end of the year.

The co-owners of an estate received shares of the revenues based upon

---

[38] Karl von Knoblauch, *Kurzgefaßte Geschichte der Familie Knoblauch von und zu Hatzbach* (Marburg, 1890), 23.

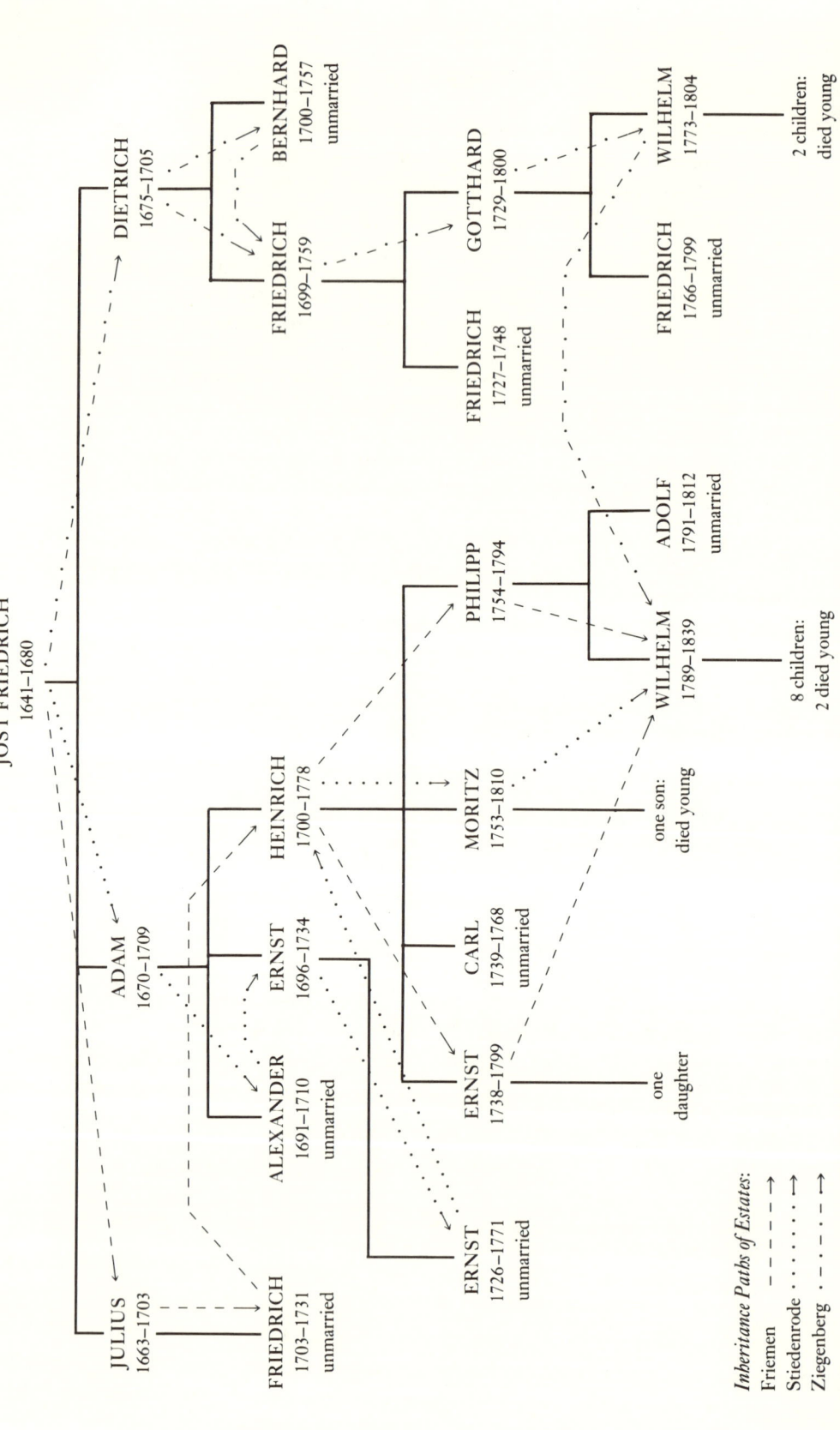

JOST FRIEDRICH
1641–1680

DIETRICH
1675–1705

BERNHARD
1700–1757
unmarried

FRIEDRICH
1699–1759

FRIEDRICH
1727–1748
unmarried

GOTTHARD
1729–1800

WILHELM
1773–1804

FRIEDRICH
1766–1799
unmarried

2 children:
died young

ADAM
1670–1709

JULIUS
1663–1703

HEINRICH
1700–1778

ERNST
1696–1734

ALEXANDER
1691–1710
unmarried

FRIEDRICH
1703–1731
unmarried

PHILIPP
1754–1794

MORITZ
1753–1810

CARL
1739–1768
unmarried

ERNST
1738–1799

ERNST
1726–1771
unmarried

ADOLF
1791–1812
unmarried

WILHELM
1789–1839

one son:
died young

one
daughter

8 children:
2 died young

Inheritance Paths of Estates:

Friemen   – – – →
Stiedenrode   · · · · · →
Ziegenberg   – · – · →

the degree of their relationship with the individual or individuals who first established the joint ownership. Therefore the size of shares did not remain constant but varied as heirs died and were replaced with differing numbers of new heirs. Like other forms of property, shares of an estate were divided equally among the sons of the original owner. If an individual died without an heir, his share was divided by his brothers.

The constant variation in the size of each individual's share is best understood by examining this process in action (see figure 3.3). In 1795 the three surviving sons of Wilhelm von Buttlar-Elberberg became co-owners of the family's two estates in Elberberg and Kirchberg, so each son received one-third of the annual profits. The eldest son (Georg) died in 1811, and his share was divided between his two minor sons, giving them each one-sixth. When the youngest of the three original brothers died unmarried in 1830, his share was divided between his one surviving brother (who now received one-half of the annual profits) and the two sons of Georg (now one-quarter each). The last of the original co-owners (Gottlob) died in 1849, and his half interest was divided among his four sons, giving them one-eighth each. The remaining half interest all belonged to Rudolf von Buttlar (1802–75) after his brother Julius died without heirs in 1855. In 1826 the family purchased a third estate and set up a *Fideikommiß* (entail) that confirmed the policy of joint ownership.[39]

Families did not always stay with one form of family settlement; instead they adopted the type of settlement most suitable for their current circumstances. For example, the six sons of Hartmann von Eschwege, who owned estates in Reichensachsen and Jestädt, became co-owners of the two estates following his death in 1770. Only one of the sons produced any heirs, and after the last of the original six sons died in 1826, the two remaining grandsons abolished the joint ownership and divided the two estates between themselves. Since each branch now possessed only one estate, the following generation again used a system of joint ownership.[40]

Instances in which only one of several sons inherited an estate were quite rare. In 1789 the three younger sons of the debt-ridden von der Malsburg-Escheberg family ceded their shares in the family's estates to their older brother Carl so that he could simplify the family's financial affairs and try to get the estates out of bankruptcy proceedings. In return the younger brothers each received a small cash settlement of 120 talers per year.[41] This violation of traditional inheritance laws and customs

[39] StAM 340 v. Buttlar-Elberberg, Nr. 13–14.

[40] StAM 340 v. Eschwege, Rechnungen.

[41] Carl failed to produce an heir, and in 1821 he bequeathed the estates to the two sons of his younger brother Friedrich (his other two brothers had not married). StAM 340 v. d.

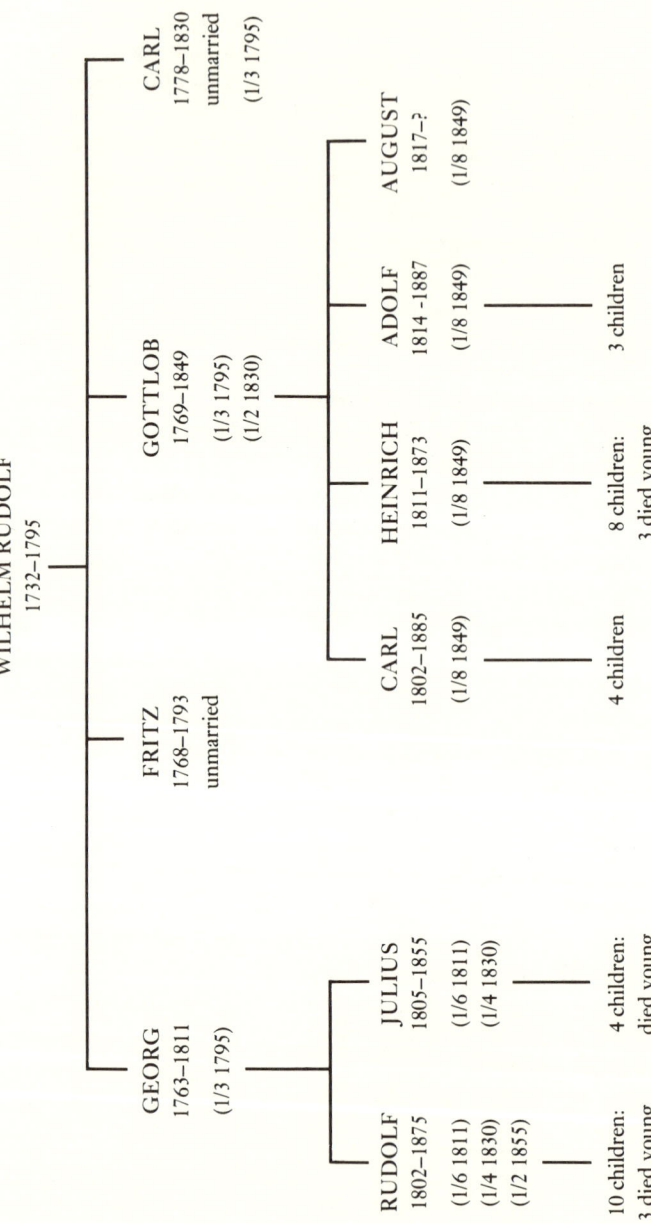

Figure 3.3. Joint Ownership of Estates in the von Buttlar-Elberberg Family. In parentheses are each individual's share of the annual profits from the estates and the year this share became effective due to the death of another heir.

was possible because the younger sons voluntarily relinquished their inheritance rights, but if a noble attempted to disinherit sons without their consent, a lawsuit was bound to result. For example, in the previously mentioned von Buttlar-Elberberg family, the father had originally bequeathed his estates to only one of his three sons in 1794. The others refused to accept this violation of the traditional inheritance procedures and therefore contested the will. The following year the supreme court (*Oberappellationsgericht*) overturned the will and named all three sons as heirs.[42]

Few nobles were willing to renounce their rights to an estate, because by doing so they also gave up their status as full-fledged members of the Ritterschaft. The statutes of the knighthood required that an individual be an owner or co-owner of a noble estate in order to be considered an active member. Nobles who could not meet this requirement could not represent the knighthood in the Hessian diet or even vote for representatives, and, more important, they were not eligible for the valuable financial benefits of the Ritterschaft's charitable foundation, the Stift Kaufungen (the benefits included low-interest loans, dowries for daughters, and annual assistance for needy widows and daughters). Thus even if an individual's share in his family estate was small and provided little income, it still brought him very tangible benefits, which is the main reason that the system of joint ownership became widespread once families had more sons than estates.

Joint ownership enabled a large number of family members to participate in the ownership of noble estates, but this was not always conducive to harmonious family relations. Meetings of the von Dörnberg family in the eighteenth century, for example, were sometimes so tense that family members are said to have taken loaded pistols with them![43]

Some families drew up agreements to regulate the inheritance of their estates not only for the next generation but also for all future generations. Such *Fideikommisse* (entails) were established to prevent the loss of any of the family's holdings, but unlike the *Fideikommisse* prevalent elsewhere in Germany, those of the Hessian Ritterschaft did not provide for primogeniture. In keeping with Hessian laws and traditions, the practice of equal inheritance rights for all sons was retained. Since most of the Ritterschaft's estates were held as fiefs and thus could not be inherited by women, alienated, or placed in debt without the consent of all other possible heirs, there was no real need for most families to set up

Malsburg-Escheberg, Verz. 2, Nr. 4/15 (family agreement of 30 May 1789); Nr. 2/30 (Fideikommiß of 14 February 1821).

[42] Hueck, "Familie von Buttlar," no. 24, p. 1.

[43] Dr. Alexander Freiherr von Dörnberg, interview with author, Hausen, 16 June 1979.

Fideikommisse prior to the nineteenth century. One family had done so as early as 1618, and several other families established entails during the eighteenth and early nineteenth centuries, but the bulk of the *Fideikommisse* in existence at the end of the nineteenth century had first been established after 1848, when the entire feudal system was abolished, forcing the nobility to seek other ways of protecting its landholdings.[44]

Daughters of the Ritterschaft were generally excluded from inheriting any of their father's property, so they received compensation in the form of cash settlements.[45] Family agreements usually provided for daughters to receive a fixed amount of cash when they reached adulthood, but in most cases daughters received only the interest on this sum until they married, at which time the entire capital was paid out as a dowry. In the seventeenth and eighteenth centuries there seems to have been little or no competition in the size of dowries among the families of the Hessian Ritterschaft, whereas inflation in dowries was quite common during this period in England and Westphalia.[46] The amount given to each daughter was approximately the same in most families and often remained unchanged for centuries, which meant that a dowry that had represented a substantial sum in the seventeenth century was no longer so impressive two hundred years later. Dowries rarely exceeded two thousand talers; the most prevalent amount was one thousand.[47] Such payments were small in comparison to the dowries obtained by some members of the Ritterschaft who married into the nobilities of neighboring states, where dowries sometimes amounted to as much as ten thousand talers.[48] However, the small size of Hessian dowries was ac-

[44] Otto Stahl, *Denkschrift über Fideikommißrecht und Fideikommißwesen im Gebiet des ehemaligen Kurhessen* (Kassel, 1902), 59–60.

[45] Hessian law required that settlements be given to noble daughters who were excluded from inheritance. Kopp and Wittich, *Landes-Verfassung und Rechte*, 1: 6.

[46] Among English nobles the size of dowries rose sharply during the seventeenth and eighteenth centuries as the supply of daughters exceeded the demand from eligible males and the nobility faced increasing competition from the squirearchy and merchants, who were offering large dowries with their daughters. Stone, *Crisis of the Aristocracy*, 645–49; G. E. Mingay, *English Landed Society in the Eighteenth Century* (London, 1963), 35–36. For the rise in the size of Westphalian dowries see Reif, *Westfälischer Adel*, 254–56.

[47] The size of dowries sometimes depended upon the number of daughters in a particular generation. For example, the von Baumbach-Lenderscheid family settlement of 1823 stated, "Each daughter of our family shall receive 1,500 talers unless there are more than four daughters in an individual branch, in which case each receives only 1,000 talers. The payment of this sum can be demanded only when the father is deceased and the daughter marries. If a daughter remains unmarried, she receives only the interest from this capital, and if a married daughter dies without children, the capital must be repaid to the male line of the family." StAM 340 v. Baumbach-Kirchheim, Nr. 99.

[48] Two of the largest dowries given to the wives of members of the Ritterschaft were the

tually advantageous for the Ritterschaft. Dowries were not much of a burden upon noble families and thus rarely caused indebtedness. In contrast, dowries represented a heavy burden for both the court nobility and the provincial nobility in eighteenth-century France.[49]

ALL IN ALL, the marriage and inheritance system practiced by the Hessian Ritterschaft was perhaps the method best suited to preserving its landholdings in the long run. The high rate of marriage by Hessian nobles reduced the chances of families' dying out, whereas nobilities that used primogeniture combined with restrictions upon marriage by younger sons usually experienced a much higher rate of extinction of families. The Westphalian nobility used adoption to prevent the disappearance of families,[50] but this method of continuing lines was not possible for the Hessian nobility before the end of the feudal system in 1848 because the state did not recognize adopted sons as legitimate vassals and would therefore take over a fief if the owning family became extinct in the male line.

Unlike nobilities using primogeniture, the Hessian Ritterschaft was not forced to compensate younger sons with large cash settlements, a situation that in France and Prussia often led to indebtedness or even the loss of part of the estate. In addition the Ritterschaft's dowries remained small, which also eliminated a potential source of debt.

Naturally the fact that all sons were entitled to inherit meant that there were few extremely wealthy Hessian nobles. In families with large numbers of sons, the individual shares of the annual profits were often quite small, forcing the heirs to rely on some other source of income (generally government offices). However, the money distributed to the heirs each year came only from the profits from the family's landholdings, leaving the principal intact. When an heir died without himself leaving any heirs, his share reverted to the rest of the family. In contrast, nobilities practicing primogeniture often gave younger sons a substantial portion of the value of the family's holdings, and these portions did not always fall back to the family after younger sons died, because the money might have been dissipated in the meantime or inherited by a

---

previously mentioned ten thousand talers brought by Marianne Gräfin von der Schulenberg into her marriage with Georg von Buttlar in 1801 and the eight-thousand-taler dowry of Hedwig von Hammerstein, who married Dietrich von Bodenhausen in 1766. Hueck, "Familie von Buttlar," no. 26, p. 1; StAM 340v. Bodenhausen, Pakct 216, Marriage contract of 13 April 1766.

[49] Forster, *Nobility of Toulouse*, 131–37; idem., *House of Saulx-Tavanes*, 132–36.

[50] Reif, *Westfälischer Adel*, 90–92.

wife or daughter (something that rarely occurred among Hessian nobles).

The most important reason for the success of the Hessian Ritterschaft's system of land transmission was its flexibility. A large number of children in one generation did not spell financial ruin for a family; it simply meant that each individual would receive less annual income (and the value of these shares gradually increased as other members of the family died without heirs). Even the division of a family's estates among several heirs was not necessarily permanent, for many lines died out within a few generations and their estates fell to relatives. There was thus a constant flow of estates between the different branches of a family as lines died out and new lines were created. As a result, few families passed on their estates from father to son to grandson until the nineteenth century (when child mortality declined substantially and a larger percentage of noblemen married), but most families were able to keep their estates in the family and preserve the family name from extinction, thereby achieving two of the most important objectives for nobles.

· 4 ·

LANDOWNING

Nobles and the Land in Prussia and Western Germany

The eighteenth and nineteenth centuries were a period of tremendous upheaval for noble landowners in many parts of Germany, particularly in Prussia. One of the most significant changes for noble landowning in Prussia was the gradual loosening of the nobility's feudal ties to the monarchy. Many estates that previously had been fiefs, requiring royal permission and the consent of relatives for mortgage or sale, became allodial in the course of the eighteenth century; the owners were thus free to dispose with their land as they pleased. Even before the advent of allodification there had been considerable mobility of estates in Prussia,[1] and once the constricting feudal ties disappeared, turnover of estates through forced or voluntary sales increased substantially because estate owners were free to contract debts or even indulge in land speculation.

Some Prussian landowners were already in a precarious financial position by the mid-eighteenth century. The Seven Years' War caused substantial damage to estates in many areas of Prussia, and after the war's end a decline in grain prices led to a short-lived but severe agricultural crisis that increased the burden of debt on many estate owners. At this point the Prussian government stepped in to help the landed nobility by issuing a three-year moratorium on the repayment of debts, beginning in 1765. In addition large sums of cash were made available to beleaguered estate owners. Nobles in Silesia received an outright gift of 300,000 talers, while the nobility of the Neumark was given 270,000 talers outright and 381,000 talers as a loan at 2 percent interest. But such actions only provided short-term relief for landowners. After the expiration of the moratorium, many estates fell victim to forced sales.[2]

The Seven Years' War was not the only source of indebtedness for

---

[1] Friedrich-Wilhelm Henning, "Die Entwicklung des Grundstücksverkehrs vom ausgehenden 18. Jahrhundert bis gegen Ende des 19. Jahrhunderts," in *Wissenschaft und Kodifikation des Privatrechts im 19. Jahrhundert*, vol. 3, *Die rechtliche und wirtschaftliche Entwicklung des Grundeigentums und Grundkredits*, ed. Helmut Coing and Walter Wilhelm (Frankfurt, 1976), 176–77.

[2] Wilhelm Abel, *Geschichte der deutschen Landwirtschaft vom frühen Mittelalter bis zum 19. Jahrhundert*, 2d ed. (Stuttgart, 1967), 293; Johannes Ziekursch, *Hundert Jahre schlesischer Agrargeschichte: Vom Hubertusberger Frieden bis zum Abschluß der Bauernbefreiung*, 2d ed. (Breslau, 1927), 3–8; Görlitz, *Junker*, 125–26.

Prussian landowners. Many nobles acquired debts as the result of luxury spending rather than improvements in their estates, so the increased burden of interest payments was not offset by rising productivity. The need to compensate relatives who were excluded from inheriting estates was yet another source of debt that did not bring any corresponding increase in income.[3] All of these factors led to a growing indebtedness of estate owners that became a serious problem once interest rates began to rise after 1768.

The first real improvement in the position of estate owners came in the 1770s with the establishment of the *Landschaften*, cooperative credit institutions that issued loans to estate owners in amounts up to one-half the value of their estates. Loans were made in the form of notes (*Pfandbriefe*) at 4 percent interest. These notes were secured jointly by all estate owners with their estates, and if a debtor failed to meet his payments, the *Landschaft* could confiscate his estate. The *Pfandbriefe* were an immediate success because they offered members of the middle class a secure form of investment with none of the problems and risks associated with normal mortgages. The notes circulated like cash and were quickly in such demand that they began to trade above their face value.[4]

The 1770s also brought a second major benefit to estate owners. Prices for agricultural products began rising strongly after 1770 and continued to do so until the early nineteenth century. As a result the value of land also began to rise, and estates became sought-after investments. Soon demand for estates pushed their prices up even faster than the rise in agricultural prices.

Although some Prussian landowners utilized the new sources of credit to make needed improvements in their estates, a growing number of nobles began to use loans from the *Landschaften* for a purpose not foreseen by the founders—speculation. The ease of obtaining low-interest loans combined with the lack of requirements to repay such loans within a specific period of time tempted landowners to take advantage of rising land values by purchasing additional estates. The resultant increase in demand for estates quickly drove land prices even higher. Soon purchasers of estates were no longer motivated by rational calculations of increased profitability but simply by speculation that prices would con-

[3] Friedrich Wilhelm Henning, "Die Verschuldung der Bodeneigentümer in Norddeutschland im ausgehenden 18. und in den ersten zwei Dritteln des 19. Jahrhunderts," in Coing and Wilhelm, eds., *Wissenschaft und Kodifikation*, 3:284, 298–99.

[4] Moritz Weyermann, *Zur Geschichte des Immobiliarkreditwesens in Preußen mit besonderer Nutzanwendung auf die Theorie von Bodenverschuldung* (Karlsruhe, 1910), 80–82, 87–88; Hanna Schissler, *Preußische Agrargesellschaft im Wandel: Wirtschaftliche, gesellschaftliche und politische Transformationsprozesse von 1763 bis 1847* (Göttingen, 1978), 82.

tinue to rise, enabling the estates to be sold again at a profit. Even nobles who were not particularly wealthy participated in this speculation by borrowing against their estates and using this capital to buy a second estate, which in turn could be mortgaged in order to buy a third. The purchasers of estates often had to pay very little in cash. Speculation in landed estates frequently reached frantic heights with some estates changing hands a number of times within the space of just a few years. Contemporary observers in both Mecklenburg and Silesia compared the atmosphere of the late-eighteenth-century land market to horse trading.[5]

Traditional ties between noble families and their estates began to disintegrate. Landed estates had previously been seen as an essential part of a noble family's prestige but had become merely commercial objects, according to one contemporary East Prussian writer, who noted, "Noble estates here are seen as a commodity to be traded. Many buy estates not to keep them but to sell them again at a profit; thus within a year an estate can pass through many hands. Everyone is willing to sell his estate if the price is high enough."[6]

Hand in hand with rising estate prices came increasing indebtedness. By 1806 the estates in the Neumark were mortgaged at an average of 72 percent of their last purchase price (106 percent of their official valuation). In the same period debts averaged two-thirds the value of estates in Silesia and over 50 percent in Mecklenburg.[7]

Like all waves of speculation, the boom in estates could not last forever. It had already begun to reach its limits by the first few years of the nineteenth century, and after grain prices plummeted in 1806 and 1807, the bottom fell out of the estate market. Prices of estates suddenly sank 50 percent or more, and those owners who tried to hold on to their estates found it increasingly difficult to meet their debt obligations once estate revenues declined. Large numbers of bankruptcies soon followed.[8]

---

[5] The Silesian war and domains councilor von Kloeber wrote in 1788, "In Silesia landed estates are being traded almost like horses" (quoted in Ziekursch, *Schlesischer Agrargeschichte*, 58), while in Mecklenburg the agricultural writer Lüder von Engel remarked, "Estates here are being traded just like horses at a public market." Quoted in Gerhard Körber, *Das Kreditwesen des ritterschaftlichen Grundbesitzes in Mecklenburg nach dem Siebenjährigen Kriege bis zur Gründung des ritterschaftlichen Kreditvereins im Jahre 1819* (Schwerin, 1929), 19.

[6] S. Holsche, *Der Netzdistrikt* (Königsberg, 1793), 171, cited by U. J. Seetzen, "Über dem Handel mit Landgüter," *Annalen der niedersächsischen Landwirtschaft* 3 (1801): 90–91.

[7] Weyermann, *Geschichte des Immobiliarkreditwesens*, 132; Ziekursch, *Schlesischer Agrargeschichte*, 56–57; Körber, *Kreditwesen des ritterschaftlichen Grundbesitzes*, 84–85.

[8] Wilhelm Abel, *Agrarkrisen und Agrarkonjunktur: Eine Geschichte der Land- und Ernährungswirtschaft Deutschlands seit dem hohen Mittelalter*, 2d ed. (Hamburg, 1966), 202–8.

The nineteenth century brought no relief from the continued up-heaval in Prussian landed society. After the end of the Napoleonic Wars, grain prices again began to climb, and the value of estates also rose. But this boom was short-lived because in 1817 grain prices started a decline that continued until 1826.[9] The number of bankruptcies rose sharply, and once again nobles began to lose estates owing to their ina-bility to meet debt payments. In 1851 a member of the Prussian diet claimed that at least 80 percent of all eastern *Rittergutsbesitzer* (owners of noble estates) lost their estates during the agrarian crisis of the 1820s.[10] Although this percentage was probably exaggerated, available figures show that the loss of estates was substantial. In East Prussia 510 of the 888 estates associated with the landowners' credit union (*Landschaft*) were owned by different families in 1829 than in 1806. More than half of these changes had resulted from forced sales.[11]

At the end of the 1820s grain prices began to recover and with them the market in estates. During the 1840s and early 1850s grain prices rose even higher, fueling a new wave of speculation in which estates again began to change hands rapidly.[12] The "great depression" of 1873 to 1896 finally brought an end to the era of speculation in landed estates.

The overall effect of the waves of speculation and crisis in the eight-eenth and nineteenth centuries upon the social composition of Prussian estate owners has not yet been studied in detail, but it is possible to draw several conclusions. First, non-nobles greatly increased their share of the ownership of noble estates. Although the sale of *Rittergüter* to com-moners was illegal in Prussia until 1807, bourgeois frequently received permission to buy noble land, and when they did not, they could always get around the law by using noble "straw men" as purchasers and by buying hereditary or extremely long leases on estates.[13] Thus at the start of the nineteenth century, bourgeois already owned between 10 and 15 percent of the noble estates in Prussia.[14] Once the restrictions upon the purchase of noble estates by commoners were removed, bourgeois be-came even more active in the land market. By 1856 they owned 42 per-

[9] Arnold Ucke, *Die Agrarkrisis in Preußen während der zwanziger Jahren dieses Jahrhunderts* (Halle, 1888), 13–14, 20–27.

[10] Abel, *Agrarkrisen und Agrarkonjunktur*, 221.

[11] Koselleck, *Preußen zwischen Reform und Revolution*, 512.

[12] Weyermann, *Geschichte des Immobiliarkreditwesens*, 182–83; Abel, *Agrarkrisen und Agrarkonjunktur*, 255–56.

[13] Martiny, *Adelsfrage in Preußen*, 34–35.

[14] Henning, "Entwicklung des Grundstücksverkehrs," 180; Koselleck, *Preußen zwischen Reform und Revolution*, 83. Mecklenburg had no restrictions upon the purchase of *Rittergüter* by commoners, so the proportion of estate owners from the bourgeoisie was probably even greater than in Prussia. Körber, *Kreditwesen des ritterschaftlichen Grundgesitzes*, 8, 75.

cent of the *Rittergüter* in Prussia.[15] A more inclusive 1888 survey revealed that bourgeois owned 48 percent of all estates over 100 hectares (250 acres), while nobles owned only 44 percent. The rest were owned by communities, churches, schools, or the state. In terms of the numbers of owners of such estates, the bourgeoisie outnumbered the nobility by an almost two-to-one ratio, for many nobles owned more than one estate, while almost all bourgeois owned just a single estate.[16]

The second major change in the composition of estate ownership in Prussia came within the nobility itself. The number of noble estate owners declined from at least 5,300 at the end of the eighteenth century to approximately 3,600 in 1885.[17] Thus even in terms of numbers alone, a substantial portion of the eighteenth-century landed nobility lost its ties to the land during the following century. However, many estate owners included in the category of nobles in the nineteenth century were probably individuals who had only recently attained noble status, so the overall change in the composition of noble landownership was probably even greater than that indicated by the one-third decline in numbers.

Much of the lower nobility's loss of estates came not at the hands of bourgeois or new nobles but at those of the wealthier members of the nobility, who were more resistant to crises and took advantage of the fluctuations in the land market to buy the estates of poorer, often heavily indebted nobles.[18] It is not possible to say exactly how extensive the alienation of the old lower nobility from the land was, but available statistics suggest that few noble families had succeeded in passing on their holdings intact from generation to generation. By 1885 only 13 percent of the estates in East Prussia had been in the hands of the same family for at least fifty years.[19] In the district of Marienwerder only twelve out of almost six hundred estates had been in the owners' families for at least one hundred years.[20]

[15] The extent of bourgeois ownership ranged from only 11 percent in Westphalia to 66 percent in the province of Prussia. K. F. Rauer, *Hand-Matrikel der im sämtlichen Kreisen des preußischen Staats auf Kreis- und Landtagen vertretenen Rittergüter* (Berlin, 1857), 451.

[16] The estates owned by the nobility were generally much larger than those owned by the bourgeoisie. J. Conrad, "Die Latifundien im preußischen Osten," *Jahrbücher für Nationalökonomie und Statistik*, 2d ser., 16 (1888): 138–43. This survey includes 16,422 estates over 100 hectares, whereas Rauer's handbook encompasses only the 12,339 estates characterized as *Rittergüter*, so it is not possible to compare the two sets of statistics directly.

[17] Koselleck, *Preußen zwischen Reform und Revolution*, 81, 672–73; Conrad, "Latifundien," p. 140; Körber, *Kreditwesen des ritterschaftlichen Grundbesitzes*, 75.

[18] Koselleck, *Preußen zwischen Reform und Revolution*, 86; Ziekursch, *Schlesischer Agrargeschichte*, 59.

[19] J. Conrad, "Agrarstatistischen Untersuchungen," *Jahrbücher für Nationalökonomie und Statistik*, 3d ser., 2 (1891): 831.

[20] Horst Mies, *Die preußische Verwaltung des Regierungsbezirks Marienwerder, 1830–1870* (Cologne, 1972), 108.

Is the Prussian example of widespread alienation of the lower nobility from the land valid for all of Germany? A precise answer must await further research, but information available on noble landowning in Hesse-Kassel and Westphalia suggests that the Prussian example should not be seen as typical. In fact Prussia, with its recurring crises in the land market, could possibly be the main exception to a general pattern of stability in noble landownership in Germany.

A vital difference between landed estates in Prussia and those in Hesse-Kassel was that most of the former had become allodial by the late eighteenth century, whereas the vast majority of estates in Hesse-Kassel were fiefs and remained so until 1848. Although holders of fiefs enjoyed all the revenues and privileges associated with their estates, their control over the land was restricted in several key areas. First, almost all Hessian fiefs (*Lehen*) were designated as *Mannlehen*, which meant they could be inherited only by males. This restriction was generally not a great handicap for the nobility, for most families wished to keep their estates in the male line anyway and set up family agreements extending this provision to estates and smaller landholdings that were not fiefs. However, when a family became extinct in the male line, the state could and did exercise its right of escheat (*Heimfall*), in which case all the nonallodial land of the family reverted to the state. A second and more important limitation of a vassal's control over his fief was the requirement to secure royal consent for loans taken out against a fief and for the alienation of a fief. Vassals who wished to sell or mortgage their fiefs also had to secure the consent of all of their male relatives who could possibly inherit the estate.

Another area of difference between Prussia and western Germany, but one that is less tangible, is the attitude of the nobility toward the land. The widespread speculation in landed estates in Prussia became possible only after nobles ceased to view their estates as an important part of their families' prestige and began to see land as an object that could be sold at a profit. Exactly when and why this change came about and the proportion of Prussian nobles who came to feel this way have not yet been determined, but the fact remains that once the ties of vassalage were removed, many Prussian nobles voluntarily alienated their estates.

Although estates in Westphalia had also become allodial by the nineteenth century, the nobility there did not enter into the waves of speculation that swept the eastern regions of Prussia. Westphalian nobles had strong ties to their estates and believed that they were acting not just for themselves but also in the name of past and future generations. Much of a family's prestige was derived from its noble estate; in many cases the family bore the same name as the estate. Therefore nobles generally would not part with land even when it was hopelessly indebted.[21]

The Hessian Ritterschaft held views virtually identical to those of the Westphalian nobility and continually sought to preserve and if possible expand its landholdings. However, this task was often difficult for the generally poor Hessian nobility, and many nobles faced the same problems that Major Gottlob von der Malsburg expressed in 1815 when he requested that the government end its long-standing bankruptcy administration of his estates: "Previously I was not able to concern myself very much with family affairs, but after the deaths of my father and my uncle, I inherited the estates and the debts of the house Malsburg. Since then it has been my goal to preserve the former and wipe out the latter."[22]

How well the nobility succeeded in its task of preserving its landholdings cannot be precisely determined because comprehensive landownership statistics do not exist for any period before the 1860s.[23] However, certain tax records provide information on changes in landownership in the late eighteenth century. The annual accounts of the knights' tax (*Rittersteuer*) reveal changes in ownership of noble land (land that was exempt from the heavy land tax known as the contribution). As with the French *taille*, liability to the contribution depended upon the status of the land, not the owner. Thus non-nobles who owned land that prior to 1655 had been in the hands of the nobility paid no contribution on this land, while nobles who purchased peasant land were subject to the contribution on this portion of their landholdings. Noble land was not completely tax-exempt but incurred the low knights' tax. The only land exempt from all taxes was that which had been royal demesne before 1655. The status of a particular piece of land could not be changed except in rare cases when land fell to the state and then was discovered to have been royal property before 1655, thus becoming tax-exempt.

The yearly accounts of the knights' tax do not list the size of landholdings, but they do include the value for tax purposes (*Steuerkapital*) of each individual's land. Since by law the total amount of noble land almost never varied, comparisons over time of the taxable value of the land owned by various groups can reveal changes in the ownership of noble

[21] Reif, *Westfälischer Adel*, 96–97.
[22] StAM 340 v. d. Malsburg-Escheberg, Verz. 2, Nr. 2/6.
[23] The eighteenth-century cadasters, which recorded the landowners in each village, do not always contain information about nobles' estates because these were frequently not considered to be part of the community being surveyed. Noble estates were recorded in the knights' tax register (*Ritterschaftliche Steuerstock*), but the sole surviving example lists only the taxable value of an estate, not its actual size.

land (which included most estates) in Hesse-Kassel during the late eighteenth century, a time when speculation in estates was rife in much of Germany and non-nobles were beginning to acquire considerable numbers of noble estates.[24]

The Ritterschaft's share of noble land, which constituted the bulk of its landholdings, gradually declined, as can be seen in table 4.1. The state profited most from this decline, because several of the wealthiest families in the Ritterschaft died out at the end of the eighteenth century,

TABLE 4.1. Ownership of Noble Land (Value of Holdings in *Steuergulden*)

	1760	1770	1780	1790	1800	1808
State[a]	137,099	158,924	188,754	194,789	247,031	330,463
	(6.8%)	(7.8%)	(9.2%)	(9.3%)	(10.7%)	(13.9%)
Princes[b]	29,461	29,461	43,178	42,492	60,157	46,042
	(1.5%)	(1.4%)	(2.1%)	(2.0%)	(2.6%)	(1.9%)
Foundations[c]	136,755	136,760	139,631	137,544	141,932	146,762
	(6.8%)	(6.7%)	(6.8%)	(6.6%)	(6.2%)	(6.2%)
Ritterschaft	1,216,270	1,191,480	1,167,232	1,143,483	1,246,170	1,187,491
	(60.5%)	(58.3%)	(57.1%)	(54.6%)	(54.2%)	(50.1%)
Other nobles	171,007	168,033	164,190	218,920	220,866	209,481
	(8.5%)	(8.2%)	(8.0%)	(10.4%)	(9.6%)	(8.8%)
Non-nobles	318,614	360,716	341,897	358,314	384,045	451,268
	(15.9%)	(17.6%)	(16.7%)	(17.1%)	(16.7%)	(19.0%)
Total	2,009,206	2,045,374	2,044,882	2,095,542	2,300,201	2,371,507
	(100.0%)	(100.0%)	(99.9%)	(100.0%)	(100.0%)	(99.9%)

NOTE: The *Rittersteuer* rolls include only the old Landgraviate of Hesse-Kassel (Upper and Lower Hesse), not the newer provinces of Hanau and Fulda.

[a] Includes only royal holdings that were subject to the *Rittersteuer*. Most royal estates were exempt from all taxes.

[b] Two cousins of the landgrave.

[c] The Stift Kaufungen, Teutonic Knights, universities of Marburg and Gießen, and several hospitals and charitable foundations.

[24] The total tax valuation (*Steuerkapital*) gradually increased due to revaluations and improvements in estates, so it is not possible to make direct comparisons of the *Steuerkapital* for a given group from one decade to another. However, the changes in the percentages of the total *Steuerkapital* provide an indication of the changes in ownership of noble land during the period. The knights' tax accounts are found in StAM, Rechnungen II, Kassel 199 and Treysa 15.

and most of their estates (those that were fiefs) fell to the state.[25] In addition, the state purchased land from several knights.

Some of the land lost by the nobility found its way into the hands of non-nobles, since unlike Prussia, Hesse-Kassel had no laws forbidding the purchase of noble estates by commoners. The share of noble land owned by non-nobles increased during the eighteenth century even though some of the most prosperous members of this group, those in the upper ranks of the bureaucracy, were ennobled and thus come under the category "other nobles" in table 4.1. In 1800, for example, families that had become noble during the eighteenth century owned land worth 46,000 *Steuergulden* (tax guilders),[26] approximately 2 percent of the total tax valuation.

Non-noble owners of noble land came from many levels of society. The vast majority were simply peasants whose family had at some time acquired a parcel of land that was free of the contribution. In 1808 the knights' tax rolls included 2,345 non-nobles; all but 75 owned noble land worth less than 1,000 tax guilders. The average holding of these 2,270 peasants and small artisans was 112 tax guilders, an amount that, depending on the quality of the land, represented at best one or two hectares. The 75 non-nobles with larger holdings of noble land owned an average of 2,620 tax guilders' worth of land each. Of these individuals, 32 were members of the state or local bureaucracy, 11 were lessees or administrators of large estates, 5 were merchants, 3 were artisans, 1 was a pastor, and 1 was an army officer, while no information is available on the occupations of 22 of these non-noble landowners.[27]

Almost all of the estates owned by the Ritterschaft were valued above five thousand tax guilders, and the majority exceed ten thousand. Several estates were worth more than thirty thousand tax guilders. Only five commoners owned estates that were comparable in value to those of the knighthood. The largest non-noble holding in 1808 was that of the merchant Carl Huschke, who owned the *Rittergut* Völkershausen valued at 19,500 tax guilders.[28] The other four estates owned by commoners ranged from 5,300 to 9,400 tax guilders in value.

[25] The allodial lands of these extinct families were inherited by the surviving daughters or by other noble families (generally also from the Ritterschaft) who were related by marriage.

[26] *Steuergulden*, each of which equaled 27/32 of a *Reichstaler*, were not actual units of currency. They were used only in official financial calculations.

[27] StAM, Rechnungen II, Kassel 199 and Treysa 15, 1808 Rittersteuer accounts.

[28] Völkershausen previously had been a fief of the von Diede family, which died out in 1807. Huschke purchased the estate from the new French administration, which was not averse to selling fiefs to commoners.

The above figures from the *Rittersteuer* accounts do not provide much evidence that a wealthy bourgeoisie was beginning to buy up the nobility's land. A few merchants had purchased noble land by the early 1800s, but the traditional bureaucracy was more active in the land market. However, the land purchases of all middle-class groups are not sufficient to account for the entire rise in ownership of noble land by non-nobles; some of the land lost by the nobility was coming into the hands of the peasantry. Peasants were not in a position to purchase entire estates, but sometimes noble estates were divided into small parcels for sale, particularly if they consisted of separate pieces of land rather than a single large holding. For example, in 1806 the allodial holdings of the heirs of Carl Emilius von Knoblauch were sold at auction for nonpayment of a debt. Local peasants from the village of Hatzbach bought the land individually.[29] This example of the breakup of a noble estate was certainly not unique, for a number of the smaller allodial estates owned by the nobility in the eighteenth century do not appear on any lists of estates from the nineteenth century, indicating that they were not sold intact to other nobles or to bourgeois but were divided into small parcels and sold to peasants.

Although commoners were allowed to buy *Rittergüter*, such purchases were not nearly as common in Hesse-Kassel as in Prussia. Nevertheless the landgrave became alarmed by the increasing number of estates being lost by the nobility to bourgeois and peasants, and at the close of the eighteenth century he began to issue ordinances aimed at restricting the purchase of noble estates by commoners. A decree of 30 January 1796 prohibited the sale or partition of a *Rittergut* without his consent, and this decree was followed by two further restrictions in 1805. The first ordered the *Lehnhof* (a section of the *Regierung*[30] in Kassel that handled all matters dealing with fiefs) not to allow bourgeois or peasants to purchase fiefs, while the second granted members of the Ritterschaft who sold allodial estates to commoners the right to reclaim such estates within ten years upon repayment of the purchase price and any improvements.[31]

---

[29] Knoblauch, *Kurzgefaßte Geschichte*, 21.

[30] The *Regierung* combined both administrative and legal functions in the eighteenth century. The most important *Regierung* was that of Kassel, which had jurisdiction over both Lower Hesse and issues that involved the country as a whole, including the regulation of fiefs. There were also *Regierungen* in Marburg, Hanau, Rinteln, and Fulda (after 1815). In 1821 the *Regierungen* lost their judicial functions to the newly created superior courts (*Obergerichte*) and became solely the administrative centers for the provinces.

[31] *Sammlung fürstlich hessischen Landesordnungen, nebst dahin gehörigen Erläuterungs- und anderen Rescripten, Abschieden, gemeinen Bescheiden und dergleichen, 1337–1806*, 8 vols. (Kassel, 1767–1816), 7: 661, 8: 223, 241 (hereafter cited as *HLO*).

William I even considered prohibiting outright the sale of allodial estates to commoners, but the Kassel *Regierung* advised against such a move, which would change a right in existence for centuries. The councilors of the *Regierung* also argued that forbidding commoners to purchase noble estates would be disadvantageous for the nobility, noting that reduced competition among potential purchasers would lead to lower prices for estates, which would not help the nobility reduce its debts. Furthermore, bourgeois would not lend money against an estate that they had no chance of acquiring, so nobles would have fewer sources of credit. Finally, the *Regierung*'s memorandum listed two reasons that continuing to permit commoners to buy noble estates would be beneficial for the state. First, the state desired profits from increased cultivation of landed estates, something that had "nothing to do with the class of the owner but rather with his wealth and knowledge of agriculture." Second, the state should try to attract wealthy foreigners to Hesse, thereby increasing the wealth of the population. Therefore the *Regierung* argued against even granting the nobility the right to repurchase their allodial estates within ten years, because foreigners were not likely to buy or lend money against land burdened with restrictions.[32] Despite the objections of the *Regierung*, the repurchase right was granted in 1805, but no use was made of it, for the following year the French occupation put an end to such restrictions.

In general there was not a very active market in estates in Hesse-Kassel during the eighteenth century. Few estates came up for sale, and most of those that did were small and belonged to noble families that were not members of the Ritterschaft. Knights were not heavily involved in buying or selling estates, the only exceptions being purchases within a particular family, either to prevent debt-burdened estates from being sold outside the family or to gain sole ownership of estates in which other branches of the family held a part interest. Sales of estates outside the family occurred only as a last resort; families would cling tenaciously to the most debt-ridden estates until the courts ordered their sale to satisfy the creditors.

INDEBTEDNESS AND SOURCES OF CREDIT

Indebtedness became a major problem for many members of the Ritterschaft in the eighteenth century. Few estates were totally free of debts, and many had debts amounting to one-half or more of their value. By

---

[32] StAM 17d Generalia, Paket. 6, memorandum of 11 April 1805.

the second half of the century indebtedness had risen to such heights that a number of noble families found themselves involved in bankruptcy proceedings. Debts were nothing new to the Hessian nobility, but the size and scope of indebtedness in the late eighteenth century appear to have exceeded previous levels.[33]

The origins of this heavy burden of debt varied from family to family and cannot always be determined, but one of the major causes seems to have been the loss of income and damage to property resulting from the Seven Years' War. Hesse-Kassel was one of the main areas of conflict for much of the war as friendly and enemy troops marched back and forth making heavy levies on the population and especially on rural estates. Many noble estate owners were thus cut off from much of their landed income during the war. Some estates were caught up in the actual fighting and suffered extensive damage, as was the case with the von Bodenhausens' castle Arnstein, which underwent two assaults and a twenty-four-hour bombardment in 1760.[34] Repairs to this and other estates damaged in the war caused the owners to run up substantial debts.

Many families' total debts were increased by the inheritance of heavily indebted estates from branches of their families that died out in the eighteenth century.[35] In such cases it was sometimes also necessary to pay large cash settlements to heirs outside the male line of the family, who could otherwise claim part of an estate. In order to settle with the allodial heirs, the new owner was generally forced to go into debt. For example, in the 1740s Ludwig von Bodenhausen inherited the estate Arnstein after a distant cousin died leaving only a married daughter. The daughter could not inherit Arnstein because most of it was a fief, but this *Rittergut* also contained considerable amounts of allodial land, which she was entitled to inherit. Therefore Bodenhausen paid 30,000 talers to acquire her rights in the estate. Several years later he inherited the estate Niedergandern from another distant cousin and again had to compensate other relatives. By 1748 Bodenhausen had paid 75,000 talers to acquire sole possession of the two estates; most of the money had

[33] The late eighteenth century seems to have been a period of financial crisis for nobles in many parts of Germany. For the precarious economic situation of nobles in Prussia and southwest Germany see Martiny, *Adelsfrage in Preußen*, 30–32; Kollmer, *Schwäbische Reichsritterschaft*, 208–44; Jerome Blum, *The End of the Old Order in Rural Europe* (Princeton, 1978), 166–70.

[34] Georg Landau, *Beschreibung des Kurfürstenthums Hessen* (Kassel, 1842), 327–28.

[35] In 1801 the von der Malsburg-Escheberg family inherited the estates Niederelsungen and Obermeiser from another branch of the family and was almost forced to sell both estates because of the debts inherited with them. The estates were even advertised for sale in the *Kasseler Commerzien Zeitung* of 5 October 1801. StAM 340 v. d. Malsburg-Escheberg, Verz. 2, Nr. 2/12.

been borrowed from a wide variety of sources at 5 percent interest. This was of course a productive debt because by acquiring the two estates he greatly increased his revenues. In 1766 the combined income from the two estates was 6,100 talers, of which approximately 3,000 talers was immediately subtracted to meet the annual interest payments on the loans.[36]

Settlements within a particular branch of a family usually did not cause much of a burden on the family's finances; the males were all owners or co-owners of the family's estates and thus did not require cash settlements, while the settlements and dowries for daughters were generally fixed at a low level by family tradition or agreement. However, a few families were in such precarious financial condition in the late eighteenth century that they could not even meet these inexpensive family obligations, forcing daughters to turn to the courts in order to obtain their promised dowries.

Another major expense that frequently led to contracting debts was the cost of educating and equipping noble sons. Those who entered the bureaucracy had to be supported through years of expensive schooling as well as a lengthy period of unpaid employment in government service. The extremely expensive custom of the "cavalier's tour" to the major cities of Europe had virtually died out in Hesse-Kassel by the late eighteenth century, but previously such tours had caused considerable debts for some families. Nobles whose sons entered the army were spared the costs of a university education, but the uniforms and equipment needed by a new officer also burdened noble families.[37] Furthermore, lower-ranking officers received such meager salaries that they often required financial assistance from their families for many years after entering the army. Some noble sons may also have increased their family's debts through luxury spending and gambling. Family archives are for the most part silent on such matters, but the army's frequent attempts to cut down on gambling by its officers suggest that the problem was serious.[38]

In many cases it is not possible to determine why or even when a family's debts originated. Some nobles were either unwilling or unable to repay loans and simply paid the interest year after year or even genera-

[36] StAM 340 v. Bodenhausen, Pakete 15, 165.

[37] For more information on the costs of educating and equipping sons see below, chapter 6.

[38] Commanding officers were required to state in their annual efficiency reports on officers whether the officers were gamblers or drinkers. For example, Lieutenant Friedrich von Urff (1769–1802) was described as "a useful officer but has a disorderly lifestyle. . . . He is addicted to drinking, debauchery, and gambling." StAM 11 (Militärkabinett), Conduitenlisten, Regiment Garde, 1795.

tion after generation.[39] If a creditor demanded repayment of his loan, the noble debtor would borrow this amount elsewhere.

Just how heavy a burden debts represented cannot easily be calculated, because accurate information on both total indebtedness and the value of estates is sparse. The valuations of estates in the tax records were quite low, which is not surprising because owners tried to downplay the value of their estates and because the nobility continually blocked proposals in the diet for a revision of the knights' cadaster.[40] At times nobles' debts greatly exceeded the official valuation of their estates. Thus in the 1760s the four lines of the von der Malsburg family owned estates and peasant dues valued at 61,000 talers, while their debts totaled at least 103,000 talers.[41] Although the tax valuation of the estates was probably much lower than the true value, the Malsburgs may well have had debts that approximately equaled the total value of their holdings, because their credit was exhausted and both the Escheberg and Malsburg branches of the family were involved in bankruptcy proceedings in the late eighteenth century.

A less extreme example of indebtedness is that of Dietrich von Bodenhausen, who in 1805 bequeathed to his sons land and possessions worth 145,000 talers upon which 68,000 talers in debts rested. Two years later the sons inherited another two estates from an uncle, and by 1818 their debts totaled 80,000 talers. The family then sold an estate that it owned in Thuringia and used most of the proceeds from this sale to reduce indebtedness. A family settlement in 1820 listed debts of only 47,700 talers on three estates valued at 249,600 talers.[42]

As the burden of debts rose, a number of noble families found themselves involved in bankruptcy proceedings (*Konkurs*) in the late eighteenth century. If an indebted estate was not a fief, the *Regierung* or the

---

[39] The yearly accounts of the Stift Kaufungen at the end of the eighteenth century include interest payments on loans that had been contracted up to two centuries earlier. In 1790, for example, the von Dalwigk family had still not repaid a debt from 1581, while Wilhelm von Berlepsch-Hübenthal was still paying interest on money borrowed by his great-granduncle in the 1680s. StAM 304, 1790 Rechnung.

[40] Lichtner, *Landesherr und Stände*, 37–38.

[41] The Escheberg line owed 49,000 talers (1771), the Malsburg line owed 38,000 talers (1767), and the Elmarshausen line owed 11,000 talers (1770). The total debts of the Niederelsungen line are not known, but land records show a debt of 5,000 talers from 1768. StAM, Rechnungen II, Kassel 199, 1760. StAM 340 v. d. Malsburg-Escheberg, Verz. 2, Nr. 2/24, 8/23; Archive of the von der Malsburg-Elmarshausen family in Schloß Elmarshausen, 3549 Wolfhagen, 1770 Rechnung. The holdings of this private archive (hereafter cited as Elmarshausen Archive) are not indexed, which makes it impossible to give precise citations.

[42] StAM 340 v. Bodenhausen, Pakete 217, 184, 303.

supreme court generally ordered its sale, especially if there seemed to be no chance that the owner could ever satisfy his creditors. Thus in 1765 the supreme court ordered the sale of Captain Wilhelm Friedrich von Berlepsch's estate in Oberurf, which was purchased by a brewer for 6,700 talers (the total debts in the bankruptcy were 13,300 talers). Berlepsch also owned several other estates, and although he sold another of them (Wickershof) in 1779, he soon found himself again involved with the courts when he was unable to meet a tax payment of 89 talers for the *Rittergut* Etzgerode in 1783. Berlepsch brought suit against his creditors in order to try to prevent bankruptcy from being declared, but his situation was hopeless. The estate was valued at only 17,500 talers but had debts totaling 41,600 talers. In 1791 the supreme court ruled against him and the bankruptcy was confirmed, which eventually led to the loss of the estate.[43]

Bankruptcy proceedings did not always lead to the sale of an estate, especially if it was a fief, which could be sold only with the consent of the ruler. In bankruptcies involving fiefs the court appointed administrators who collected all incomes and gave the owners a small yearly payment while using the remaining profits to help settle the creditors' demands. Such bankruptcy administrations often lasted twenty or more years and provided little income to the noble families involved, but this process enabled several families to save their estates from forced sales. Most of the post–Seven Years' War sequestrations ended in the 1780s or 1790s, when debts had been reduced by the court-appointed administrators and estate owners were able to obtain low-interest loans from the state to satisfy their creditors.

Until the late eighteenth century, the largest single source of credit for members of the Ritterschaft was the Stift Kaufungen, which in addition to supporting widows and daughters of knights actively participated in the capital market. The government did not permit the Stift to use the profits from its landholdings to purchase additional land, so the Stift invested its capital by providing loans to members of the Ritterschaft as well as to individual peasants or even to entire villages. Only one other source of credit, the *General-Depositen- und Landes-Assistenzkasse* in Kassel, was available for peasants, and this state-run bank's main function was to provide small loans to farmers who had lost animals. Therefore the Stift Kaufungen became a major source of credit for agriculture in the course of the eighteenth century. Members of the Ritterschaft received loans at a lower rate of interest than other borrowers (in 1779 knights paid an average of 4.3 percent interest, others 5 percent), but outstand-

[43] StAM 261 (Oberappellationsgericht), Ältere Akten, B:581, 585, 595, 598.

ing loans to peasants and villages soon greatly exceeded those to nobles (see figure 4.1). Many of the peasants who borrowed from the Stift Kaufungen resided in the four surrounding villages, but the Stift made loans to peasants all over Lower Hesse.[44]

Although the Stift Kaufungen was owned by the knighthood and administered by knights, members of the Ritterschaft generally could not satisfy all their credit needs by borrowing from the Stift. The officials of the Stift were not free to grant loans as they pleased, because the government set strong requirements for collateral as a condition for receiving loans over fifty guilders from the Stift. Even if knights were able to meet these requirements, they still needed the consent of the landgraves of both Hesse-Kassel and Hesse-Darmstadt, for the Stift Kaufungen was under the sponsorship of both rulers until 1810. Such consent was usually granted, but the process was often time-consuming and served to deter potential noble borrowers. An additional and even more important reason that the Stift could not satisfy all the credit needs of the Ritterschaft was the size of its loans. For much of the eighteenth century, loans from the Stift Kaufungen rarely exceeded ten thousand talers and generally amounted to between two and four thousand talers (see table 4.2).[45]

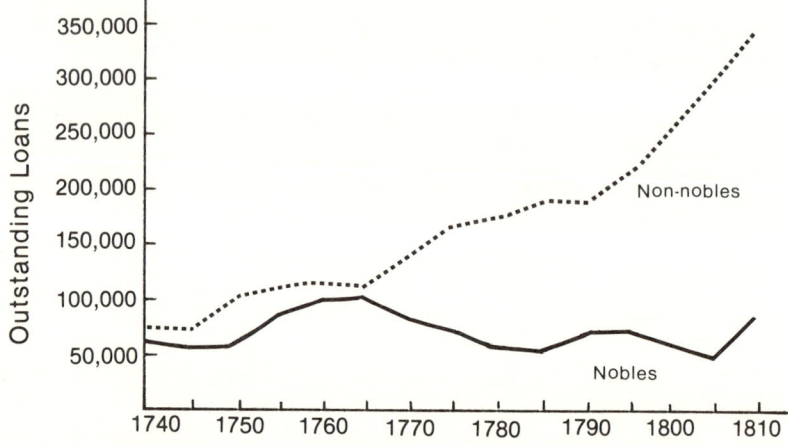

Figure 4.1. Borrowers from the Stift Kaufungen (in *Reichstaler*).

[44] Gilsa, *Wirtschaftliche Entwicklung des Stiftes Kaufungen*, 45–63. The annual accounts of the Stift Kaufungen are found in StAM 304, Jahresrechnungen.

[45] Loans to knights were much larger than those to non-noble borrowers. In 1770 the 41 noble debtors owed the Stift Kaufungen an average of 2,028 talers each, while the other 1,316 borrowers owed an average of 108 talers each. Gilsa, *Wirtschaftliche Entwicklung des Stiftes Kaufungen*, 57.

Such amounts were not sufficient to meet the rising credit needs of the Ritterschaft, whose members therefore borrowed from a wide variety of sources. Many charitable institutions actively participated in the loan market because they wanted to invest the profits from their landholdings and peasant dues. Foremost among such institutions were the state hospitals (*Landeshospitäler*) at Merxhausen and Haina, but many smaller foundations also made loans. Unfortunately for credit seekers, loans from these sources were usually even smaller than those from the Stift Kaufungen, so nobles requiring large amounts of capital were forced to turn to private individuals as well. Since most loans from individuals were also small, nobles were frequently in debt to one or more foundations and a host of private creditors, generally nobles or bourgeois in the upper levels of government service, merchants, and Jews. The maximum rate of interest that lenders could charge was set by law at 5 percent for Christian and 6 percent for Jewish lenders.[46]

Lists of creditors from bankruptcy proceedings illustrate the wide range of sources of credit for many noble families. In 1773 Wilhelm von Buttlar-Elberberg, a high-ranking court official, owed more than 145,000 talers to fifty-two creditors. Not all of these debts had been contracted in the form of loans; Buttlar owed a total of 3,400 talers to ten merchants and artisans for unpaid bills and 7,000 talers to the treasury for an unpaid account. Four additional debts were obligations to other members of his family (15,800 talers in all), which left 96,700 talers in capital and 21,200 talers in back interest owed to thirty-seven different

TABLE 4.2. Loans Made by the Stift Kaufungen to Members of the Ritterschaft (In *Reichstaler*)

	Number of New Loans	Total Amount	Average Loan
1740–1749	7	14,766	2,109
1750–1759	8	50,500	6,312
1760–1769	1	500	500
1770–1779	4	7,800	1,950
1780–1789	3	15,580	5,193
1790–1799	2	17,000	8,500
1800–1809	6	43,300	7,217

[46] *HLO*, 6:13 (23 May 1760).

creditors (see table 4.3).[47] None of Buttlar's loans had come from the Stift Kaufungen.

Another bankruptcy from the same period, that of the von der Malsburg-Escheberg family in 1771, also lists no debts to the Stift Kaufungen. The family owed 49,100 talers (not including back interest), and, as with Wilhelm von Buttlar, the major creditors were other nobles (six individuals who had loaned a total of 21,500 talers). In both cases loans were obtained primarily from nobles who were not members of the Ritterschaft, which suggests that many knights were not in a position to extend credit in the eighteenth century. Only three of the ten noble Buttlar creditors and one of the six noble Malsburg creditors were members of the Ritterschaft; most of the other nobles were high-ranking army officers. The Malsburgs also owed 5,261 talers to five *Schutzjuden* (Jews who were permitted to reside in the territory of a noble landlord in return for paying an annual "protection" fee). Unlike Wilhelm von Buttlar, the Malsburgs had received substantial loans from charitable institutions (including 67,000 talers from the Haina Hospital) and had no large debts to merchants, just a number of small unpaid bills.[48]

The bankruptcy of one of the poorest families in the Ritterschaft, the

TABLE 4.3.

Creditors of Wilhelm von Buttlar-Elberberg in 1773 (In *Reichstaler*)

Creditors	Total Capital	Avg. Debt/ Individual	Number of Loans	Average Loan
10 Nobles	39,620	3,926	19	2,066
8 Bourgeois civil servants	17,090	2,136	12	1,424
6 Bourgeois court employees	12,124	2,021	16	758
5 Merchants	15,202	3,040	6	2,534
5 Jews (*Schutzjuden*)	11,149	2,230	13	858
1 Bourgeois (profession unknown)	1,000	1,000	1	1,000
2 Charitable institutions	875	438	3	292
37 Total	96,700	2,614	70	1,381

[47] StAM 340 v. Buttlar-Elberberg, Nr. 451.
[48] StAM 340 v. d. Malsburg-Escheberg, Verz. 2, Nr. 8/30.

von Löwenstein-Wickershof family, reveals a different pattern of sources and amounts of credit than the above two examples. In 1775 the Löwensteins' total debt was 16,600 talers, of which 14,200 talers were loans and the rest were unpaid bills and wages. Only three of the creditors were nobles, and only one of these, Sophie von Griesheim, had loaned over 300 talers (she was owed 3,500 talers). A Jewish trader had loaned 2,270 talers and the Stift Kaufungen had provided 600 talers, but most of the loans were in small amounts. The remaining thirty creditors had loaned a total of 8,643 talers, for an average of 288 talers each. Fourteen of these smaller creditors were *Schutzjuden*, who together loaned 4,530 talers.[49] The fact that such a large proportion of the Löwensteins' debt was to Jews indicates that the family was unable to obtain credit elsewhere; borrowing from Jews was generally a measure of last resort because of the higher rate of interest on such loans.

Not all members of the Ritterschaft were in such dire financial straits. Some knights, particularly those holding high government offices, not only had no debts but were themselves sources of credit for other nobles or for local peasants. For example, when Geheimer Rat Hans Wilhelm von Baumbach-Ropperhausen died in 1805, his estate included almost ten thousand talers' worth of debts owed him by local peasants and townsmen. The annual rate of interest on these loans averaged 3.85 percent, so Baumbach had extended credit at very reasonable rates.[50]

Beginning in the 1770s those nobles who did need credit no longer experienced difficulty in obtaining loans large enough to meet their needs. The Hessian government had begun to play an active role in the loan market in order to invest the huge surpluses in the treasury obtained by selling the services of the Hessian army to England during the American Revolution. Between 1776 and 1784 England paid Hesse-Kassel over nineteen million talers (over three million pounds sterling). After subtracting the costs of salaries, equipment, and mobilization, the landgrave still was left with a profit of eleven million talers.[51] Landgrave Frederick II invested most of this wealth outside Hesse-Kassel in loans to other European princes (always to states not larger than his own), but beginning in the 1770s he also allowed members of the nobility, officer corps, and bureaucracy to borrow from the treasury (*Kriegskasse*). At first the rate of interest on these loans was the usual 5 percent interest, but by the 1780s most loans from the treasury were made at 4 or even 3.5

---

[49] StAM 340 v. Löwenstein, Paket 55. See also Friedrich Schunder, *Die von Löwenstein: Geschichte einer hessischen Familie*, 3 vols. (Lübeck, 1955), 1:257–59.

[50] Elmarshausen Archive, list of income for the heirs of Geheimer Rat von Baumbach, 1805.

[51] Both and Vogel, *Landgraf Friedrich II*, 95.

percent interest. Members of the Ritterschaft began increasingly to take advantage of this new, inexpensive source of credit (see table 4.4).[52]

Not only were loans from the treasury much larger than those which knights had been able to obtain in the past,[53] but the rate of interest was even lower than that of the Ritterschaft's own Stift Kaufungen, so the treasury soon became the leading source of credit for knights. In 1789 Landgrave William IX decided to make loans available to members of the Ritterschaft at still lower rates,[54] and for more than a decade most loans to nobles were made at 3 or 3.5 percent interest. As a result, nobles were able to reduce the burden of interest payments by taking out a large loan from the treasury in order to pay off numerous older debts, which were almost always at 5 or even 6 percent interest. In some cases nobles used loans from the treasury to conclude advantageous settlements with their creditors, who were willing to settle for less than what was owed them in order to avoid having their funds tied up in bankruptcy proceedings, which often dragged on for decades. In 1786 Georg von Buttlar-Elberberg justified a request for a large loan from the treasury by saying that because his estates were under sequestration, he saw no chance of satisfying his creditors, but that if he were to receive a large loan, he could reach an agreement with them. Buttlar added that he had already contacted his creditors and reported, "Virtually all have already

TABLE 4.4. Loans Made by the Treasury to Members of the Ritterschaft (In *Reichstaler*)

	Number of Loans	Total Amount	Average Loan
1770–1779	15	117,166	7,811
1780–1789	10	214,200	21,420
1790–1799	23	237,500	10,326
1800–1806	4	58,300	14,575

[52] Joseph Sauer, *Die Finanzgeschäfte der Landgrafen von Hessen-Kassel* (Fulda, 1930), 36. Information on loans by the treasury (*Kriegskasse*) is contained in StAM, Rechnungen II, Kassel 51, 52; 12 (Kriegsministerium), Kriegszahlamt Rechnungen, Nr. 8300–8342; 300 Abt. 11, C 8, Nr. 5; 17c Generalia, Nr. 229.

[53] Several of the loans were immense. In 1785 Pandolphus Freiherr von Dörnberg, a Prussian and former Hessian minister of state, received 115,000 talers at 2.5 percent interest. The next largest loan was for 50,000 talers, but most loans were much smaller.

[54] StAM 17d Generalia, Paket. 6, William IX to Erbmarschall von Riedesel, 18 April 1789.

agreed to cancel a substantial portion of my debts if they immediately receive the balance in cash."[55]

By the end of the eighteenth century the majority of the families in the Ritterschaft had obtained loans from the treasury, and twenty-two families had borrowed over ten thousand talers each. Heavy indebtedness to the state led to serious problems for some noble families after the French occupied Hesse-Kassel in 1806. The new Kingdom of Westphalia, which was now the holder of the former treasury obligations, was constantly in need of large sums of capital to finance the costs of reforms and Napoleon's wars. The new government could not simply demand payment of the loans, because most contained long-term repayment plans (frequently 1 percent of the capital per year) and could not be called in without cause. To encourage debtors to repay their loans immediately, the government offered to cancel a large portion of the debt.[56] However, few nobles were able to take advantage of the offer because their economic situation had deteriorated owing to the loss of virtually all of their former legal and financial privileges. In addition, noble landowners were forced to make "voluntary" loans to the Westphalian state by buying its bonds, which drained most excess capital.[57]

Some families even began to experience difficulties in meeting the required interest and capital payments. Once payments were in arrears, the Westphalian government was able to call in loans. This occurred to the von Buttlar-Elberberg family after it was unable to maintain payments on a debt of 39,000 talers on the *Rittergut* Ermschwerd. In 1808 the family managed to pay both the required 1,550 talers in interest and 450 talers in capital, but for the next two years only the interest was paid.[58] Finally in 1811 the family was unable to make either payment, and the government ordered the sale of the estate. Ermschwerd, along with two smaller estates, was sold at auction in 1813 to Hofrat Christian Heimbach, who agreed to pay the family's debts to the state from all its estates (163,600 talers) and also 22,000 talers in cash. In return the Buttlars pledged to settle all other outstanding debts on the property that had been sold.[59] The Buttlars had thus been forced to sell the prize of their

[55] StAM 340 v. Buttlar-Elberberg, Nr. 455.

[56] Sauer, *Finanzgeschäfte*, 105–7.

[57] Margarete Hildebrand, *Die Finanzwirtschaft des Königreichs Westfalen* (Marburg, 1925), 130–40.

[58] The family's steward informed the government that he had been unable to collect the estate's incomes from the peasants because the abolition of seigneurial justice had robbed him of the means to collect arrears swiftly. StAM 340 v. Buttlar-Elberberg, Nr. 455.

[59] Heimbach in turn sold the estates to the French general Jacob Alix. When the elector returned from exile, he declared the original sale invalid because the estates were fiefs and could not be alienated without his consent. The estates were confiscated without compen-

estates, which had been in their possession since the early sixteenth century, but this sale would probably have occurred eventually even without the change in governments, owing to the family's hopeless financial situation.

Nobles indebted to the treasury were not the only debtors to feel the pressure of the Kingdom of Westphalia's need for funds. In 1808 the Westphalian government confiscated all the holdings of the Stift Kaufungen, and because the Stift had also provided support for nobles in Hesse-Darmstadt, which was still independent and an ally in the Confederation of the Rhine, Westphalia paid Hesse-Darmstadt 100,000 talers in compensation for the lost rights and incomes. In order to raise this amount, most of the Stift's outstanding loans were called in. In 1810 nobles owed the Stift 87,600 talers, but by 1814 this debt had been cut down to 14,120 talers. Non-nobles' debts sank from 340,000 to 143,500 talers during the same period.[60]

The economic squeeze on the landed nobility caused by higher taxes, forced loans, loss of privileges, and limitation and recall of credit eased after the Westphalian government collapsed at the end of 1813. However, the elector's attempt to eradicate virtually all traces of the Kingdom of Westphalia's existence caused further economic harm to some nobles. All landowners had been forced to buy the bonds of the Westphalian government, and these obligations were repudiated by the elector, making them worthless. A number of individuals, including a few nobles, also lost heavily when the elector confiscated without compensation all former state property that had been sold by the Westphalian government.[61]

Although seigneurial jurisdiction was not restored, the nobility did regain its remaining rights as landlords, and nobles' economic situation gradually began to improve. But the first two decades following the return of the elector from exile brought renewed difficulties for many landowners due to catastrophic harvests in 1816 and 1817 and then a pe-

sation, which led to a long lawsuit by General Alix and his heirs against the state. The Buttlars again became the nominal owners of the estates but were told that their debts to the state were also considered to be in existence again. Within two years the family reached an agreement with the elector under which the estates became royal property in exchange for the cancellation of all the family's debts to the treasury. StAM 340 v. Buttlar-Elberberg, Nr. 128, 130, 135.

[60] Gilsa, *Wirtschaftliche Entwicklung des Stiftes Kaufungen*; StAM 304, 1810 and 1814 Rechnungen.

[61] In 1812 Geheimer Rat Carl Otto von der Malsburg-Escheberg paid more than 65,000 talers for land and peasant dues that had previously belonged to the state. All of this property was confiscated in 1814. Otto Kuhring, *Das Schicksal der westflischen Domänenkäufer* (Kassel, 1913), 130, 134.

riod of extremely low grain prices in the 1820s. During this period the Ritterschaft lost a number of estates as hopelessly indebted families such as the Freudenthal and Gilserhof lines of the von Baumbach family were forced to sell all their landholdings. Some other families who possessed several estates sold one in order to reduce or eliminate their debts. In such cases the estate chosen for sale was generally located far from the family's main estates or had not been in the family very long.[62] As in the past, families were unwilling to consider selling their ancient estates except for sales between branches of the same family.[63]

In the first half of the nineteenth century there was less credit available to estate owners than in the past. Depleted by the Westphalian government and by the campaigns of 1814 and 1815, the treasury (*Kriegskasse*) no longer provided large, low-interest loans. A few smaller government treasuries such as the *Militär-Witwen-Kasse* (Military Widows' Treasury) continued to make credit available but in small amounts with no reduction in rates of interest for the nobility.[64] As a result, nobles once again turned to the Stift Kaufungen and to private individuals for loans.

Families that were in good financial condition began to acquire estates, especially those which became available after two of the richest families in the Ritterschaft, von Diede and von Meysenbug, died out at the beginning of the nineteenth century. Their fiefs fell to the state, but some of the allodial estates came on the market. The von Baumbach-Nentershausen family bought the estate Frielingen in 1810 from the von

[62] For example, in 1818 the Bodenhausens sold the estate Niedertrebra in Brunswick to its peasants and used the proceeds to reduce their debts considerably (StAM 340 v. Bodenhausen, Pakete 186). Wilhelm von der Malsburg-Elmarshausen inherited the estate Glimerode from his uncle, Johann von Gohr, in 1817 and sold it five years later for 17,000 talers to Heinrich Rivière. Elmarshausen Archive.

[63] In 1821 the von Baumbach-Ropperhausen family sold the estate Obermöllrich, which had been theirs for only a generation, to the closely related von Baumbach-Lenderscheid family, while in 1850 Wilhelm von Gilsa (Mittelhof line) sold his estate in Gilsa to Otto von Gilsa (Unterhof line). Buttlar-Elberberg, *Stammbuch*: von Baumbach, Tafel V; von Gilsa, Tafel II.

[64] Rates of interest often varied according to the state of the loan market. In 1819 Wilhelm von der Malsburg-Elmarshausen had promised to lend his cousin, Carl Otto von der Malsburg-Escheberg, 8,000 talers but found himself without sufficient capital due to "the greatly depressed value of my government bonds" (especially the Westphalian obligations that he had been forced to buy). Malsburg then suggested an alternate source of capital to his uncle: "I owe the Military Widows' Treasury in Kassel 8,000 talers at 4 percent and have announced the repayment of the 8,000 talers to the institute. These 8,000 talers are thus available and, I have reason to believe, can be had at 4 1/2 percent." StAM 340 v. d. Malsburg-Escheberg, Verz. 2, Nr. 2/6, Wilhelm v. d. Malsburg to Geheimer Rat Carl Otto v. d. Malsburg, 10 September 1819.

Diede allodial heirs for 18,000 talers and later acquired a second estate in the same village for 11,000 talers. Even the von Buttlar-Elberberg family, which had been forced to sell three of its estates because of debts in 1816, managed to recoup some of its losses just a decade later when it purchased the nearby estate Riede (formerly a fief of the von Meysenbug family) from the elector for 34,000 talers.[65]

Although the purchase of whole estates was more spectacular, most noble families who acquired land did so in the form of small purchases designed to increase the size and value of their existing estates; such purchases were made primarily from the peasantry. The process of rounding out and expanding an estate was slow and laborious, often involving acquisitions of less than one acre of land. Noble families that were not burdened with debts began to acquire peasant land in the 1820s, when falling grain prices hurt many peasants financially, but the bulk of the Ritterschaft's land purchases from the peasantry did not occur until after the enactment of the first Redemption Law (*Ablösungsgesetz*) in 1832.

NOBLE LANDOWNERSHIP AFTER THE REFORMS OF 1832 AND 1848

The Redemption Law gave peasants the right to abolish the dues and services owed to landlords by paying twenty times the annual value of such obligations. All redemptions (*Ablösungen*) were voluntary and could take place only at the request of the peasant, not the landlord. Few peasants were able to make such large payments all at once, so the legislature established a new credit institution, the *Landeskreditkasse* (State Credit Bank), to provide low-interest loans to the peasantry. Loans from the *Landeskreditkasse* enabled large numbers of peasants to free themselves from the most burdensome of their dues and services, the labor services (*Dienste*) and tithes (*Zehnte*). These two obligations were redeemed by whole villages rather than by individual peasants, and most villages took this step in the 1830s and 1840s. However, many peasants did not redeem their individual obligations to landlords, such as quitrents (*Grundzinsen*) for hereditary land, so these dues frequently remained in effect until 1848, when the second Redemption Law abolished the entire system of fiefs and hereditary leases under the same terms of compensation for landlords as in 1832. The loans made by the *Landeskreditkasse* for the purpose of redeeming peasant dues and services illustrate this process (see figure 4.2).[66]

---

[65] Baumbach, *Familie von Baumbach*, 94; StAM 340 v. Buttlar-Elberberg, Nr. 98.

[66] The rate of interest for loans to redeem services was 3 percent, tithes 3.5 percent, and

The Hessian state received the lion's share of the redemption payments because it was the landlord for approximately two-thirds of the peasantry, but noble landlords also took in large amounts of this capital. For most noble families the total amount received as indemnification for lost dues and services amounted to less than fifteen thousand talers, but a few families with extensive landholdings received much more. The dues and services owed to the von Berlepsch family, for example, were redeemed by payments amounting to more than forty thousand talers.[67]

Noble landlords did not always have immediate access to the funds being borrowed by peasants from the *Landeskreditkasse* to redeem dues and services, for the law establishing this bank contained several important restrictions upon the payment of redemption funds to landlords. If a landlord had pledged peasant dues (such as a village's tithe) as collateral on a loan from a third party, the redemption payments for these dues were retained by the *Landeskreditkasse* until the debt had been paid or the landlord asked that the redemption capital be paid directly to his creditor. A second and more important restriction was that if a peasant obligation had been held by the landlord as a fief from the state, the capital

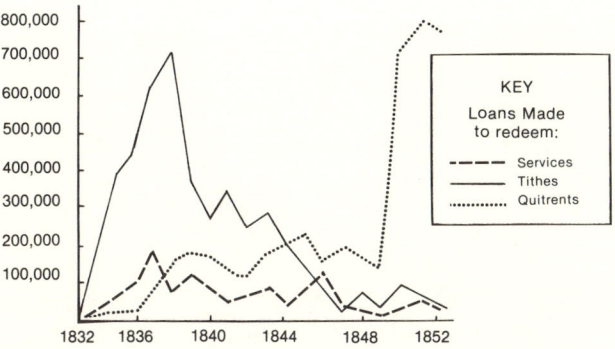

Figure 4.2. *Landeskreditkasse* Loans to Peasants (in *Reichstaler*).

---

quitrents 3.75 percent. A. Schleicher, "Das kurhessische Landescredit-Institut und seine dreissigjährige Wirksamkeit," *Jahrbücher für Nationalökonomie und Statistik* 1 (1863): 413. The most comprehensive statistics on loans made by the *Landeskreditkasse* to peasants are found in Sakai, *Kurhessische Bauer*, 145–46.

[67] StAM 225 (Landeskreditkasse), Nr. 1765. The redemption payments (*Ablösungskapitalien*) for noble families are found in StAM 225, Nr. 4–2364 and in StAM 45b (Oberfinanz Kammer, Kommission für die Ablösungen), Nr. 1–372.

was not to be paid out until a law was enacted to regulate the whole system of lord-vassal relationships, which did not occur until 1848. Since many peasant dues and services, especially the tithes, were fiefs or parts of estates that were fiefs from the state, a large portion of the peasantry's redemption payments were retained by the *Landeskreditkasse* and thus did not immediately come into the hands of the nobility. When the *Landeskreditkasse* held capital belonging to landlords, it paid the owners 3.75 percent interest annually.[68]

In 1835 the government began to allow vassals whose redemption payments were being retained by the *Landeskreditkasse* to obtain their capital through a process known as surrogation, whereby a vassal purchased land equal in value to the fief that had been redeemed and offered this as a substitute. If accepted by the government, the new land thus became a fief from the state, and the vassal received his capital from the *Landeskreditkasse*. Later it also became possible to receive the redemption capital itself as a cash fief (*Geld-Lehen*), but most substitutions were made with land.[69]

The continued existence of the feudal system after 1832 coupled with the government's insistence that fiefs that had been redeemed be replaced by land of equal value provided a powerful incentive for the nobility to invest in land. Additional pressure to use the redemption payments in this manner came from family agreements and entails (*Fideikommisse*), which often stipulated that land or incomes that were lost as a result of the reforms had to be replaced by more land so that the total value of the family's entailed holdings would not be diminished. For example, the closely related Nentershausen and Kirchheim branches of the von Baumbach family established a joint *Fideikommiß* in 1826. By 1851 the two houses had received more than 32,000 talers in redemption payments, so they drew up a new agreement confirming the entailed nature of all their wealth. Each branch bound itself to invest its share of the capital in land, which would then become part of the *Fideikommiß*. The Nentershausen branch, which had already used some of its redemption capital to purchase a large peasant holding in Hoheneiche in 1834, spent much more on land than the 16,000 talers required by the agreement of 1851. By the end of the decade this family had paid over 23,000 talers to enlarge its holdings in Hoheneiche and to purchase four

[68] *Sammlung von Gesetzen*, 6 (1832): 160, 170.

[69] The government acted to prevent the loss of fiefs that had formerly been peasant dues and services because it did not want to lose the fees that it received from fiefs and especially because it did not wish to forfeit the possibility of acquiring a fief outright when a vassal's family became extinct in the male line. A list of all substitutions for fiefs (*Lehns-Surrogationen*) between 1834 and 1841 is found in StAM 17c, Generalia, Paket 227.

large peasant landholdings in Dens, which were placed together to form an estate.[70]

Other families from the Ritterschaft were also active in acquiring peasant land in order to satisfy requirements set by a *Fideikommiß* or the government. The von Buttlar-Elberberg family, which had once again gone into debt to buy an entire estate for 34,000 talers in 1826, spent another 40,000 talers on land purchases in the four decades following the Redemption Law of 1832. Virtually all of these purchases were small parcels of peasant land. Kammerherr Karl von der Malsburg-Escheberg bought 5,400 talers' worth of land from peasants between 1835 and 1841 and tried repeatedly to get the government to accept this land along with a newly built granary worth 2,700 talers as a substitute for 9,000 talers in redemption payments (for former tithes) being held by the *Landeskreditkasse*.[71]

The primary use of redemption capital by noble families was thus to buy land, in most cases from the peasantry because entire estates came on the market infrequently. The other primary use of these payments was to pay off inherited debts. Many families were forced to use the payments in this manner, since by law landlords could not otherwise obtain the use of capital from incomes that had been pledged as collateral for loans. The only other widespread way in which redemption payments were used was to purchase bonds, but even in this respect the nobility remained traditional, buying government issues rather than the new bonds or stock of railroads and other private companies.

Government bonds were nothing new to the members of the Ritterschaft, for all landowners had been forced to buy Hessian and Westphalian bonds between 1807 and 1813. Some families also acquired bonds from other German states in the early nineteenth century. After 1832 all noble families became heavily involved with government bonds when they began to receive *Landeskreditkasse* obligations in exchange for funds being retained. In the decades that followed, there were so many noble families attempting to invest their newly acquired capital in land at the same time that there was probably insufficient land on the market to satisfy all of them, causing many nobles to turn to bonds as a means of investing at least part of their capital.

Families who held bonds generally owned those of several different states. The issues of Austria, Prussia, and Hesse-Darmstadt were the most popular foreign bonds, but some families also purchased bonds

[70] StAM 340 v. Baumbach-Nentershausen, Acc. 1942/20, Nr. 45; Acc. 1948/41, Nr. 15.

[71] StAM 340 v. Buttlar-Elberberg, Nr. 96; StAM 340 v. d. Malsburg-Escheberg, Verz. 2, Nr. 2/27, 9/14.

from smaller states or even *Standesherren*. Occasionally a family loaned money to a local firm; however, such firms were not new industries but traditional ones that had arisen from the family's own estate manufactories. For example, during the years 1840–45 the Ziegenhagen glassworks received 13,000 talers from its owners, the von Buttlar-Elberberg family. Other obligations held by this family in 1847 were 5,000 guilders in Austrian bonds, 650 talers in *Landeskreditkasse* obligations, 200 guilders in Hesse-Darmstadt bonds, 50 guilders in Nassau bonds, and 4,125 talers in loans to fourteen individuals, mostly from the surrounding villages.[72] These loans to peasants show that the nobility remained an important source of local credit during much of the nineteenth century.

The Hessian nobility's three main uses of the redemption payments—acquisition of land, repayment of debts, and purchase of bonds—correspond exactly with those of the mediatized princes of western and southern Germany.[73] This is not surprising because the poorer Hessian nobles were in even less of a position than the *Standesherren* to risk investing their capital in railroads and industry. Like the *Standesherren*, most members of the Hessian Ritterschaft did not even consider forms of investment that were not in keeping with traditional noble practices, although there were a few exceptions. Most of the handful of noble "industrialists" in the mid-nineteenth century owned nothing more than an expanded estate manufactory such as a brickyard or distillery, but one of the newest families in the Ritterschaft, the Freiherren Waitz von Eschen, was quite active in industry. After studying mineralogy in Marburg and Göttingen, Carl Sigismund Freiherr Waitz von Eschen (1795–1873) purchased the first of several coal mines in 1817 and established a large chemical factory in the 1830s. Waitz was also very interested in railroad development and served on the boards of directors of several railroad companies.[74]

Despite the large influx of capital from the peasantry after 1832, some noble families still found it necessary to seek credit, at times because of difficulties in obtaining the use of the redemption payments themselves rather than just the interest. However, obtaining credit in the 1830s and 1840s was not an easy task for estate owners, not because there was no

[72] By 1859 loans to the glassworks totaled 30,000 talers and the family held a total of 54,000 talers in obligations, of which only 320 talers were in Hessian railroad bonds. StAM 340 v. Buttlar-Elberberg, Nr. 379, 414.

[73] Winkel, *Ablösungskapitalien*, 150–61.

[74] Möker, *Nordhessen im Zeitalter der industriellen Revolution*, 192–94; *Die Firma von Waitzsche Erben KG, Kassel, unter besonderer Berücksichtigung des Braunkohlenbergbaues am Hirschberg bei Großalmerode* (Kassel, 1977), 1–3.

capital available—although the *Landeskreditkasse* made loans only to peasants in this period, the Stift Kaufungen had plenty of funds on hand from the huge redemption payments it was receiving from its peasants—but because the elector's consent for loans suddenly became extremely difficult to obtain. Most of the estates of the Ritterschaft were still fiefs prior to 1848, and all loans against these estates required the consent of the elector.

The new ruler after 1831, Frederick William, was far less inclined than his predecessors to allow vassals to mortgage their fiefs. In order to control borrowing by vassals more closely, the elector asked the interior ministry in 1835 for a complete list of all loans to vassals that his father had approved. Minister Hassenpflug supplied this information and noted, "The wealth of the majority of your Royal Highness's vassals has declined owing to various unfavorable circumstances, dating in part from the Westphalian period." Hassenpflug praised the activities of the *Landeskreditkasse* and added, "Your Royal Highness certainly does not wish to deny its benefits to the nobility, which is no less loyal to its illustrious ruler than any other class."[75] But Hassenpflug's plea for more credit for the nobility (as long as this credit was coupled with rational repayment plans) fell on deaf ears, and in 1841 the elector seriously restricted credit for vassals by instructing the interior ministry to enforce a 1766 decree that prohibited vassals from mortgaging the substance of their fiefs. Only the annual income could be pledged as collateral. The interior minister argued that in practice this restriction had frequently been ignored, especially after 1817, but the elector insisted that the decree be strictly enforced in the future, thus preventing many nobles from applying for credit.[76]

The Ritterschaft's frustration with the scarcity of credit was summed up by Otto von Trott zu Solz at the annual conference in 1847:

> Urgently needed royal consent for taking out loans has even been denied in cases in which the wealth and fate of whole families is at stake, when it was known that the loans were not being sought frivolously but were necessary to avoid bankruptcy; in addition, there was no possibility of escheat [*Heimfall*] owing to the large number

[75] StAM 300, Abt. 11, C 8, Nr. 5, Hassenpflug to Elector Frederick William, 11 May 1835. Despite numerous requests by nobles in the 1840s for permission to borrow from the *Landeskreditkasse*, the government reaffirmed its policy that such loans were to be granted only for the purpose of commuting peasant dues and services. StAM 17c (Regierung Kassel, Lehensrepositur), Generalia, Nr. 229, interior ministry protocol of 21 November 1845.

[76] StAM 300, Abt. 11, C 8, Nr. 5, Elector Frederick William to interior ministry, 21 June 1841; 17c, Generalia, Nr. 229, Lehnhof to interior ministry, 29 September 1841.

of relatives. Royal consent has been virtually unobtainable, even though it was clear that through orderliness, thrift, and intelligence, nobles have been trying to improve their fiefs, which had often been inherited in ruinous condition. The result is essentially a complete absence of credit for vassals. The *Landeskreditkasse*, whose benefits are enjoyed by every other class, exists for the estate owner only in order to hold on to the redemption payments at low interest for as long as it takes him to redeem them laboriously by purchasing expensive allodial land.[77]

The end of the feudal system in 1848 eliminated the nobility's credit difficulties. Nobles no longer had to find substitutes for redemption payments that were being held by the *Landeskreditkasse* because the payments were for peasant dues that had been fiefs granted to noble landlords by the state. Once estate owners compensated the government for its loss of the right of escheat, they received all the payments owed them for former fiefs. Those nobles who needed even more capital also had no more problems after 1848, because the allodification of estates ended the necessity of obtaining the elector's consent for loans. As a result, the number of knights who borrowed from the Stift Kaufungen jumped from only four in the 1840s to seventeen in the 1850s.[78] Nobles also received a new source of credit at this time. Once most peasant dues had been redeemed, the *Landeskreditkasse* began to make loans in substantial amounts to landowners and other borrowers at reasonable rates (4 to 4.5 percent interest).[79] Some of the loans obtained by noble estate owners in the 1850s and 1860s were used to repay old debts in order to obtain a more favorable rate of interest. However, many nobles asked for credit in order to purchase more land, and one noble, Rudolf von Keudell, borrowed twenty thousand talers from the Stift Kaufungen to set up a beet sugar factory on his estate.[80]

By using capital from redemption payments and loans to purchase ad-

[77] ARSK, Rep. VI, Gef. 2–3, Nr. 7.

[78] StAM 304, Jahresrechnungen.

[79] Between 1851 and 1865 the *Landeskreditkasse* made thirty-four loans totaling 507,000 talers to members of the Ritterschaft. Most of the loans (twenty-one) were for less than 10,000 talers, but ten loans exceeded 20,000 talers, the highest being a loan of 100,000 talers to the von der Malsburg zu Malsburg family in 1863. However, the loan to this hopelessly indebted family was probably made in order to consolidate the family's debts so that the government would become the sole creditor and could take over the estates when the family forfeited on the loans, which occurred by the end of the decade. The next largest loan was only for 50,000 talers. StAM, Rechnungen II, Kassel 230, 1851–65.

[80] StAM 304, Rep. IV, Gef. 2–5, Nr. 78. Requests for loans to purchase land are found in numbers 84, 86, 87, 96, and 100.

ditional property, many nobles increased the size of their landholdings substantially. In the second half of the nineteenth century noble landowners gained even more land when they received a share of the communal lands of neighboring villages. The division of the commons was closely linked to consolidation (*Verkoppelung*), a program of land reform designed to end the irrational, quiltlike patterns of tiny peasant landholdings by exchanging land and bringing parcels together. Laws calling for both the division of common lands and the consolidation of landholdings were enacted in 1834, but these laws required the villages involved to approve and initiate the process. Prior to Hesse-Kassel's annexation by Prussia in 1866, few villages had taken this step. Prussian legislation greatly accelerated the process, although some villages did not reform their landholdings until the mid-twentieth century.[81]

The lack of comprehensive statistics for noble landowning before the 1860s makes it difficult to determine exactly to what extent the nobility was able to enlarge its estates through purchases of peasant land and the division of the commons, but the changes in size of fifteen noble estates for which information is available indicate that many estates grew substantially in the nineteenth century, while very few estates declined in size (see table 4.5).[82]

The extent of noble landowning in the 1860s is revealed in detail by a survey of noble landowners conducted to determine eligibility for election to the legislature. The total amount of land owned by the nobility was 65,000 hectares (161,000 acres). This represented approximately 7 percent of the total area of Hesse-Kassel. Most of the nobility's holdings consisted of forest, as can be seen in table 4.6.[83]

The largest landholdings were those of the *Standesherren*. Three branches of the Ysenburg-Büdingen family together owned more than

[81] Kurt Scharlau, "Landeskulturgesetzgebung und Landeskulturentwicklung im ehemaligen Kurhessen seit dem 16. Jahrhundert," *Zeitschrift für Agrargeschichte und Agrarsoziologie* 1 (1953): 144–45.

[82] Eighteenth-century estate size is compiled from the cadasters, most of which were drawn up in the 1770s and 1780s. StAM Kataster I, Schachten 1777 B 1, Gilsa 1781 B 2–3, Niederurf 1786 B 2–8, Obermöllrich 1794 B 1, Betzigerode 1778 B 2, Wulmersen 1767 B 1, Kirchheim 1770 B 1, Reichensachsen 1745 B 2, Abgunst 1767 B 1, Lenderscheid 1783 B 1–3, Arnstein 1766 B 1, Groß-Ropperhausen 1783 B 2–5, Oberhone 1787 B 4, Aue 1770 B 2–4, Harmuthsachsen 1780 B 3. The nineteenth-century figures are found in StAM 30 (Statistische Kommission), Rep. II, Kl. 6, Nr. 9 (1863), and *Handbuch des Grundbesitzes im deutschen Reiche*, vol. 11, pt. 1, *Regierungsbezirk Kassel* (Berlin, 1895), 1–109. The dates of acquisition for the estates are based on information contained in Heinrich Reimer, *Historisches Ortslexikon für Kurhessen* (Marburg, 1926). The estates of the Westphalian nobility grew even more during the nineteenth century. Estates in 1890 were on the average 156 percent larger than in 1830. Reif, *Westfälischer Adel*, 478.

[83] StAM 30, Rep. II, Kl. 6, Nr. 7, 9.

TABLE 4.5. Changes in Estate Size (Nonforest Land Only)

Estate	Owner	Owned since	Size in Hectares:			Net Change in 19th c.
			18th c.	1863	1895	
Schachten	v. Schachten	1234	168	405	474	+306 ha. (+182%)
Gilsa	v. Gilsa	1359	131	131	283	+152 ha. (+116%)
Niederurf	v. Urff	1309	129	143	264	+135 ha. (+105%)
Obermöllrich	v. Baumbach	1793	32	61	60	+28 ha. (+88%)
Betzigerode	v. Hesberg	1778	78	84	131	+53 ha. (+68%)
Wülmersen	v. Stockhausen	1550	112	117	184	+72 ha. (+64%)
Kirchheim	v. Baumbach	1588	115	115	181	+66 ha. (+57%)
Reichensachsen	v. Eschwege	1435	51	74	74	+23 ha. (+45%)
Abgunst	v. Stockhausen	1629	88	95	127	+39 ha. (+44%)
Lenderscheid	v. Baumbach	1701	87	104	112	+25 ha. (+29%)
Arnstein	v. Bodenhausen	1434	201	232	237	+36 ha. (+18%)
Ropperhausen	v. Baumbach	1701	262	292	274	+12 ha. (+5%)
Oberhone	v. Eschwege	1436	56	57	57	+1 ha. (+1%)
Aue	v. Eschwege	1424	113	145	110	−3 ha. −3%
Harmuthsachsen	v. Hundelshausen	1363	178	212	122	−56 ha. (−31%)
Total			1,801	2,267	2,690	+889 ha. (+49%)

TABLE 4.6.
Land Owned by the Nobility in 1863

Hessian Ritterschaft	40,600 ha.	(61% forest)
Schaumburg Ritterschaft	1,900 ha.	(18% forest)
Former *Reichsritterschaft*	4,400 ha.	(77% forest)
Standesherren	12,300 ha.	(72% forest)
Other nobles	5,900 ha.	(not given)

11,000 hectares of land. However, many families from the Ritterschaft also owned huge tracts of land (primarily forest). The Freiherren von Dörnberg possessed over 5,200 hectares, and the von Buttlar-Elberberg and von der Malsburg-Escheberg families each owned approximately 2,400 hectares. The average holdings of a noble house amounted to 650 hectares; the median was 280 hectares. Many estates were jointly owned by several members of a family, so it is also useful to compare each individual's share. By these standards the largest landowner in the Ritterschaft in the 1860s was Hans Carl von der Malsburg-Escheberg, who was the sole owner of his family's 2,400 hectares. Six other knights owned over 1,000 hectares each, but since many families, especially the poorer ones, had a number of owners for only one or two estates, the average individual holding was only 230 hectares, and the median holding was only 99.[84]

The size of the individual estates of the nobility varied greatly. Some were scarcely larger than the holdings of a well-to-do peasant, while others covered thousands of acres. The largest single estate was that of the Freiherren von Riedesel in Ludwigseck, which totaled over 3,200 hectares (almost 8,000 acres, but of this land all but 560 acres were forest). The estate Weierhof, owned by a *Standesherr*, was smaller (1,600 hectares) but more valuable because almost half the estate was arable land. The next largest estates were Escheberg (1,450 hectares) and Elberberg, both of which were primarily forest and belonged to families in the Ritterschaft. The majority of estates were under two hundred hectares in size, and 32 of the 202 estates owned by nobles in 1865 were smaller than fifty hectares (see figure 4.3). When only nonforest land is considered, three estates stood head and shoulders above the rest: Prince Ysenburg-Büdingen's Weierhof (714 hectares), the Schenck zu

[84] StAM 30, Rep. II, Kl. 6, Nr. 9.

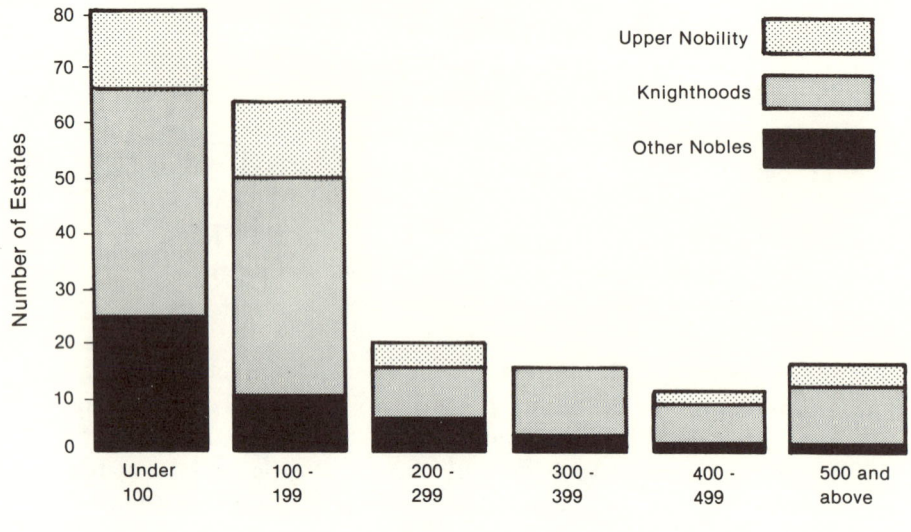

Figure 4.3. Size of Estates Owned by the Nobility in 1865.

Schweinsberg estate in Schweinsberg (520 hectares), and the Schachtens' estate in Schachten (380 hectares).[85]

Relatively few bourgeois owned large tracts of land in this period. In 1865 only 5 bourgeois held estates with more than 200 hectares of land. In contrast, 54 estates owned by nobles were at least this large, and most of these were substantially larger. By the end of the nineteenth century, the number of estates in bourgeois hands had increased considerably. In 1895 non-nobles owned 259 estates over 50 hectares in size, while the nobility held only 183 such estates. The state owned an additional 147 large landholdings, which were primarily extensive tracts of forest. Although non-nobles held the majority of the estates above 50 hectares, their estates were generally smaller than those of the nobility. Only 2 estates owned by bourgeois exceeded 300 hectares; almost 70 percent were under 100 hectares in size. In contrast, almost 80 percent of the nobility's estates were over 100 hectares; 12 estates even exceeded 1,000 hectares (see table 4.7).[86]

The nobility predominated in ownership of those estates designated as *Rittergüter*. Only 27 of the 133 *Rittergüter* in existence in 1895 were not in the hands of nobles, and most of these 27 were smaller estates.

---

[85] StAM 30, Rep. II, Kl. 6, Nr. 5, Übersicht der größeren Ökonomien in Kurhessen, 1865.

[86] Ibid; *Handbuch des Grundbesitzes*, 11: 1–109.

TABLE 4.7. Estates in Private Hands

Size in ha.	1865		1895	
	Nobles	Non-nobles	Nobles	Non-nobles
50–99	48	85	38	176
100–199	63	32	56	69
200–299	20	5	34	12
300–399	14	0	10	1
400–499	10	0	10	0
500–599	2	0	8	1
600–699	2	0	7	0
700–799	3	0	3	0
800–899	1	0	4	0
900–999	0	0	1	0
1,000 +	7	0	12	0
Total	160	122	183	259

Very few of the bourgeoisie's gains in estates in the late nineteenth century came from the Ritterschaft. Between 1863 and 1895 knights lost a total of 17 out of the 101 estates that they had owned in 1863, but only 7 of these estates were sold to bourgeois or subdivided and sold to peasants; the other 10 were purchased by nobles. During the same period members of the Ritterschaft added 7 new estates to their holdings, making the total number of estates owned in 1895 by knights 91. Therefore the knighthood as a whole owned only 10 fewer estates than in 1863. The 84 estates that had been continuously in the possession of the same families between 1863 and 1894 increased substantially in size through land purchases and the division of common lands. In 1863 these 84 estates contained a total of 10,278 hectares of nonforest land; by 1895 the total had increased 22 percent to 12,554 hectares.[87]

The continuity of the Ritterschaft's landownership was much greater than that of non-nobles during this period. In an 1851 survey of large landholdings excluding those of the Ritterschaft, non-nobles owned 186 estates above fifty hectares in size. An 1895 survey lists the owners of 123 of these estates and reveals that only 49 were still owned by the same family as in 1851. Of the 74 estates that had changed hands during this

[87] StAM 30, Rep. II, Kl. 6, Nr. 9 (1863); *Handbuch des Grundbesitzes*, 11: 1–109.

period, 57 were owned by other non-nobles, 1 by the state, and 16 by nobles (including four knights).[88]

The strength of the knighthood's bonds to its estates was not a new phenomenon. Most of the estates owned by knights in the nineteenth century had been in the possession of the same family for much longer, frequently three or four hundred years. Only 21 of the 101 estates owned by knights in 1863 had been owned by different families in 1760 (the eighteenth-century owners of 8 estates cannot be determined).[89]

Despite the turmoil of the early twentieth century in Germany, the Ritterschaft's total landholdings remained amazingly steady. In 1929 knights owned eighty-seven estates, only four fewer than in 1895. However, the turnover in estates had been increased by the extinction of several noble houses. Between 1895 and 1929 the Ritterschaft lost twelve estates (nine to non-nobles) and gained eight estates. Knights were no longer able to expand the size of their estates in this period, but few estates shrank in size. The seventy-nine estates owned continuously by the same families between 1895 and 1929 declined from 12,282 hectares of nonforest land in 1895 to 11,569 hectares in 1929, a shrinkage of only 6 percent.[90]

Why was the Hessian Ritterschaft so successful in preserving its landholdings in the eighteenth and nineteenth centuries? One of the main reasons was the direct and indirect influence of the state. In the late eighteenth century, which seems to have been a period of economic crisis for both the Hessian and the Prussian nobilities, the Hessian government made large amounts of capital available at low interest to assist beleaguered noble estate owners in consolidating their debts and reducing the burden of interest payments. Most of these loans were made under the condition that the recipient repay a fixed portion of the loan each year, a condition that was often lacking in Prussian loans.

During the same period in Prussia, nobles also received substantial amounts of credit from the newly created *Landschaften*, but many Prussian landowners used these loans to speculate in estates, a development that had been made possible by the allodification of most fiefs. In contrast, the rulers of Hesse-Kassel clung to the feudal system as long as possible, which prevented any widespread speculation in estates because most were fiefs and could not be sold or even mortgaged without

[88] StAM 30, Rep. II, Kl. 6, Nr. 12, Verzeichnis der 100 und Mehr Acker haltenden Güter und Grundbesitzungen von Privaten mit Ausschluß der Ritterschaft, 1863; *Handbuch des Grundbesitzes*, vol. 11.

[89] StAM Rechnungen II, Kassel 199; Treysa 15.

[90] Noble landownership for 1929 was compiled from *Niekammers landwirtschaftliche Güter-Adreßbücher*, vol. 6, no. 2, *Regierungsbezirk Kassel* (Leipzig, 1929).

royal consent. The feudal system lasted quite long in Hesse-Kassel; nobles' fiefs did not become allodial until 1848.[91]

Although the Hessian government's activity (low-interest loans) and
passivity (retention of the feudal system) helped nobles to retain their
landholdings, these policies had not been motivated primarily by a desire to assist the nobility. Landgrave Frederick II made loans available
in the late eighteenth century primarily because he had received tremendous amounts of capital from England and wished to invest his funds.
At first he made loans only outside Hesse-Kassel, and even after he began providing credit for the nobility, he did not initially offer a special
rate of interest. Although the landgrave claimed in 1789 that he was
making low-interest loans available in order to assist the Ritterschaft, it
may well have been the case that the market for loans at 4.5 to 5 percent
interest was already satiated and only lower interest rates would attract
new borrowers desiring to refinance their debts. The government's retention of the feudal system was also due to its own interests rather than
to a desire to help the nobility. The state, not the nobility, was the greatest recipient of feudal dues and services from the peasantry and thus
benefited the most from their retention. Furthermore, the government
wished to retain its final rights of ownership to nobles' fiefs, which reverted to the state if the family died out in the male line.

Even had the ties of fiefdom not bound most Hessian nobles to their
estates, it is doubtful that many knights would have voluntarily alienated their landholdings. Most families had owned their estates for centuries, and many nobles bore the same names as their estates. The long-
lasting ties between noble families and their estates were made possible
by the unrestricted marriage system of the Hessian nobility. Without
primogeniture and its attendant limitations on marriage by younger
sons, families did not become extinct as quickly as in other parts of Europe. Even though individual branches died out, the family as a whole
lived on and maintained strong bonds with its estates. In Prussia, however, estates changed families through inheritance more frequently.
Many new owners did not feel close ties to their recently inherited estates and were thus willing to alienate estates voluntarily. So by the late
nineteenth century, very few Prussian estates had been in the same family for at least a century, whereas continuous ownership of an estate

---

[91] Many nobles recognized the importance of the feudal system for the preservation of
their landed estates. A member of the Treusch von Buttlar-Märkershausen family wrote
in 1830, "I see feudal ties as the only support of our families; if these ties end, then in 100
years merchants, tenant farmers, and shepherds will have our estates and the old nobility
will have vanished." StAM 340 v. Baumbach-Kirchheim, Paket 102.

for three or four centuries was quite common among Hessian noble families.

Long before the end of the feudal system in Hesse-Kassel in 1848, many families took steps to protect their landholdings by establishing binding inheritance agreements or *Fideikommisse*, and once all estates became allodial, most of the remaining noble families acted to preserve their estates in this manner. At the end of the nineteenth century there were seventy-one *Fideikommisse* within the former Electorate of Hesse-Kassel (now *Regierungsbezirk* Kassel). Forty-two were owned by members of the Ritterschaft, eleven by *Standesherren* or members of the former ruling family, thirteen by other nobles, and only five by bourgeois.[92] The forty-two *Fideikommisse* owned by knights frequently consisted of several estates, so by the late nineteenth century most of the Ritterschaft's ninety-one estates were entailed, which served as a continuing guarantee of stability in noble landownership.

[92] Stahl, *Fideikommißrecht und Fideikommißwesen*, 57–58.

· 5 ·

THE LANDED ESTATE

Most nobles did not manage their estates themselves, either because they held offices that required them to be absent most of the time or because the estate was jointly owned by several members of a family, which made an impartial administration the best means of collecting and distributing the revenues. A noble family therefore generally appointed a steward to look after the daily affairs of its holdings. The steward, called a *Rentmeister* or *Verwalter*, collected all of the family's incomes from leases, peasant dues, and wood and grain sales; paid salaries, bills, and interest on debts; supervised the family's other employees on the estate; and kept all necessary accounts for the estates and incomes.

Even though most nobles were absentee landlords, they usually kept a close eye on the affairs of their estates through correspondence, supervision of the account books, and periodic visits. Unlike French court nobles, most Hessian nobles in government service did not live far from their estates and thus could visit them frequently. Army officers were sometimes able to spend extended periods of time on their estates during the eighteenth century, because at times much of the army was furloughed to reduce expenses. Noble civil servants also received periodic leaves of absence to attend to the affairs of their estates. But the day-to-day affairs of most estates were handled by stewards, not the owners.

Like the French estate agents of the eighteenth century,[1] the Hessian steward was strongly loyal to the family that he served and generally remained in his office until he died or old age forced him to retire. Some families even gave their stewards lifetime contracts, and it was not unusual for a son to follow his father as a noble family's steward.[2]

[1] Robert Forster, *"Seigneurs* and Their Agents," in *Vom Ancien Régime zur französischen Revolution*, ed. Ernst Hinrichs, Eberhard Schmitt, and Rudolf Vierhaus (Göttingen, 1978), 169–97. For the administration of estates in England see Mingay, *Landed Society*, 59–71; F.M.L. Thompson, *English Landed Society in the Nineteenth Century* (London, 1963), 151–83; David Spring, *The English Landed Estate in the Nineteenth Century: Its Administration* (Baltimore, 1963).

[2] Two generations of the Becker family served as stewards for the Freiherren von Dörnberg in the late eighteenth century, and both Wilhelm Dacke and his son Friedrich received lifetime contracts as steward for the von der Malsburg-Elmarshausen family. StAM 340 v. Dörnberg, Nr. 374, 1008–9; Elmarshausen Archive, employment contracts of 16 June 1825 and 12 September 1844.

103

Stewards generally came from the bourgeoisie and often were university graduates. Individuals with legal training proved particularly useful for managing estates, and in the eighteenth century many noble families hired lawyers to serve as both steward and seigneurial judge. Thus the administrators of the Dörnberg estates had all acquired considerable legal experience as lawyers before being hired by the family; several of these individuals had even earned doctorates of law.[3] Even in families where the position of seigneurial judge and administrator were not united, lawyers or former civil servants often served as stewards.[4]

Two stewards for the von Buttlar-Elberberg family in the eighteenth century were also university graduates and had been appointed *Rentmeister* after first holding another office in the family's service. The theology student Johann Bockwitz became the tutor for the family's children in 1742 and later served as the steward. He was replaced in the 1790s by Johann Noessel, the family's seigneurial judge. Not all administrators had attended a university. The next steward for the Buttlars was Carl Conradi; his selection in 1827 reflected the growing emphasis on forests in the nineteenth century, for he had previously been the family's forester.[5] Members of leaseholders' families also sometimes became stewards. In 1826 Ernst von Stockhausen reported to his brother that he had selected as his new steward the eighteen-year-old son of a former leaseholder, "whom I can train completely according to my methods."[6]

Most stewards received substantial salaries. The cash portion of the salary was not overly large, ranging from fifty to two hundred talers, depending on the size of the family's landholdings, but stewards also received free lodging and considerable amounts of wood and produce.[7]

[3] For the personnel records of the Dörnbergs' stewards see StAM 340 v. Dörnberg, Nr. 374–75, 1008–9.

[4] For example, Friedrich Schmidt, a former junior-level civil servant, became the steward for the *Rittergut* Elmarshausen in 1795, and a lawyer administered the estates Wülmersen and Abgunst in the late eighteenth century. Elmarshausen Archive, employment contract of 29 May 1795; StAM 340 v. Stockhausen, Nr. 322. French estate agents in the eighteenth century also frequently possessed legal training. Forster, *House of Saulx-Tavanes*, 61.

[5] Hueck, "Familie von Buttlar," no. 48, p. 5; StAM 340 v. Buttlar-Elberberg, Nr. 412, employment contracts of Johann Noessel (18 November 1789) and Carl Conradi (1 November 1827).

[6] StAM 340 v. Stockhausen, Nr. 99, letter of 2 February 1826.

[7] Steward Johann Noessel's 1789 contract with the von Buttlar family specified the following salary: 124 *Reichstaler* in cash, 8 *Viertel* of rye, 12 *Viertel* of oats, 4 *Viertel* of barley, 2 *Viertel* of wheat, 4 cords of wood, 12 geese, 24 chickens, 24 roosters, 200 eggs, and free pasturage for two pigs. (Note: the grain quantities were in Gudensberg *Viertel*, which were 17 percent larger than Kassel *Viertel* and equaled 188 liters or 5.25 bushels; see appendix E.) In addition Noessel received free lodging and 2.5 percent of all the grain that he col-

Thus the total value of a steward's salary at the end of the eighteenth century often exceeded three or four hundred talers, which was better than the pay of many junior councilors in the bureaucracy. However, a steward normally could not advance any higher unless he eventually saved enough money to lease an estate.

The steward collected three types of income for his noble employer: (1) income from the estate itself, usually in the form of rent, (2) peasant dues and services, and (3) profits from the sale of wood from the often extensive forest holdings. In the eighteenth century the main estate, rather than peasant dues or the forests, was generally the single most important source of income for noble families.

Estate owners could choose from three alternatives in deciding how their estates should be utilized. Those landowners who did not hold full-time offices could run their estates themselves, as was frequently the case in Prussia, but such individuals were in the minority in Hesse-Kassel. Most estate owners therefore faced the choice of either hiring administrators to run each of the family's estates (in addition to the steward, who collected the family's other incomes, although he might administer one estate as well) or leasing the estates.

Arguments could be found in favor of both courses of action. In 1795 the sons of Wilhelm von Buttlar inherited the *Rittergut* Elberberg, which just five years before had been freed from a bankruptcy administration by means of a large loan from the treasury. The brothers held differing opinions on how to best utilize the estate. Gottlob von Buttlar argued strongly in favor of leasing the estate:

> The present administration has produced little or no profit; at year's end the expenses often exceed the income, so we frequently have had to supplement Amtmann Noessel's treasury with cash or produce, and this was already the case when our late father administered the estate himself. Now that our offices prevent us brothers from going to the estate very often, even less supervision is possible. Thus the disadvantages of administering the estate become even more apparent. . . .
>
> It is well known that a large burden of debt was bequeathed to us brothers; in addition to the previous debts on the estate there is the interest from the 40,000-taler loan, which must be paid from the

---

lected from the peasants. StAM 340 v. Buttlar-Elberberg, Nr. 412. Service as a steward could also bring benefits that were less tangible but still very important. In 1799 the Buttlars rewarded Noessel's faithful service by asking the landgrave to grant him the title *Commissions-Rat*. The request was granted, and the Buttlars paid the necessary fees. StAM 5, Nr. 722, Buttlar-Elberberg to Landgrave William IX, 11 February 1799.

estate revenues. Furthermore, there are still several large dowries to be paid, and we need something for our own living expenses. All these needs can be met only by improving the financial condition of the estate, and herein lies the importance of leasing. The rent from such a large estate will be at least 500 talers, and to this must be added the 2–3,000-taler deposit made by the future lessee for the inventory. With this capital we can immediately pay off some of our debts and avoid several lawsuits, and in this manner we can head off bankruptcy proceedings, which are otherwise quite likely.[8]

Another brother, Georg von Buttlar, expressed the opposite viewpoint:

If I were convinced that by renting Elberberg we would receive as many benefits as my brother promises himself, nothing would be more natural than for me to agree with his opinion. . . . But I cannot yet convince myself that he is right. I firmly believe that through rational administration we can obtain more income and can better preserve the estate by keeping the fields in good condition as well as improving those which are in poor condition.[9]

This particular debate was solved by government intervention. To assure that the Buttlars would continue to be able to meet their capital and interest payments to the treasury, the *Regierung* ordered that the estate be leased. Even without government pressure, the family probably would have decided to lease the estate, because both brothers held government offices and had neither the time nor the training to administer their estates or to supervise a hired administrator (the third brother was a minor, but he later entered government service as well). For similar reasons most other nobles also chose to lease their estates.

To offer an estate for lease, a family's steward placed advertisements in the *Commerzien Zeitung* in Kassel and in similar agricultural and commercial newspapers in neighboring states so that as many potential leaseholders as possible could be attracted. Those interested were invited to examine the estate and submit bids. In the eighteenth century the estate was normally rented to the highest bidder.[10]

Leasing an estate required a substantial capital outlay, because the new leaseholder had to purchase the inventory of animals and grain from

[8] StAM 340 v. Buttlar-Elberberg, Nr. 160, memorandum of 10 August 1795.

[9] Ibid., memorandum of 30 October 1795.

[10] Examples of this process, including newspaper advertisements and correspondence with prospective leaseholders, can be found in StAM 340 v. Buttlar-Elberberg, Nr. 160, 162–164, 166 and 340 v. d. Malsburg-Escheberg, Verz. 2, Nr. 11.

the previous lessee or the owner and also make a large security deposit as a guarantee against damage to the estate or failure to pay the rent. An estate's inventory normally amounted to one or two thousand talers, but the inventory of a large estate could be worth up to four thousand talers. Therefore a leaseholder had to possess considerable wealth in his own right, making it impossible for a peasant, even a relatively prosperous one, to rent an entire estate. Leaseholders were thus members of the middle classes and included former members of the bureaucracy, such as building commissioner Georg Borheck from Göttingen, who rented the *Rittergut* Elberberg in 1805; lawyers like Wilhelm Krug, leaseholder of the Dörnbergs' estate Hohnstadt in 1784; and even former artisans such as Johannes Dippel, who amassed a fortune of ten thousand talers as a master mason and used this capital to lease the royal estate Marien-rode in 1803.[11] It is frequently impossible to determine the original background of applicants for leases because they were already experi-enced as lessees or administrators of large estates. In the nineteenth cen-tury, members of the new economic bourgeoisie, the manufacturers, were also interested in the possibilities of leasing estates, if not for them-selves, then for their offspring. In 1821 the paper manufacturer Johann Becker of Kassel wrote to the Malsburgs' steward to ask about the avail-ability of the estate Oedinghausen, "since I have been considering the possibility of a lease for my son."[12]

Applications for leases frequently came from administrators or lessees of estates located outside of Hesse-Kassel, generally in Hanover and Prussia. This suggests that leaseholders of large estates were a mobile professional group. Estate owners recognized this fact and advertised the availability of their estates in newspapers outside their own region.

The most common length of a lease was nine or twelve years, but oc-casionally estates were given out for only six or even three years. Lessees attempted to obtain as long a lease as possible, while estate owners were concerned that long leases would deprive them of possible higher rents in the future. An unusually long lease was that of the *Rittergut* Elmars-hausen, which was to run eighteen years starting in 1802.[13] Leases fre-quently contained a provision known as a *Wechseljahr*, under which either party could end the lease by giving proper advance notice at a

[11] In 1826 Dippel applied to lease the *Rittergut* Elberberg, and the owners asked a de-mesne official about his background. StAM 340 v. Buttlar-Elberberg, Nr. 163.

[12] StAM 340 v. d. Malsburg-Escheberg, Verz. 2, Nr. 11, #10.

[13] Neither party had the right to break this contract. If the leaseholder died, one of his sons (to be chosen by the estate owner) would take over the lease. However, the lease-holder had the right to end the lease after nine years, if he desired. Elmarshausen Archive, lease of 15 January 1802.

specified point in the contract, generally after three or six years. At the start of a lease, the new leaseholder had to take over the inventory of animals and grain from the previous lessee or the owner and also pay a security deposit. The owner of the estate paid the lessee 5 percent interest annually on this sum and returned the deposit at the end of the lease. Leaseholders were not responsible for repairs to buildings or fences unless the damage had resulted from their own negligence. Thus estate owners had to bear the often considerable repair and construction costs.[14]

Many rental contracts granted leaseholders a degree of protection against losses resulting from disasters such as extremely bad harvests, hailstorms, floods, and acts of war. In such leases estate owners promised to return part of the annual rent, depending on the severity of the damage. For example, the rental contract for the estate Elmarshausen in 1799 stated that generally "the good harvest of one year balances out the bad harvest of another and the high grain prices of one year compensate for the low prices of the next," but in the case of unusually bad circumstances the lease specified, "If two impartial experts estimate the loss to be the whole harvest, so that not even enough grain for sowing is obtained, then the lessee receives two-thirds of the rent back; if the damage is assessed at two-thirds of the harvest, the lessee receives one-third of the rent, and any smaller losses must be born by the lessee alone."[15]

Along with the fields and pastures belonging to estates, leases gave their holders control over subsidiary estate activities, such as breweries or distilleries and occasionally taverns or mills. Leases also generally included part of the dues and services owed by local peasants to the estate owner. The labor services of the surrounding villages were almost invariably part of the contract, because the estate owner had no use for them once his estate was rented. Sometimes leases contained the tithes of one or more villages, but most tithes remained under the control of noble landlords and were collected by their stewards.

The gradual rise in grain prices in the late eighteenth century, coupled with the system of competitive bidding for leases, drove rents up-

[14] Some typical leases containing such provisions are found in StAM 340 v. Bodenhausen, Paket 167, lease of Arnstein (1833); 340 v. d. Malsburg-Escheberg, Verz. 2, Nr. 11, leases of Escheberg: items 5 (1793), 7 and 23 (1799), 9 (1814), Oedinghausen lease: item 10 (1821); 340 v. Buttlar-Elberberg, leases of Elberberg: Nr. 160 (1796), Nr. 162 (1805), Nr. 164 (1827), Nr. 166 (1839), Nr. 166a (1863), Nr. 166b (1873); 340 v. Baumbach-Kirchheim, Nr. 17: Binsförth lease (1791), Kirchheim leases (1791, 1803); Elmarshausen Archive, leases of 1799, 1802, 1831.

[15] Elmarshausen Archive, lease of 23 February 1799.

ward at each renewal. The rise in rents was for the most part gradual until the late 1790s, when the speculation in land that was raging in northern and eastern Germany also began to affect Hesse-Kassel as leaseholders from Hanover and Prussia turned to central Germany for what seemed to be bargains in leases and outbid the local leaseholders. This development can be seen clearly in the leases of the estates Escheberg and Oedinghausen. In 1787 a local leaseholder, Johann Sprenger, received the estates for six years at 1,000 talers per year. At the end of this lease a new contract was signed giving Sprenger the estates again, but for 1,383 talers. The lease was to run for nine years, although at the end of each three-year period either party could end the lease. In 1799, after six years of the contract had passed, the von der Malsburg family canceled Sprenger's lease in favor of a leaseholder from Hanover, who offered 1,850 talers per year. August Reinmann was given a twelve-year contract with no provision for terminating the lease earlier.[16]

Reinmann's hopes that the rising grain prices would bring him large profits were quickly dashed, and he soon began to have difficulty in meeting his annual rent payments. In 1802 he wrote to the estate owner describing his problems:

Owing to last year's poor harvest, which is the third in a row, I am again unable to pay the rent on time. Even though this year grain prices are quite high, I have discovered that such high prices (if they are caused by a bad harvest) bring more harm than good for a leaseholder, since he harvests very little. A medium-level price, coupled with a good harvest, is much more advantageous, because in the case of a bad harvest, the leaseholder has little grain left over to sell and everything that he must purchase for his household is much more expensive, which has been the case for me for the last two years.

Reinmann asked that the lease be changed to make every third year a *Wechseljahr*, enabling him to break the lease without penalty, so that "if I see that despite all my endeavors I cannot succeed, then at least I can salvage some of my wealth and protect myself and my family from impoverishment."[17] The Malsburgs denied Reinmann's request, but the following year they allowed him to ease some of his problems by subletting one of the estates.

[16] StAM 340 v. d. Malsburg-Escheberg, Verz. 2, Nr. 11, #5, leases of 1787, 1793, and 1799.
[17] Ibid., #7, Reinmann to Geheimer Rat von der Malsburg, 11 August 1802.

Reinmann was not the only leaseholder having difficulties in the early years of the nineteenth century. Many foreign leaseholders found that they had miscalculated the profit that could be obtained from Hessian estates. In Prussia the bottom fell out of the land market when grain prices sank in 1806 and 1807, and the corresponding decline in Hessian grain prices caused a number of speculators to decide to cut their losses by breaking their leases (see figure 5.1).[18]

Broken leases caused considerable problems for Hessian landlords because they had to find a new leaseholder at an unfavorable time due to low grain prices, as in 1808 and 1810. But this was not the only problem that resulted from leasing estates to the highest bidder. Even if the lease remained intact, the lessee might simply run the estate into the ground in order to obtain as much profit as possible without concern for the future condition of the land. This occurred to Hans David von Knoblauch after 1815, when he rented his estate in Hatzbach to a stranger who outbid the previous lessee but later had difficulty paying the rent. The new leaseholder kept the estate for only five of the agreed-upon twelve years, ruining it in the process.[19]

Some noble families recognized these dangers and did not rent their estates to the highest bidders, preferring to keep reliable lessees at somewhat lower rents. Thus when the lease of the Dörnbergs' estate Hausen expired in 1798, steward Jacob Becker wrote to the owner recommending that the current leaseholder be allowed to retain the estate, noting, "Since Otto is a good farmer, he should be given preference over all other interested individuals, particularly because he has truly improved the condition of the fields and pastures." The owner, Wilhelm Freiherr von Dörnberg, agreed and replied, "Although I am convinced that public bidding would drive the rent even higher, I am in favor of Otto's re-

[18] The values of leases for noble estates are found in the following rental contracts and estate account books: Elmarshausen Archive, 1770–1880 Rechnungen; StAM 340 v. Eschwege, B. Amtsbücher, 1770–1879 Reichensachsen Rechnungen, 1799–1875 Aue Rechnungen; StAM 340 v. Buttlar-Elberberg, Nr. 160, 162–64, 166 and 1781–1880 Rechnungen; Archiv der Freiherrlichen Familie von Dörnberg, Haus Breitenbach, 6440 Bebra 1, Hausen Rechnungen, 1775–1875 (hereafter cited as Dörnberg Archive; the holdings of this small family archive, mainly estate account books, may recently have been transferred to the Staatsarchiv Marburg—if so, they would probably be located in 340 v. Dörnberg, Amtsbücher). A complete set of grain prices for sales by the Landeshospital Merxhausen in the years 1625 through 1857 is contained in StAM Materialsammlung 1 (Landau), Nr. 570. These prices correspond very closely to the prices I have calculated for the grain sales of the von Buttlar-Elberberg family in the years 1781–1850 (see below, figure 5.2).

[19] Knoblauch, *Kurzgefaßte Geschichte*, 22. The lease is found in StAM 340 v. Knoblauch, F VIII, Nr. 1.

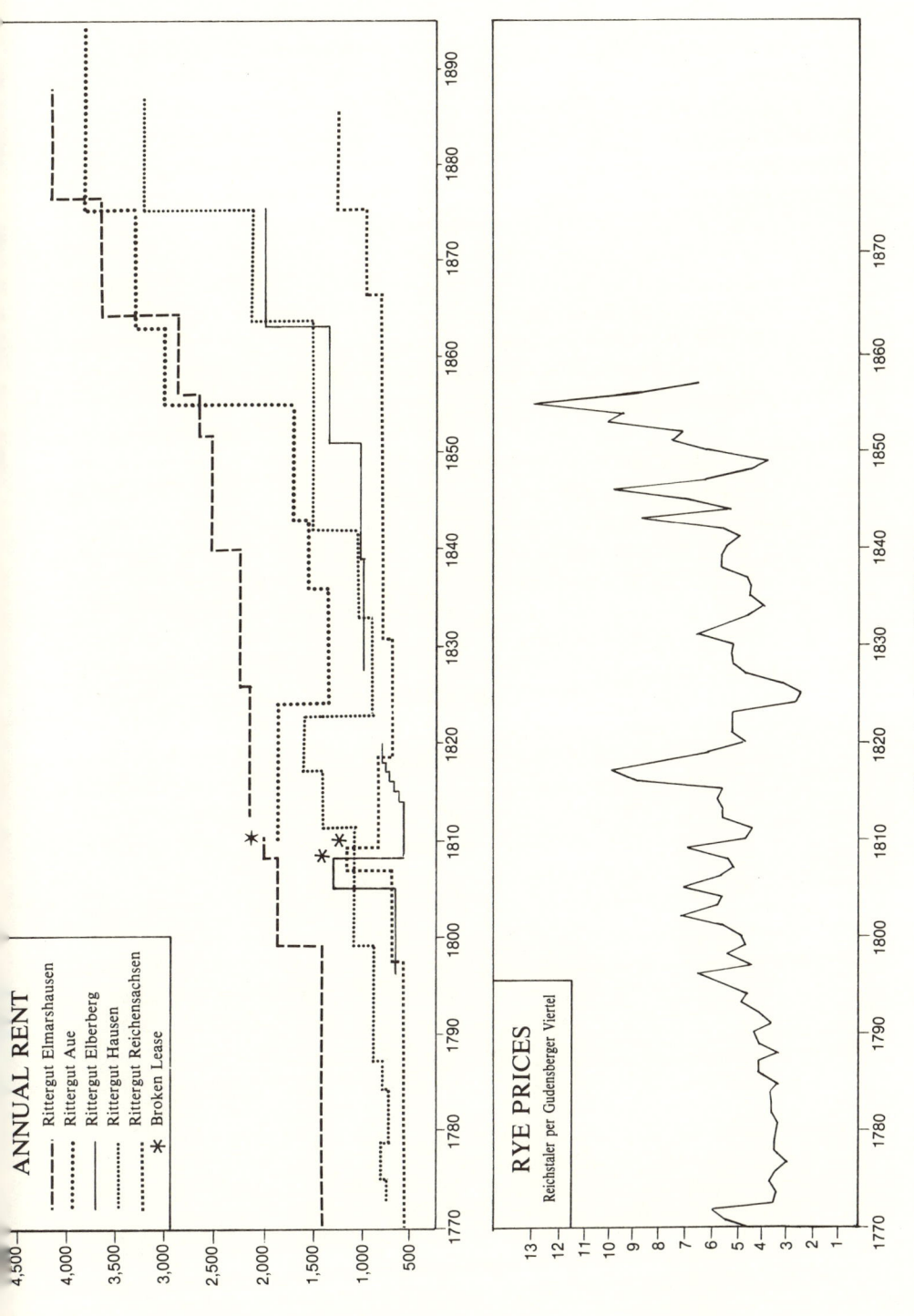

ANNUAL RENT

Rittergut Elmarshausen
Rittergut Aue
Rittergut Elberberg
Rittergut Hausen
Rittergut Reichensachsen
* Broken Lease

Reichstaler

4,500
4,000
3,500
3,000
2,500
2,000
1,500
1,000
500

1770 1780 1790 1800 1810 1820 1830 1840 1850 1860 1870 1880 1890

RYE PRICES

Reichstaler per Gudensberger Viertel

Reichstaler

13
12
11
10
9
8
7
6
5
4
3
2
1

1770 1780 1790 1800 1810 1820 1830 1840 1850 1860 1870

Figure 5.1. Leases of Noble Estates.

taining the estate, because I know he is an upright individual and a good farmer."[20]

Families that had experienced difficulties with new leaseholders began to move away from the former highly competitive system of bidding during the nineteenth century. Leaseholders were offered longer leases, generally twelve years, and in most cases the current lessee was able to continue when his lease came up for renewal, although rents gradually rose as economic conditions improved. Even though the current leaseholder generally received preference, if his offer was not high enough the owners could always threaten to open up bidding to the public.

The leases of the von Buttlar-Elberberg family, whose attempts to obtain the highest possible rents led to severe problems at the start of the nineteenth century, provide a good illustration of this change in leasing policy. In 1805 a new lessee from Hanover took over the estate Elberberg after bidding 1,300 talers in rent (the previous lease was only for 730 talers), but after three years he broke the lease, citing as his reason the decline in grain prices and the failure of the estate's distillery to produce the profits he had anticipated.[21] The leaseholder who followed, foundry manager Schreiber, received the estate at a much lower rate (590 talers for the first six years, then rising gradually to 800 talers during the last six), but evidently he exploited the estate for all it was worth. The 1823 estate account book notes, "In 1820 we the owners of Elberberg were forced to take over the estate after the lease expired in order to keep it from deteriorating any further."[22] In 1826 the estate was again leased (for twelve years), and when this contract expired, a new leaseholder, Ludwig Raffin, took over the estate at the same price. Raffin remained as leaseholder for thirty-three years, receiving three twelve-year leases (although he had to end the third lease after nine years because of poor health).[23] Another Buttlar estate, Kirchberg, experienced even less turnover in leaseholders during the nineteenth century. August Ruelberg leased the estate in 1818 for nine years and received it for another nine years in 1827. After his death in 1836, his widow and sons renewed the lease for another twelve years, and then one of the sons took over the estate for two consecutive twelve-year leases. The half-century tenancy of the Ruelberg family in Kirchberg and Ludwig Raffin's thirty-three years as lessee of Elberberg demonstrate the complete change in the leas-

[20] StAM 340 v. Dörnberg, Nr. 2398. Amtmann Becker to Wilhelm Freiherr von Dörnberg, 13 June 1798, Dörnberg to Becker, 29 July 1798.

[21] StAM 340 v. Buttlar-Elberberg, Nr. 162, Borheck to the Buttlars, 21 January 1808.

[22] StAM 340 v. Buttlar-Elberberg, 1823 Rechnung.

[23] StAM 340 v. Buttlar-Elberberg, Nr. 166 and 166a (leases of 1839, 1851, and 1863).

ing policies of the von Buttlar family after its disastrous experiences with competitive bidding at the start of the century.[24]

Except for a brief decline in the 1820s resulting from low grain prices, rents rose steadily in the nineteenth century, and when grain prices soared to new heights in the 1850s and early 1860s, rents advanced accordingly. But in contrast to the early 1800s, higher rents now generally came from the current leaseholders, who knew the value of their estates and were eager to keep them. However, the large fluctuations in the grain market caused some leaseholders to demand safeguards against a disastrous decline in grain prices before they would sign long leases. Thus the 1819 and 1831 leases (twelve and nine years respectively) of the *Rittergut* Willingshausen contained clauses calling for a reduction of the rent if grain prices fell below a certain level.[25]

How much profit leaseholders made is difficult to determine, because they kept their records separate from the estate papers that have been deposited by noble families in archives. Occasionally leaseholders became quite wealthy from their leased estates, as was the case with Wilhelm Pfeiffer, who leased the estates Ermschwerd, Stiedenrode, and Friemen from Georg Friedrich von Buttlar-Elberberg from 1747 until his death in 1810. By the late eighteenth century Pfeiffer had become a major creditor for Buttlar and exploited this favorable financial position by pressuring Buttlar into granting him an extremely favorable lease that was to run for the unheard-of length of twenty-four years.[26] Most leaseholders did not amass as much of a fortune as Pfeiffer did but still probably earned a good return on their investment unless agricultural conditions were unusually bad.

Not all *Rittergüter* were leased in their entirety to bourgeois tenant farmers. Some estates, particularly those which consisted of many scattered pieces of land, were rented in parcels to local peasants.[27] Although splitting an estate into parcels could bring in more rental income, it could also lead to much more difficulty in collecting rent, so most estate owners opted for the simpler and safer solution of renting the whole es-

[24] StAM 340 v. Buttlar-Elberberg, 1818–70 Rechnungen. The Bodenhausens' estate Arnstein was also placed in the hands of a single family, the Suntheims, for much of the nineteenth century, as the leaseholder was succeeded first by his wife and children and later by his son alone. StAM 340 v. Bodenhausen, Nr. 187–88, 191, 202–4 (1820–59 Rechnungen).

[25] StAM 340 v. Schwertzell, 1819 and 1831 Rechnungen.

[26] StAM 340 v. Buttlar-Elberberg, Nr. 132.

[27] See the list of tenants for the estate Niederelsungen in 1799, StAM 340 v. d. Malsburg-Escheberg, Verz. 2, Nr. 11, #3. One of the von Löwenstein family's two small estates in Römersberg was also leased to a number of peasants after 1801. 340 v. Löwenstein, Paket 45, 1801 Rechnung.

tate to a single individual. An 1865 survey of estates reveals that the vast majority of noble estate owners chose this method of renting their estates (see table 5.1).[28]

Table 5.1 also indicates that a number of nobles had become interested in agriculture by the mid-nineteenth century and had decided to administer their estates themselves rather than rent them. In the von Stockhausen family, for example, Carl von Stockhausen (1767–1838) resigned his commission as an army officer in 1799 in order to administer the estates Wülmersen and Abgunst. His son Ernst (1807–61) also became involved in administering the family's estates after he completed his legal studies at the universities of Marburg and Göttingen.[29] One of the most successful noble estate owners was Friedrich von und zu Schachten (1788–1866). He studied cameralism at the universities of Marburg and Göttingen and then took over the family estate after his father's death in 1817. Schachten not only greatly enlarged the holdings of the estate; he made it world famous for its sheep raising. His sheep were exhibited at world's fairs and were exported all over the world.[30]

Another nobleman actively involved in running his own estate was Karl Rabe von Pappenheim. In 1872 he took over the family estate in Liebenau, breaking a 150-year tradition of renting it to bourgeois tenant farmers. During the decades that followed, he greatly improved the es-

TABLE 5.1. Management of Noble Estates

Size of Estate without Forest (In *Acker*)	Run by Owner	Run by Administrator	Leased as a Whole	Leased in Parcels
1,500+	1	0	1	1
1,200–1,499	1	0	3	0
900–1,199	0	1	6	1
600–899	6	5	21	0
300–599	13	2	53	3
Under 300	6	1	50	3
Total	27	9	134	8

[28] StAM 30, Rep. II, Kl. 6, Nr. 5, Übersicht der größeren Ökonomien in Kurhessen.
[29] StAM 340 v. Stockhausen, Nr. 323–25.
[30] Karl Poppe, *Geschichte des Geschlechtes derer von und zu Schachten* (Göttingen, 1933), 55–56.

tate by working out agreements with local peasants to consolidate land-holdings, bringing new land into cultivation through drainage and clearing projects, planting more trees, and refurbishing the estate's mill. He even electrified the entire estate in 1892.[31]

In addition to nobles who administered their own estates, it was not unusual in the nineteenth century for a noble who was a co-owner of an estate to lease it from his family. In such cases the lessee/owner paid rent to the family's steward but received part of it back at the the end of the year, along with his share of the family's other revenues, when the annual profits were divided among the owners. Not all nobles proved successful as leaseholders. During Major Ludwig Freiherr von Dörnberg's six-year lease (1817–23) of his family's estate Hausen, he was frequently in arrears in payments and several times had to request cancellation of part of the annual rent. When Dörnberg's lease expired, the estate was again rented outside the family.[32] Dörnberg had had the misfortune to begin his career as a leaseholder at an unfavorable time, for the period of his lease was marked by a catastrophic decline in grain prices. Other nobles who leased estates in the nineteenth century were more successful, in part because of better preparation, which sometimes included the study of agriculture or economics at a university. Increased interest in agriculture among nobles during the nineteenth century was not confined to Hesse-Kassel. Similar changes in attitudes occurred among nobles in Westphalia and Bavaria,[33] and the Junkers of eastern Prussia had long been actively involved in running their estates.

Peasant Dues and Services

Alongside the income that nobles received from their estates in the form of rent, they derived considerable revenue from lands that once had belonged to them but over the centuries had been given out to peasants as fiefs or hereditary tenancies. Such land tenure existed in a bewildering variety of forms in Hesse-Kassel, but by the late eighteenth century all forms of hereditary tenure and fiefs were recognized by the courts as being the true property of the peasant holders. However, landlords (both nobles and the state) retained some rights of ownership or over-lordship (*Obereigentum* or *dominium directum*, in contrast to the peasants'

---

[31] Wilhelm Hopf, "Karl Rabe von Pappenheim," in *Lebensbilder aus Kurhessen und Waldeck, 1830–1900*, ed. Ingeborg Schnack, 6 vols. (Marburg, 1939–58), 5:239.

[32] StAM 340 v. Dörnberg, Nr. 646; Dörnberg Archive, 1817–23 Hausen Rechnungen.

[33] Reif, *Westfälischer Adel*, 222–23; Hubert Glaser, ed. *Krone und Verfassung: König Max I. Joseph und der neue Staat: Beiträge zur Bayerischen Geschichte und Kunst, 1799–1825*, 2 vols. (Munich, 1980), 2: 433.

right to use the land, known as *dominium utile*) to such land and were thus still entitled to collect all dues and services connected with hereditary tenures and fiefs.[34]

The most common obligations owed by peasants to landlords were the quitrents (*Grundzinsen*), which were paid not only in cash but also in grain, poultry, and eggs. The amount of quitrents resting on a particular piece of hereditary peasant land had generally been fixed centuries earlier and was recorded in both the village cadaster and the landlord's *Salbuch* (register of landholdings). The landlord could neither increase the rents from hereditary holdings nor change the types of rent owed to him (from cash to produce, for example).[35] Since the amount of the quitrents had been fixed so long ago, inflation had substantially eroded the value of the cash portion of the payments, making the produce portion of quitrents far more important to landlords than the cash.

In addition to the *Grundzins* resting on a peasant's landholding, each house in a village paid a *Hauszins* (hearth rent) to its landlord, generally a small amount of money and poultry. For example, each of the ten houses in the village of Blankenbach that were under the jurisdiction of the von Baumbach-Nentershausen family paid the following *Hauszins*: one *Albus* ($\frac{1}{32}$ taler), one goose, one chicken, two roosters, and sixty eggs. Each item was due at a different time of the year on a particular religious holiday.[36]

Many peasants also owned land that was subject to the tithe (*Zehnt*). Unlike quitrents, the tithe was not a fixed annual payment but rather a fixed percentage of the total yield of a particular field. Thus tithes represented an important source of income for landlords, because tithes, in

[34] For detailed information on the development of hereditary peasant land tenure in Hesse-Kassel see Sakai, *Kurhessische Bauer*, 10–12; Hans L. Rudloff, "Die gutsherrlich-bäuerlichen Verhältnisse in Kurhessen," *Schmollers Jahrbuch* 41 (1917): 116–24; Hans Lerch, *Hessische Agrargeschichte des 17. und 18. Jahrhunderts* (Hersfeld, 1926), 12–23. Much of the peasantry's land was held as fiefs from noble landlords, and even in the nineteenth century the peasant holders of such land were called "vassals" in their leases. See for example the investiture document (*Lehnbrief*) of 22 December 1841 in Karl von Baumbach, "Geschichte der Familie von Baumbach-Nentershausen vom 18. Jahrhundert bis zur Mitte des 19. Jahrhunderts: Kulturell, sozial und wirtschaftlich" (typescript, 1948), 34. This manuscript is located in StAM 340 v. Baumbach-Nentershausen, Acc. 1950/35. For a comprehensive survey of peasant dues and service in other parts of Europe see Blum, *End of the Old Order*, 50–79.

[35] In Westphalia landlords could choose whether they wanted peasant dues paid in cash or produce, so they selected the most advantageous method of payment based on the current level of grain prices. Reif, *Westfälischer Adel*, 59.

[36] Baumbach, "Familie von Baumbach-Nentershausen," 23–24.

contrast to the cash portion of quitrents, had not declined in value over the centuries.

The amount of tithe collected varied greatly from village to village. Quite often the proportion was not one-tenth but one-eleventh of the harvest, occasionally as low as one-twentieth or one twenty-second. Moreover, many villages were totally exempt from tithes.[37] Where it was levied, the tithe represented a heavy burden on peasants. The burden was greatest in areas with poor soil (which required large amounts of seed grain), because the landlord's tithe was collected from the gross harvest without taking into consideration the costs of cultivation or other burdens on the land.[38]

To avoid the considerable costs of supervising the amount of grain harvested, collecting the necessary percentage of tithe, and transporting and storing this grain, many landlords worked out agreements with local villagers to sell them the tithe in return for a fixed amount of cash or grain. This process was known as *vermaltern* and usually took place before the harvest. Often a particular tithe was sold for two or three years at a time, so in effect the landlord was leasing the tithe to the local peasants.[39] *Vermaltern* brought advantages to both sides. Landlords were spared the expense of collecting and storing the tithe (and many did not have adequate grain storage facilities anyway), while the peasants were generally able to buy the tithe at a reasonable price because they agreed among themselves not to bid against each other and drive up the price.[40] However, landlords occasionally sold a tithe to an outsider. In 1815 forestry official Friedrich von Osterhausen was the highest bidder in the

[37] The amount of tithe paid by a particular village is listed in the introduction (*Vorbeschreibung*) of its cadaster. The following examples of villages with noble landlords illustrate the wide range of tithes paid, even within a particular village. The villages of Willingshausen, Schweinsberg, Hausen, Elberberg, Ropperhausen, and Lenderscheid all paid one-eleventh of the harvest, except for some fields in Lenderscheid at one twenty-second. The villages of Schachten, Gilsa, Betzigerode, and Solz owed one-tenth of the harvest, although some portions of Solz owed only one-eleventh, while a few parcels of land were subject to no tithes at all. Finally, the villages of Nentershausen, Kirchheim, Reichensachsen, and Aue were exempt from all tithes. StAM, Kataster I, *Vorbeschreibungen* of the cadasters of the above villages.

[38] As a result, peasants sometimes did not bother to cultivate marginal land that was subject to the tithe, since little or no yield would remain after subtracting the tithe and the costs of cultivation. Sakai, *Kurhessische Bauer*, 23; Lerch, *Hessische Agrargeschichte*, 68.

[39] In 1820 the von Buttlar family owned fifteen tithes. Two were leased along with the main estate, and the other thirteen were sold in advance of the harvest (*vermaltert*), eight for a fixed amount of grain, five for cash. The conversions to a fixed amount of grain were set annually; those to grain, every three years. StAM 340 v. Buttlar-Elberberg, Nr. 215.

[40] Lerch, *Hessische Agrargeschichte*, 65–66.

sale of the tithe in Bessa (jointly owned by the von Buttlar and von der Malsburg families). Osterhausen then gave each of the local peasants the choice of delivering a fixed amount of grain or the required one-eleventh of the harvest.[41]

By the eighteenth century, serfdom to all intents and purposes no longer existed in Hesse-Kassel. In those villages whose inhabitants were still called serfs (*Leibeigene*), all that was required of these individuals was a small annual cash payment to their lord (*Leibherr*), a payment if they moved away, and a special payment called the *Besthaupt* following the death of a "serf." Even this extremely mild form of serfdom was found only in certain parts of the country (primarily Upper Hesse and Schaumburg), and it was gradually dying out because it was often transmitted only through the male line. Serfs could also purchase their freedom from these obligations.[42]

A much greater burden for peasants came from the labor services (*Dienste*) owed to landlords. Labor services were not associated with serfdom in most cases; instead they were a burden connected with the hereditary use of a peasant farm or piece of land. Peasants with larger farms who owned draft animals were required to perform *Spanndienste* (team services: plowing or transporting items with a team of animals), and all peasants performed *Handdienste* (hand services) such as sowing, fertilizing, and reaping. In most villages the services required of each peasant were exactly specified, but occasionally peasants were required to perform any services that the landlord demanded, the so-called *ungemessene Dienste* (unlimited services). In return for their labor, peasants were generally provided with food and drink, often in substantial amounts, which in many communities were recorded in the cadaster along with the types and amounts of services owed to the landlord. For example, the peasants of the village of Schwebda had to perform a wide variety of services for their landlords (two branches of the von Keudell family), but in return they received ample food and drink, as can be seen in table 5.2.[43] The two days per year spent working in the Keudells' brewery must have been particularly popular, for along with two hearty

[41] StAM 340 v. Buttlar-Elberberg, Nr. 217, Osterhausen's proclamation of 29 July 1815.

[42] Hugo Brunner, "Rittergüter und Gutsbezirke im ehemaligen Kurhessen," *Jahrbücher für Nationalökonomie und Statistik* 115 (1920): 52–54; Sakai, *Kurhessische Bauer*, 9–10.

[43] StAM Kataster I, Eschwege B 2 (1750). Other lists of food and drink provided for services are found in StAM 340 v. Bodenhausen, Paket 54, and in the following eighteenth-century cadasters: Aue, Betzigerode, Bischhausen, Harmuthsachsen, Kirchheim, Nentershausen, Schachten, Solz, and Stammen. When the peasant services were part of an estate's lease, the leaseholder was obligated to provide the required food and drink. See for example the lease of 6 November 1791 in StAM 340 v. Baumbach-Kirchheim, Nr. 17.

TABLE 5.2. Labor Services in the Village of Schwebda

Labor Services	Food and Drink
1½ days planting and picking vegetables	2 loaves of bread, 4 cheeses, 2 liters of beer per day
3 days reaping, combing, and soaking flax	2 loaves of bread, 4 cheeses per day
Spinning 8 *Pfund* of oakum to make 12–14 reels of yarn	6 *Heller* per reel
1 day cutting and binding grass 3 days repairing fences 2 days digging ditches 1 day clearing fields 1½ days cleaning sheep stalls	2 loaves of bread, 2 cheeses, and 2 hot meals of soup and vegetables per day
½ day washing sheep	½ loaf of bread, 1 liter of beer
2 days mowing grass, 8 days drying it	Total of 16 liters of beer, 6 loaves of bread, 3 large cheeses, ½ pound of lard
4 half days mowing hay, 8 days drying it	Per half day: ½ pound of meat, and vegetables, 1 loaf of bread, 2 cheeses, 2 liters of beer. When drying: ½ loaf of bread, 1 cheese per day
2 days working in brewery	1 meal of soup, vegetables, and meat, 1 meal of soup and dumplings, 9 liters of beer, 4 glasses of brandy
1 trip as a messenger, 8–9 *Meilen* (74–83 kilometers)	Per *Meile*: 1 *Albus*, 4 *Heller* Upon return: ½ loaf of bread, 1 liter of beer, 1 cheese

meals each peasant received a total of nine liters of beer and four glasses of brandy!

The quality of the work performed by peasants providing their annual services was normally not very high, a situation recognized by many landlords, who therefore reached agreements with their peasants to convert the labor services into small annual cash payments.[44] By the

[44] Peasants did not always prefer cash payments over the actual performance of service, for they could not always count on having hard cash available. Thus in the late eighteenth century the peasants of the villages of Ottrau and Willingshausen, who had the choice of

end of the eighteenth century most of the services owed by peasants to royal manors (whose leaseholders preferred to use more efficient wage laborers) had been converted to cash payments, as had been the services owed by peasants to many noble landlords.[45]

Landlords who continued to require the performance of services often had difficulty in obtaining the cooperation of their peasants in the late eighteenth and early nineteenth centuries. The problem worsened in 1808 when the new Westphalian government abolished all remnants of serfdom and with them the requirement to perform services that either were associated with serfdom or were not precisely spelled out as to type and amount of services owed. Peasants refused to make distinctions between different kinds of services and consequently ceased performing all services, causing tremendous problems for both the government and private landlords in collecting the harvest of 1808. Further decrees in the summer of 1809 ordered peasants to continue to perform fixed services, but peasant resistance to services continued to plague landowners for the rest of the Westphalian government's existence.[46]

Although the return of the elector from exile at the end of 1813 brought the restoration of the pre-1806 rural order, landlords continued to have problems with peasants over labor service. This frequently led to lawsuits aimed at forcing peasants to perform services. Landlords had to take this step because they no longer possessed the right of seigneurial justice.[47]

---

working twenty-five days a year for the von Schwertzell family or paying 1 taler, 20 albus in cash, all chose to perform the services. StAM 340 v. Schwertzell, 1789–95 Rechnungen.

[45] By the late eighteenth century, conversion of services to cash payments had already been carried out by the von Trott zu Solz, von Schenk zu Schweinsberg-Fronhausen, von Urff, von Dörnberg, von und zu Gilsa, and von Baumbach-Nentershausen families, for example. StAM Kataster I, *Vorbeschreibungen* of the cadasters of Solz, Fronhausen, Niederurf, Hausen, Gilsa, and Nentershausen. For the conversion of services by leaseholders of royal manors see Lerch, *Hessische Agrargeschichte*, 42. The monetization of services was also becoming common in other areas of Germany. See Friedrich Lütge, *Die mitteldeutsche Grundherrschaft und ihre Auflösung*, 2d ed. (Stuttgart, 1957), 157–58; Wolfgang von Hippel, *Die Bauernbefreiung im Königreich Württemberg*, 2 vols. (Boppard am Rhein, 1977), 1:200; Reif, *Westfälischer Adel*, 221.

[46] Brunner, "Rittergüter," 63–65. Michael Schunk, lessee of the von Knoblauch family's estate in Hatzbach, wrote to the owners several times to complain that the peasants were not performing the fixed services as part of his lease. On 2 September 1809 he stated, "None of our *Dienstleute* are performing any more services, neither the team nor the hand services. I have heard that the peasants of all our villages have bound themselves not to perform any more services." Over two years later (21 March 1812) Schunk wrote that the peasants were not performing services because a local government official had told them that they did not have to do so. StAM 340 v. Knoblauch, F 111, Nr. 11.

[47] For example, the villagers of Reckershausen refused to perform services after 1815, which led to a lawsuit by the landlord. StAM 340 v. Bodenhausen, Paket 53, memoran-

One additional payment, which unlike most others was not due every year, was *Lehngeld* (transfer fee). When peasant land changed hands through sale or inheritance, the new owner had to pay the landlord a certain percentage of the value of the land. The most common amount owed to noble landlords was 10 percent, although in some villages the transfer fee consisted only of 5 percent of the value. In many villages transfer fees could be collected only from land that changed hands in a sale, not through inheritance, and the land in some villages was exempt from transfer fees.

For the landlord, *Lehngeld* represented an important portion of the cash income from peasants, but the amount received each year varied greatly. Between 1779 and 1808 the von Baumbach-Kirchheim family received a total of 1,335 talers in transfer fees from three villages. In seven of these thirty years, no peasant land changed hands, so no fees were collected, but in 1787 the Baumbachs' transfer fees totaled 142 talers.[48]

Lehngeld was one of the most unpopular obligations to peasants, particularly when it was collected after a peasant died and his children inherited his land. Just as with other peasant dues, landlords occasionally had trouble collecting transfer fees in the nineteenth century. For example, beginning in 1825 the peasants of Kirchberg refused to pay any more transfer fees, forcing the village's landlord, the von Buttlar family, to start a lawsuit, which dragged on for years.[49]

Because of the many varieties of hereditary peasant leases and fiefs, there was little uniformity in the distribution of peasant dues and services in the late eighteenth century. Some individuals or even entire villages were still "serfs" and had to make certain payments, but they were the exception rather than the rule in Hesse-Kassel. The amount of quitrents paid by individuals also varied widely, for these payments had been fixed by leases originally drawn up generations or even centuries earlier. In some villages no land was subject to the tithe, while in others some land was free of tithes but other land was not, with amounts ranging from one twenty-second to one-tenth of the harvest. The amount and types of services owed to landlords varied from village to village or

dum of administrator Bachmann, 25 August 1819. Other examples of lawsuits arising from refusal to perform services can be found in StAM 270f, Verz. 1 (Regierung als Gericht), B–242, B–249, E–27, E–28, O–11, O–19, S–86; Verz. 2 (Obergerichtsakten), M–4, O–3, O–4.

[48] StAM, 340 v. Baumbach-Kirchheim, Nr. 17.

[49] Ten years later the case had advanced to the superior court (*Obergericht*), but in the meantime the Buttlars had not received any transfer fees. StAM, 340 v. Buttlar-Elberberg, 1835 Rechnung.

even within a particular village, because frequently the inhabitants were subject to different landlords.[50] Even an individual peasant might have different landlords for his various parcels of land. By the end of the eighteenth century, most peasants no longer performed services in person but paid a cash fee instead, but for those peasants who still had to serve, the amount of food received in return varied from landlord to landlord.

The situation was not much simpler for landlords. Unlike the East Prussian estate owners, Hessian nobles were seldom sole landlords (*Grundherren*) for entire villages. Instead nobles had overlordship (*Obereigentum*) over certain plots of land in villages, while the peasant holders of other parcels of land gave their dues and services to other nobles (sometimes different branches of the same family) or to the state, which was the largest landlord in Hesse-Kassel. An individual noble family therefore collected revenues from a wide range of villages, but not necessarily from all the villages in the area around its estate (and also not from all the inhabitants of a particular village). For example, villagers in Niedermeiser owed quitrents and tithes to the von der Malsburg family, located over fifteen kilometers away in the *Rittergut* Elmarshausen, yet the inhabitants of a dozen other villages located far closer to the estate owed no dues or services to this family.[51]

The frequent division of peasant holdings through inheritance led to the splintering of the dues and services owed to landlords, a process that over the centuries resulted in tremendous bookkeeping problems. Thus some of the peasants in the villages around the town of Homberg owed the von Baumbach-Nentershausen family quitrents of only one-half or even one-eighth of a chicken each year, and the annual hearth rents also included fractions of an egg![52]

Although the amounts of produce owed as quitrents or tithes by individual peasants were generally not large, the total quantities (particularly of grain) collected by landlords from their numerous peasants were often quite substantial. It was through this grain rather than that produced by their own estates that nobles participated in the grain market, because the estates were usually leased and provided only cash income.

[50] For example, the inhabitants of the village of Aue owed quitrents to the state, the hospital in Eschwege, the local church, and two noble families (Eschwege and Keudell). StAM Kataster I, Aue B 2 (1770). The village of Borken had a total of sixteen different *Zinsherren* (landlords for quitrents) in the eighteenth century. Heinrich Albrecht, ed., *Borken 1777*, Hessische Ortsbeschreibungen, vol. 4 (Marburg, 1962), 43–44.

[51] StAM Kataster I, Kassel D 1–10, Ritterschaftliches Steuer Catastrum der Legestadt Cassel (1800), vol. 4.

[52] Seventy-four peasants from six villages owed a total of 6½ geese, 10½ chickens, 56 roosters, and 52½ eggs. Baumbach, "Familie von Baumbach-Nentershausen," 29–30.

Tithes were frequently rented along with estates or sold in advance of the harvest for cash, so the main source of grain for landlords was the annual quitrents from local villagers. In addition, some noble families also received considerable amounts of grain from mills that had been given out on hereditary leases.[53] Not all the grain collected from the peasantry found its way to the market. Most of the employees of noble families received part of their salaries in the form of produce, and noble households sometimes consumed part of the grain and poultry collected each year.[54]

Since the quantities of grain available for sale were not overly large, noble landlords were generally involved only in the local grain market, with sales being made either to neighboring villagers or to millers and bakers from nearby towns. Occasionally administrators or leaseholders of local estates also purchased grain, probably to supplement their own grain supplies in order to participate in large grain transactions.[55]

The pattern of grain sales could change radically when harvests were poor and prices were high. The Buttlars' steward in Elberberg normally sold the family's grain to local villagers in small amounts, but when prices rose and grain was scarce, bakers and wholesale grain merchants from Kassel began to scour the countryside in search of all available grain supplies and therefore purchased large quantities of grain from the Buttlars. In the 1780s, when prices for rye (the main cereal crop) began to approach five talers per *Viertel* after remaining below four talers for most of the decade, the baker Josef Wiegand from Kassel purchased substantial amounts of grain in Elberberg. For the next five years prices remained relatively steady and no purchasers from Kassel appeared in Elberberg, but after rye prices soared to seven talers per *Viertel* in 1795, a Jewish wholesaler from Kassel bought 100 *Viertel*. Prices again approached seven talers in 1802, and another Jewish merchant, Abraham Sussmann from Kassel, purchased 210 out of the total of 277 *Viertel* of

[53] The von Buttlar family received 249 *Viertel* of rye each year in quitrents for parcels of land and 56 *Viertel* from hereditary leases of mills. The tithes were sold in advance of the harvest (*vermaltert*), and those which were sold for fixed amount of grain yielded an average of 48 *Viertel* of rye between 1781 and 1820. StAM 340 v. Buttlar-Elberberg, 1781–1820 Rechnungen.

[54] Between 1790 and 1799 the steward of the von der Malsburg family collected almost five hundred *Viertel* of rye each year. An average of 11 percent was delivered to the owners, 4.5 percent went for salaries, 2 percent was lost through spoilage, and over 80 percent of the rye was sold. StAM 340 v. d. Malsburg-Escheberg, 1790–99 Rechnungen.

[55] The von Eschwege family's steward sold all fifty *Viertel* of rye available in 1783 to the lessee of one of the family's estates. In 1800 a nearby estate owner, Wilhelm von Keudell, purchased most of the available rye. In 1807 and 1811 leaseholders and administrators of estates in the area bought moderate amounts of grain, although the largest purchaser was a merchant from a nearby town. StAM 340 v. Eschwege, 1783–1814 Rechnungen.

rye sold by the Buttlars that year. Later in the decade the leaseholders of the Buttlar estates began to purchase much of the family's surplus grain, and this occurred frequently in the following two decades. In the most severe crisis to hit Hesse-Kassel, that of 1816–17, leaseholders and a baker from Kassel made a number of large purchases in 1816, but the following year, when grain prices were even higher, most of the family's grain was sold in small quantities to local villagers or to the government's emergency granary (*Notspeicher*), probably on order of the government.[56]

In times of crisis the government stepped in to dictate when and to whom grain could be sold. When grain prices rose sharply in 1784, the Kassel *Regierung* ordered the von Buttlar family to sell forty-one *Viertel* of its surplus rye to four neighboring villages.[57] In the nineteenth century, government measures consisted mainly of decrees forbidding the export of grain during crisis years.[58]

Noble landlords were seemingly in an excellent position to reap huge profits from bad harvests and high grain prices, for most of their grain payments from peasants were fixed in amount (quitrents and hereditary mill leases). Only the tithes were related to the size of the harvest. In reality, however, landlords received substantially less grain in periods of scarcity, because many peasants were not able to make the required payments. Landlords also sometimes reduced the size of payments owed to them in periods of bad harvest.[59]

Despite the lower quantity of grain available, noble landlords reaped their greatest profits in periods of high prices. Between 1790 and 1830 income from rye sales by the Buttlars exceeded 2,000 talers in only eight years (the average annual income during this period was 1,615 talers). In six of these years grain prices were unusually high (six or more talers per *Viertel*), as can be seen in figure 5.2.[60] However, in certain years when unusually large amounts of grain were received, income was high despite relatively low prices. This frequently occurred in a year with a

[56] StAM 340 v. Buttlar-Elberberg, 1781–1830 Rechnungen.

[57] Ibid., 1784 Rechnung.

[58] The villagers of Harmuthsachsen complained that during the crisis year 1847 their landlord, Oberforstmeister Moritz von Hundelshausen, not only refused to give any grain to the village's poor but "loaded his grain in a hay-filled wagon and drove to to Sooden to sell it, in violation of the government regulation that no grain should be taken out of its village but should be sold there." StAM 16 (Ministerium des Innern), Rep. IX, Kl. 1, Nr. 85, petition of 8 April 1848.

[59] For example, the Buttlars reduced the tithe of the village of Bessa by one-third in 1781 after a hailstorm caused extensive crop damage. StAM 340 v. Buttlar-Elberberg, 1781 Rechnung.

[60] Ibid., 1781–1830 Rechnungen. Bad harvests affected noble landlords less than the leaseholders of their estates because much of the landlords' income in grain was fixed.

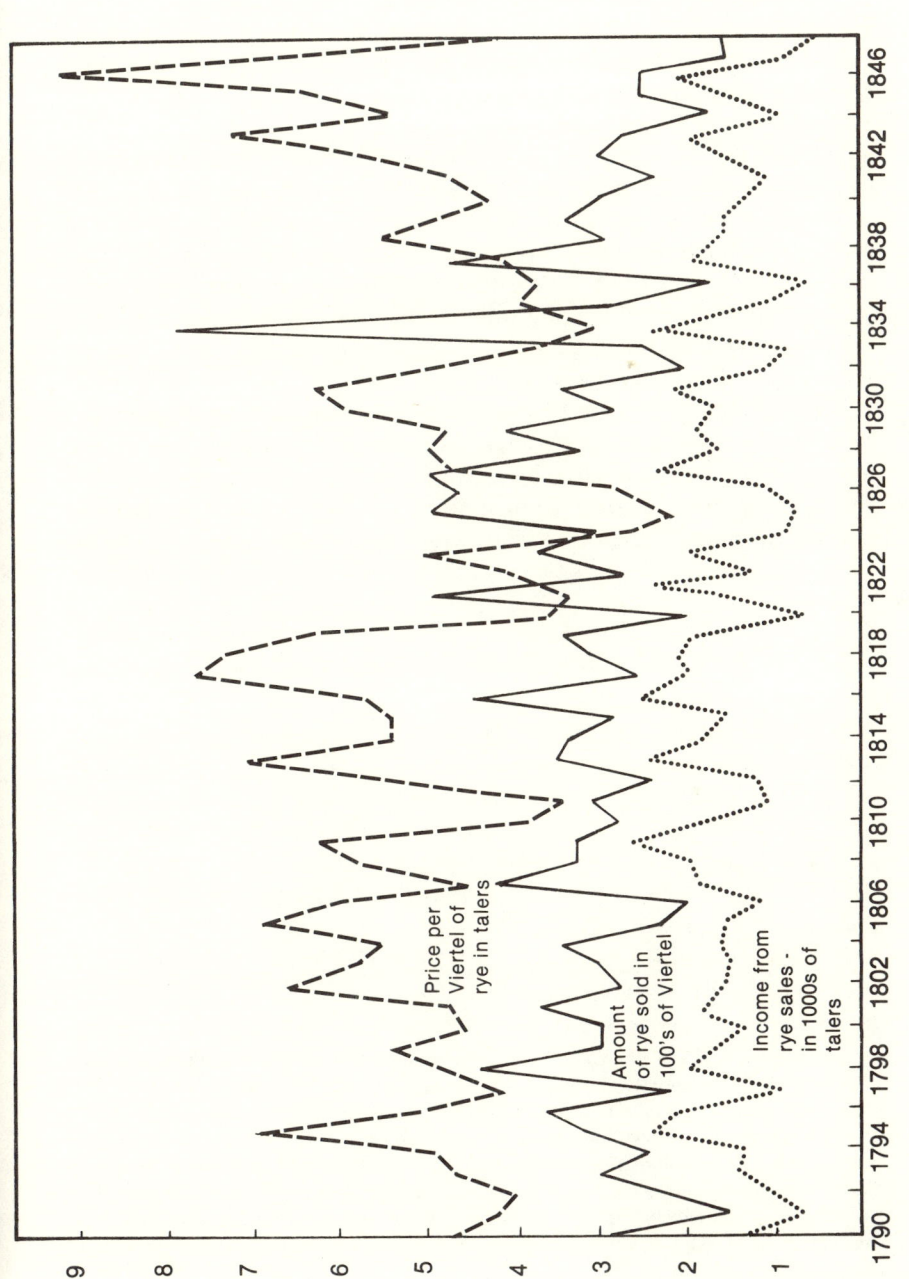

Figure 5.2. Grain Sales of the von Buttlar-Elberberg Family.

good harvest that followed a period of high grain prices. In such years peasants began to make up the deficits in grain deliveries that had occurred during the bad harvests. As shown in figure 5.2, the amount of rye sold by the Buttlars rose sharply in 1821 and 1834, years with good harvests following extended periods of scarcity and high prices.

The proceeds from grain and poultry sales (all from peasant dues) along with the cash payments by peasants made up a substantial portion of most noble landlords' income. The percentage of the total income varied from landlord to landlord, because some nobles collected dues and services from a large number of villages, while others had few peasants under their overlordship. The value of nobles' own holdings also varied greatly, but in general peasant dues constituted between one-third and two-thirds of the annual landed income of noble families at the end of the eighteenth century, as can be seen in table 5.3.[61] For the von Buttlar-Elberberg family, income from peasant dues averaged 2,890 talers per year between 1781 and 1805, which amounted to 51 percent of the total annual income. Grain deliveries represented the most important part of the peasant dues; income from grain sales averaged 2,330 talers annually. In contrast, the cash income from the various forms of quitrents brought in only 125 talers per year.[62] The importance of peasant dues

TABLE 5.3. Income from Peasant Dues and Services

Family	Period	Annual Income	% from Dues and Services
v. d. Malsburg-Escheberg	1790–1799	2,884 talers	62
v. Löwenstein-Wickershof	1801–1804	645 talers	53
v. Buttlar-Elberberg	1781–1805	5,655 talers	51
v. Löwenstein-Römersberg	1790–1804	700 talers	48
v. d. Malsburg-Elmarshausen	1770–1789	2,635 talers	37
v. Eschwege-Reichensachsen	1770–1774	1,500 talers	35
v. Baumbach-Nentershausen	1804–1805	2,050 talers	28

[61] StAM 340 v. d. Malsburg-Escheberg, Rechnungen; 340 v. Löwenstein, Paket 44–46; 340 v. Buttlar-Elberberg, Rechnungen; 340 v. Eschwege, Rechnungen; 340 v. Baumbach-Nentershausen, Acc. 1948/41, Nr. 33; Elmarshausen Archive, Rechnungen.

[62] The main crop was rye, but the Buttlars also received deliveries of oats, barley, and wheat. The average annual revenues from peasant dues were as follows (in talers): *Dienstgeld* (cash payments instead of service), 22; *Schutzgeld* (from Jews), 15; *Lehngeld*, 122; tithes (from those which were sold in advance of the harvest), 193; sale of poultry, 151; hereditary mill leases, 33; and sale of fish, 5. Income from the family's own holdings consisted of the following average amounts: rent from the main estate, 906 talers; revenue

for the von Buttlar family actually is underrepresented by the above figures for annual income, because not all of the produce from peasant dues was sold. Some of this produce was used by the noble household itself or given to servants and employees of the family as part of their salary and thus does not figure into the family's grain sales. In addition, the labor services of the local villages as well as several tithes were leased along with the main estate, so part of its value as a rental object came from peasant dues and services.

With peasant dues constituting such a large proportion of nobles' landed income, it would be natural to assume that all noble landlords categorically opposed any attempt to alter the system of "feudal" dues, but this was not the case. Although many nobles favored the status quo, a growing number of nobles recognized the drawbacks of the traditional system. Not only were the compulsory labor services by peasants notoriously inefficient, but the meals that had to be given in return were sometimes more valuable than the labor received. Furthermore, peasant dues were becoming harder to collect. Part of the difficulty in collecting peasant dues lay in the extensive bookkeeping effort required to keep track of tiny amounts of dues owed by large numbers of individuals, a problem that was constantly being aggravated by the peasant practice of dividing land equally among all heirs after the owner's death. However, the greatest problem in collecting peasant dues lay in the changed attitudes of the peasantry. In the eighteenth century, particularly after the French Revolution, peasants began to question the right of landlords to collect seigneurial dues, and cases of refusal to pay dues became more and more common. Once landlords lost their right of seigneurial justice, they were forced to bring suit in the state courts to obtain payment of arrears by peasants, but this was often a long and costly process.

Because of these problems, there was already a strong tendency on the part of noble landlords to convert peasant dues and services into annual cash payments by the early nineteenth century. This trend was furthest advanced in the area of labor services, but tithes were also on their way to becoming a cash payment as landlords increasingly sold tithes in advance to local peasants, often for several years at a time. Some landlords even began to explore the possibility of converting the produce portion of quitrents into cash payments or abolishing quitrents entirely in return for compensation, but such proposals met with resistance from peasants, perhaps because they did not have enough cash or credit to be able

from the forests, 1,824 talers; and income from sheep raising, 35 talers, for a total of 2,765 talers. StAM 340 v. Buttlar-Elberberg, 1781–1805 Rechnungen.

to make such large lump-sum compensation payments.[63] The willingness of nobles to consider changes in the traditional system of peasant dues and services had been greatly increased by the shocks of the French Revolution and the attempts made by the Kingdom of Westphalia to abolish most peasant obligations.

Since many nobles had already taken steps to put all their dealings with the peasantry on a cash basis, the 1831 constitution's call for the redemption of many peasant dues and services was not really a massive blow to the nobility. In the following year, when laws to regulate the process of redeeming the dues and services of the peasantry were drawn up, noble deputies did not attempt to block such legislation but simply tried to obtain the most favorable terms possible. The final result, compensation based upon twenty times the annual value of the dues or services involved, was favorable to the landlords, although less than the compensation in Bavaria and Prussia, where landlords received twenty-five times the annual value of the peasant dues and services being abolished.[64]

Despite the reforms of the 1830s, the relationships between landlords and peasants often remained strained, especially because the Redemption Law of 1832 did not abolish some of the most hated burdens such as transfer fees (*Lehngeld*). Disputes over wood prices and peasant rights of use in noble forests provided an additional source of tension. When news of the uprisings in Paris reached Hesse-Kassel at the end of February 1848, riots broke out in the cities of Hanau and Kassel, and the unrest quickly spread to the countryside, as peasants sought to rid themselves once and for all of hated burdens. The peasants adopted the townsmen's cry for freedom of the press, but as a contemporary government report noted, "Freedom of the press is understood to be freedom from all dues, namely those to landlords, which is why most of the acts of violence have been directed against noble estate owners."[65]

One of the first noble families to be terrorized by angry peasants was the von Rau family, whose castle at Nordeck was stormed by a mob on

---

[63] In 1821 the von Löwenstein family asked the inhabitants of several of its villages if they were in favor of abolishing their quitrents by making compensation payments. The peasants all rejected the idea. StAM 340 v. Löwenstein, Paket 12.

[64] "Die Ablösungsgesetze und andere Gesetze zur Erfüllung der Forderungen des Liberalismus," *Deutsche Vierteljahrsschrift* (1854): 186–220; Blum, *End of the Old Order*, 392. For details of the nobility's stand during the debates on the reform of the system of dues and services see below, chapter 7.

[65] StAM 16, Rep. VII, Kl. 2, Nr. 52, Bd. I, Regierung Marburg to interior ministry, 3 April 1848.

the evening of 14 March. According to the family's steward, the crowd was in an ugly mood:

> The rebels broke up part of a wall and demolished a picket fence, and they also shot at me while I was speaking to them from the window, trying to soothe the rebels and get them to leave. We then had to accept their demands, even the most ridiculous ones, and afterward they extorted a sum of money from Herr von Rau, demolished the entryway, and forced tenant Schultheiß to give them liquor. It was not until three o'clock in the morning that the last rebels finally ceased drumming, breaking walls, kicking doors, and shouting.[66]

Although the actions of peasant mobs generally did not extend beyond making loud threats, forcing open doors, or breaking windows, several noble landlords underwent harrowing experiences in March and April 1848. Ludwig von Baumbach, a sixty-nine-year-old retired army officer, was confronted by a mob of nearly two hundred peasants at his estate Siebertshausen on the evening of 23 March. The peasants threatened to destroy all his belongings and forced him to sign a list of concessions regarding wood rights and prices. Baumbach noted afterward, "I was able to protect myself against attacks upon my person only by placing a barrel of gunpowder in front of me and stating that if anyone came too close, I would ignite the powder and blow up all the occupants of the room."[67]

Similar forced concessions were obtained from other landlords such as the von Hundelshausen, von Buttlar-Elberberg, and von Eschwege families.[68] In many cases nobles were not present at their estates when

---

[66] StAM 16, Rep. VII, Kl. 12, Nr. 52, Bd. I, Rentmeister Rang to Regierung Marburg, 15 March 1848.

[67] StAM 16, Rep. IX, Kl. 1, Nr. 85, Lt. Col. von Baumbach-Siebertshausen to interior ministry, 26 March 1848.

[68] On 18 March the inhabitants of Harmuthsachsen presented Oberforstmeister Moritz von Hundelshausen with a long list of demands, including the abolition of quitrents and transfer fees, which he was forced to accept verbally. This did not completely satisfy the peasants, who returned and awakened him at one o'clock in the morning in order to obtain written acceptance of their demands (StAM 16, Rep. IX, Kl. 1, Nr. 85, Hundelshausen to interior ministry, 29 March 1848). Rudolf von Buttlar-Elberberg was forced to make a number of concessions to a large mob of peasants who came to his estate on the evening of 16 April and again on the following day (StAM 340 v. Buttlar-Elberberg, Nr. 42, Buttlar's memorandum of 18 April 1848). The commander of one of the "mobile columns" of troops sent to restore order in the Werra valley reported, "The mood of the inhabitants of Reichensachsen is favorable toward the government but not so favorable for the local landlord, Obervorsteher von Eschwege. However, according to prominent inhabitants, this will not lead to criminal acts." Despite these assurances, a large number of peasants from

the unrest broke out, so the burden of dealing with angry peasants frequently fell upon administrators. The strain felt by many stewards during the tumultuous days of March and April 1848 can be seen in the following report by the Malsburgs' *Rentmeister*, Friedrich Wilhelm Dacke, on 21 April:

> Life is miserable here; at night sleep is out of the question. One cannot trust anyone anymore. Two men circle the courtyard the entire night standing guard. This morning I was able to change my clothes for the first time since Monday, and I threw myself onto the bed still fully dressed, not letting the sword out of my hand, the loaded pistols on the table. The devil take this life! Either it will soon get much better here or else it will become even worse. But we are hoping for the best.[69]

Frequently estate agents were much more unpopular than the estate owners themselves, who had less contact with the peasants. In such cases one of the main peasant demands was the removal of a hated administrator.[70] In general, however, mob actions against noble landlords or their administrators were few in number in Hesse-Kassel and were not nearly as violent and destructive as the peasant protests against landlords in other parts of Germany or even the actions of Hessian peasants and townsmen against Jews in 1848.[71] The commutation of many peasant dues and services after 1831, along with the establishment of the *Landeskreditkasse* to assist peasants in carrying out this process, had removed most of the former sources of tension between landlords and peasants.

Although the peasants invariably called for the overthrow of the old feudal order in their petitions, in many cases it was they who were de-

---

neighboring villages massed at Eschwege's estate later that same day and made threats of arson and violence (StAM 11, C 9 gg, p. 191, Major von Borck to Kriegsministerium, 28 March 1848; p. 209, Carl von Eschwege to Captain Bennecke of the mobile column).

[69] Elmarshausen Archive, Rentmeister Dacke to Forstmeister von der Malsburg, 21 April 1848.

[70] The peasants of Elben demanded the firing of the Buttlars' administrator, Heinrich Heerdt, while the peasants of Oberlistingen and Niederlistingen insisted that the Malsburgs' forester be replaced. StAM 340 v. Buttlar-Elberberg, Nr. 42; Paul Heidelbach, *Deutsche Dichter und Künstler in Escheberg und die Beziehung der Familie von der Malsburg-Escheberg zu den Familien Tieck und Geibel* (Marburg, 1913), 58.

[71] Eckhart G. Franz, "Vormärz und Revolution in den kurhessischen Landen am 'Werra Strom,'" in *Festschrift zum 60. Geburtstag von K. A. Eckhart*, ed. Otto Perst (Marburg, 1961), 266–70. For the violent protests by peasants in other parts of Germany see Theodore S. Hamerow, *Restoration, Revolution, Reaction: Economics and Politics in Germany, 1815–1871* (Princeton, 1966), 107–9; Hippel, *Bauernbefreiung*, 1: 485–98.

fending traditional rights and privileges against changes made by noble landlords seeking to increase revenues. One of the most widespread grievances in 1848 was high wood prices. In the 1830s and 1840s some noble landlords attempted to increase income by auctioning wood rather than selling it at traditional low prices, and in 1848 peasants clamored for a return to the system of fixed wood prices.[72] In some cases peasants demanded not only retention of their traditional rights but also new rights of use in nobles' forests.[73]

As a result of the unrest, the Landtag ended all remaining peasant dues in the second Redemption Law. Although the compensation payments for lost peasant dues temporarily provided landlords with considerable income, in the long run noble families would be dependent on the income from their estates and forests.

FOREST INCOME

Many noble families owned extensive tracts of forest, which provided much of their annual landed income. But in the eighteenth and early nineteenth centuries, nobles were unable to exploit their forest holdings to the fullest because local peasants retained considerable rights to the use of the forest. Peasants could collect fallen branches and let their pigs root in nobles' forests, and in many communities peasants also were guaranteed the right to purchase wood at traditional fixed prices. By the late eighteenth century such artificially low wood prices were becoming a source of conflict between villages and noble forest owners seeking to limit this right. In the 1780s the von der Malsburg family attempted to restrict the right of the villagers of Oberlistingen to buy as much wood as they wanted at twenty-four *Albus* per cord. The Malsburgs proposed an annual limit of one cord per peasant landowner (*Bauer*) and one-half cord per cottager, but the government reaffirmed the village's traditional right.[74] One family that did have limits on the amount of wood its peas-

---

[72] The inhabitants of Elben demanded that the von Buttlar family end all wood auctions and set prices at the low level that had prevailed between 1801 and 1815. These new prices were to remain in effect forever. StAM 340 v. Buttlar-Elberberg, Nr. 42, petition of 17 April 1848.

[73] See the report of the Dörnbergs' administrator in Hausen, Amtsschultheiß Gundlach, to the interior ministry on 28 March 1848. StAM 16, Rep. VII, Kl. 12, Nr. 52, vol. I.

[74] In 1788 a government commission recommended setting a limit of two cords for a peasant with a full holding, one cord for a peasant with a half holding, and one-half cord for a cottager, but the *Regierung* rejected this proposal. StAM 17d, v. d. Malsburg, Nr. 20, 22. Note: the actual amounts were in *Klafter*; a *Klafter* is slightly larger than a cord (see appendix E).

ants could buy at low fixed prices, the Freiherren von Dörnberg, rejected peasants' complaints of high prices in 1802, stating:

> The above traditional wood prices have existed since time immemorial and have not been raised. Every peasant can get by with the established quantity of wood, and over three-quarters of the peasants have not only enough firewood but too much of it and each year sell a half or even a whole cord. We are not required to give our subjects more than required; those subjects who cannot get by with the traditional amount, such as wealthy peasants and especially distillers, must request wood, and because this wood is our property, they must pay the prices that we have set. Since, as is well known, the prices of all objects have risen and the population increases each year, we have no scruples about raising the price of that wood which we are not required to supply, and we do so primarily for economic reasons—to motivate the peasants to improve their fireplaces and reduce wood consumption.[75]

The nineteenth century saw a change in the attitude of nobles toward their forests. Previously many nobles had not attempted to achieve as much revenue as possible from their forests and had often taken a paternalistic attitude toward the needs of the local peasants. Thus in 1797 the von Buttlar family rejected a request by the city of Kassel to sell it large quantities of wood, stating, "We must consider the needs and welfare not only of the villages under our jurisdiction but also of our vassals in other villages, and we would not like to refuse to sell them wood, which we have done for years."[76] However, two decades later this same family began to look for ways to increase the profits from the sale of wood to peasants. In 1820 and 1821 the Buttlars issued decrees forbidding the sale of wood to peasants who had not yet paid for previous purchases. Henceforth mayors and village councils would have to provide lists of persons from their villages who were capable of paying for the wood. In the case of nonpayment, the village would be liable for the debt.[77]

Five years later the mayors and village councils of seven villages wrote to the government to complain that their villages had previously received wood from the Buttlars' forests but the family no longer wished to make deliveries because too many inhabitants had not paid and law-

[75] StAM 17d, v. Dörnberg, Paket 11, Freiherren von Dörnberg to Regierung Kassel, 1 October 1802.

[76] StAM 340 v. Buttlar-Elberberg, Nr. 250, Buttlars to Fürstlich Hessische Holz-Versorgungs-Commission der Residenzstadt Cassel, 12 July 1797.

[77] StAM 340 v. Buttlar-Elberberg, Nr. 250, Forest Regulation of 23 August 1820; Buttlars to Forester Conradi, 30 May 1821.

suits to collect these arrears were too expensive. Consequently the family now intended to sell wood at auction or to large purchasers for cash only. The mayors added that this change would be a disaster for these seven villages, because the state forests could not supply the necessary wood. Therefore the villages asked the government to extend the provisions of two decrees from 1815 and 1823 to the Buttlars' forests. These decrees established simplified, inexpensive court procedures for cases involving arrears in payments for wood from state forests. The government approved the request the following year, ending for the time being the difficulties between the villages and the Buttlars.[78]

The wood sales of the von Buttlar family did retain certain paternalistic aspects. The villages of Elberberg, Elben, and Kirchberg, which prior to 1807 had been under seigneurial jurisdiction of the Buttlars, always received their firewood at a lower price than the inhabitants of other villages. In 1827 the Buttlars' forester/steward recommended eliminating these special prices because the reason for their existence had disappeared, but the family rejected his proposal.[79] The lower prices for these villages remained in effect even after all remaining seigneurial ties were severed in 1848.

Prices for firewood from the Buttlars' forests remained fairly steady in the first half of the nineteenth century. In 1810 a cord of beech cost five talers, but during the next two decades the price gradually declined, reaching four talers in 1835, before returning to five talers in the 1840s.[80] Beginning in the late 1830s, the Buttlars started auctioning wood used for construction purposes rather than selling it at fixed prices like firewood. This change immediately led to higher prices and complaints from the peasants.[81] The auctions were stopped in 1848 because they were one of the main causes of the peasant unrest in the surrounding villages in March 1848.

Attempts to increase revenues from forests involved not only changes

[78] Ibid., mayors and village councils of Kirchberg, Gleichen, Dorla, Obervorschtz, Werckel, Wehren, and Haddamer to Kreisamt Fritzlar, 25 November 1826; StAM 17d Generalia, Paket 8, decision of Regierung Kassel, 13 January 1827.

[79] StAM 340 v. Buttlar-Elberberg, Nr. 250, Conradi to Buttlars, 9 September 1827.

[80] StAM 340 v. Buttlar-Elberberg, 1810–1850 Forstrechnungen. The price for the inhabitants of Elben, Elberberg, and Kirchberg was generally one-half taler less per *Klafter* of beech.

[81] The village of Elben complained that it was being robbed of an ancient prerogative, but Forester Conradi replied that the cadaster simply stated that the village purchased its wood from the Buttlars; this did not give the village the right to purchase wood at low fixed prices. StAM 340 v. Buttlar-Elberberg, Nr. 250, mayor and village council of Elben to Kammerherr von Buttlar, 4 March 1841; Forester Conradi to the mayor of Elben, 29 March 1841.

in pricing and selling policies but also efforts to increase the amount of wood for sale. In the nineteenth century noble landowners and their foresters began to utilize more scientific methods of forestry, instead of leaving the forests in their natural state. Some nobles even studied forestry and became experts in the field. One such landowner, Rudolf von Buttlar-Elberberg (1802–75), not only greatly increased the quality and yield of his family's forests but also developed a new method of planting seedlings that brought him renown in forestry circles all over Germany. In 1853 he published a book detailing his methods of forestry.[82]

Income from forests took on added importance for nobles after the agrarian reforms abolished peasant dues and ended most nobles' involvement with the grain trade. Forests were now one of the most important remaining sources of income, so nobles began to devote more attention to improving the quality and yield of their forests. For example, in 1852 the von Baumbach-Nentershausen family commissioned a forester to develop a plan that would greatly improve the composition of its forests. However, the continued existence of certain peasant rights was an obstacle to the accomplishment of parts of the plan, so in 1853 the family began to reach agreements with local peasants abolishing their forest rights in return for a yearly payment of six talers each.[83] The abolition of peasants' forest rights did not become widespread in Hesse-Kassel until after 1867, when the new Prussian government enacted a law enabling forest owners to end such rights by compensating the villages.[84]

Increased demand for timber, resulting in part from the needs of railroads and other new industries,[85] gradually drove wood prices up, and these higher prices, in conjunction with the larger yields resulting from improved methods of forestry, led to huge profits for noble forest owners in the nineteenth century. For example, in the late eighteenth century, revenue from the Elberberg forest ranged between one and two thousand talers annually. At the start of the nineteenth century, the size of the forest increased somewhat after the Buttlars purchased the holdings of another branch of the family. Afterward the annual forest income generally exceeded four thousand talers, but in the 1840s profits soared to above ten thousand talers per year, only to drop sharply after

[82] Hueck, "Familie von Buttlar," Nr. 12, pp. 7–9; *Allgemeine deutsche Biographie*, 56 vols. (Leipzig, 1875–1912), 3: 655–56 (hereafter cited as *ADB*).

[83] Baumbach, "Familie von Baumbach-Nentershausen," 74.

[84] Bähr, *Hessische Wald*, 17–18.

[85] For example, the Buttlars sold 1,400 talers' worth of wood to the Friedrich-Wilhelm-Nordbau railroad construction company in 1845. StAM 340 v. Buttlar-Elberberg, 1845 Forstrechnung.

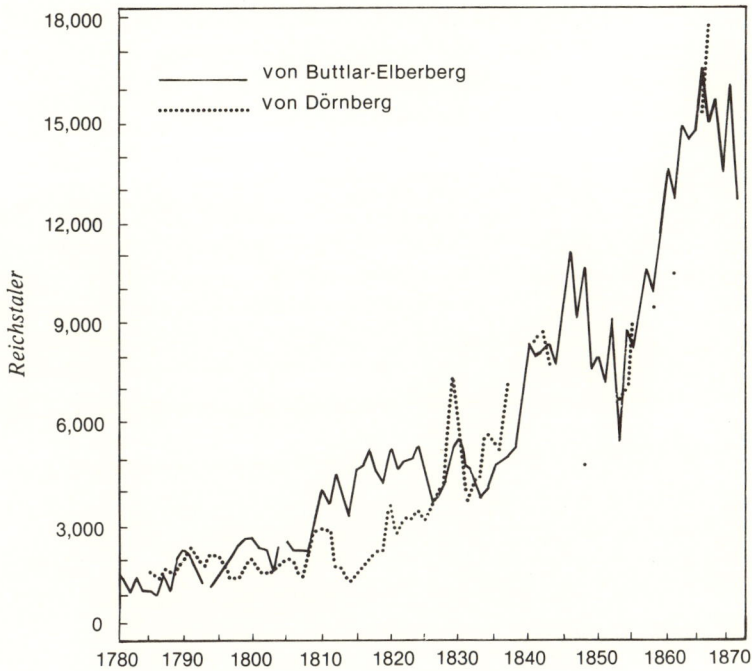

Figure 5.3. Annual Income from Forests (in *Reichstaler*).

1848. This decline was only temporary, however, and the Buttlars' forest income rose to new heights in the 1850s and 1860s.[86]

Similar improvement in earnings was obtained by the Freiherren von Dörnberg (see figure 5.3), who began to convert their forests from a natural state to one based upon rational forestry principles at the end of the eighteenth century. In order to finance the costs of large-scale planting, the family sold one of its smaller estates (Frankershausen) in 1811. Within fifty years the profits from the Dörnbergs' forests quadrupled, averaging 7,700 talers annually in the early 1850s in contrast to an average of only 1,900 talers per year between 1785 and 1804. A little more than a decade later forest income had again doubled, averaging 16,700 talers.[87] Other families with less extensive forest holdings also experienced a boom in forest income. At the start of the nineteenth century,

[86] Ibid., 1781–1866 Forstrechnungen.
[87] Dörnberg Archive, 1785–1804, 1853–55, 1865–66 Rechnungen.

135

the Nentershausen forest yielded only seven hundred talers per year for the von Baumbach family, but by the 1850s the annual forest income was approaching two thousand talers.[88]

PROFITS

A *Rittergut*, along with its attached forests and peasant dues, often proved very lucrative for its owners. Since the main estate was generally leased, the owners had few estate-related expenses. Salaries for the administrator, the forester, and perhaps one or two subordinates normally did not amount to more than a few hundred talers plus some produce and wood, and the tax burden was extremely low in the eighteenth century. For example, the estate Elmarshausen had a total income of over 3,600 talers per year in the 1780s but paid only 73 talers in taxes. The cash portion of the salaries for the estate's employees totaled only 140 talers.[89]

The most important estate-related expenses of noble estates were the costs of construction and repairs. Maintenance expenses for buildings and fences could be quite high at times. Between 1770 and 1789, for example, the costs for repairs and materials at Elmarshausen averaged 575 talers annually but ranged as high as 1,430 talers in 1771.[90]

For some families, however, the estate-related expenses were dwarfed by the burden of interest payments and capital amortization from debts resting on estates. Thus the von Buttlar family paid 1,200 talers annually in interest during the 1790s, a period in which its average profits amounted to slightly over 1,600 talers per year. Many estates were also burdened for periods of time by obligations within the owner's family, particularly payments to widows and sisters. The size of such expenses in the late eighteenth century is illustrated by table 5.4.

Despite the burden of interest payments and other expenses, most estates provided sufficient profits to enable the owners to supplement their income from government offices or even to live without outside income in some cases. Many estate owners also gradually reduced the size of their debts. During the nineteenth century the financial situation of most estates improved noticeably, a development that was assisted by the increasing revenues generated by most estates.

[88] StAM 340 v. Baumbach-Nentershausen, Acc. 1948/41, Nr. 33 (1804–5, 1808, 1821, 1828–29, 1839, 1853, and 1856 Rechnungen).

[89] Elmarshausen Archive, 1780–95 Rechnungen. In the nineteenth century taxes became a larger burden after the nobility lost many of its previous exemptions. Elmarshausen paid an average of 277 talers annually in taxes of all kinds in the 1820s.

[90] Elmarshausen Archive, 1770–89 Rechnungen.

TABLE 5.4. Income and Expenses of Noble Estates at the End of the
Eighteenth Century (In *Reichstaler*)

Estate	Average Annual Income	Major Expense Items					Average Annual Profit
		Family	Tax	Wages	Repairs	Interest	
Elberberg	5,522	634	126	398	591	1,200	1,639
Hausen	5,232	395	96	297	231	270	3,276
Escheberg	4,781	0	93	299	537	232	3,300
Elmarshausen	3,653	0	73	138	577	672	1,293
Reichensachsen	1,609	100	35	87	46	490	787
Solz	1,355	150	36	46	8	0	819
Römersberg	962	0	16	27	40	390	345
Wickershof	591	0	28	32	11	0	490

The amount of income from peasant dues and services generally remained constant, the only important variation taking place in the income from grain sales, which depended on grain prices and the amount of grain available for sale. But the income from nobles' own holdings rose substantially during the nineteenth century. Rents moved gradually higher, with sharper increases in the 1850s and 1860s, but the most dramatic improvements in income came from nobles' forest holdings.

Since most of the increased income from estates in the nineteenth century came from the nobles' own property (demesnes and forests), the loss of peasant dues and services was not as great a setback as it would have been in the eighteenth century. Even if the interest and capital from redemption payments are not counted, most noble estates had a higher income without peasant dues after 1848 than they had had with peasant dues at the start of the century. For example, income from all sources for the *Rittergut* Elmarshausen averaged 3,900 talers at the end of the eighteenth century; by the 1860s the average income had climbed to 9,200 talers (excluding income from the redemption payments). Even a small estate like Wickershof showed substantial improvement in income, which rose from 600 talers at the end of the eighteenth century to 1,100 talers in the 1850s (not including redemption payments).[91]

Perhaps the most dramatic example of improvement in the fortunes of noble landowners is the von Buttlar-Elberberg family, which stood on the brink of economic ruin at the end of the eighteenth century. The an-

[91] Elmarshausen Archive, 1781–1800 and 1861–70 Rechnungen; StAM 340 v. Löwenstein, Paket 45, 1794–1804 and 1856–57 Wickershof Rechnungen.

nual profit from the landholdings of this family rose from less than one thousand talers in the early 1790s to twelve thousand talers in 1865.[92] Most other estate owners did not register such extraordinary gains but still had a much higher landed income in the mid-nineteenth century than at the end of the eighteenth century. For example, the von der Malsburg-Elmarshausen family received an average of 1,400 talers a year in profit from its main estate at the end of the eighteenth century; by the 1860s the annual profit averaged 2,900 talers.[93]

The estates of the Westphalian nobility also registered strong gains in income during the nineteenth century despite the loss of peasant dues and services,[94] so the "peasant emancipation" (*Bauernbefreiung*) did not lead to the economic ruin of noble landlords, at least not in Hesse-Kassel and Westphalia. The nobles in these two states survived and profited because they had substantial landholdings of their own and thus were not cut off from all landed income when the reform legislation ended nobles' landlordship over peasant land. In contrast, many nobles in Eastern Europe, who had little or no demesne, were ruined by the reforms.[95]

LIFE ON A NOBLE ESTATE

One of the most interesting aspects of any study of the nobility is the actual lifestyle of the nobles themselves. Unfortunately the available records of the Hessian nobility provide little information about the daily lives of nobles on their estates or in their town houses, in contrast to the detailed records kept of the economic affairs of many noble estates. The following account of the lifestyle of the nobility is therefore primarily impressionistic. Coverage of the nobility is far from complete, for only a handful of memoirs and contemporary accounts are available, but this information does provide a glimpse at the style of life for some members of the Hessian nobility, who may have been typical of many others.

The lifestyles of noble families on their estates varied tremendously, both from family to family and within families from generation to generation. The poorest members of the nobility lived on small country estates with few if any of the luxuries such as ornate coaches, numerous servants, or expensive clothing normally associated with the noble style

[92] The Buttlars added a third estate to their holdings in 1826, which accounts for part of the rise in landed income, but the bulk of the increased profit came from the main estate Elberberg and its extensive forests. StAM 340 v. Buttlar-Elberberg, 1790–1866 Rechnungen.

[93] Elmarshausen Archive, 1781–1800 and 1861–70 Rechnungen.

[94] Reif, *Westfälischer Adel*, 230–36.

[95] Blum, *End of the Old Order*, 425–26.

of life. More prosperous families generally enjoyed such luxuries, but at times their lives underwent considerable change. In the von der Malsburg-Elmarshausen family, for example, Friedrich Anton von der Malsburg (1695–1760) lived very well. He completely remodeled the family's historic castle and filled all the rooms with expensive tapestries. His son Gottlob (1735–88) continued to make improvements to the castle and also maintained an expensive lifestyle. In the next generation, Heinrich (1775–1847) was unable to continue the lifestyle of his father and grandfather. Already as a student he had written to his mother in 1792, "If you get a good chance to sell the silver, then do so, because we can eat just as well from porcelain as from silver, and cash earns interest; dishes do not." Although he attempted to live more frugally, as was necessitated by his modest salary as a forestry official, Heinrich did have one area of extra expenditures—his generosity to poor children. On a number of occasions he took in poor or orphaned children and raised them in his family, later assisting them in getting started in a career. Thus Fritz Weizenfeld (so named because he had been found abandoned in a wheat-field) was raised by the Malsburgs, who later purchased citizenship rights for him in the city of Hamburg, so he could follow a trade there. The family also financed a local youth's university education and paid to have a girl trained as an opera singer. Heinrich von der Malsburg's many expenses caused him to begin piling up debts. By the 1830s almost all of the costly furnishings acquired by previous generations had been sold, and the castle was beginning to fall apart. Finally in 1834 Heinrich turned over the debt-ridden estate to his son Otto in return for a modest yearly payment. Only the influx of capital from the redemption payments, particularly after 1848, saved the family from financial ruin.[96]

Some families resided full-time on their estates, but the government careers of many nobles kept them away from their estates for most of the year; they therefore resided in the city or town where they worked. Even so, ties to estates remained strong, and estate owners and their families endeavored to spend as much time as possible on their estates. In such cases the estate often served as a gathering place for family celebrations or even a vacation home where the family spent the summer.

As joint ownership became increasingly common among Hessian nobles, more and more individuals were part owners of their estates, which could lead to problems if they all decided to exercise their rights of ownership and visit the estate at the same time. Some families worked out arrangements for the communal use of their estates. Thus in 1855 the Nentershausen branch of the von Baumbach family drew up an agree-

[96] Malsburg, "Aufzeichnungen," 17–25.

ment for the use of the estate Nentershausen, whose manor house was large enough to accommodate many family members at the same time. Two female members of the family (the sisters Julie von Baumbach, a spinster, and Sophie von Eschwege, a widow) lived there permanently along with a staff of servants. The salaries of the housekeeper and the maids were paid by the family as a whole, but Julie was responsible for the salary of her personal servant. Julie received an allowance of fifty talers annually from the family so she could keep the house ready for a steady stream of guests. Under the terms of the family agreement, brothers and sisters and their spouses and children did not pay anything for short visits but would have to pay a reasonable amount of board for visits over four weeks, the actual amount to be worked out with Julie. Julie and Sophie's brother Reinhard leased the estate from the family as a whole and lived in the *Pächterhaus* (leaseholder house), while the two sisters lived on the second floor of a wing of the manor house, leaving the remaining rooms available for other family members when they came to visit.[97]

As the previous example shows, estate owners and their families were not the only individuals residing on estates, and the exact numbers are often hard to determine. The estate itself required a number of employees such as an administrator, a forester, their assistants, and other hired hands, and if the landholdings of the estate were leased, the leaseholder and his family also resided on the estate, generally in a separate house set aside for this purpose. The manor house required a staff of servants if the family was in residence. Depending on the wealth of the family, these would include a cook, a housekeeper, several maids, a coachman, and one or more manservants. In addition many noble households also included a tutor and a governess for the children. Although primarily land records, some of the eighteenth-century cadasters also provide details on household size in the eighteenth century. In 1745, for example, residents on the estate Reichensachsen consisted of the owner, Hartmann Wilhelm von Eschwege; his wife, two sons, and a daughter; three male servants and four maids; a hunter and his family of three; and a shepherd with his family. The staff of the estate Willingshausen consisted of a housekeeper, a gardener, two servants, a cook, a blacksmith, a coachman, a postilion, a stable boy, and a night watchman, along with several female servants for the unmarried sister of the owners—Georg, Carl, and Bernhard von Schwertzell. Even one of the poorer families in the Ritterschaft, that of Johann Ludwig von Berlepsch, maintained four male servants and four maids on its estate at Wickershof during the same period.[98]

Servants often spent many years in a family's service and became much more than just employees. Carl Ludwig von Baumbach-Nassenerfurth reported that after his father's death in 1774, his mother no longer wished to employ a long-serving manservant named Meyer. But Meyer replied, "Even if you do not want to keep me on as a servant, I cannot stay away from the children of my master—I must look out for them. I do not require any wages, if you cannot give me any. My needs are simple, and all I require is food." Meyer remained in the family's service (with wages, after all) and accompanied Baumbach during his university studies in Leipzig. When Meyer died in 1799, he bequeathed his savings to the individuals he had served so faithfully, Carl and Henriette von Baumbach.[99]

For many nobles living on or visiting their estates, hunting was the most important leisure-time activity. The diaries of Heinrich Wilhelm von Stockhausen, for example, are full of descriptions of the hunts he went on whenever he visited his brother on the family estate Wülmersen. Even when he was there on extended visits, he went hunting virtually every day. Stockhausen's hunts were often not particularly successful—all he would shoot was a squirrel or a rabbit—but the purpose was more exercise and recreation than the provision of meat for the table. This pattern continued for the rest of his life until old age finally caught up with him. At age seventy, just two years before his death in 1840, he noted in his diary, "This year I was not on a single real hunt—the first time since 1786."[100]

Besides the importance attached to hunting by individuals, hunts also served an important social function. Major hunts complete with beaters (in a *Treibjagd*) would bring together friends, relatives, and neighbors from the nobility as well as important local bourgeois such as leaseholders or stewards. For example, a large hunt hosted by the von Baumbach-Nentershausen family on 30 October, 1846 involved eighteen individuals: eleven nobles from five different families, three bourgeois, and three of the Baumbachs' foresters. The group succeeded in shooting fifty-one rabbits. Other group hunts were even more successful. The letters sent

[98] StAM, Kataster I, Reichensachsen B2, Reptich B5, Willingshausen B2.

[99] Baumbach, *Lebensbild*, 10.

[100] StAM 340 v. Stockhausen, Nr. 115, 9: 492; 11: 267, 271, 316, 331–32, 335–36, 338–39; for the importance of hunting to nobles in southern Germany see Hans Wilhelm Eckardt, *Herrschaftliche Jagd, bäuerliche Not und bürgerliche Kritik: Zur Geschichte der fürstlichen und adligen Jagdprivilegien, vornehmlich im südwestdeutschen Raum* (Göttingen, 1976), 37–76, 268–84.

to student Carl von Buttlar-Elberberg by his mother in the early 1840s always contained the news of the latest hunts. For example, on 11 November 1840 his uncles Julius and Carl along with a neighbor, Rudolf von Keudell, shot seventy-eight rabbits, one fox, and two stags. The following day they added forty-eight more rabbits, one fox, one stag, and two snipes.[101]

The lifestyle of some nobles included considerable consumption of alcoholic beverages. Records of the abuse of alcohol by nobles are scanty, for this was not a topic to be treasured in family archives. Some clues about alcohol abuse are contained in the evaluation reports of army officers, such as that of Captain Carl von Dalwigk-Hof in 1788, which stated, "He is very fond of brandy and is therefore poor in managing his finances."[102] More detailed information about drinking habits is available for the brothers Gottlob and Carl von Buttlar-Elberberg in 1813. During a stay in Kassel to negotiate the sale of their estate Ermschwerd because of heavy debts, they ran up a bill for 248 talers at the inn "Zum römischen Kaiser" in less than four weeks. Of this total only 63 talers were for meals, lodging, and firewood; the rest went for luxuries like "coffee with extra sugar" and in particular beer, wine, and brandy. These totals included memorable days such as 28 February 1813, when the Buttlars and one other individual washed down their breakfast with a bottle of strong, sweet Malaga wine, one-quarter bottle of table wine, and three cups of coffee; drank with their noon meal a total of three bottles of Rudesheimer wine, four bottles of old (1776) Rhine wine, one bottle of table wine, and eight portions of coffee with extra sugar; and followed up with three bottles of table wine and four large mugs of beer for dinner.[103]

One other area of potentially dangerous luxury spending was gambling. Gambling for large sums of money generally occurred in cities and towns rather than on noble estates. For some nobles gambling may have spelled financial ruin, but one noble, Carl von Gilsa, seems to have been very fortunate. At the gambling casinos in Leipzig during the late 1790s, he won enough money to purchase all the necessary tools and inventory to farm his family's estate and also make numerous improvements to the estate buildings. He retained his interest in gambling and later remarked jokingly, "There is only one king, and that is King Pharaoh [a popular card game]."[104]

[101] Baumbach, "Familie von Baumbach-Nentershausen," 79; Hueck, "Familie von Buttlar," no. 1, p. 2.

[102] StAM 11, Conduitenlisten, Landgrenadier Regiment Schreiber, 1788.

[103] StAM 340 v. Buttlar-Elberberg, Nr. 133.

[104] C. F. von Gilsa, *Der Oberstallmeister von Gilsa: Ein Lebensbild aus dem achtzehnten und neunzehnten Jahrhundert* (Berlin, 1862), 15.

If a noble active in the bureaucracy or civil service did not set up residence in one of the cities or towns, he was often away from his family for extended periods of time. At such times the management of both the estate and the family fell to the wife, assisted by the family employees and sometimes also other relatives. Thus when Geheimer Rat Carl Ludwig von Baumbach-Nassenerfurth had to be away on business for a long time, his wife asked one of her sisters or other relatives to come stay with her for company and assistance.[105]

The wife's role on a noble estate was thus very important. The supervision of a large household of family members and servants took considerable time, and when the husband was absent, the wife also became responsible for the management of the entire estate. Wives also paid close attention to the education of the children, often conducting the lessons themselves if a tutor was temporarily unavailable. Many wives also cultivated hobbies such as gardening, painting, or embroidery. Julie von Buttlar-Elberberg even wrote a cookbook that was very popular in Marburg and surrounding areas.[106]

For all members of the family the arrival of friends or relatives brought a welcome variety to life on a country estate. Marriages, wedding anniversaries, and birthdays all provided occasions to invite friends and relatives to the estate, often for several days. Even when no special occasion was at hand, relatives or aquaintances often came to visit. Such visits provided a welcome change of pace for nobles and their families.[107]

Nobles living in towns or cities undoubtedly led different lifestyles from their rural counterparts, for cultural and social opportunities were much more readily available in an urban setting. Some nobles holding high-ranking offices at court or in the bureaucracy maintained elaborate residences in the capital city. Unfortunately it has been impossible to locate records of the lifestyles of such families.

[105] Baumbach, *Lebensbild*, 153.

[106] Gilsa, *Oberstallmeister von Gilsa*, 36.

[107] Some of these visitors could be termed "professional house guests." Lacking a permanent residence of their own, they traveled from estate to estate, visiting friends and relatives. See below, p. 149.

· 6 ·

CAREERS OF NOBLES

CAREER CHOICES

Although the Hessian Ritterschaft was by definition a landed nobility, almost all of its members followed careers not involved with the land, primarily in government service. The reasons that so many nobles held government offices are rooted in the economic and social systems of Hesse-Kassel.

Economic necessity drove some nobles to seek careers. Income from landed estates varied from year to year and for some families was not sufficient to cover expenses, especially if the family was laboring under a burden of debt. The problem of inadequate landed income was most apparent in families in which a number of nobles jointly owned one or two estates, for in many such families each individual's share was too small for him to live independently. Furthermore, the system of joint ownership was almost always accompanied by the leasing of the estate, so most if not all members of the family had nothing to do with the day-to-day affairs of the estate. The lack of a function to fulfill on their estates was thus motivation to seek a career even for nobles who did have sufficient landed income.

Economic considerations were often important in making a noble seek a career, but they seldom played a role in determining what kind of a career he chose. Such decisions depended primarily upon the traditions of the nobility and of individual families, and nobles therefore followed the same kinds of careers for centuries: army officer, civil servant, forestry official, and courtier.

Why were so many nobles drawn to government service? The answer does not lie in the Hessian legal code, for by the eighteenth century it no longer contained laws threatening the loss of noble status for individuals engaged in trade or commerce.[1] Nevertheless, nobles continued to adhere to the traditional, socially acceptable careers in the army, in the bureaucracy, or at court.

Government service attracted many nobles because it often brought with it high prestige. The high status of government service was reflected in and reinforced by the *Rangordnung*, a table of ranks that estab-

---

[1] Only the Hessian exclave Schaumburg still had restrictions on the occupations of nobles in the eighteenth century. A decree of 1615 prohibited nobles from following a "buergerliche Nahrung." Kopp and Wittich, *Landes-Verfassung und Rechte*, 1:100.

144

lished the order of precedence for officials. The table of ranks provided a prestige system independent of the traditional orders of birth, because bourgeois who held high offices in the army or bureaucracy took precedence over members of old noble families who held no office or one of lesser rank. At first the table of ranks did not completely ignore differences in social status. The ordinance of 1710, which listed twenty-one different ranks, placed noble *Geheime Räte* (privy councilors) in the eighth rank, while bourgeois *Geheime Räte* were only in the tenth rank. Noble *Regierungsräte* outranked their bourgeois counterparts by four ranks. Such differences were eliminated by the ordinance of 1762, which ranked all government officials by position only, not by social station.[2]

High positions in the military or bureaucracy brought non-nobles status approaching that of the nobility. Ordinances of 1756 and 1768 declared the marriage of a noble daughter to a bourgeois in the rank of at least major or *Geheimer Rat* to be *standesgemäß* (socially acceptable); all other marriages outside the nobility were considered a misalliance and caused the loss of the bride's dowry from the Stift Kaufungen.[3] Beginning in 1762 bourgeois in the upper six classes of the table of ranks (captains, councilors, professors, and above) were allowed to appear at court without the special permission normally required of non-nobles.[4]

The desire to avoid being "outranked" by members of the bourgeoisie provided additional impetus for members of the nobility to enter government service once the table of ranks had become an important determinant of social prestige. In the nineteenth century members of the Ritterschaft who held no government office eagerly sought to gain a place in the table of ranks through appointment as a *Titular Kammerherr* (titular chamberlain), a position that was unsalaried but occupied a place in the fourth category of the table of ranks (actual chamberlains were in the third category).[5]

---

[2] *HLO*, 3: 656–57, 6: 42–44.

[3] See above, p. 43.

[4] *HLO*, 6: 37.

[5] In 1829 Wilhelm von Baumbach-Sontra, a former junior-level civil servant (*Regierungsassessor*) who had turned to administering his estate, wrote to the elector, "Although many estate owners who have never served your Most Serene Ruling House have had the good fortune to be named chamberlains, this highest of all honors has still not managed to reach down to me. I have hoped for this most gracious promotion for eight years and therefore presume most humbly to lay this request at your Royal Highness's feet—most graciously to promote me to *Titular Kammerherr*." The elector granted this request. StAM 300, Abt. 11, B 1, Nr. 19, 8 February 1829. Similar requests from other nobles are found in numbers 17, 20–23, 25, and 28.

For some nobles the high prestige associated with government service was the only reason that they served, so changes in the table of ranks were very important to them. Thus in 1855 Ernst Freiherr von Dörnberg, a member of a wealthy family with a long tradition of government service, resigned his position as a legation secretary after it was downgraded to only the seventh category of the table of ranks. His letter of resignation from the foreign ministry stated:

> I told myself that diplomatic service requires not only the same degree of education, the same mental and physical qualities as other state service, but also a certain degree of wealth and a special family background. I thought I fulfilled all these requirements, since your Royal Highness accepted me for the diplomatic corps. I knew that my salary would never be sufficient for my needs, that I would never particularly like living in large cities, and that my duties as such would never completely satisfy me, but there still remained the thought of the honored position that my services would bring me. This thought was destroyed by the table of ranks of 20 April 1854. Since then nothing more binds me to the service.[6]

The aristocracy's continued preference for careers in government service throughout the eighteenth and nineteenth centuries can be seen in table 6.1, which lists the occupations of 729 male members of the Ritterschaft born between 1730 and 1849.[7] Not surprisingly, the army was the main career choice for nobles; in almost every generation approximately one-half of the men became army officers.

The bureaucracy was the second most popular career choice for nobles. Up to the mid-nineteenth century the number of knights entering the upper bureaucracy (positions that required university study) gradually increased, only to decline again in the cohort born 1830–49. Very few nobles took positions that did not require a university education once the offices previously reserved for members of the Ritterschaft—*Landrat* and *Rittersteuerobereinnehmer*—were abolished in the late eighteenth century. In the decades that followed, only a few knights served in the lower bureaucracy in positions such as tax collector or road construction supervisor. Although the forestry service was part of the finance ministry in the nineteenth century, it is listed separately in table

---

[6] StAM 9a (Ministerium des kurfürstlichen Hauses und der auswärtigen Angelegenheiten), Nr. 440, 1 October 1855.

[7] Information on nobles' careers was compiled from genealogies, personnel records of the army and bureaucracy, and the *Hessen-Casselischer Staats- und Adresskalender*, in the nineteenth century known as the *Kurfürstlich hessisches Hof- und Staats-Handbuch* (Kassel, 1764–1866), hereafter cited as *Staatshandbuch*.

TABLE 6.1. Career Choices

	Cohort Born:						
	1730–1749	1750–1769	1770–1789	1790–1809	1810–1829	1830–1849	Total
Army	47 (47%)	67 (67%)	78 (61%)	71 (51%)	58 (39%)	56 (48%)	377 (52%)
Upper bureaucracy	16 (16%)	15 (15%)	15 (12%)	20 (14%)	28 (19%)	15 (13%)	109 (15%)
Lower bureaucracy	7 (7%)	2 (2%)	3 (2%)	3 (2%)	1 (1%)	0	16 (2%)
Forest	5 (5%)	3 (3%)	11 (9%)	9 (6%)	9 (6%)	2 (2%)	39 (5%)
Court	10 (10%)	6 (6%)	9 (7%)	5 (4%)	10 (7%)	1 (1%)	41 (6%)
Officials of nobility	3 (3%)	3 (3%)	2 (2%)	2 (1%)	2 (1%)	1 (1%)	13 (2%)
Other	1 (1%)	1 (1%)	0	1 (1%)	3 (2%)	5 (4%)	11 (2%)
Emigrants	0	0	0	3 (2%)	10 (7%)	8 (7%)	21 (3%)
None	10 (10%)	3 (3%)	9 (7%)	25 (18%)	26 (18%)	29 (25%)	102 (14%)
Total	99 (99%)	100 (100%)	127 (100%)	139 (99%)	147 (100%)	117 (101%)	729 (101%)

6.1 because nobles monopolized the upper-level forestry positions and the entry requirements were much less stringent than for the regular bureaucracy.

The number of nobles who were able to obtain court offices declined in the nineteenth century as many of the smaller German courts went out of existence after their states were taken over by Prussia. Most Hessian knights sought employment at their own court, but its size was reduced in the nineteenth century. The Prussian annexation of Hesse-Kassel in 1866 virtually ended the possibility of finding positions at court.[8]

[8] The number of knights listed in table 6.1 as holding court offices in the nineteenth cen-

147

A few nobles in each generation were employed as officials of the nobility itself. In most cases they served as directors of the Stift Kaufungen (and thus as the leaders of the knighthood), but one knight headed the foundation for noblewomen in Wallenstein, while another directed the Marburg chapter of the Teutonic Order prior to its dissolution at the start of the nineteenth century. Most nobles who served as officials of the nobility had originally followed careers in some form of government service.

Only 11 of the 729 individuals studied followed careers that were not typically associated with the nobility. Adolf von Baumbach-Lenderscheid (1742–66) and Wilhelm Freiherr von Verschuer (1842–78) left home at an early age to become sailors, both Philipp von Canstein (1753–94) and Hans von Dalwigk-Schauenburg (1820–78) held professorships, Hans Hermann von Stockhausen (1809–36) became a pastor, Heinrich Freiherr von Dörnberg (1831–1905) was an artist in Dresden, and Ernst von Schenck zu Schweinsberg (1833–1918) earned a doctoral degree and became an engineer. Two members of one of the newest families in the Ritterschaft, the Freiherren Waitz von Eschen, were active as entrepreneurs, directing and expanding the activities of their family's coal mines and chemical factory. Finally, two knights held positions in agriculture that were normally filled by bourgeois; they administered estates that did not belong to their families.[9]

For centuries some nobles in each generation left Hesse to seek careers in other German states, but in most cases they returned to their estates upon retirement. Beginning in the 1830s, however, nobles began to leave Europe entirely, in most cases never to return. The goal of the majority of these emigrants was the United States, where sixteen out of the twenty-one emigrants from the Ritterschaft settled. The other five went to South America, another area where Germans were beginning to concentrate. In some cases the noble emigrants had already attempted to begin careers before deciding to leave. Four emigrants had attended a university, and two of these individuals had held nonsalaried offices in the bureaucracy. Most of the noble emigrants were members of the poorest families in the Ritterschaft[10] or of families in which a large number of

---

tury may be overstated because it is not always possible to distinguish between individuals holding honorary court titles and those who were actually active as members of the court.

[9] Wilhelm Heinrich von Gilsa (1816–99) administered an estate of the von der Decken family in Hanover, and Gustav von Biedenfeld (1838–1909) ran the *Rittergut* Kurbitz of the von Feilitzsch family in Saxony.

[10] Thus two out of the four sons of Major Carl von Baumbach-Gilserhof, who lost all his land because of debts in the 1830s, emigrated to the United States in the nineteenth century, as did two members of the impoverished von Löwenstein-Römersberg family.

males were co-owners of the family's land, making each individual's share small. But emigration was not limited to just a few families. The twenty-one emigrants came from fifteen different family lines. As a result of the Hessian system of equal inheritance, the emigrants were not simply younger sons who had not inherited anything; in fact eleven out of the twenty-one emigrants were eldest or only sons. Most emigrants gave up their interest in their families' holdings in return for a cash settlement, but a few remained co-owners of estates and continued to receive their shares of the profits.

For a number of members of the Ritterschaft in each generation, no occupation can be found. Some of these individuals were active in the administration of their estates, while others may simply have had sufficient income from the land and other investments to enable them to live as *rentiers*. A few nobles with no steady income but good social connections became virtual "aristocratic gypsies," going from estate to estate visiting relatives and acquaintances. Such visitors were often a welcome diversion to nobles on isolated country estates and would stay weeks or even months, joining in on the hunts and telling fascinating tales of their journeys through Hesse and neighboring states.[11] However, some individuals for whom no occupation could be found in genealogies or government handbooks came from the poorest families of the knighthood. These nobles were certainly not *rentiers* or constant house guests, and they probably eked out a meager living on their small landholdings in a lifestyle that differed little from that of the more prosperous members of the peasantry. Unfortunately almost no records of these poorest nobles survive.

The career choices of the Hessian Ritterschaft followed essentially the same pattern as those of the other types of nobles in Hesse-Kassel in the nineteenth century. Approximately nine out of every ten nobles listed in the roll of nobles of 1835 were involved in some form of government service (see table 6.2).

The traditions or financial circumstances of particular families frequently caused certain careers to predominate. This tendency was most evident in families that turned primarily to the military for careers. Nineteen out of the twenty-six males of the von Stein-Liebenstein family became army officers in the eighteenth and nineteenth centuries

[11] See for example the memoirs of Heinrich Wilhelm von Stockhausen (1768–1840) in the early nineteenth century. He had no residence of his own and divided his time among visits to his two brothers on their estates and to other friends and relatives both inside and outside Hesse. StAM 340 v. Stockhausen, Nr. 115, "Bruchstücke aus dem Leben von Hans Heinrich Wilhelm von Stockhausen von ihm selbst geordnet," 9 vols. (hereafter cited as Stockhausen Memoirs). For wandering nobles in Westphalia see Reif, *Westfälischer Adel*, 276.

TABLE 6.2. Occupations of Nobles in 1835

	Hessian Ritterschaft	Schaumburg Ritterschaft	Former *Reichsritterschaft*	Other Nobles
Army	92 (51%)	14 (54%)	13 (72%)	113 (47%)
Upper bureaucracy	35 (19%)	6 (23%)	1 (6%)	64 (27%)
Lower bueaucracy	1 (1%)	0	0	13 (5%)
Forestry	13 (7%)	2 (8%)	2 (11%)	19 (8%)
Court	17 (9%)	2 (8%)	1 (6%)	3 (1%)
Officials of nobility	6 (3%)	0	0	2 (1%)
Other	0		0	7 (3%)
None	17 (9%)	2 (8%)	1 (6%)	19 (8%)
Total	181 (99%)	26 (101%)	18 (101%)	240 (100%)

SOURCE: *Adelsmatrikel* of 1835 in StAM 300, Abt. 11, C 32, Nr. 6.

(three held other government offices; the remaining four held none). Nine out of ten von Hesbergs were officers, and eleven members of the von Schenk zu Schweinsberg-Fronhausen family[12] made the military their career in contrast to only one civil servant, one emigrant, and three without careers. In twenty-four out of the forty-nine lines studied, the overwhelming majority of sons became army officers, while in another eight lines more sons went to the army than to any other career, but a substantial minority became civil servants. The bureaucracy was the leading career choice for the members of six lines, and in the remaining eleven lines no particular career predominated.

There is no direct correlation between a family's wealth and the tendency for its members to choose a particular career except in the case of families in which civil servants predominated. Five out of these six families were among the wealthiest in the Ritterschaft, which is not surprising because the high costs of university education combined with the long period of service at little or no salary required of beginning civil servants made it extremely difficult for the poorer families of the Ritterschaft to send their sons into the bureaucracy.

[12] The Fronhausen branch of the von Schenck zu Schweinsberg family, along with a branch residing in Hesse-Darmstadt, spells its name "Schenk" rather than "Schenck."

Virtually all noble houses (forty-seven out of forty-nine) had at least one member who entered the army officer corps, making military service the career most widely represented among members of the Ritterschaft. Even nobles who held high-ranking positions in the bureaucracy generally sent at least one of their sons into the army.

EDUCATION

Almost all Hessian nobles received their early education from private tutors called *Hofmeister* or *Hauslehrer*, a common form of education for young nobles throughout Europe. By educating their children at home, nobles sought to maintain distance between themselves and the lower classes, especially when the family lived on its rural estate and the closest school was in the neighboring village. In such cases it was unthinkable that noble children be placed in the same class with their future subjects and servants, the children of the peasantry. Furthermore, the quality of the education provided by such tiny rural schools often left much to be desired.

Most private tutors were unemployed theology students. Since there were far too many qualified candidates for the few pastorates that became vacant each year, theology graduates generally earned their living as village schoolteachers or private tutors while waiting for an opening in a church. Serving as a tutor for a noble family brought with it the possibility that the family might later use its influence to gain a position for the tutor, particularly because many noble families were the patrons of churches in the surrounding villages and thus could appoint or approve candidates to fill vacant pastorates, as long as such candidates had studied at least two years of theology.[13]

Occasionally employment as a tutor led to a more important and higher-paying position in a noble family's service, as was the case for the theology student Johann Daniel Bockwitz, who was hired to tutor Wilhelm von Buttlar-Elberberg in 1742 and later became the administrator of the family's estates. Bockwitz's religious training proved to be a poor preparation for the duties of an administrator, however, and his successor, former seigneurial court justice Johann Noessel, later described the results: "The lavish and unlimited confidence which the most noble family von Buttlar, especially its head, placed in the former tutor (later superintendent) Johann Daniel Bockwitz, a depraved and ignorant the-

---

[13] For example, the von der Malsburg family appointed Johann Christoph Losse as pastor in Oberelsungen after he had served for six years as *Hauslehrer* in Schloss Elmarshausen. Gerhard Bätzing, *Pfarrergeschichte des Kirchenkreises Wolfhagen von den Anfängen bis 1968* (Marburg, 1975), 183.

ologian, led to the family's decline and indebtedness and finally resulted in bankruptcy proceedings."[14]

The quality of the education provided by private tutors varied greatly. Nobles with positions in the bureaucracy generally lived in Kassel or Marburg and could almost always find well-qualified tutors, because the supply of possible candidates was largest in the capital city and at the university. However, nobles living on their estates in the countryside were often less fortunate in their choice of tutors, as can be seen in Julie von Buttlar-Elberberg's description of her husband Gottlob's education in the late eighteenth century:

> As a child and youth he enjoyed the extremely spotty education of a so-called *Hauslehrer*, which barely amounted to more than a little reading, writing, and arithmetic; alongside this a so-called French governess taught him a few of the most common French expressions; however, a Frenchman would have had great difficulty understanding them. Thus equipped with this very scanty learning, as was the case for most Hessian nobles at that time, he was sent at age sixteen or seventeen to a forester in Holzhausen in the Reinhard Forest to learn forestry and hunting.[15]

Some of the poorer noble families could not afford a full-time private tutor, so their children, like Carl Friedrich von Baumbach-Freudenthal (1777–1825), received their early education in the form of private lessons from the village pastor or schoolteacher.[16] Both of these positions were poorly paid, and their holders constantly sought outside sources of income.[17] During intervals when no tutor was available for a rural noble family, the wife often took over the responsibility for the education of the children, although many noble wives had themselves not received much schooling. The education of noble daughters was often not accorded a very high priority.

One exception to the overall low level of education for noblewomen in Hesse was Karoline von Loewenstein (1772–1822), who was raised by her uncle, Dietrich von Milchling zu Schönstadt, following the death of her parents. She received a good education from tutors and private schools and then became a lady-in-waiting at the court of the Duchy of

---

[14] Hueck, "Familie von Buttlar," no. 48, p. 5.

[15] Ibid., no. 26/27, p. 1.

[16] Friedrich Wilhelm Strieder et al., *Grundlage zu einer hessischen Gelehrten, Schriftsteller und Künstler Geschichte vom 16. Jahrhundert bis auf gegenwärtigen Zeiten*, 21 vols. (Kassel, 1781–1863), 19: 11.

[17] Wilhelm Wolff, *Die Entwicklung des Unterrichtswesens in Hessen-Kassel von 8. bis zum 19. Jahrhundert* (Kassel, 1911), 457.

Nassau until it was disbanded in 1809. She then moved to Arolsen in the principality of Waldeck, where she authored a number of anonymous newpaper and journal articles and tutored young noblewomen in French, literature, and other subjects.[18]

Although tutors normally served as the primary source of education for noble children, parents also played an important role. The contributions of both parents and tutors to the education of Reinhold von Baumbach-Nassenerfurth in the early nineteenth century can be seen in his recollections of his childhood:

> For breakfast, which for us children consisted mostly of milk and white bread, we gathered in the dining room, and Mother then read us a hymn. Our tutor and governess, who had breakfasted in their rooms, were also allowed to participate in this small ceremony but generally did not. Our lessons began at eight o'clock and continued until noon except for a brief pause to eat our second breakfast, which most times consisted of bread and butter or a piece of cake. When we were not receiving instruction or doing lessons supervised by the tutor, we played outside or, when the weather was bad, in the many rooms of the house. . . . For a special treat we children were taken now and then to zoos or riding shows or other sights, and in order to interest us in plants and animals as well as minerals, the tutor encouraged the children to start collections of all kinds. . . . Governess Jacot from Switzerland encouraged us to build our own tools and toys, and the girls received everything needed to sew dolls. When we went on walks or trips, we were always shown items of technology or were told stories to stimulate our imagination or increase our knowledge of history. Often the stories stretched over several days and were therefore told in installments. Mother excelled at this. With her sewing sock in hand, surrounded by her children, she wandered through gardens, fields, and forests, never tiring of telling new, fascinating stories. Father also often gathered the little band around him and gained our complete attention with his tales of his own experiences or an occasional horror story.[19]

Despite the emphasis on education in this family, there still remained time for play with other children, including those of the peasants, whose roles in these games, however, were designed to prepare them for the subordinate roles they would play as adults. Thus for the Baumbach

---

[18] Strieder et al., *Gelehrten, Schriftsteller und Künstler Geschichte*, 19: 407–9.
[19] Baumbach, *Lebensbild*, 151–53.

children, "one of our favorite games, which was always preceded by lengthy preparations, was playing soldiers. My brother Ernst was usually the commander of one mob of peasant boys and I, Reinhold, author of these reminiscences, led the other one. When the two sides were not at war, we all gathered peacefully in a large tent; our sisters then dispensed lots of pieces of buttered bread, on birthdays also chocolate and cake."[20]

During the eighteenth century most noble youths were predestined by their parents for a military career and therefore ended their schooling at home at an early age. For some nobles, appointment as a *Fähnrich* (ensign) was preceded by several years as a page at court, where the possibilities for further education were good, but as a rule a noble youth joined a regiment as a *Fahnenjunker* (standard-bearer) in his early teens and then advanced to *Fähnrich* before becoming a lieutenant at approximately age seventeen. Such young nobles received their education from the officers of their regiments, and as a result, their knowledge outside of military drill was scanty. As one former officer, Ludwig von Baumbach-Nentershausen, wrote in 1799, "Young nobles need a broad range of knowledge, but how can parents expect this from their sons when they enter the military as *Junker* at age 15½? Where are they supposed to learn the subjects so necessary for their social station—mathematics, geometry, history, and languages—when their garrison is located in a small country town where children barely even learn how to write? As a result, the knowledge of these young nobles never extends beyond that of a sergeant, which means they only learn how to drill."[21]

In order to improve the educational level of new officers, Landgrave Frederick II established a military academy in 1778. Educational standards at the new military academy were high, for its cadets also received instruction from the faculty of the Collegium Carolinium, a new school established by the landgrave to give the capital city of Kassel its own institution of higher education. Only the nobility benefited from the educational opportunities provided by the military academy, for entry into the cadet corps was limited to individuals of noble birth.[22]

New cadets were accepted between the ages of eight and fifteen, and at age seventeen or eighteen cadets were commissioned as officers. Life as a cadet was spartan. Cadets rose at five o'clock in the summer and six in the winter, they were allowed to have only a small amount of spend-

---

[20] Ibid., 154.

[21] ARSK, Rep. VI, Gef. 17, Nr. 3, Baumbach to the Stift Kaufungen, 31 December 1799.

[22] Friedrich Wilhelm Strieder, *Grundlage zur Militär-Geschichte des landgräflich hessischen Korps* (Kassel, 1798), 227–28.

ing money (so that there would be no differences in wealth among the cadets), and they could receive visitors only on Sunday afternoons. The main subjects taught were French, military science, mathematics, riding, and fencing. Training in French was heavily emphasized; lessons from all subjects had to be translated into French by the cadets, and one instructor reported, "As far as possible, nothing but French is spoken here."[23]

The military academy was closed when the French occupied Hesse-Kassel in 1806, but after the collapse of the Kingdom of Westphalia and the return of Elector William I from exile, the cadet corps was reestablished. Entry requirements in 1815 differed from those of 1778. Admittance was no longer limited to nobles; members of the bourgeoisie were now able to send their sons to the military academy by paying a yearly fee of 250 talers. There were eighteen vacancies for paying cadets (*Pensionäre*), both noble and bourgeois, and twelve positions as Royal Cadets (*Kurfürstliche Kadetten*), which were free of cost and were reserved for sons of the nobility, who also served as pages at court. Despite the introduction of bourgeois cadets, the majority of cadets came from the nobility until the 1850s.[24]

New cadets had to be at least thirteen years old and be able to read and write as well as know elementary mathematics, history, and geography. The total period of study was four years. Cadets received a better-balanced education than in the eighteenth century because the list of subjects taught had been expanded and now included German, French, religion, nature, geography, history, mathematics, military science, freehand drawing, and military drafting. In addition cadets received instruction in fencing, dancing, and riding several times a week and participated in supervised gymnastics during their free time. Upon completion of their four years of study, cadets had to pass an examination before becoming officers, generally at age eighteen.[25]

The establishment of the military academy and the continual im-

[23] Quoted in "Kurzgefaßte Beschreibung des hochfürstlich hessischen Kadettenkorps zu Cassel," *Hessische Beiträge zur Gelehrsamkeit und Kunst*, 2 vols. (Frankfurt, 1785–87), 2: 373, 384–86. The heavy emphasis on French at the military academy was part of Landgrave Frederick II's overall preference for the French language. As one former cadet during this period reported, "Nothing but French was spoken at the court of Frederick II." Stockhausen Memoirs, 1: 8.

[24] The ratio of noble to bourgeois cadets was as follows: 1820, 15–2; 1830, 14–7; 1840, 17–8; 1850, 12–13; 1860, 14–10; 1866, 12–15. *Staatshandbuch*, 1820–66. For the development of the Hessian cadet corps in the nineteenth century see Bernhard von Poten, *Geschichte des Militär Erziehungs- und Bildungswesens in den Landen deutscher Zünge*, 5 vols. (Berlin, 1889–99), 2: 159–61.

[25] Poten, *Militär Erziehungs- und Bildungswesens*, 2: 166–67.

provement of its curriculum in the nineteenth century benefited many members of the Ritterschaft, because most knights who made the army their career had attended the academy.[26] Almost all of the remaining knights who became officers did so by serving a brief period in the ranks of their regiment and then advancing to ensign, but a handful of noble officers received their education from yet another source, a university. During the eighteenth century the University of Marburg offered courses in military science, and several nobles became officers after attending the university. In the nineteenth century a few nobles became officers after having been enrolled in law at a university, which suggests that they had been unsuccessful in their studies and had therefore turned to the military for a career. One such individual was Carl Friedrich von Baumbach-Lenderscheid, who later described his educational background as follows:

> My father had been selected at an early age for a military career by his father, and therefore his intellect received very little development. As a result, he could not reach any firm decision on how his children should be educated and thus was always unfortunate in his choice of a tutor to direct their education. I therefore received little basic knowledge, and this naturally bore little fruit at the higher schools which I attended. Consequently I had to leave the University of Göttingen just three-quarters of a year after entering it. Through the help of my father's brother, who was a government minister, I received a position as an ensign in the Carabinier regiment.[27]

For nobles who did not enter the military, the period of education by private tutors was often followed by additional schooling away from home, especially if they planned to enter a university. By the end of the eighteenth century, attendance at a secondary school (*Gymnasium*) was preferred or even required by most universities, and since the number of knights attending universities rose steadily in the late eighteenth and early nineteenth centuries (see table 6.3),[28] more and more members of the Ritterschaft were schooled for at least a few years at a Gymnasium.

---

[26] At least forty-nine out of the eighty-one Hessian officers from the Ritterschaft born between 1800 and 1849 had been cadets.

[27] StAM 340 v. Baumbach-Kirchheim, Paket 103, Nr. 1, undated autobiographical essay.

[28] Statistics on university attendance by nobles have been compiled from the following sources: Max E. Habicht, ed., *Suchbuch für die Marburger Universitäts-Matrikel von 1653–1830* (Darmstadt, 1927); StAM 305a (Universität Marburg), Acc. 1950/9, Nr. 722–29, Marburg matriculation lists for 1824–68; Götz von Selle, ed., *Die Matrikel der Georg August*

Nobles who entered a Gymnasium after receiving their early education from private tutors were often at a disadvantage in comparison to students who had attended city schools. Thus the Gymnasium in Hersfeld informed Franz Ludwig von Baumbach-Lenderscheid in 1795 that his son Carl lacked "many very necessary elementary bits of knowledge. . . . It would be better if he had made more progress for his age."[29] But despite the frequent deficiencies of the tutorial system, nobles residing in the countryside continued to receive their early education from private tutors even in the second half of the nineteenth century. For example, two *Landräte* of the 1890s, Werner von Trott zu Solz (born in 1849) and Wilhelm von Schwertzell (born in 1854), were schooled at home by tutors before entering Gymnasia, the former at age ten, the latter at sixteen.[30]

TABLE 6.3. University Attendance by Members
of the Ritterschaft

Cohort Born	Total Males	Attended University
1730–1749	99	25 (25%)
1750–1769	100	23 (23%)
1770–1789	127	33 (26%)
1790–1809	139	46 (33%)
1810–1829	147	57 (39%)
1830–1849	117	27 (23%)

Universität zu Göttingen, 1734–1837 (Hildesheim, 1937); Wilhelm Ebel, ed., *Die Matrikel der Georg August-Universität zu Göttingen, 1837–1900* (Hildesheim, 1974); August Woringer, ed., *Die Studenten der Universität zu Rinteln* (Leipzig, 1939); Georg Erler, ed., *Die jüngere Matrikel der Universität Leipzig*, vol. 3, 1709–1809 (Leipzig, 1909); Paul Hintzelmann, ed., *Die Matrikel der Universität Heidelberg*, vols. 4–7, 1704–1870 (Heidelberg, 1916); Ottfried Praetorius and Friedrich Knöpp, eds., *Die Matrikel der Universität Giessen: Zweiter Teil, 1708–1807* (Neustadt, 1957); Franz Kössler, ed., *Register zu den Matrikeln und Inscriptionsbüchern der Universität Giessen, WS 1807/8–WS 1850* (Giessen, 1976); Karl Wagner, ed., *Register dur Matrikel der Universität Erlangen* (Munich, 1918); Karl Rügemer, ed., *Kösener Korps-Listen von 1798 bis 1904* (Starnberg, 1905). Because some of the matriculation lists do not include all of the nineteenth century, it is possible that not all university attendance by knights has been included, particularly in the cohort born 1830–49. But because many students attended several universities, the amount of underrepresentation is probably not significant.

[29] StAM 340 v. Baumbach-Kirchheim, Paket 104, Lehrer Werneburg to Franz Ludwig von Baumbach, 19 April 1795.

[30] StAM 165, Nr. 6180, 6181.

The growing numbers of Hessian nobles attending Gymnasia and universities in the early nineteenth century reflected the increased value placed upon education by the nobility as a whole. On several occasions during the 1830s, the delegates of the knighthood discussed the need for raising the educational level of the nobility when they met at the annual conference in the Stift Kaufungen. In 1839 Ludwig von Baumbach-Ropperhausen, a high-ranking civil servant, urged the other delegates to recall how important the nobility had been in previous centuries and then stated that "the present Ritterschaft is but a shadow of its former self," which Baumbach attributed in part to the "inadequate intellectual preparation" of many of its members. He called for more members of the knighthood to give their sons a good education, especially in the field of law, so that:

> It will again be possible for the Ritterschaft to play a larger role in the country's administration and in the Landtag to expose and destroy the chicaneries and sophistries of the lawyers; it is even likely that if the princes of the royal houses and the *Standesherren* allow themselves to be represented by members of the Ritterschaft, which is bound to happen if we are well qualified, then allied with the peasants, with whom we have common interests, we will have a majority in the legislature.[31]

In order to increase the number of nobles studying law, Baumbach proposed the establishment of scholarships for sons of the Ritterschaft. Such scholarships would cover the costs of attending both a Gymnasium and a university and would also provide financial support during the period without pay as a probationary civil servant (*Referendar*). Response to the proposal was mixed. Some delegates noted that their families had already set up scholarship funds for their sons and therefore believed that action by the knighthood as a whole was unnecessary. Carl von Eschwege, one of the directors of the Stift Kaufungen, disagreed with Baumbach's contention that the nobility's decline was due to inadequate education; for Eschwege the causes were to be found in "the rise of standing armies and the influence of the French Revolution in Germany." He agreed that intelligence and financial improvement were necessary for the nobility but noted that the knighthood's situation in both areas had actually improved during the nineteenth century. Therefore scholarships should not be restricted to legal studies but should include other subjects as well.[32]

[31] ARSK, Rep. VI, Gef. 20, Nr. 11, minutes of the 1839 conference.
[32] Ibid.

Action on the proposed scholarship fund was slow in coming; the first scholarship was granted in 1857, when Friedrich von Trott zu Solz was awarded two hundred talers annually for four years of university study. The fund that had been established was sufficient to support only one student at a time, so the award of a new grant had to wait until the previous holder finished his studies. Unlike Baumbach's 1839 proposal, the Ritterschaft's scholarship supported knights only while at a university, not in a Gymnasium or during the period of unpaid service as a *Referendar*. Naturally, the awarding of one scholarship every three or four years did not have a significant impact upon the overall educational level of the nobility.

As nobles became more serious about university attendance and improved their preparations by attending a Gymnasium prior to beginning their university studies, the average age of nobles entering a university rose. Up to the mid-eighteenth century, nobles often received no formal schooling outside that from their tutors before matriculating at a university and therefore began their studies at an early age, generally sixteen or seventeen, although students as young as fourteen could be found. By the nineteenth century the average age at entrance had risen almost three years because students needed to attend a Gymnasium for at least a few years prior to enrolling at a university (see table 6.4).[33]

The university most often attended by members of the Ritterschaft

TABLE 6.4.
Age of Knights Entering a University

Cohort Born	Average Age	Cases
1730–1749	16.9	21
1750–1769	17.4	20
1770–1789	17.8	30
1790–1809	18.4	45
1810–1829	19.3	52
1830–1849	19.8	24

NOTE: Three knights who did not begin their studies until late in life are not included in the above averages.

[33] For the overall rise in the age of matriculation of university students in Germany during the nineteenth century see Konrad H. Jarausch, *Students, Society, and Politics in Imperial Germany: The Rise of Academic Illiberalism* (Princeton, 1982), 84, 91–92.

was the state university at Marburg. Many knights chose Marburg because it was not far from home and the cost of living there was lower than in larger German university cities. But the main reason for Marburg's popularity was that study at Marburg was specified as a precondition for service in the Hessian bureaucracy. In 1771 Landgrave Frederick II declared that all Hessian students had to study at least two years at one of the two state universities (Marburg and Rinteln) if they wanted to enter the Hessian bureaucracy.[34] The landgrave took this step to protect the state universities against the increasing competition from the newer and more renowned Hanoverian university in Göttingen. However, even before this decree was issued, noble students who planned to enter government service spent at least part of their university study in Marburg in order to learn the Hessian legal system.

Göttingen attracted many students from the Hessian Ritterschaft because the new university enjoyed an excellent academic reputation and was a center of aristocratic social life.[35] Furthermore, many nobles had estates in the area around Kassel, and for these individuals Göttingen was more conveniently located than Marburg.

In the nineteenth century noble students began to travel greater distances in order to study, and one of their main goals was the University of Heidelberg, which was famous for its legal faculty. Other students attended universities in Berlin, Leipzig, Jena, or Bonn for part of their schooling. Although students from the Ritterschaft were more mobile in the nineteenth century than they had been previously, most did not attend more than two universities (see table 6.5).

The overwhelming majority of noble students studied law, either as their only specialty or together with cameralism (see table 6.6). Few nobles studied cameralism alone because, as in Prussia, the study of law was virtually a prerequisite for entry into not only the judiciary but also the administration. Even the foreign ministry sought only young nobles with a completed legal education.[36] Cameralism was the preferred

[34] Otto Berge, "Beiträge zur Geschichte des Bildungswesens und der Akademien unter Landgraf Friedrich II von Hessen-Kassel (1760–1785)," *Hessisches Jahrbuch für Landesgeschichte* 14 (1954): 247. After the university at Rinteln (in the Hessian exclave Schaumburg) closed in the early nineteenth century, Marburg was the only remaining state university.

[35] Charles E. McClelland, "The Aristocracy and University Reform in Eighteenth Century Germany," in *Schooling and Society: Studies in the History of Education*, ed. Lawrence Stone (Baltimore and London, 1976), 150–58.

[36] The elector himself recommended that future civil servants study law. When Geyling von Altheim told Elector William I in 1803 that his ward, Wilhelm von Stein, had just started studying cameralism in Marburg, the elector replied, "It would be better if you had him study law because a jurist can be used all over." StAM 5, Nr. 12403. For the necessity for prospective members of the Prussian administration to study law see Wilhelm Bleek,

TABLE 6.5. Universities Attended by Knights

Cohort Born	Marburg	Göttingen	Heidelberg	Gießen	Berlin	Leipzig	Rinteln	Jena	Bonn	Tübingen	Erlangen	Other	Total	Number of Students	Average No. of Univ. attended
1730–1749	20	8	0	1	0	0	1	0	0	0	3	0	33	24	1.4
1750–1769	14	12	0	3	0	2	4	0	0	0	0	1	36	23	1.6
1770–1789	25	14	2	2	0	1	0	2	0	0	0	0	46	33	1.4
1790–1809	34	30	8	0	0	1	0	0	1	0	0	0	74	44	1.7
1810–1829	36	23	15	3	5	0	0	1	3	2	0	0	88	54	1.6
1830–1849	17	5	12	0	3	4	0	2	0	1	0	0	44	25	1.8

TABLE 6.6. Subjects Studied by Knights

Cohort Born	Law Only	Law and Cameralism	Cameralism Only	Forestry	Philosophy	Natural Sciences	Military Science	Other	Unknown
1730–1749	8	0	0	0	0	0	0	0	16
1750–1769	14	0	1	0	0	0	1	1	6
1770–1789	18	2	7	1	0	0	1	0	4
1790–1809	22	5	13	2	0	1	0	0	3
1810–1829	31	5	6	5	3	1	0	1	5
1830–1849	10	7	2	0	1	2	0	1	4

course of study only for the financial branch of government, and few nobles sought to enter this portion of the bureaucracy. The only other area of study that attracted more than a handful of noble students was forestry, once more scientific methods of forestry began to make the old system of apprenticeship to a forester obsolete. In the nineteenth century the interests of noble students began to expand, and some nobles studied subjects such as philosophy, natural sciences, and mathematics. One knight even studied theology and became a pastor.

The nineteenth century also brought a change in the lifestyle of noble students. Previously university study had generally been quite expensive for nobles because of the way in which they attended universities. During the eighteenth century the typical young noble did not attend a university alone; he was accompanied by his tutor and one or more servants. For example, Ludwig Rabe von Pappenheim (1750–86) entered the University of Göttingen in 1767 at the age of sixteen accompanied by his tutor, J. H. Stippius (a recent law graduate), and a servant. In Göttingen they rented four rooms plus a small room for the servant and settled into academic life. Living expenses for an aristocratic student in Göttingen were rather high in 1767. Stippius reported to Pappenheim's

Von der Kameralausbildung zum Juristenprivileg: Studium, Prüfung und Ausbildung der höheren Beamten des allgemeinen Verwaltungsdienstes in Deutschland im 18. und 19. Jahrhundert (Berlin, 1972), 114–17. At the University of Göttingen in the late eighteenth century, two-thirds of all noble students were enrolled in the field of law. McClelland, "Aristocracy and University Reform," 157; idem., *State, Society, and University in Germany, 1700–1914* (Cambridge, 1980), 47–48, 194. In the nineteenth century approximately four-fifths of nobles entering universities chose law as their field of study. Jarausch, *Students, Society, and Politics*, 87. Law remained the preferred course of study for diplomats under the German Empire as well. Cecil, *German Diplomatic Service*, 26–27.

father that for the first three months their everyday expenses such as food and lodging amounted to 156 talers, while the cost of books, lecture fees, dancing and fencing lessons, and entertainment totaled 138 talers.[37] Thus the cost of education for a noble studying at a university in the aristocratic style of the seventeenth and eighteenth centuries (with tutor and servant) could amount to one thousand or more talers per year.

Despite the high cost of Pappenheim's education, he at least omitted the extremely expensive institution of the "cavalier's tour" to the major cities of Europe after completing his studies. Traditionally the cavalier's tour had been seen by many European nobilities as the final stage in a young noble's education. During his stay in the major cities and courts of Europe he would encounter nobles from all over the continent, thereby broadening his horizons.[38]

Information about cavalier's tours by Hessian nobles is sparse, and very likely few Hessian nobles took grand tours to all the major cities of Europe, although shorter tours to various German cities were not unusual. One of the last of the large-scale cavalier's tours taken by a member of the Hessian Ritterschaft was that of Wilhelm Rudolf von Buttlar-Elberberg (1732–95). After he completed his studies at the University of Marburg, he left for Switzerland, arriving in Bern in July 1753. Following a stay in Geneva, he crossed over into France and spent more than a year visiting cities such as Lyons, Marseilles, Montpellier, Orléans, and especially Paris. Finally, after visiting Brussels and Utrecht, he returned home in January 1755. The total cost of this cavalier's tour was 19,646 talers (equivalent to the value of a medium-sized estate), and the resultant debts were an important factor in his bankruptcy in the 1760s.[39] Buttlar's extravagant and expensive cavalier's tour probably marked the end of this traditional European noble practice in Hesse-Kassel. Soon after his return the Seven Years' War began, which ruptured ties with France and damaged the nobility's economic standing. Even if no war had occurred, however, the cavalier's tour would have died out, for fewer and fewer families were able to expend so much money in such a short period of time.[40]

By the nineteenth century nobles attending a university were doing

---

[37] Gustav Rabe von Pappenheim, "Aus der Studienzeit eines hessischen Edelmannes in den Jahren 1767–1770," *Hessenland* 19 (1905): 269.

[38] Stone, *Crisis of the Aristocracy*, 692–702; Reif, *Westfälischer Adel*, 153–56.

[39] Hueck, "Familie von Buttlar," no. 48/52, p. 1.

[40] Most other German nobilities also abandoned the cavalier's tour in the eighteenth century, but such tours remained common—although somewhat smaller in scope than in the past—among members of the Westphalian *Stiftsadel* until the 1830s. Reif, *Westfälischer Adel*, 364.

so in a more frugal manner. They were no longer accompanied by tutors and in most cases did not bring servants with them. As a result, the expense of university study was considerably lower, despite the higher cost of living. Whereas Ludwig von Pappenheim spent as much as 1,000 talers per year in Göttingen in 1767, Wilhelm von Baumbach-Sontra's annual expenses at the same university fifty years later were only 520 talers, since he attended the university alone and lived frugally.[41]

Although in general the education of nobles involved career-oriented subjects such as law and cameralism, many knights took a lively interest in the arts and literature. Several noble families were active as patrons of literary and artistic circles. The Malsburgs' estate Escheberg, located near Kassel, became a well-known rendezvous for artists, musicians, scholars, and statesmen from Hesse and neighboring states. The concerts, readings, and plays performed at Escheberg under the sponsorship of Kammerherr Carl Otto von der Malsburg (1790–1855) were occasions at which Hessian and Westphalian nobles mingled with leading artists and scholars.[42] Malsburg's older brother, Ernst Otto (1786–1824), had himself achieved literary renown as a poet and translator of Spanish poetry.[43] Another branch of the Malsburg family was also very active in the arts during the nineteenth century. Caroline von der Malsburg-Elmarshausen, whose husband held a high court office (*Oberhofmarschall*), hosted a salon in Kassel for leading musicians.[44]

Another important cultural center during the nineteenth century was the von Schwertzell estate in Willingshausen. Friedrich von Schwertzell (1784–1858) attended the same Gymnasium in Kassel as Wilhelm Grimm, and the two families soon had frequent contact. Grimm often visited Willingshausen and later carried on extended correspondence with several of Friedrich's sisters, especially Karoline, who helped collect Hessian fairy tales for the Grimm brothers' famous book. Another of the sisters married the artist Gerhard von Reutern, who, along with Wilhelm Grimm's younger brother Ludwig, founded an artists' colony at Willingshausen.[45]

[41] StAM 340 v. Baumbach-Nentershausen, Paket 12.

[42] Heidelbach, *Dichter und Künstler in Escheberg*; idem., "Karl Otto von der Malsburg," in Schnack, *Lebensbilder*, 3: 288–93.

[43] Although he was famous for his poetry, Malsburg's field of study had been law. He advanced to the rank of *Regierungsrat* in the bureaucracy before becoming chargé d'affaires at the Hessian embassy in Dresden. Strieder et al, *Gelehrten, Schriftsteller und Künstler Geschichte*, 19: 437–41; *ADB*, 20: 148.

[44] Jakob Hofmeister, *Hessische Erinnerungen: Aus den Papieren eines verstorbenen kurhessischen Offiziers* (Kassel, 1882), 48–51; Malsburg, "Aufzeichnungen," 5.

[45] Wilhelm Schoof, "Georg Ludwig Wilhelm von Schwertzell, Wilhelmine von Schwertzell," in Schnack, *Lebensbilder*, 5: 376–86; Wilhelm Maurer, *Aufklärung, Idealismus*

OFFICER CORPS

The Hessian officer corps of the eighteenth century was never so exclusively aristocratic as that of Prussia, where 90 percent of all army officers were nobles as late as 1806.[46] In Hesse-Kassel large numbers of nonnobles served as officers, some attaining high rank. It was even possible for noncommissioned officers (none of whom were nobles and probably few of whom could even be called bourgeois) to become officers, especially in times of full mobilization.[47] In preparation for the campaign in America in 1776, the army commissioned eighty-eight new *Fähnriche* (ensigns): seven (all nobles) had been pages at court, twenty (nine of whom were nobles) were young officer aspirants (*Fahnenjunker*), thirteen (five of whom were nobles) had served as *Freikorporale* (individuals who were from classes exempt from military service but who enlisted to become officers after serving approximately one year in the ranks), twenty-eight (of whom sixteen were nobles) were individuals without previous military experience, and twenty (none of them from the nobility) were noncommissioned officers.[48] Thus 58 percent of the new ensigns were nonnobles.

Under normal conditions the ratio of non-nobles to nobles among the junior officers was not quite so large, but throughout the late eighteenth century non-nobles constituted almost one-half of the Hessian officer corps (see table 6.7). An almost exclusively aristocratic officer corps such as that of Prussia was not possible in Hesse-Kassel because the Hessian nobility was simply not large enough to supply a sufficient number of officers for the army, which was quite large in relation to the size of the population.[49] In the eighteenth century approximately 60 per-

---

und Restauration: Studien zur Kirchen- und Geistesgeschichte in besondere Beziehung auf Kurhessen, 1780–1850, 2 vols. (Giessen, 1930), 2: 118.

[46] Karl Demeter, *Das deutsche Offizierkorps in Gesellschaft und Staat, 1650–1945*, 4th ed. (Frankfurt, 1965), 5.

[47] W. Grotefend, "Die Ergänzung des hessischen Offizierkorps zur Zeit Landgraf Friedrichs II," *Hessenland* 14 (1900): 2–4.

[48] *Casselischen Polizei und Commerzien Zeitung*, 1 July 1776, 8 July 1776, 15 July 1776 (located in StAM, Zeitschriften). Many of the non-noble *Fähnriche*, including the bulk of the former noncommissioned officers, were placed in the *Garnison* (garrison) regiments. If these militialike units are excluded, only 44 percent of the new ensigns were non-nobles. For more information on the Hessian officer corps in the late eighteenth century see Rodney Atwood, *The Hessians: Mercenaries from Hessen-Kassel in the American Revolution* (Cambridge, 1980), 36–51.

[49] In the eighteenth century there was one soldier for every nineteen inhabitants in Hesse-Kassel, in contrast to only one for every twenty-three in Prussia. Wolf von Both and Hans Vogel, *Landgraf Wilhelm VIII von Hessen-Kassel: Ein Fürst der Zopfzeit* (Munich, 1964), 63. Even in the nineteenth century Hesse-Kassel was second only to Prussia in

TABLE 6.7. Social Composition of the Officer Corps

| Year | Nobles | | Non-nobles | | Total |
	No.	%	No.	%	
1764	260	43	341	57	601
1770	247	52	224	48	471
1780	313	55	253	45	566
1790	284	56	225	44	509
1800	256	53	223	47	479
1806	307	57	229	43	536
1814	164	37	282	63	446
1820	131	46	156	54	287
1830	133	43	173	57	306
1840	130	51	127	49	257
1850	146	53	130	47	276
1860	161	55	133	45	294
1866	162	55	130	45	292

SOURCE: *Staatshandbuch, 1764–1866.*

NOTE: The following garrison or militia units are not included in the above totals: *Garnisons Regimenter* (1764, 1770, 1780, 1806); *Land-Regimenter* (1800, 1806); *Landwehr* (1814, 1820); *Schützen Corps der Stadt Cassel* (1820, 1830). The ratio of noble to bourgeois officers in these units was as follows: 1764, 20:96; 1770, 20:97; 1780, 21:102; 1800, 14:109; 1806, 14:256; 1814, 31:111; 1820, 5:51; 1830, 3:32. In all of the other years listed in the table the army did not have such units.

cent of the members of the Hessian Ritterschaft made the army their career, and the percentage of officers among the other groups of the nobility was probably at least that high.[50] During the same period in Prussia, when every effort was made to get as many nobles as possible into the officer corps, the percentage of nobles who became officers was generally 60 to 65 percent at best.[51] If these Prussian figures can be seen as representing approximately the maximum proportion of officers that a nobility is capable of supplying, then there was little room for expansion

terms of the percentage of the population in the army. Georg von Viebahn, *Statistik des zollvereinten und nördlichen Deutschlands*, 3 vols. (Berlin, 1858–68), 3: 319.

[50] In 1835, 51 percent of all members of the Hessian Ritterschaft were active or former officers, and the percentage of officers among the other groups of the nobility was similarly high. See table 6.2 above.

[51] Otto Büsch, *Militärsystem und Sozialleben im alten Preußen, 1713–1807: Die Anfänge der sozialen Militarisierung der preussisch-deutschen Gesellschaft* (Berlin, 1962), 95–96.

of the number of officers coming from the Hessian nobility. Therefore the Hessian army had no other choice than to accept large numbers of non-noble officers. Moreover, many of the noble officers were not from Hesse-Kassel.

Bourgeois in the officer corps always enjoyed the same status as noble officers, in contrast to the bureaucracy, where an official's rank depended upon both the position he held and his social station until the mid-eighteenth century. All officers commanded high prestige in Hessian society, as can be seen in the table of ranks, where a lieutenant general took precedence over a government minister in the eighteenth century. High-ranking bourgeois officers were virtually on a par with the nobility, for marriages between bourgeois in the rank of major or above and noblewomen were not considered misalliances and high-ranking officers from the bourgeoisie were often ennobled.[52] But overall the bourgeoisie was not strongly represented in the upper ranks of the officer corps. In 1806, for example, only seventeen of the eighty field-grade officers (major and above) were bourgeois, and another two officers had been ennobled during their careers.[53] Four other high-ranking noble officers were the sons of individuals who had been ennobled, but the remaining fifty-seven nobles in the rank of major and above came from old noble families.

Opportunities for bourgeois to advance in the army increased greatly after the French occupied Hesse-Kassel in 1806 and then incorporated it into the new Kingdom of Westphalia. As in the French army, talent rather than birth was to be the criterion for the selection and promotion of Westphalian officers, but the new kingdom's brief existence did not allow enough time for a complete transformation of the officer corps. Trained soldiers and officers were needed for the campaigns of Napoleon, so the army of Hesse-Kassel was incorporated into the new Westphalian army. Out of loyalty to the elector, some officers from the Ritterschaft refused to serve in the Westphalian army, but the majority of the Hessian officers continued their military careers after 1806. Most officers, nobles and bourgeois alike, needed their salaries, and the nobles were also reluctant to anger the new regime, which might take action against their property. Those Hessian officers who at first remained loyal to the elector were imprisoned in Luxemburg.[54] By 1808 most for-

---

[52] Both and Vogel, *Landgraf Wilhelm VIII*, 64; idem., *Landgraf Friedrich II*, 100.

[53] Maj. Gen. Carl von Motz had been ennobled in 1780, and Lt. Col. Adam von Ochs received his patent of nobility in 1802. A third new noble, Major Wilhelm von Heimrod, cannot be considered a member of the bourgeoisie. He was ennobled as an infant because he was an illegitimate son of the crown prince (later Elector William I).

[54] For a detailed description of the events of this period by a Hessian officer imprisoned

mer Hessian officers were serving in the Westphalian army, although the following year a small group of these officers took part in an abortive uprising led by Colonel Wilhelm Freiherr von Dörnberg.[55]

The Napoleonic campaigns cost the nobility heavy casualties on the battlefields of Spain and Russia but also provided dazzling careers for many officers. Carl Otto von der Malsburg was still a cadet when the French occupied Hesse-Kassel, and in 1807 he became a second lieutenant in the Westphalian army. During the next seven years he saw action in Spain and Russia and was one of the survivors of the retreat from Moscow. When the Kingdom of Westphalia collapsed in 1813, Malsburg had already attained the rank of lieutenant colonel, although only twenty-four years of age. After the return of the elector, who attempted to restore the conditions of 1806, Malsburg had no desire to become a junior officer again and therefore resigned from the army.[56] In so doing Malsburg was an exception; most Hessian nobles in the Westphalian officer corps found no difficulty in changing sides in 1813 to join the campaign against their former French allies.

At the end of the Napoleonic Wars non-nobles occupied 63 percent of the officer positions in the Hessian army (in contrast to only 43 percent in 1806), but in the decades of peace that followed, the percentage of non-noble officers shrank. During this period the Hessian army declined tremendously in size because the state could no longer rely on foreign subsidies to finance a large standing army, as had been the case in the eighteenth century. In the much smaller peacetime officer corps, nobles regained numerical superiority over bourgeois by 1840. In the remaining twenty-six years of Electoral Hesse's existence, the percentage of nobles rose slightly, reaching 55 percent in 1866.[57]

Despite the large number of bourgeois officers, at times even a majority, the nobility continued to dominate the officer corps, a situation most clearly demonstrated by the differences in the ratio of nobles to non-nobles at various ranks. At the lower end of the officer corps, the bourgeoisie was quite well represented, but each step up the ladder of ranks was characterized by a higher percentage of nobles (see table 6.8).

The top-ranking positions in the army were virtually monopolized by the nobility throughout most of the eighteenth and nineteenth centuries.

---

in Luxemburg see the diary of Lieutenant Colonel Heinrich Wilhelm von Stockhausen in Stockhausen Memoirs, vols. 3–9. Stockhausen entered Westphalian service in 1808. At the end of 1812 he was taken prisoner in Russia and joined the Russian-sponsored German Volunteer Corps to fight against Napoleon.

[55] See below, chapter 7.

[56] Heidelbach, "Karl Otto von der Malsburg," in Schnack, *Lebensbilder*, 3: 289–90.

[57] *Staatshandbuch*, 1814–66.

TABLE 6.8.
Social Composition of the Officer Corps by Rank
(Ratio of Noble to Bourgeois Officers)

	1764	1780	1800	1814	1830	1850	1866
Lt. Gen.	7:0	13:0	4:0	1:0	—	0:1	—
Maj. Gen.	13:1	11:1	7:0	7:1	3:1	3:3	6:0
Colonel	12:4	20:5	12:0	6:0	6:2	4:4	7:0
Lt. Col.	22:4	21:9	8:2	14:2	5:3	11:9	6:5
Major	26:7	24:14	15:14	20:9	14:7	9:6	15:5
Captain	41:29	29:17	42:19	34:25	24:43	28:34	35:31
Staff Capt.ª	30:32	40:58	34:32	19:44	—	—	—
1st Lt.	43:74	38:27	35:38	24:56	23:43	37:31	29:39
2nd Lt.	36:132	74:74	66:90	39:145	58:74	54:42	64:50
Fähnrich	30:58	45:48	33:28	—	—	—	—
Total	260:341	313:253	256:223	164:282	133:173	146:130	162:130
% Noble	43	55	53	37	43	53	55
% Noble (Col. or above)	86	88	100	93	75	47	100

NOTE: This table does not include members of the Hessian ruling family and foreign princes granted honorary generalships in the Hessian army.

ª *Stabskapitaine*; sometimes also translated as "captain-lieutenant."

In the late eighteenth century, seven-eighths of the officers in the key command ranks (colonel and above) were nobles, and by 1800 nobles filled all of these high-ranking positions. The percentage of bourgeois in the upper ranks rose somewhat thereafter, but only in 1850 did the percentage of bourgeois in the top officer ranks equal or exceed the percentage of bourgeois in the officer corps as a whole, probably as a result of personnel changes following the 1848 revolution. This triumph of the bourgeoisie was only fleeting; within a decade the nobility again held four-fifths of the top ranks. Six years later, in 1866, all colonels and generals were noblemen. Furthermore, unlike the eighteenth century, when some of the top-ranking noble officers were bourgeois who had been ennobled by the emperor or the landgrave, almost all high-ranking noble officers in the nineteenth century had been born noble. For example, in 1866 none of the thirty-four nobles in the rank of major and above had been ennobled, and only three were the sons of individuals who had been ennobled. Three others were third-generation nobles, but most of the high-ranking officers were from old noble families; nineteen were members of the Hessian or Schaumburg Ritterschaft.

The nobility also tended to concentrate in the most glamorous branch of service, the cavalry, which was a noble stronghold in most German states. Few nobles were to be found in the more technical artillery and engineer branches, which even in Prussia were a preserve of the bourgeoisie.[58] During wartime the nobility's monopoly on positions in the cavalry declined; thus at the end of the Seven Years' War and again at the end of the Napoleonic Wars, nobles occupied only about one-half of the officers' positions in this most elite branch of service, but in the decades of peace that followed, the nobility once again dominated the cavalry. By 1850 over four-fifths of all Hessian cavalry officers were nobles (see table 6.9).

Nowhere was the monopoly of the nobility stronger than in the two elite guards regiments, the *Garde du Corps* cavalry regiment and the guards infantry regiment (called variously *Erste Garde*, *Regiment Garde*, and *Leibgarde Regiment*). These two units were stationed in the capital, and some of their officers also held positions at court. The guards regiments remained exclusively noble until 1830, when six out of seven guards cavalry officers but only twenty-six out of thirty-seven guards infantry officers were nobles. Thereafter the percentage of bourgeois officers declined, and by 1866 the *Garde du Corps* again had only noble officers, and all but two of the thirty-nine guards infantry officers were nobles.

The nobility's predominance in the elite regiments, in the cavalry,

TABLE 6.9.
Branches of Service (Ratio of Noble to Bourgeois Officers)

	1764	1780	1800	1814	1830	1850	1866
Cavalry	82:79	92:41	63:25	47:46	29:22	39:8	40:9
Nobles	51%	69%	72%	51%	57%	83%	82%
Infantry	174:232	218:186	189:173	115:207	98:136	93:94	106:94
Nobles	43%	54%	52%	36%	42%	50%	53%
Artillery and engineers	4:30	3:26	4:25	2:29	6:15	5:23	7:23
Nobles	12%	10%	14%	6%	29%	18%	23%

[58] Demeter, *Offizierkorps*, 15–16, 30–31.

and in the upper ranks of the army even as late as 1866 shows that there was no trend toward a *Verbürgerlichung* (bourgeoisification), at least in terms of numbers, of the officer corps, in contrast to most other German states, where the bourgeoisie continually increased its representation in the officer corps during the nineteenth century.[59] However, despite the strongly aristocratic composition of the Hessian officer corps, its political outlook was more liberal than that of the Prussian officer corps. In Hesse-Kassel all officers swore an oath to the constitution after 1831, and when Elector Frederick William tried to undermine the constitution in 1850, all but 36 of the 277 Hessian officers, noble and bourgeois alike, turned in their resignations in order to avoid violating their oaths to the constitution.[60]

Members of the Ritterschaft who became army officers started their careers much earlier than did those who entered the bureaucracy. Most new lieutenants were under twenty years old even in the nineteenth century, while beginning civil servants were well into their twenties because of their lengthy period of education. Furthermore, young army officers immediately received salaries, while beginning civil servants worked for years without pay, normally not advancing to salaried positions until in their late twenties or early thirties. Despite their earlier salaries, however, young army officers were not much better off financially than their counterparts in the bureaucracy. The expenses of low-ranking officers almost invariably exceeded their salaries, especially in the cavalry, where the cost of purchasing and maintaining horses and equipment was quite high. Service in the elite guards regiments also proved expensive. Captain Heinrich Wilhelm von Stockhausen reported in 1808 that he had run up considerable debts as a junior officer because of low pay and the "costs of purchasing the expensive guards uniforms, which changed twenty times during my twenty years in the Hessian Guards."[61]

In order to meet their expenses, most younger officers required supplemental income from their families or estates, and for many families the need to supplement the salaries of their officer sons caused a heavy strain on their finances. In 1857 retired Major Carl von Löwenstein applied for financial assistance from the Stift Kaufungen to educate his daughter and justified his request by stating, "The education of my children has already caused heavy expenses for me, and these have been substantially increased by the costs of equipping my two sons as offi-

[59] Ibid., 29–50. In Prussia, for example, the proportion of officers from the nobility declined from 65 percent in 1860 to 30 percent in 1913.

[60] See below, p. 239.

[61] Stockhausen Memoirs, 1: 23.

cers, especially since my eldest son joined the cavalry against my wishes. Aside from all this, I must give my sons considerable financial support, as is generally the case for young officers."[62]

Although it was possible for a junior officer to live solely from his salary, he was then able to afford only the bare necessities of life, particularly if he had to support a family. As a result, many junior officers from the Ritterschaft who had families turned to the Stift Kaufungen for financial aid, as did First Lieutenant Friedrich von Rau in 1834:

> My wife brought no wealth into our marriage and I have no idea when I will come into the possession of my own. My father's property consisted solely of the estates, which to this day are sequestered in order to satisfy his creditors. Thus I am cut off from any support from this source and must therefore live from my salary, which is sufficient to secure a modest, humble existence but simply does not permit any extra expenditures for the education of my children.[63]

Officers first received a salary adequate to support a family comfortably when they attained the rank of captain. In the mid-nineteenth century a second lieutenant received between 270 and 350 talers depending on his length of service, the location of his garrison, and his branch of service. Officers of guards units stationed in the capital received slightly higher pay, as did cavalry officers. The salary of a first lieutenant ranged between 380 and 480 talers. A captain in the second pay class received 670 to 780 talers, and a captain in the first pay class earned 1,000 to 1,080 talers. High-ranking officers were well paid. A full colonel received 1,900 talers, and generals' salaries amounted to 2,500 talers or more.[64]

While the salary of a captain or major was sufficient to ensure a reasonably comfortable existence, it took officers a long time to reach these ranks because promotions were based on seniority and occurred very slowly in the junior ranks. Normally an officer spent the first ten to eleven years of his army career as a second lieutenant, followed by an additional seven to eight years in the rank of first lieutenant. Many officers thus ended their careers in the rank of captain, but those who remained in the army and continued to advance did so at a more rapid pace.[65]

---

[62] StAM 304, Rep. II, Gef. 11–13, Nr. 31.

[63] Ibid., Nr. 18.

[64] StAM 300, Abt. 11, E 8, Nr. 28 (1846).

[65] Members of the Ritterschaft who became officers between 1815 and 1839 spent an average of 11.1 years as second lieutenants, 7.4 years as first lieutenants, 6.9 years as cap-

Although service as an army officer in the nineteenth century was not a path to riches, it still provided many knights with the chance eventually to obtain positions of high status without having to undergo the lengthy and expensive education required for the bureaucracy. Furthermore, for many nobles military service was the profession most suited to the nobility's ancient martial traditions. Therefore the Ritterschaft and the other families of the nobility continued to send many of their sons to the army, and these nobles dominated the Hessian officer corps.

BUREAUCRACY

The Hessian nobility had a long tradition of service in the bureaucracy prior to the nineteenth century. In some families members of each succeeding generation attended universities and then entered the university.[66] At the same time some bourgeois families also began to develop into *Beamtenfamilien* (civil service families). Since non-nobles were allowed to own noble estates, many of these bourgeois families purchased land or received fiefs from the landgrave over the course of time and thus began to move closer socially to the nobility. During the seventeenth and eighteenth centuries, most of these bourgeois civil servants were ennobled.[67]

By the eighteenth century the Hessian bureaucracy had begun to expand in size and had become completely separate from the court. The provincial *Regierungen* still exercised both administrative and judicial functions, but a supreme court (*Oberappellationsgericht*) had emerged by mid-century. The trend toward the separation of the judiciary and the administration became more apparent in 1785, when the largest and most important of the *Regierungen*, that of Kassel, established two subdivisions, one for judicial functions (the *Justizsenat*) and one for administrative functions (the *Verwaltungssenat*). However, the final separation

---

tains, 2.9 years as majors, and 4.7 years as lieutenant colonels before being promoted. Promotion times for younger officers accelerated somewhat in mid-century; knights who entered the officer corps between 1840 and 1854 remained second lieutenants only 7.9 years and first lieutenants only 5.9 years. StAM 11 and 300, Conduitenlisten. Similar lengthy periods of service in the junior officer ranks were common in the Prussian army during this period. See Manfred Messerschmidt, "Die preußische Armee," in *Handbuch zur deutschen Militärgeschichte, 1648–1939*, ed. Friedrich Forstmeier and Hans Meier-Welcker, 9 vols. (Munich, 1964–79), vol. 4, pt. 2, p. 25.

66 Wolfgang Metz, "Das Eindringen des Bürgertums in die hessische Zentralverwaltung" (Ph.D. diss., University of Göttingen, 1947), 55.

67 Idem, "Zur Sozialgeschichte des Beamtentums in der Zentralverwaltung der Landgrafschaft Hessen-Kassel bis zum 18. Jahrhundert," *Zeitschrift des Vereins für hessische Geschichte und Landeskunde* 67 (1956): 138–48.

of the administration and the judiciary did not occur until 1821, when the *Regierungen* became purely administrative bodies while their judicial functions were taken over by the newly created superior courts (*Obergerichten*).[68]

In 1760 Landgrave Frederick II attempted to create a more efficient central financial bureaucracy by uniting the *Rentkammer*, *Oberforstamt*, and *Kriegspfennigamt* into a new *Kriegs- und Domänenkammer* (War and Domains Board). This imitation of the Prussian bureaucracy did not prove successful, and after Frederick's death in 1785, his son William IX abandoned the attempt to remodel the Hessian bureaucracy along Prussian lines.[69]

Landgrave Frederick II also imitated another Prussian institution, the *Landrat* (county councilor), in the 1770s. As in Prussia, the *Landräte* were selected exclusively from the landed nobility and were officials of both the diet and the government. Like the War and Domains Boards, the *Landrat* system did not long survive its creator; in 1793 William IX restored the former system of numerous independent towns and districts (*Ämter*). Larger subdivisions of the provinces did not come into existence until 1821, when the country was divided into twenty-two counties (*Kreise*), each headed by a *Kreisrat* (also called a *Landrat*, although the office was no longer limited to nobles, as it had been in the eighteenth century).

Under Landgrave Frederick II the number and percentage of nobles in the upper bureaucracy increased steadily. At the time of his death in 1785, the number of nobles actually exceeded the number of bourgeois in the most important departments of the upper bureaucracy (see table 6.10).[70] As the strength of the nobility in the officer corps also increased during Frederick's reign, it appears that the landgrave was imitating his namesake Frederick the Great's preference for nobles as officers and civil servants.[71] The sharp rise in the proportion of nobles in the Hessian bureaucracy during Frederick II's reign was due both to increased recruitment of members of older noble families and to ennoblement of bour-

---

[68] Kurt Dülfer, "Fürst und Verwaltung: Grundzüge der hessischen Verwaltungsgeschichte im 16.–19. Jahrhundert," *Hessisches Jahrbuch für Landesgeschichte* 3 (1953): 190–92.

[69] Ibid., 205–7.

[70] Departments studied: *Staatsministerium*, *Oberappellationsgericht*, *Kriegs- und Domänenkammer* (*Oberrentkammer* after 1785), *Rentkammer* Hanau (1790 on), *Steuerkollegium*, *Regierungen* in Kassel, Marburg, Rintlen, and Hanau (1790 on). *Oberappellationsräte* are included in the category *Geheimer Rat*. *Staatshandbuch*, 1764–1805.

[71] As crown prince, Frederick spent four years in Prussian service during the Seven Years' War and was greatly impressed by Frederick the Great. After Frederick became landgrave in 1760, many of his closest advisers were Prussian nobles. Both and Vogel, *Landgraf Friedrich II*, 18–20.

TABLE 6.10.
Social Composition of the Bureaucracy in the Eighteenth Century

	1765			1775			1785			1795			1805		
	ON	NN	B	ON	NN	B	ON	NN	B	ON	NN	B	ON	NN	B
Staatsminister	1	2	0	5	0	0	6	0	0	3	0	0	1	2	0
Präsident/Direktor	1	2	0	1	1	1	1	1	0	0	5	0	1	3	2
Geheimer Rat	4	0	6	4	0	5	4	2	6	2	3	8	1	8	9
Rat	5	1	20	5	1	22	7	7	16	8	7	24	6	9	18
Assessor	4	1	8	3	0	4	5	1	6	5	7	7	6	3	10
Total	15	6	34	18	2	32	24	11	28	18	22	39	15	25	39
Percentage	27	11	62	35	4	62	38	17	44	23	28	49	19	32	49

ON = Old noble; NN = New noble (1st or 2nd generation); B = Bourgeoisie

geois civil servants. Upon recommendation by the landgrave, the emperor ennobled a number of prominent bourgeois families active in the civil service. In some cases two generations of a family were serving in the bureaucracy at the same time, so a single ennoblement could change the status of more than one civil servant. For example, when Geheimer Rat Johann Daniel Schmerfeld was ennobled in 1780, his three sons (two *Regierungsräte* and a *Kriegs- und Domänenassessor*) automatically became nobles also.

Table 6.10 does not include all bourgeois civil servants. The position of secretary in the various departments was always held by non-nobles, as were the overwhelming majority of offices in the technical *Berg- und Salzwerk Direktion* (Directorate of Mines and Saltworks). However, such positions were lower in rank than offices in the judicial, administrative, and financial bureaucracy and were therefore less prestigious.

Although virtually all of the leading positions in the bureaucracy (minister of state and presidents or directors of the various departments) were filled by nobles, this does not mean that talented members of the bourgeoisie could never attain the highest offices in the bureaucracy, for it was not unusual for high-ranking bourgeois officials to be ennobled in the eighteenth century. Of the eighteen individuals who served as minister of state between 1764 and 1805, only one, Jacob Sigismund Waitz, was not a noble when he became a minister (in 1764, he was ennobled shortly thereafter), but two other ministers had been elevated into the nobility earlier in their careers.[72] Three members of the Hessian Ritterschaft served as ministers of state during this period, and another two noble ministers were elected into the knighthood while in office.[73]

By the end of the eighteenth century the newest families of the nobility had become quite important for the bureaucracy. Thus in 1801 eight of the forty nobles holding offices in the key departments of the bureaucracy had been ennobled during their careers, while another seventeen were the sons of individuals who had been ennobled. Five of the new noble families were represented by two generations of civil servants (sixteen individuals in all). The most prominent of these families was the von Motz family, which included two department directors, a supreme court justice, three councilors, and an assessor in 1801.[74]

[72] The two new nobles were Moritz von Althaus (ennobled 1766) and Carl Wilhelm von Meyer (ennobled 1779). Both men had been ennobled by the emperor. Frank, *Standeserhebungen*, 1: 17, 3: 235.

[73] The three ministers from older families of the knighthood were Johann von Fleckenbühl genannt Bürgel, Carl von Berlepsch, and Wilhelm von Baumbach-Lenderscheid. Martin von Schlieffen and Friedrich Freiherr Waitz von Eschen were selected to join the Ritterschaft in 1781 and 1804 respectively.

[74] *Staatshandbuch*, 1801. Information on new nobles was obtained from Frank, *Standes-

The Hessian Ritterschaft's share of the offices in the upper bureaucracy during the eighteenth century was much smaller than that of the new nobles. Between 1765 and 1805 there were never more than nine knights in the key departments of government at any one time. One reason for the small number of knights in the upper bureaucracy during this period was the availability of a number of offices that were reserved for members of the Ritterschaft and did not require a university education or a long period of service without pay. Four *Rittersteuerobereinnehmer* supervised the collection of the tax on noble land, and all eleven *Landräte* were drawn from the ranks of the knighthood. Since these offices could be filled only by members of the Ritterschaft, they are not included in table 6.10. However, even though these positions did not require a university education, they were sometimes filled by knights who had received legal training and were already serving in the upper bureaucracy. For example, Hans Freiherr von Dörnberg (1755–1803) resigned from his office as war and domains councilor in 1798 in order to take on the much less demanding post of *Rittersteuerobereinnehmer*, which left him plenty of time to pursue his interests in historical research and writing.[75] When the new office of *Landrat* was created in 1774, approximately one-half of the positions were filled by knights who had already received a complete legal education and were serving in the junior grades of the upper bureaucracy. Noble civil servants were eager to become *Landräte* because the salary of one thousand talers greatly exceeded that of other councilors, and nobles could advance to *Landrat* much more quickly than to any other high-paying office. After the office of *Landrat* was abolished in the 1790s, most of its holders were retired with pensions, although a few well-qualified individuals returned to the regular bureaucracy. One former *Landrat*, Wilhelm von Baumbach-Lenderscheid, even advanced to the rank of minister of state by the end of his career.

The nobility was most strongly represented in the judicial and administrative branches of government (the *Regierungen* and the supreme court), and throughout the eighteenth century members of older noble families preferred to enter these two fields of government rather than the financial bureaucracy. In 1765 only two out of the fifteen civil servants from older noble families served in the financial bureaucracy; forty years later this proportion had increased only to four out of fifteen. Thus most of the nobles in the financial bureaucracy were members of new families (in 1805 thirteen out of the total of seventeen nobles).[76]

---

erhebungen; Gritzner, *Standes-Erhebungen*; *Gothaisches genealogisches Taschenbuch der briefadeligen Häuser*; Deutsches Adelsarchiv, *Genealogisches Handbuch des Adels*.

[75] Strieder et al., *Gelehrten, Schriftsteller und Künstler Geschichte*, 2: 94–96.

[76] *Staatshandbuch*, 1765–1805.

Despite close ties to the court, members of the nobility received little or no preference for entry into the bureaucracy. They were not exempt from the requirement to pass an entrance examination; nobles who wrote to the landgrave requesting positions in the bureaucracy for their sons were always told to send their sons to the Examination Commission. The members of this commission were high-ranking bourgeois civil servants who were some of the top legal experts in Hesse. They administered comprehensive written and oral examinations in Latin on complicated points of law. These tests proved to be the undoing of some noble candidates, despite their legal training. In 1799 Landrat Johann von Baumbach-Amönau wrote to the landgrave requesting that his son Wilhelm, who had just completed his studies, be given a position as an assessor. The landgrave passed this request on to the *Regierung*, which ordered Wilhelm to report to the Examination Commission. The commission found him unqualified because of flaws in both his legal arguments and his Latin. Six months later, upon his request, Baumbach was reexamined and again found unqualified, so he left Hesse and joined the bureaucracy of the Duchy of Baden, where he eventually advanced to the rank of *Geheimer Rat*.[77]

Nobles also generally received no preference for promotion in the lower and middle ranks of the bureaucracy during the late eighteenth century. Advancement through the rank of councilor (*Rat*) was based almost exclusively on seniority. In order for someone to be promoted, the position he sought had to be vacant as the result of a death, promotion, or transfer. Thus when a noble assessor wrote to ask for a promotion to councilor, he would generally refer to a vacant position and state that he was the senior assessor. Occasionally civil servants received promotions in the form of the title of the next higher rank without the corresponding salary, which was not granted until additional funds were appropriated (often years later). Only at the very highest levels of the bureaucracy was favoritism toward nobles evident. Throughout the second half of the eighteenth century, virtually all of the ministers of state and heads of the main government departments were nobles, although some of these individuals had been ennobled at some point in their careers.

Young nobles entered the administrative and judicial bureaucracies in the rank of assessor without vote, an unsalaried position. The next higher office was assessor with vote, which brought with it a small salary. Above this level came the offices of *Justizrat* and then *Regierungsrat*.[78] Senior councilors were often honored with the title *Geheimer Rat*,

---

[77] StAM 5, Nr. 4749; Baumbach, *Familie von Baumbach*, 60.

[78] The offices of *Justizrat* and *Regierungsrat* were not equal in rank or salary in the eight-

and distinguished jurists could advance to the position of supreme court justice (*Oberappellationsrat*). The top posts beneath the ministerial level were the president of the supreme court, the president of the *Regierung* in Kassel, and the directors of the *Regierungen* in Marburg, Hanau, Rinteln, and Fulda (after 1815). Most bourgeois civil servants also followed this path of advancement, although some bourgeois with long service as a secretary in one of the departments were promoted to the rank of councilor.

Salaries in the mid-eighteenth century were high and included substantial amounts of produce in addition to the cash payments. In 1760 the four supreme court justices received salaries ranging from 663 to 1,063 talers per year plus 50 *Viertel* of rye, 62 of oats, 27 of barley, 3 of wheat, and 2 of peas. This produce was worth approximately 650 talers at that time. Councilors in the *Regierungen* received between 239 and 739 talers and a somewhat smaller amount of produce.[79] During the late eighteenth century salaries became more uniform for particular ranks but declined substantially in value because produce was no longer included. By 1804 salaries had been fixed at the following levels: *Oberappellationsrat*, 850–950 talers; *Regierungsrat*, 635 talers in Kassel, 535 in Marburg; *Justizrat*, 300 talers; and assessor with vote, 100 talers.[80] The salaries of the top officials were not fixed and usually were the subject of negotiations between the government and the individual. Thus when Wilhelm von Baumbach-Lenderscheid was named minister of state in 1803 with a salary of 4,600 guilders (3,067 talers), he soon wrote to the elector saying that his salary was the lowest any Hessian minister had ever received and noting that he had had to engage a private secretary in order to protect his failing eyesight. Baumbach mentioned that his predecessor had received 7,200 guilders, but he would be satisfied with 6,000 guilders (4,000 talers), which another minister was receiving. The elector granted his request.[81]

Upper-level bureaucrats such as presidents and directors received sal-

---

eenth century. The former office only ranked in the sixth class of the table of ranks, while the latter was in the fourth class. *HLO*, 8: 120 (1803 Rangordnung). Following the separation of the judiciary from the administration in 1821, the office of *Justizrat* disappeared from the normal career progression. Those councilors in the *Regierungen* who exercised administrative functions after 1821 retained the title *Regierungsrat*, and those councilors who transferred to the newly formed superior courts received the title *Obergerichtsrat*. At the same time the division of the office of assessor into those without and those with a vote ceased. New civil servants served their unsalaried training period in the rank of *Referendar*, while the rank of assessor was the first salaried position in the upper bureaucracy.

[79] StAM 5, Nr. 14997, Kammer Besoldungs-Etat, 1760.
[80] StAM 5, Nr. 5354.
[81] StAM 5, Nr. 4826, Baumbach to elector, 6 November 1804.

aries ranging between 1,500 and 2,000 talers at the end of the eighteenth century and often held other offices such as director or member of various foundations and committees that required little work and brought in extra income. An additional source of income for all judicial officials above the rank of assessor without vote was provided by the court fees (*Sporteln*), although the lion's share of these fees went to the director of the court. In 1785 the councilors and assessors of the *Regierung* in Marburg wrote to the landgrave asking for an increase in their salaries (*Rat*, 400 talers; *Justizrat*, 300 talers; assessor, 100 talers) and stated that the director received approximately 550 talers in fees annually in addition to his 800-taler salary, while the other members of the *Regierung* received only 80 talers apiece in fees.[82]

Although the high-ranking members of the bureaucracy were well off financially, most of the younger civil servants were not. Beginning officials had to work between two and six years before they received their first salaries, which generally amounted to only 100 talers per year. An extreme case is that of Moritz August von Trott zu Solz (1770–1842), who became an assessor without vote in the *Regierung* in Marburg in April 1791. After two years he wrote to request a promotion or at least a small salary because "in the present expensive times it is impossible for me to live any longer from my family's resources, for my parents have other children to support too." This request was denied, and in November Trott was transferred to the *Regierung* in Hanau, still in the same unsalaried rank. The following month he again requested a promotion because he had been further burdened by the expenses of the move to Hanau. His request was denied on the grounds that he was unqualified for promotion because he did not yet know Hanau's laws. A renewed request for advancement was granted in May 1794, and he became an assessor with vote, although no salary was awarded to him. Finally, in May 1796 he received his first salary (200 guilders, or 133 talers) after five years of service. Four years later Trott was given a 100-guilder raise, and the following year (1801) he became a *Justizrat*. However, the remaining 100 guilders of the 400-guilder salary for this position were not granted to him until two and one-half years later. In 1806 he asked for another promotion or at least a raise because "with my present salary I cannot even buy the most essential necessities of life."[83]

The slow pace of promotions and meager salaries caused some of the most talented civil servants to seek positions in other German states. For

[82] StAM 5, Nr. 4486, Councilors and assessors of the Regierung Marburg to landgrave, 26 February 1785.

[83] StAM 5, Nr. 4540, Trott to Landgrave William IX/Elector William I, 1 November 1793, 4 December 1793, 3 May 1794, 23 April 1796, 4 March 1800, 17 June 1806.

example, Ferdinand von Schenck zu Schweinsberg, who had joined the *Regierung* in Marburg in 1784 and had advanced to *Regierungsrat* after fourteen years of service, resigned in 1803 to accept a position as *Geheimer Rat* and director of the *Regierung* of the Bishopric of Fulda at a salary of 2,000 guilders (1,333 talers). His superior, Regierungsdirektor Franz Rieß, informed the elector that the government was losing one of its most capable men.[84]

Hesse-Kassel's absorption by the new Kingdom of Westphalia in 1808 did not interrupt the careers of most noble civil servants, because the Hessian bureaucracy was incorporated into the new Westphalian bureaucracy. Unlike a number of noble army officers, who refused to serve in the Westphalian army out of loyalty to the elector, noble bureaucrats had no qualms about serving the new state. Of the seven civil servants from the Ritterschaft in 1806, at least six entered Westphalian service, and another two knights who finished their studies after 1806 also served the new regime. Virtually all other noble and bourgeois members of the Hessian bureaucracy also joined the Westphalian civil service.[85]

For most nobles, service in the Westphalian bureaucracy brought with it higher salaries and faster promotions. Thus Louis von Heydwolff, who had received only 100 talers per year as a Hessian *Regierungsassessor*, became a Westphalian judge in 1808 at a salary of 643 talers.[86] Most nobles remained in the Westphalian bureaucracy until its collapse in 1813, although Ludwig von Baumbach-Ropperhausen, a former Hessian assessor who had advanced to *Präfectur-Rat*, resigned after two years because he had felt he "could no longer help his fellow citizens."[87] One young knight, August von Trott zu Solz (1783–1840), became a loyal supporter of the new government and quickly advanced to the rank of prefect as a reward for his opposition to the Dörnberg uprising of 1808, which had included many fellow members of the Ritterschaft. Unlike most noble civil servants, Trott did not resign from Westphalian service after the French defeat at Leipzig in 1813. He remained loyal to King Jerome and even followed him to Paris. Trott's faithfulness to the Westphalian government destroyed his chances of returning to the Hes-

[84] StAM 5, Nr. 4526. When Fulda was incorporated into Hesse-Kassel after the Napoleonic Wars, Schenck returned to the Hessian bureaucracy and eventually became the justice minister.

[85] *Staatshandbuch*, 1866; *Almanach royal de Westphalie* (Kassel, 1810–13).

[86] Other junior officials made similar gains. Justizrat Carl von Hanstein (1806 salary: 200 talers) became a public prosecutor at 1,287 talers. The salary increases for higher officials, who generally remained in their old offices, were not quite so spectacular but were still substantial. The salary of Regierungsdirektor Rieß rose from 1,200 to 1,673 talers, and Regierungsrat Vultejus's salary increased from 550 to 1,055 talers. StAM 5, Nr. 4489.

[87] StAM 5, Nr. 4753, Baumbach to elector, 8 December 1813.

sian bureaucracy, and the elector even ordered his arrest in 1816, despite the general amnesty that had been granted to all former Westphalian officers and officials the previous year. Trott was eventually allowed to leave Hesse, and he entered the bureaucracy of Württemberg.[88]

When the elector returned from exile in December 1813, he ordered all former Hessian officers and officials to return to the posts that they had held in 1806, an act that was later sharply criticized by the historian Heinrich von Treitschke, who called William I the "seven years' sleeper" and noted that "majors became lieutenants again; councilors, assessors."[89] However, the order for officials to return to their 1806 positions was probably necessary to restore order following the chaos caused by the collapse of the Westphalian government, and it should be noted that these demotions were only temporary. Within the next few months most officials received one or more promotions in order to fill the many vacancies that had occurred in the bureaucracy since 1806. Thus within a year or two, most civil servants had advanced to positions equal or nearly equal to those they had held under King Jerome, although the salaries of Hessian civil servants were much lower than those paid by the Westphalian government.

In 1821 the government underwent a far-reaching reorganization. The traditional division of the country into various kinds of principalities, each with its own administrative and legal system, was replaced by a unified system with four provinces, which in turn were divided into a total of twenty-two *Kreise* (counties). At the same time the administrative and judicial branches of government were finally separated. The *Regierungen* lost their judicial functions to the newly created *Obergerichten* (superior courts) and became simply the administrative bodies for the provinces. The early nineteenth century also brought another change in the bureaucratic structure when the diplomatic service became part of the civil service as the new foreign ministry. Previously diplomats had been considered part of the court.

In the new, enlarged bureaucracy after 1821, the nobility played a smaller role numerically but still held the majority of the top positions such as ministers, presidents, and directors until the 1840s (see table 6.11). Although the total number of nobles in the bureaucracy was not much larger than the number of noble civil servants at the end of the eighteenth century, older noble families had increased their representation in the bureaucracy because ennoblement, which had played such a

[88] *ADB*, 38: 659–60.

[89] Heinrich von Treitschke, *Deutsche Geschichte im neunzehnten Jahrhundert*, 5 vols. (Leipzig, 1928), 3: 510.

TABLE 6.11. Social Composition of the Bureaucracy in the Nineteenth Century

	1825			1835			1845			1855			1865		
	ON	NN	B	ON	NN	B	ON	NN	B	ON	NN	B	ON	NN	B
Staatsminister	1	1	0	1	1	1	1	1	0	1	0	2	1	1	2
Staatsrat[a]	2	1	3	0	0	0	0	2	2	2	1	0	2	0	1
Präsident/Direktor	3	5	7	7	1	7	4	0	10	1	0	6	3	0	9
Geheimer Rat[b]	1	2	12	2	4	25	4	0	30	6	0	15	4	0	20
Rat[c]	11	0	66	4	2	71	11	2	53	16	0	37	14	1	47
Assessor[d]	1	1	35	10	0	33	11	2	34	9	0	30	5	0	38
Referendar[e]	4	0	19	13	2	22	10	0	43	4	1	57	10	0	76
Total	23	10	142	37	10	159	41	7	172	39	2	147	38	2	193
Percentage	13	6	81	18	5	77	19	3	78	21	1	78	16	1	83

ON = Old noble; NN = New Noble (1st or 2nd Generation); B = Bourgeois

SOURCE: Staatshandbuch, 1825–66. Departments studied: Interior Ministry, including Regierungen and Landratsämter; Justice Ministry, including Oberappellationsgericht and Obergerichte; Finance Ministry; and Foreign Ministry.

[a] Individuals who headed a ministry without receiving the title minister; a Staatsrat (sometimes called Ministerialrat) usually outranked a department director in the Table of Ranks.

[b] Includes Oberappellationsräte

[c] Includes Landräte

[d] Includes Kreissecretäre

[e] Apprentice; nonsalaried position

prominent role in swelling the ranks of noble civil servants during the previous century, had become much less prevalent. Thus in 1805 twenty-five of the forty nobles in the bureaucracy belonged to new families, whereas in 1865 all but two of the forty noble civil servants were in at least their third generation of nobility. The number of civil servants from the Ritterschaft rose from eight in 1805 to seventeen in 1865.

The continued importance of the nobility in the Hessian bureaucracy was most evident at the ministerial level. Thirteen of the twenty-four individuals who became finance, interior, justice, or foreign minister between 1821 and 1866 were of noble birth, and another four ministers had been ennobled earlier in their careers. All but one of the eight war ministers came from the nobility. A total of six members of the Ritterschaft rose to the rank of minister after 1814: one as war minister, three as foreign minister, and two as justice minister.[90] It is perhaps revealing of the liberal political leanings of many of the officials from the Ritterschaft that the only appointments of knights to the leadership of a ministry outside the traditional noble strongholds of war and diplomacy came as the result of popular unrest. Thus the liberal Ferdinand von Schenck zu Schweinsberg was named justice minister in 1830 after widespread disturbances swept Hesse following the July revolution in France. He served ten months before being fired by the elector for his liberal views. In 1848 Moritz von Baumbach-Kirchheim became justice minister in the "March Ministry" (*Märzministerium*)—the liberal government formed as a result of the March 1848 revolution. Two years later he was replaced by the strongly conservative bourgeois politician, Ludwig Hassenpflug.[91]

In addition to the actual ministers, twenty-six individuals were placed in charge of ministries, sometimes for a number of years, without ever receiving the title of minister. Only six out of the nineteen provisional directors of ministries other than the war ministry were nobles, but four

[90] For lists of the ministers in the nineteenth century see Thomas Klein, ed., *Hessen-Nassau (einschließlich Vorgänger-Staaten)*, Grundriß zur deutschen Verwaltungsgeschichte, vol. 11 (Marburg, 1979), 52–60. For biographical information about ministers who served from 1831 to 1866 see Harald Höffner, "Kurhessens Ministerialvorstände der Verfassungszeit" (Ph.D. diss., University of Gießen, 1981), 73–361.

[91] Günter Franz, "Ferdinand Freiherr von Schenck zu Schweinsberg (1765–1842), Kurhessischer Staatsminister," in Schnack, *Lebensbilder*, 4: 331–37. For Baumbach see *ADB* 3: 154–56. Another member of the *Märzministerium* was the head of the foreign ministry, Wilhelm von Schenck zu Schweinsberg (son of Ferdinand), whom the elector chose as a counterweight to the liberal ministers in the cabinet. To the elector's dismay, Schenck turned out to be even more liberal than the others. Losch, *Geschichte des Kurfürstentums*, 239, 258–59.

CAREERS OF NOBLES

out of the seven officers who temporarily headed the war ministry without later advancing to war minister were nobles.

The nobility was strongly represented in all branches of government in the nineteenth century. After the 1821 reorganization, the number of nobles was largest in the judiciary and smallest in the administration, but this relationship was reversed in the decades that followed. Nobles also generally held approximately one-quarter of the positions in the financial bureaucracy and soon completely monopolized the diplomatic corps (see table 6.12).

As with the nobility as a whole, members of the Ritterschaft also began to shift from careers in the judiciary to careers in the administrative and diplomatic bureaucracies.[92] Part of the increased number of knights in the administration came in the office of county councilor (*Kreisrat* or *Landrat*). In the eighteenth century only members of the Ritterschaft could become *Landräte*, but when the office was reestablished in 1821, no nobles were appointed to this position, which now required a university education and prior service in the bureaucracy. In the decades that followed, young knights who entered the bureaucracy began to prepare themselves for the office of *Landrat* by asking to serve part of their probationary time as an unpaid *Referendar* in a *Kreisamt* (county office), working under a *Landrat*. This prepared them for later advancement to a salaried position as *Kreissecretär* (county secretary) and eventually to *Landrat*, as was the case for Julius von Buttlar-Elberberg. He became

TABLE 6.12. Social Composition of the Bureaucracy by Ministry

Ministry	1825 N	1825 B	1835 N	1835 B	1845 N	1845 B	1855 N	1855 B	1865 N	1865 B
Justice	13	50	18	75	14	88	7	81	12	122
Interior	7	66	11	59	17	57	18	54	15	54
Finance	8	24	9	23	9	26	8	12	6	16
Foreign	4	2	8	1	9	0	7	0	7	1

N = Nobles; B = Bourgeois

[92] Civil servants from the Ritterschaft served in the following ministries:

	1825	1835	1845	1855	1865
Justice	6	5	6	4	3
Interior	3	4	4	5	5
Finance	2	3	3	3	4
Foreign	1	2	4	5	5

Kreissecretär in Fritzlar in 1838 after seven years as a *Referendar*, the last two in the *Kreisamt*. Following an additional seven years' service as county secretary, Buttlar advanced to *Landrat*.[93] This pattern was followed by other nobles, and the number of noble *Landräte* gradually increased, although they never outnumbered their bourgeois counterparts until after Hesse-Kassel's annexation by Prussia in 1866.[94]

An even larger number of knights began to enter the diplomatic service in the nineteenth century, as the foreign ministry began to recruit nobles with legal training for diplomatic posts. Applicants for positions in the foreign service could not apply directly after completing their studies; they had to serve at least one year as a probationer at a provincial government or superior court (*Regierungs-* or *Obergerichtsreferendar*).[95] In 1842 the foreign ministry drew up the following list of "Necessary Characteristics for a *Referendar* in the Foreign Ministry":

1. Good political (monarchical) sentiments
2. Especially trustworthy character
3. Thorough legal education
4. Fluency in writing and speaking the French language
5. Nobility
6. Independent wealth[96]

The foreign ministry was quite successful in attracting members of the Ritterschaft. After 1821 eight knights joined the diplomatic service. Six of these had previously been Hessian *Obergerichtsreferendare*, one had been an *Obergerichtsassessor* in Württemberg, and one had previously served eight years as a cavalry lieutenant, although he had completed his

---

[93] StAM 16, Rep. I, Kl. 9a, Nr. 17.

[94] Social composition of the Hessian *Landräte*:

	1825	1835	1845	1855	1865
Nobles	0	1	3	6	5
Bourgeois	22	20	17	14	14

Source: *Staatshandbuch*, 1825–65

In Prussia the office of *Landrat* remained a preserve of the nobility. In the eighteenth century all *Landräte* were aristocrats, and in the nineteenth century almost three-quarters of the *Landräte* were nobles prior to 1848. Even as late as 1901, 65 percent of the *Landräte* came from the nobility. Hubert C. Johnson, *Frederick the Great and His Officials* (New Haven, 1975), 288; Koselleck, *Preußen*, 689.

[95] StAM 9a, Nr. 239, requirements for applicants, 1833.

[96] StAM 9a, Nr. 228, memorandum of 1 November 1842. The predominance of nobles in foreign service remained strong throughout the nineteenth century not only in Germany but in other European countries as well. See Cecil, *German Diplomatic Service*, 58–78.

legal studies and had served briefly as a legal apprentice (*Rechtspracticant*) before volunteering for the campaign against Denmark in 1849.[97] The knights who had been recruited from the ministry of justice had worked there between two and four years without pay, but soon after their transfer to the foreign ministry, they were promoted to salaried positions. Philipp Freiherr von Dörnberg, for example, became a legation secretary in 1842 just two months after joining the foreign ministry; his total period of unpaid service was only slightly more than two years.[98] In contrast, beginning civil servants in the judiciary and administration served three to four times as long without pay.

The foreign ministry provided tremendous opportunities for advancement to members of the Ritterschaft. Three knights rose to the rank of foreign minister before 1866, although one of them had not previously served as a diplomat.[99] Promotions in the foreign ministry occurred much faster than in the other branches of the bureaucracy. Nobles not only quickly advanced to the position of legation secretary; they also moved up to legation councilor (*Legations-Rat*) within another four or five years.

Diplomats' salaries were high. A legation secretary received 900 talers, while a councilor received 1,200 talers plus a supplementary diplomatic salary that depended upon the city to which he was posted. This extra income was often several times the normal salary, giving most ambassadors a total income of between five and six thousand talers per year. But the very expensive mode of living associated with foreign diplomatic posts ensured that ambassadors could not save much if any of their salaries and were often forced to rely on their personal wealth or contract debts. In 1864 the Hessian ambassador to France, Eduard von Goeddaeus (not a knight), resigned stating that "no ambassador can live properly in Paris on less than ten thousand talers per year."[100] No member of the Ritterschaft left the diplomatic corps for financial reasons, but the Paris ambassadorship caused Philipp Freiherr von Dörnberg to contract substantial debts in the 1850s.[101]

One example of a knight's career in the foreign ministry is that of Alexander von Baumbach-Ropperhausen (1814–94), who studied law at

---

[97] The personnel records of the knights in the foreign ministry are contained in StAM 9a and 250 (Justizministerium), Acc. 1880/20.

[98] StAM 9a, Nr. 227, 373, and 387.

[99] Friedrich von Trott zu Solz had been a *Geheimer Rat* in the justice ministry before becoming foreign minister in 1832.

[100] StAM 9a, Nr. 471, diplomatic protocol of 3 August 1864.

[101] StAM 9a, Nr. 373. For the financial problems of diplomats in the late nineteenth century see Cecil, *German Diplomatic Service*, 47–53.

the universities of Marburg, Berlin, and Göttingen from 1832 to 1836 and then entered the bureaucracy. After three and one-half years as an *Obergerichtsreferendar*, Baumbach was recruited by the foreign ministry in 1840. The following year he became legation secretary in Vienna with an annual salary of one thousand talers. Two years later he was transferred to Munich as interim chargé d'affaires. In 1849 Baumbach was promoted to *Legations-Rat* and returned to the foreign ministry in Kassel. In September 1850 he was appointed to head the ministry (in the rank of *Geheimer Legations-Rat* rather than minister) as part of the conservative Hassenpflug government, and in 1853 he was formally named minister. When Hassenpflug left office two years later, Baumbach resigned as minister. For the next eleven years he served as ambassador to France and then to Austria before being pensioned by the Prussians in 1866.[102]

Nobles serving in the administrative, judicial, and financial bureaucracies did not advance as rapidly as their contemporaries in the diplomatic service, and the period of service without pay was also much longer. In Hesse-Kassel, as in Prussia, the number of applicants for positions in the bureaucracy grew much faster than the number of salaried positions as the universities turned out more and more educated individuals.[103] As a result, the number of unpaid *Referendare* rose from twenty-three in 1825 to eighty-six in 1865, and the time prospective civil servants spent as *Referendare* grew longer and longer. The period of unpaid service by members of the Ritterschaft is shown in table 6.13.

Even after civil servants were promoted to salaried positions in the nineteenth century, their financial worries were not over. The starting salary for an assessor in the 1830s and 1840s was only 400 talers, increasing to 600 talers after several years. Councilors earned between 800 and 1,200 talers as late as 1848, even though all the councilors of the *Regierung* in Kassel had signed a petition back in 1815 protesting against their totally inadequate salaries and claiming that the lowest salary on which a councilor could live was 1,200 talers.[104] At that time *Regierungsräte* were still getting a share of the court fees, but the government reorganization of 1821 ended this practice while at the same time increasing salaries to make up for most of the loss.[105]

[102] StAM 9a, Nr. 3700; Losch, *Geschichte des Kurfürstentums*, 260, 297.

[103] By the 1850s Prussian *Referendare* generally served between ten and twelve years before advancing to their first salaried positions. John R. Gillis, *The Prussian Bureaucracy in Crisis, 1840 to 1860* (Stanford, 1971), 42–43.

[104] StAM 5, Nr. 4457, memorandum of 10 September 1815.

[105] Obergerichtsrat Ludwig von Baumbach-Ropperhausen complained that the loss of

TABLE 6.13.
Period of Service without Pay

	Born	Became Referendar	Years without Salary	First Salaried Position
JUDICIARY				
Moritz v. Schenck zu Schweinsberg	1801	1823	4½	Obergerichts-assessor
Ernst v. Baumbach-Kirchheim	1804	1825	5½	Obergerichts-assessor
Friedrich v. Urff	1805	1829	10	Obergerichts-secretär
Edwin v. Bischoffs-hausen	1810	1833	4½	Justizamts-assessor
Georg v. Hesberg	1819	1847	4½	Unterstaats-procurator
Heinrich v. Heydwolff	1823	1849	9	Justizamts-assessor
ADMINISTRATION				
Hermann v. Baumbach-Kircheim	1809	1830	7	Kreissecretär
Julius v. Buttlar-Elberberg	1805	1831	7	Kreissecretär
Eduard v. Baumbach-Lenderscheid	1814	1839	5	Kreissecretär
Carl v. Eschwege	1826	1853	8	Kreissecretär
FINANCE				
Wilhelm v. Schwertzell	1800	1827	5	Oberzoll-assessor
Hermann v. Dörnberg	1813	1839	4	Oberfinanz-assessor
Ernst v. Eschwege	1818	1846	9½	Oberfinanz-assessor

Not all nobles who entered the bureaucracy were able to work their way up the ladder to the rank of councilor or higher. Some were not able to obtain a position as an assessor in one of the central departments and instead had to settle for the office of *Justizbeamter* (justice of the peace), a position equal in rank to that of an assessor and somewhat better paid but offering very few chances for advancement.

Nobles without a university education could no longer seek the well-paid prestigious offices that once had been reserved for members of the Ritterschaft, *Landrat* and *Rittersteuerobereinnehmer*, because by the nineteenth century the former office required a university education and the latter had been eliminated. As a result some nobles entered the lower bureaucracy in low-paying positions such as *Strassenbaukommissar* (road construction supervisor) or tax collector.[106] These nobles must have taken these positions out of financial necessity, for there was no prestige to be gained from such offices.

In the nineteenth century many knights began to complain that the Ritterschaft had been deprived of the substantial influence it had previously enjoyed in the bureaucracy. In the 1820s Wilhelm von Baumbach-Sontra, who had resigned from the bureaucracy after one year in order to administer his estate, wrote, "In Hesse the nobility is not asking for preference over the bourgeoisie for positions in the bureaucracy but simply for an equal chance. Unfortunately this goal is still far removed."[107] At the annual conference of the Ritterschaft in 1847, Carl von Eschwege presented a list of the former rights and privileges that had been taken away from the Ritterschaft in recent times. Eschwege described the small number of nobles, especially knights, in the upper bureaucracy and stated, "In contrast one can find members of the Ritterschaft among the actuaries, secretaries, lower road and tax officials, foresters, and forest overseers, something which did not occur previously, and the cause of this does not lie solely in their lack of qualification. It would be inter-

---

Sporteln signified a financial loss for him, because before the change he had received a salary of 785 talers plus 266 talers in fees for a total of 1,051 talers but his new salary amounted to only 1,000 talers. StAM 16, Rep. I, Kl. 4, Nr. 17, Baumbach to interior ministry, 6 April 1828.

[106] For example, Wilhelm von Schutzbar genannt Milchling (1794–1863) served as a *Strassenbaukommissar*, and Louis von Trott zu Solz (1819–88) was a *Wege- und Brückengelderheber*.

[107] StAM 340 v. Baumbach-Kirchheim, Nr. 12, undated memorandum (1820s). At this time the Ritterschaft and Elector William II were on extremely bad terms because of the Countess Reichenbach scandal and Wilhelm's infringement of important rights of the knighthood (see below, chapter 7), so the elector may actually have been discriminating against members of the Ritterschaft.

esting to compare the composition of the upper bureaucracy with that of other German states to see if anywhere else the nobility, especially the Ritterschaft, is so poorly represented."[108]

Despite such complaints, the Ritterschaft and the other types of nobles in Hesse-Kassel continued to play an important role in the upper bureaucracy during the nineteenth century. Although the percentage of noble civil servants declined as the bureaucracy expanded, the number of nobles rose, and nobles held the majority of the top posts in government until the middle of the century. As for the Ritterschaft in particular, the number of its members in the upper bureaucracy gradually increased. In 1825 there were ten knights in salaried positions and another two as *Referendare*; by 1865 these totals had increased to thirteen and four respectively.

The Prussian annexation of Hesse-Kassel in 1866 was at first a major blow to the members of the Ritterschaft in the bureaucracy, because many were serving in the foreign ministry and were dismissed by the Prussians. Nobles in the finance, interior, and justice ministries were more fortunate, as they were all taken over into the new Prussian bureaucracy for the *Regierungsbezirk* (administrative district) Kassel. However, during the first decades after the annexation, possibilities for advancement were much more limited because nobles could no longer hope to advance to the rank of minister, and even the remaining top positions were filled by Prussian officials. Thus in 1875 there were only five members of the Hessian Ritterschaft in the bureaucracy of *Regierungsbezirk* Kassel: two *Regierungsräte*, two *Landräte*, and one assessor. In the decades that followed, the number of knights in the bureaucracy increased, and by 1900 one was *Regierungspräsident*, while two others were councilors (one in the *Regierung*, the other in the *Oberlandesgericht*) and two were assessors. But the biggest gain for the Ritterschaft came in the position of *Landrat*, an office held by eight knights in 1900. Eight of the remaining fourteen *Landräte* were also nobles, which clearly demonstrates the Prussian preference for nobles in this office.[109]

---

[108] ARSK, Rep. VI, Gef. 2–3, Nr. 7.

[109] *Königlich preußischer Staatsdienst-Kalender für den Regierungsbezirk Kassel* (Kassel, 1867–1914). The percentage of *Landräte* from the nobility was higher in *Regierungsbezirk* Hesse-Kassel than in other districts in western Prussia but not as high as in the eastern provinces. Thus in the years 1890–1918 nobles filled 86.7 percent of the positions as *Landräte* in Pomerania but only 41.5 percent in the Rhineland. Lysbeth W. Muncy, "The Prussian *Landräte* in the Last Years of the Monarchy: A Case Study of Pomerania and the Rhineland in 1890–1918," *Central European History* 4 (1973): 307, 317.

FORESTRY AND COURT OFFICES

A career as a forestry official was also quite socially acceptable for a noble. The forestry service had close ties to the court, and during the eighteenth century senior forestry officials served simultaneously in the court as the monarch's chief hunting officials. As a result, nobles monopolized the upper-level forestry positions. The top officials, the *Oberjägermeister* and the *Landjägermeister*, as well as all of the seven to eight forest inspectors (*Oberforstmeister* and *Forstmeister*) were nobles, while non-nobles occupied all of the lower-ranking positions: senior forester (*Oberförster*), forester (*Förster*), and forester's assistant (*Forstläufer*), with 23, 153, and 458 individuals respectively at the end of the eighteenth century. The lines between the upper and lower forestry services were strictly drawn, so non-nobles could not expect to advance beyond the rank of *Oberförster* in the eighteenth century. Similarly, young nobles who entered the forestry service during this period did not start out in the lower ranks but were named *Jagdjunker* or *Forstjunker* and placed as unpaid trainees in forestry offices. Their first salaried position was as a forest inspector, not a forester.[110]

In contrast to young civil servants, nobles in the forestry service were able to advance more quickly to salaried positions although, as in the regular bureaucracy, salaries for junior officials were quite low. For example, Gottlob von Buttlar-Elberberg became a *Jagdjunker* in 1788 at the age of nineteen and the following year was granted an annual allowance of 70 talers. In 1793 he also received a court appointment as a *Kammerjunker* at 100 talers per year, and three years later he was promoted to *Forstmeister* with an initial salary of 400 talers. In 1799 Buttlar became an *Oberforstmeister*, and within five years his total salary was 900 talers.[111]

Like Buttlar, many noble foresters also held court appointments at some point in their careers, and some nobles managed to combine careers in the forestry service and at court, advancing simultaneously up both ladders of promotion. Ferdinand von Baumbach-Ropperhausen (1786–1862) became a *Jagdjunker* in 1803 after studying forestry at the universities of Marburg and Göttingen. Following service as a forester during the Westphalian administration, he became a *Forstmeister* in 1814 and that same year was named a *Kammerjunker* at court. Three years

[110] Between 1764 and 1800 there was only one instance of a non-noble holding an office in the upper forestry service, and during the same period no nobles held low-ranking forestry positions. *Staatshandbuch*, 1764–1800 (checked at five-year intervals).

[111] StAM 5, Nr. 18378. Buttlar was exiled for his part in the 1809 anti-French uprising, but he became the *Landforstmeister* after the elector's return from exile. Hueck, "Familie von Buttlar," no. 26.

later he was promoted to *Oberforstmeister* and shortly thereafter received the title *Kammerherr* at court. Further promotions to *Hofjägermeister* and *Oberjägermeister* followed in 1821 and 1831 respectively, although these positions were now purely court appointments.[112]

Despite the lack of formal educational requirements for foresters in the eighteenth century, many noble forestry officials had attended a university. Five out of the fourteen members of the Ritterschaft born between 1730 and 1779 who became forestry officials had been students, and the proportion of students was even higher among the knights who entered the forestry service in the nineteenth century: sixteen out of twenty-five (born between 1780 and 1849) had attended a university. The increased educational level of foresters was due to the introduction of new scientific methods of forestry and to the government's adoption of stricter entrance requirements for foresters following the establishment of a forestry institute in Fulda in 1816. All candidates for the forestry service had to attend the institute for at least two years or pass its examination.[113]

Along with improvements in the educational level of forestry officials, the nineteenth century saw an end to the nobility's total domination of the upper forestry service. In the 1820s a bourgeois, Ernst Hartig, was named to head the service as *Landforstmeister*, while another bourgeois, Ferdinand Ortlöpp, was named one of the five *Oberforstmeister* (this was, however, a special case because Ortlöpp had not risen through the ranks but had received his appointment by virtue of being the brother of the elector's mistress). In addition, three non-nobles became forest inspectors (*Forst-Inspektoren*), a new position that had the same function and occupied the same place in the table of ranks as the office of *Forstmeister*. However, the five noble forest inspectors also bore the title *Forstmeister*, a distinction that none of their non-noble colleagues shared.

The breakdown of class barriers in the forestry service continued in the 1830s as more non-nobles began to receive the titles of *Forstmeister* and *Oberforstmeister*. Furthermore, nobles who entered the forestry service no longer advanced immediately to *Forstmeister* after completing their training; instead they served as *Oberförster* or even *Förster*. However, differences in birth did not completely disappear from the forestry service. All noble trainees received the title of *Forstjunker* during their appren-

---

[112] In the eighteenth century the *Oberjägermeister* headed both the forestry office (*Ober-Forst-Amt*) and the court hunting office (*Hofjägerei*), but by the nineteenth century this position had become solely a court appointment; the forestry service was headed by the *Landforstmeister*. Ferdinand von Baumbach's records are contained in StAM 5, Nr. 12399, 12405; StAM 300, Abt. 11, B 1, Nr. 37.

[113] *Sammlung von Gesetzen*, 1 (1816): 51–52; 2 (1818): 42–44.

ticeship and retained this title during their service as *Förster* and *Ober-förster*. Since a *Forstjunker* was in the sixth class of the table of ranks while even an *Oberförster* was only in the eighth class, noble foresters continued to enjoy higher status than their non-noble colleagues.

The number of nobles in the upper forestry service remained fairly constant in the nineteenth century, but the percentage of nobles declined sharply in the 1850s, when the number of forest inspectorships almost tripled as the result of a reorganization of the forest districts. Despite this massive influx of non-nobles, the upper forestry service maintained its aristocratic tone. In 1860 the *Landforstmeister* and both *Ober-forstmeister* were members of the Ritterschaft, all six noble forest inspectors were *Forstmeister* while only two of the sixteen non-noble forest inspectors bore this title, and the four noble trainees were all *Forstjunker* but the one bourgeois trainee was not.[114]

The nobility had thus remained quite powerful in the upper forestry service during the nineteenth century, and it is not surprising that nobles also continued to control the royal court in this period. Positions at court remained reserved for nobles from old, distinguished families. Individuals who made the court their career often advanced through a specific progression of ranks just as in the bureaucracy. The first appointment was generally as an unpaid *Hofjunker*; after this came the salaried offices of *Kammerjunker* and then *Kammerherr*. There were only six high-level positions at court. The senior official was the *Oberkammerherr*, and the names of the other positions varied but generally included the *Hof-marschall*, *Oberjägermeister*, *Oberstallmeister*, and *Oberschenk*.

Members of the Ritterschaft frequently received court appointments as the result of service in one of the elite guards regiments. Like many officers from the knighthood, Carl Ludwig von Gilsa (1753–1823) served as a page at court before becoming an officer in the *Garde du Corps* cavalry regiment stationed in Kassel. Soon afterward he was named a *Hofjunker* and granted a salary of 264 talers to supplement his meager pay as a lieutenant. Further promotions to both *Rittmeister* (cavalry captain) in the army and *Kammerjunker* at court followed, and in 1788 Gilsa became one of the landgrave's adjutants and was named a *Kammerherr*. Shortly thereafter Gilsa's active military career ended, but he continued to rise at court and was *Oberstallmeister* at the time of the French takeover. Gilsa continued his career under King Jerome and became *Großhofmeister* to the queen.[115]

The most widely held court office was that of *Kammerherr* (chamber-

---

[114] *Staatshandbuch*, 1814–66.
[115] StAM 5, Nr. 12381, 12386. For a biography see Gilsa, *Oberstallmeister von Gilsa*.

lain). This title was frequently granted to nobles in middle- or high-level positions in the bureaucracy or forestry service, although without any additional salary. In addition, several nobles were full-time chamberlains in residence at court and received a salary of 1,200 talers, which was equivalent to that of a senior councilor.

Although the court remained exclusively the province of the nobility in the nineteenth century, the small number of full-time court offices meant that few nobles were able to make a career in court service. However, those who did could eventually advance to positions of high salary and status.[116]

THE ABOVE STUDY of the offices held by the Hessian nobility presents a seemingly static picture: the types of careers chosen by members of the Ritterschaft in the nineteenth centuries were identical to those chosen in previous centuries, the nobility dominated the Hessian officer corps as strongly in 1866 as at any time in the preceding one hundred years, and the court continued to be a preserve of the nobility. Only in the bureaucracy and the forestry service did the nobility lose its numerical advantage over the bourgeoisie, and this resulted in both cases primarily from expansion. Even though the proportion of officials from the nobility declined in these careers, the number of nobles remained steady. Thus the overall position of the Hessian nobility as a service aristocracy remained essentially the same in the nineteenth century as it had been in the eighteenth.

This apparent lack of change is, however, misleading, for society had undergone considerable transformation during this period. Emphasis was now placed on qualifications for office rather than birth in most areas of government service. Thus the Hessian nobility's continued ability to secure large numbers of government offices resulted not from sheer inertia but from the nobility's efforts to adapt to new requirements and changing circumstances. Increasing numbers of nobles attended Gymnasia and universities in preparation for careers in the bureaucracy or forestry service, while others sought and gained admission to the military academy to prepare themselves for careers in the army.

The Hessian nobility's success in securing government offices far out of proportion to its numbers was not an isolated phenomenon. Elsewhere in Germany nobles also continued to play an important role in government service during the nineteenth century. In Prussia, for ex-

---

[116] In the 1830s the *Oberkammerherr* and *Oberhofmarschall* received an annual salary of 3,000 talers each and ranked in the highest class of the table of ranks. StAM 7a/1 *Oberhofmarschallsamt*, Fach 35, Nr. 1 a–c.

ample, the proportion of nobles in the administrative bureaucracy increased substantially after 1825, particularly in the leading positions, and the nobility also continued to dominate the upper ranks of the officer corps. Nobles were also strongly represented in the top levels of the Bavarian bureaucracy.[117] But many of the nobles holding government offices in these and other German states in the nineteenth century were new nobles, whereas in Hesse-Kassel, with its low level of ennoblement, older noble families had succeeded in maintaining their position as a service aristocracy.

[117] For the nobility's influence in the Prussian and Bavarian bureaucracies see Koselleck, *Preußen zwischen Reform und Revolution*, 434–36, 680–90; Gillis, *Prussian Bureaucracy*, 206, 209–12, 254; Nikolaus von Preradovich, *Führungsschichten*, 104–23; Muncy, *Junker in the Prussian Administration*, 158–219; Walter Schärl, *Die Zusammensetzung der Bayerischen Beamtenschaft von 1806 bis 1918* (Kallmünz, 1955), 32–49. For the nobility's role in the officer corps see Demeter, *Offizierkorps*, 29–50; Preradovich, *Führungsschichten*, 124–53; Hermann Rumschöttl, *Das bayerische Offizierkorps 1866–1914* (Berlin, 1973), 61–143.

· 7 ·

THE POLITICS OF THE NOBILITY

The political outlook of the Hessian nobility defies easy characterization because nobles held a wide range of political opinions. Some nobles were, as is to be expected, extremely conservative, clinging desperately to all of their traditional privileges or even trying to turn the clock back to undo reforms already in existence. Other nobles were more pragmatic, seeking to defend their interests if possible but willing to bow to the inevitable once times changed. Some nobles not only accepted reforms but worked actively to achieve them. These liberal nobles were almost all university-educated and, for the most part, served in the bureaucracy where they worked side by side with members of the bourgeoisie and learned to place the interests of the state above those of individual classes.[1]

Contacts between nobles and bourgeois were not limited solely to their work together in the bureaucracy or other government service such as the officer corps. By the late eighteenth century, members of the nobility and bourgeoisie were meeting together in art academies, reading societies, social clubs, and the exclusive *Société des Antiquités* (a new learned academy). Furthermore, at least in the capital city, the two groups were also frequently neighbors, building their houses in the same areas.[2] And the increasing rate of intermarriage was yet another sign of the frequent contacts between nobles and bourgeois.

Another significant source of social contact between nobles and bourgeois, and in many cases also a vehicle for the spread of liberal ideas, was freemasonry. In the second half of the eighteenth century a number of masonic lodges came into existence in Hesse-Kassel, particularly in the capital. Their membership consisted of both nobles and bourgeois, generally high-ranking officers, civil servants, and court officials. In addition to the masonic lodges, nobles and bourgeois were active together in Rosicrucian circles and in the radical Illuminati. This latter organization

[1] The liberal views of both noble and bourgeois members of the bureaucracy in the eighteenth century are stressed by Charles W. Ingrao, "Barbarous Strangers: Hessian State and Society during the American Revolution," *American Historical Review* 87 (1982): 963–64.

[2] Hans Erich Bödeker, "Strukturen der Aufklärungsgesellschaft in der Residenzstadt Kassel," in *Mentalität und Lebensverhältnisse: Beispiele aus der Sozialgeschichte der Neuzeit: Rudolf Vierhaus zum 60. Geburtstag* (Göttingen, 1982), 58–67.

was directed by a noble, the Hessian assessor Adolf Freiherr von Knigge.[3]

Such secret societies had an up-and-down existence in Hesse-Kassel. Landgrave Frederick II strongly supported freemasonry and was himself a member of the lodge "Friedrich zur Freundschaft." But the French Revolution made his successor extremely suspicious of secret societies, and in 1793 Landgrave William IX banned freemasonry in Hesse-Kassel. The lodges reopened after the country's conquest in 1806 and soon became closely associated with the French and Westphalian governments. When William returned from exile, he immediately reimposed the ban on freemasonry, but by the end of 1814 Oberhofmarschall Friedrich Wilhelm von Bardeleben, a leading mason but also one of William's top court officials, was able to persuade the elector to lift the ban. For the next ten years nobles and bourgeois again met together in masonic lodges, and then in 1824 Elector William II, highly suspicious of all secret societies after receiving threatening letters from a so-called Revenge Society, banned freemasonry. Except for a brief revival during the revolution of 1848, freemasonry remained illegal in Hesse-Kassel until the Prussian takeover in 1866. But during the periods when freemasonry was banned, many former masons continued their previous contacts in social clubs.[4]

In addition to urban nobles' contacts with bourgeois in secret societies, learned academies, and social clubs, there was also considerable social contact between nobles and bourgeois in the countryside. Bourgeois leaseholders and estate administrators and their families often appear on guest lists for noble dinners, weddings, or hunting parties.[5] The overall level of contact between nobles and bourgeois is difficult to assess. Nobles having frequent social contacts with the bourgeoisie may have been in the minority, but it was these individuals who were often among the most influential members of the nobility, in particular because of their high positions in government service. The two groups had not merged into a single elite, for there were still instances of antipathy to be found.[6]

[3] Bödeker, "Strukturen der Aufklärungsgesellschaft," 68–69. For more details of the membership of Hessian masonic lodges see Adolf Kallweit, *Die Freimauererei in Hessen-Kassel: Königliche Kunst durch zwei Jahrhunderte von 1743–1965* (Baden-Baden, 1966), 12–14, 63–64; Wilhelm Kolbe, *Zur Geschichte der Freimaurerei in Kassel* (Berlin, 1883), 10–12, 14–15, 18, 29; Richard van Dulmen, *Der Geheimbund der Illuminaten: Darstellung, Analyse, Dokumentation* (Stuttgart, 1975), 43–44, 58–74.

[4] Kallweit, *Freimauererei*, 14–34.

[5] For example, see the lists of guests at hunting parties and dinners on the estate Wülmersen of the von Stockhausen family in the early nineteenth century. Stockhausen Memoirs, 2: 317, 332; 9: 334–37, 394–96.

[6] As the young wife of a bourgeois civil servant in Kassel wrote in 1781, "Here there is

But the Hessian nobility was bound to be affected by its high level of contact with the bourgeoisie. Even nobles who were not active in clubs or societies had some personal contact with bourgeois, due to service in the officer corps or bureaucracy. While the bulk of the nobility probably maintained an essentially conservative outlook, most nobles did not view the bourgeoisie as their enemy and thus frequently proved receptive to reform.

The wide range of political opinions within the nobility as a whole was reflected in the views of the delegates it sent to the Hessian diet in the eighteenth century, although moderate and liberal deputies were probably somewhat overrepresented because nobles frequently chose delegates who had attended a university, in particular government officials. Thus over one-half of the delegates from the nobility to the diets held during the reign of Landgrave Frederick II (1760–85) had attended a university, whereas less than one-quarter of the nobility as a whole had done so.[7]

Under Frederick II the diet played a surprisingly progressive role. Thanks to the huge profits reaped from the subsidy treaties with England, the landgrave was free from financial pressures and therefore did not need to make heavy demands on the estates. During his reign he even canceled or reduced a number of taxes. As a result the estates were not forced into the role of opposition to the monarchy, as was the case in many other German states. The Hessian estates actually cooperated well with the government, and their numerous petitions and requests to the landgrave frequently served as the inspiration for important social and economic reforms.[8]

The progressive activities of the diets under Frederick II could not have been possible without the support of the nobility, for it still dominated the Landtag in the eighteenth century. Although nobles controlled only one of the two chambers of the diet (the prelates' and knights' estate), they had certain advantages over the delegates from the towns. Decisions of the diet required the approval of both estates. When differences arose, representatives of the government (the *Landtagskom-*

nothing but antipathy between the upper bourgeoisie and the nobility." Erich Ebstein, ed., *Gottfried August Bürger und Philippine Gatterer: Ein Briefwechsel aus Göttingens empfindsamer Zeit* (Leipzig, 1921), 127.

[7] Ingrao, "Barbarous Strangers," 966; see above, table 6.3.

[8] For a recent reevaluation of the relationship between Landgrave Frederick II and the Hessian diet see Charles W. Ingrao, *The Hessian Mercenary State: Ideas, Institutions, and Reform under Frederick II (1760–1785)* (Cambridge, 1987). On Frederick's political activities see also Karl-Hermann Wegner, "Landgraf Friedrich II—Ein Regent der Aufklärung," in *Aufklärung und Klassizismus in Hessen-Kassel unter Landgraf Friedrich II, 1760–1785* (Kassel, 1979), 10–22.

missare) negotiated with both chambers of the diet to try to achieve a compromise. These negotiations were conducted in writing, and all petitions and requests from either chamber went first to the diet's hereditary presiding official, the *Erbmarschall*, who was also the hereditary leader of the Ritterschaft. As a result, the nobility knew in advance what the proposals of the towns were and could attempt to counteract unfavorable motions by immediately sending its own counterproposals. In contrast, the towns' chamber rarely knew in advance what the nobles were going to propose to the government.[9]

The death of Landgrave Frederick II greatly changed both the role of the estates and the stands taken by the nobility within the diet. Like his father, William IX was not dependent on the diet for funds, thanks to the profits from the subsidy treaties with England, but the strongly conservative William was less inclined than his father to work together with the diet. Since he did not need the estates for funding, he simply did not convene them. The estates had met shortly before his father's death in 1785, and William convened them only once during the next twenty years (in 1797), even though the estates were supposed to meet at least once every six years.

By the time the diet of 1797 met, the spirit of cooperation with the landgrave had vanished; furthermore, the atmosphere in Hesse-Kassel had been transformed by the French Revolution. The nobility had become increasingly concerned about threats to its privileged position, threats from both below and above. Just two years earlier the landgrave had attempted to squeeze more money out of the nobility by threatening to revive the feudal *Ritterpferde* (personal service by vassals). The knights had refused to comply, saying that the matter needed to be discussed at a diet.[10] In addition, government officials had frequently infringed upon traditional rights and privileges of the nobility. The threat from below had been made all too clear by the events of the French Revolution, and in the diet the nobility soon found itself confronted by a group of delegates from the towns who were much more assertive than in previous diets and thus more willing to challenge the privileges of the nobility.

Faced with such threats to its position, the nobility in 1797 chose delegates who were more conservative than those elected during the reign of Frederick II. The new delegates also possessed less education than the nobles in previous diets; only one of the delegates elected by the Ritterschaft had attended a university.[11]

[9] Demandt, "Hessischen Landstände," 43–44.

[10] See above, p. 29.

[11] The five delegates were Lieutenant Colonel August von Pappenheim (who had attended the University of Göttingen), Captain J.J.F. von Boyneburg, Captain Friedrich

Most of the nobles' efforts in the Landtag of 1797–98 were devoted to protecting the nobility's tax exemptions and other fiscal advantages. The nobles successfully opposed demands by the towns for a revision of the knights' cadaster, even though evidence abounded that some noble property was not listed in this tax register through oversight or conceal-ment. But the knights' protest against the government's attempts to curb abuses of the privilege of *Tafelfreiheit* (tax exemption for much of the in-come from knights' estates) was rejected by the landgrave.[12]

The noble deputies were also unsuccessful in their attempt to prevent the abolition of the office of *Landrat*. The ten *Landrat* positions (filled solely by members of the Ritterschaft) had been created in 1774 to serve as officials of both the government and the diet but had gradually come to serve only the former, though the diet continued to pay their salaries. During the diets of 1779 and 1785 the towns had proposed the elimina-tion of this office but had been successfully opposed by the knights. However, by 1797 criticism of this institution had become much stronger, and the landgrave decided to abolish it.[13] A key factor in his decision was the recommendation of the *Regierung* in Kassel against re-taining the office of *Landrat*. The vice-president of the *Regierung*, Ge-heimer Rat Wilhelm von Baumbach-Lenderscheid (who had served as a *Landrat* for fifteen years), showed that he placed the interests of the country above those of his class when he wrote, "Although my mem-bership in the Hessian Ritterschaft and the interests of my relatives give me good reason to wish that this office continue in existence, higher re-sponsibilities force me to accept the fact that the country can best use its funds elsewhere."[14]

The nobility lost yet another significant battle in the diet of 1797–98. At issue was the *Kleezehnt*, a tithe on clover planted on fields left fallow. This tithe was highly controversial, even within the nobility. Many gov-ernment officials (including the noble *Landräte*) had strongly criticized the clover tithe because it discouraged peasants from planting clover, a practice that enriched the soil and provided fodder for animals. The landgrave had already abolished this tithe for peasants under his control

---

von Heydwolff, Major Rudolph von Trott zu Solz, and Kammerherr Friedrich von Dörn-berg. The other members of the Ritterschaft in the Landtag, Obervorsteher Carl von Scholley and Erbmarschall Ludwig Freiherr von Riedesel, were university graduates. StAM Urkunden, Landtagsabschied 1798.

[12] Lichtner, *Landesherr und Stände*, 36–40.

[13] Ibid., 41–48; StAM 73 (Landstände), Acc. 1898/6, Nr. 119, Fasc. 1, Nr. 26b; StAM, Urkunden: Landtagsabschied of 15 May 1779, p. 16; Landtagsabschied of 14 March 1798, p. 72.

[14] StAM 5, Nr. 14748, Votum of 23 January 1798.

in 1790, and most nobles also recognized the need for its elimination, but the majority of the delegates from the Ritterschaft refused to support abolition of the clover tithe unless landlords were compensated for their loss. The delegates were not swayed by Erbmarschall Ludwig Freiherr von Riedesel's plea for immediate abolition of the tithe in order to head off possible unrest: "It is well known that foolish ideas are becoming commonplace among our subjects and are making them rebel against their masters. We nobles must therefore take steps to prevent this unrest and draw our subjects closer to us."[15] Only one knight supported Riedesel; the others continued to hold out for compensation, which they did not receive when the clover tithe was abolished by the landgrave in the summer of 1798.[16]

Although the nobility's position in this debate can hardly be termed liberal, the nobles were not simply clinging desperately to traditional privileges. They were willing to accept reform of the clover tithe if they would be compensated for their financial losses. The nobility took a similar stand when the question of the abolition of peasant labor services was raised. Nobles were well aware of the inefficiency of such labor, and many noble landlords had already concluded their own agreements with local villages to convert labor services into small cash payments. Therefore the delegates from the nobility were quite willing to support the elimination of services in return for compensation, and in January 1798 they joined with the delegates from the towns to ask the landgrave to issue such a decree. But the landgrave, who was the largest recipient of peasant services, was not inclined to go this far and simply recommended that noble landlords follow the example of the royal demesnes, where many peasant services had already been commuted to cash payments.[17]

The nobility was always ready to support progressive measures that benefited its own interests. As a result, noble delegates frequently advocated free trade. In the diet of 1785 they pressed for the removal of restrictions upon the export of wool because many nobles maintained large flocks of sheep during this period,[18] and in 1797 nobles again spoke out in favor of free trade, even citing Adam Smith. This time the issue

[15] Cited in Lichtner, *Landesherr und Stände*, 6.

[16] For the nobility's position on the clover tithe issue see StAM Urkunden, Landtagsabschied of 14 March 1798, pp. 47–52.

[17] Lichtner, *Landesherr und Stände*, 62. The joint request (Desiderium Commune XIX of 9 January 1798) can be found in StAM 5, Nr. 14749.

[18] StAM 73, Acc. 1898/6, Nr. 119, Fasc. 1, Desideria 16. For the nobility's involvement in the wool trade see Ottfried Dascher, *Das Textilgewerbe in Hessen-Kassel vom 16. bis 19. Jahrhundert* (Marburg, 1968), 100, 166–67.

was the grain trade. As large grain producers, the nobles wanted the landgrave to remove restrictions upon the export of grain. At first the towns refused to support the nobility, citing the need for limitations upon exports during periods of scarcity and high grain prices, but after the nobility agreed to support the towns' request for the construction of granaries to alleviate the effects of bad harvests, both chambers united in advocating free trade.[19]

In addition to free trade, the nobility supported easing restrictions on artisans. But the towns, anxious to protect their traditional monopoly, refused to consider any alteration of the Guild Ordinance of 1730, which restricted artisans to the towns.[20] Neither the towns nor the nobility supported liberalization of the controls on distilleries. Both groups were active producers of spirits, and in separate requests to the landgrave, each asked that the number of stills of the other be reduced.[21]

When no vital interests were at stake, the two chambers were willing to work together for reforms. Joint desiderata (*Desideria*) requested a reduction in the size of the army, the removal of the restrictions on admission to the university at Marburg, the abolition of the frequently misused annual efficiency reports (*Konduitenlisten*) for civil servants, and an increase in the salary of members of the judiciary so that they would be less dependent upon court fees and fines.[22]

Overall the nobility's attitude in the diets of the late eighteenth century had been a mixture of conservatism and liberalism. The former was most evident in issues involving traditional rights and privileges of the nobility, although even in such cases some nobles advocated reforms while others were willing to accept change as long as nobles were compensated for their losses. When the interests of the nobility were not at stake, most noble delegates were willing to work together with the bourgeoisie for reform.

The diet of 1797–98 was the last meeting of the estates prior to the French occupation of Hesse-Kassel in 1806, even though they were supposed to meet every six years. Landgrave William IX (Elector William I) had faced so much opposition from the knights and towns in 1798 that he decided not to convene the diet unless it was absolutely necessary.[23]

---

[19] Lichtner, *Landesherr und Stände*, 64–65.

[20] Ibid., 66–67. For conflicts between towns and nobles over artisanal monopolies elsewhere in Germany see Mack Walker, *German Home Towns: Community, State, and General Estate, 1648–1871* (Ithaca, 1971), 115.

[21] StAM Urkunden, Landtagsabschied of 14 March 1798, pp. 62, 72.

[22] StAM 5, Nr. 15868.

[23] Volker Press, "Landtage im Alten Reich und im Deutschen Bund: Voraussetzungen

In 1804, when the elector took no steps toward convening a diet even though one was due, the Ritterschaft's chief official, the *Erbmarschall*, polled the other knights to see if they believed a diet was necessary. Opinions were divided, although supporters of the need for a diet slightly outnumbered opponents.[24] Since the elector had no pressing need for funds, he did not convene the estates.

The French occupation of Hesse-Kassel and its subsequent incorporation into the new Kingdom of Westphalia brought many unpleasant changes for the Hessian nobility. The new constitution eliminated a number of traditional noble privileges, and the Westphalian reforms often caused economic hardship for noble landowners. But overall the social and economic power of the nobility remained intact. The new regime needed the services of the many nobles in the Hesssian officer corps and bureaucracy, and King Jerome sought to give his rule more legitimacy by maintaining an elaborate court filled with members of the old nobility.

Nobles' reactions to the dramatic turn of events after 1806 were divided. Many knights refused to serve in the new government, and some of them eventually turned to armed resistance. But the majority of the members of the Hessian Ritterschaft collaborated with the Westphalian government, most out of financial necessity or the desire to continue to advance professionally, a few (mostly younger nobles) out of deep-felt acceptance of the liberal ideals of the French Revolution. Even some nobles who had originally strongly opposed the new government found themselves forced to seek service with it as time passed. When Captain Heinrich Wilhelm von Stockhausen was released from French captivity in January 1808, he was initially contemptuous of the Hessian junior officers who had taken service with the French after 1806 (only staff officers had been imprisoned in 1806). On his return home he stayed in the same inn as several former Hessian officers in French service and recorded in his diary:

> Because I treated them so coolly, you might even say scornfully, they tried to prove to me that they had entered into French service only out of sheer necessity. I responded that I believed that some of them might have been forced by financial need to take this step but others had acted out of their own personal interest in order to advance higher, and that I had been very upset to meet two members

---

ständischer und konstitutioneller Entwicklungen 1750–1830," *Zeitschrift für Württembergische Landesgeschichte* 39 (1980): 111.

[24] StAM 73, Acc. 1898/6, Nr. 130. Lichtner states (*Landesherr und Stände*, 76) that only a few knights favored holding a Landtag, but the actual survey shows otherwise.

of the Hessian Ritterschaft, namely Captain von Hesberg and Lieutenant von Gilsa, who owned estates in Hesse and therefore could not have been forced by financial necessity to enter French service; in so doing they have completely forgotten their duty as vassals of their prince and have brought eternal shame upon themselves.[25]

Yet a few weeks later even he began to look for a position in the newly forming Westphalian army (which to him was different from service in the regiments raised in Hesse by France prior to the establishment of the new regime in 1808), although he noted, "if my financial situation were better, I would never take the slightest step toward seeking a position, but during my twenty-nine years of Hessian service I have used up most of my wealth and have even gone deep into debt."[26]

By having a foot in both pro- and anti-French camps, the Ritterschaft was well positioned to survive no matter who triumphed. The advantages of this divided loyalty were clearly demonstrated in the Dörnberg uprising of 1808. By the spring of 1808 many nobles were active in a conspiracy to kidnap King Jerome and overthrow his government at a time when anti-French uprisings were expected throughout Germany in conjunction with Austria's planned return into the war against Napoleon. One of the main centers of the conspiracy in Hesse was the foundation for noblewomen (*adliger Damenstift*) at Wallenstein, where noble conspirators could meet without raising the suspicions of the authorities while visiting friends or relatives among the residents. Among the conspirators were Georg von Schmerfeld, Staatsrat Friedrich von Witzleben, Louis von Trott zu Solz, Carl von Baumbach-Amönau, Gottlob von Buttlar-Elberberg, Georg von Dalwigk, Carl von Eschwege, Gottlob von der Malsburg, Moritz Wolff von Gudenberg, and Philipp Wolff von Gudenberg. On 23 April 1808 Colonel Wilhelm Freiherr von Dörnberg, commander of a Westphalian guards battalion, led an uprising of poorly equipped peasants and townsmen. An eyewitness and wife of one of the participants, Julie von Buttlar, reported the confused atmosphere in which the revolt began:

As evening approached, the horns called everyone together. Horses and riders dashed through the street, men shouted and cursed, wives and children cried and called out a farewell to a husband, father, son or brother, perhaps never to see him again; finally the unorganized mob, completely untrained in all the skills necessary for

[25] Stockhausen Memoirs, 6: 247–48.
[26] Ibid., 6: 264.

warfare, gathered together and, following the flying banners and gaily sounding horns, left the town on the road to Kassel.[27]

The following morning Julie and the other inhabitants of Homberg were awakened by the sound of cannon fire, and soon the first panic-stricken ex-rebels came streaming back through the town. Dörnberg's mob had been no match for the well-armed and well-trained government troops sent out to intercept the insurgents. Several nobles holding high offices in the Westphalian government were later blamed for having betrayed the conspirators, but in reality knowledge of the forthcoming uprising was so widespread that government officials easily learned of it in advance. Dörnberg was able to flee the country, but many of his fellow conspirators were not so fortunate. Two Westphalian soldiers captured among the insurgents were subsequently executed, and a number of nobles arrested for participation in the plot were sentenced to death by the Westphalian government.[28]

These death sentences were never carried out, for the condemned men had friends and relatives who still held high offices in King Jerome's court and bureaucracy. Due to their intercession, as well as that of friendly French officials, King Jerome commuted the death sentences to exile or imprisonment. Prison proved fatal to one of the females involved in the conspiracy, fifty-nine-year-old Sophie von Baumbach-Lenderscheid; furthermore, her young niece Caroline, who had embroidered the flag used in the uprising, never completely recovered her health after being released from prison and died in 1814.[29]

Hessian nobles continued to serve the Westphalian government for another five years, but their loyalty did not run very deep. By the end of 1813 most nobles serving in the Westphalian army and bureaucracy were able to see which way the political wind was blowing and therefore resigned their offices to take up service under the returning elector. Only a few nobles remained loyal to King Jerome. For this they earned the undying enmity of Elector William I, thus forfeiting any chance of returning to Hessian service. Although some nobles had remained loyal to the elector throughout the entire period of exile, William was not

[27] Julie von Buttlar, "Der Dörnbergsche Aufstand 1809," in Hueck, "Familie von Buttlar," no. 26/27, p. 5.
[28] Karl Lyncker, *Geschichte der Insurrectionen wider das westfälische Gouvernement* (Kassel, 1857), 127–62; Dörnberg, *Wilhelm von Dörnberg*, 34–53; Heinz Heitzer, *Insurrektionen zwischen Weser und Elbe* (Berlin, 1959), 163.
[29] Lyncker, *Insurrectionen*, 157–58. The death sentence against Julie von Buttlar's husband Gottlob was commuted to two years' exile after her father, Carl Ludwig von Gilsa, a high court official, asked King Jerome for clemency for his son-in-law. Hueck, "Familie von Buttlar," no. 26/27, pp. 12–13; Gilsa, *Oberstallmeister von Gilsa*, 22–23.

pleased with the high degree of collaboration shown by many Hessian nobles, and on several occasions he had pro-French nobles arrested or banished to their estates.[30]

William I's return to power was characterized by a determined effort to eliminate all traces of the Kingdom of Westphalia and turn the clock back to 1806, although he did retain a few favorable changes such as the elimination of seigneurial justice and the addition of some new taxes. William could not, however, restore the monarchy's former financial independence, for the extravagance of the Westphalian government and the high costs of the Napoleonic Wars had drained the Hessian treasury. He therefore convened the diet in March 1815, hoping to obtain its speedy acquiescence to his financial demands. But the elector's hopes were soon dashed as the estates began pressing for important changes: more control over taxation, a precise accounting of the country's finances, and a written constitution. William himself had contributed to this last demand by joining with other German princes in the fall of 1814 at the Congress of Vienna to promise constitutions for their states, although the term used—*landständische Verfassungen* (estate-based constitutions)—was open to many interpretations.[31]

The new diet differed considerably from those of the eighteenth century, for William had added a new estate—the peasants—to the traditional two. He hoped thereby to create a counterweight to the nobles and towns, who had frequently opposed his policies.[32] Voting remained by estate, with decisions of the diet requiring the approval of all three chambers. Unlike the previous ones, however, the new Landtag also had occasional joint sessions, where all three chambers sat together and voted by head.[33]

Recognizing the importance of this diet, the knighthood elected a highly qualified group of delegates. All five were university-educated, and two of them were high-ranking civil servants. The other three deputies consisted of a forestry official, an estate owner, and the former head of the Marburg chapter of the Teutonic Order. Despite their similar educational backgrounds, these five deputies held differing political

[30] Losch, *Kurfürst Wilhelm I*, 335, 349, 351.

[31] Ibid., 333–40; idem., *Geschichte des Kurfürstentums*, 95.

[32] Losch, *Kurfürst Wilhelm I*, 334.

[33] The dissolution of the Teutonic Order's chapter in Marburg in 1809 had reduced the size of the prelates' and knights' chamber by one, so it now consisted of five delegates from the Ritterschaft and one representative each from the Stift Kaufungen and the University of Marburg. The towns continued to have eight delegates, and the new peasants' estate consisted of five deputies. Carl Wilhelm Wippermann, *Kurhessen seit dem Freiheitskriege* (Kassel, 1850), 26, 39.

views. Forestry official Franz von Rau and estate owner Carl von Eschwege were the most conservative members of the group; Geheimer Rat Carl Otto von der Malsburg-Escheberg generally took conservative stands, although he advocated reforms in government; and the two remaining delegates from the Ritterschaft, former Teutonic Order official Ernst von Baumbach-Nentershausen and Geheimer Rat Carl von Dalwigk (president of the supreme court of the Duchy of Nassau) were moderates. Despite differences in their attitudes toward reforms, all five were determined to defend the privileged position of the nobility.

Before the diet opened, the newly elected noble deputies began receiving a wide range of opinions from members of the knighthood. The strongly liberal Friedrich Ludwig von Berlepsch, who had been a high-ranking Westphalian official, wrote to demand that the estates draw up a constitution for Hesse-Kassel. He also called for the end of the feudal system and the financial privileges of the nobility.[34]

Such radical views found little echo among the nobility as a whole. In the Fulda district, for example, several knights drew up highly conservative sets of instructions for their deputy, Ernst von Baumbach. The first set concentrated mainly on the many privileges lost by the nobility under the Westphalian government and not restored by Elector William I after his return from exile.[35] A second set of instructions also complained of lost privileges but went much further in its 126 pages of text. The authors refused to recognize the legality of the diet because it included an illegal extra chamber, the peasants. Deputy von Baumbach was therefore instructed to "work together with the other delegates from the two legitimate chambers to bring the assembly to a speedy close." As long as the diet remained in session, however, Baumbach was told to use it to protest against unfair actions taken by the government since the elector's return. The final instruction for Baumbach was to "undertake nothing that was not in the best interests of the country or in particular the Ritterschaft."[36]

Despite its overall highly conservative nature, this petition also contained a number of progressive instructions for Baumbach. The authors called for improvements in the judicial system, abolition of customs duties within the country, and full civil rights for Jews (although this last

[34] StAM 73, Acc. 1898/6, Nr. 286, #12, Berlepsch to Estates, 3 January 1815. For a biography of Berlepsch see *ADB*, 2: 403–4.

[35] Hellmut Seier and Winfried Speitkamp, eds., *Akten zur Entstehung und Bedeutung des kurhessischen Verfassungsentwurfs von 1815/16* (Marburg, 1985), 1–8.

[36] Ibid., 16, 42. The full version of this document—"Instruction für den Ritterschaftlichen Deputirten des löblichen Fulda-Stroms zu den auf den 1. März ausgeschriebenen Landtag"—is contained in StAM 340 v. Baumbach-Nentershausen, Nr. 151.

demand was coupled with a desire to limit the spread of Jews within the country).[37]

A list of instructions for the deputy from the Schwalm district (Dalwigk), signed by a number of knights, went even further in calling for reforms that benefited the country as a whole rather than just the Ritterschaft. Although these instructions began with a call for the restoration of the Ritterschaft's lost privileges, most of the instructions consisted of requests for progressive reforms. The knights called for a written budget, the separation of the monarch's private wealth from that of the state, higher salaries for junior army officers and civil servants, an end to the practice of making fines part of judges' salaries, no restoration of the guild system, a uniform system of weights and measures, and more control for the diet over lawmaking.[38]

After the diet opened in March 1815, the efforts of the delegates from the nobility concentrated on attempting to regain lost rights and privileges, particularly seigneurial justice. This was the subject of the knights' first desideratum on 21 March and a second, proposed desideratum in April.[39] This second request was, however, withdrawn in favor of a more general statement by all three chambers on 17 April. The joint desideratum criticized the elector's failure to provide a complete listing of the country's finances and called for the restoration of the "constitution" in effect in 1805, that is to say the traditional system of rights and privileges.[40] This latter demand was part of a new tactic by the nobility to call for the restoration of the "traditional constitution" until a new one was enacted by the diet.[41]

---

[37] Ibid.

[38] Seier and Speitkamp, *Akten*, 42–46. The probable primary author of this draft list of instructions, Oberstallmeister Carl von Gilsa (1753–1823), had fallen out of favor with Landgrave William IX in the 1790s for making "radical" (at least in the eyes of the landgrave) remarks. During a ride with the landgrave, conversation turned to the French Revolution, and the landgrave remarked that if he were in Paris, he would drive the Jacobins out with a stick. Gilsa's attempt to view the situation realistically—he pointed out that Paris alone had twice as many inhabitants as the entire state of Hesse-Kassel—was not well received by the landgrave, who soon removed Gilsa from his court office. Under King Jerome Gilsa again held a high court office, which he immediately lost when the elector returned from exile at the end of the Napoleonic Wars. Gilsa, *Oberstallmeister von Gilsa*, 9–10.

[39] Seier and Speitkamp, *Akten*, 55–56; StAM 73, Acc. 1900/33, L-73, Protokolle der Landtagsverhandlungen von 1815, 2. Anlagenband, Anl. 94, Fol. 147–49 (April 1815).

[40] Seier and Speitkamp, *Akten*, 80–81.

[41] See for example the statement by Deputy Franz von Rau on April 17, 1815: "Since an improved constitution has been rejected, despite all previous promises, even to the Congress of Vienna, the elector should restore the country to the conditions and consti-

The temporary union of all three estates did not last very long, for the peasants were not really interested in turning the clock back to 1805. At the beginning of May the peasants presented their own desideratum opposing the restoration of seigneurial justice and the nobility's tax exemptions. In reply the first chamber (prelates and knights) drafted a memorandum criticizing the existence of a separate chamber for the peasants. While conceding that the peasantry deserved representation, the nobles stated that the peasants should be part of the second chamber (the towns), not a separate estate. As in all previous statements from the first chamber, the memorandum called for the restoration of seigneurial justice and the nobility's tax exemptions. This call was once again contained in the first chamber's final memorandum before the diet recessed in July.[42]

Overall the debates of 1815 had shown a tremendous divergence of interests among the three chambers. The gulf between the nobility and the peasants was particularly large because the nobles wanted to bring back aspects of the traditional system that were extremely unpopular with the peasants—seigneurial justice and tax exemptions for the nobility. The only significant unanimity of opinion among the estates came on the issue of the country's finances. All three estates had joined to press the elector to give a detailed accounting of the country's financial situation before any new taxes could be approved and to separate his personal wealth from that of the state.

Although the attention of the first estate had thus far focused primarily on regaining lost privileges, the noble delegation was far from united in its political outlook. Thus on 10 July 1815 the conservative deputy Carl von Eschwege reported to his constituents, "We have powerful enemies—even, I am ashamed to say, in the ranks of our own estate. I hope that everyone will recognize them and find them unworthy to associate with us any longer."[43]

During the debates of 1815 the elector had put off the estates' requests for a constitution by saying they should first wait for the constitution for all of Germany that was under consideration at the Congress of Vienna. But no such constitution came to pass, and the elector then appointed a

---

tution of 1805." Ibid., 78. See also the draft memorandum of the prelates' and knights' chamber, 5 May 1815. Ibid., 89.

[42] *Beurkundete Darstellung der Kurhessischen Landtagsverhandlungen mit Blicken auf die Vergangenheit, Gegenwart und Zukunft* (Kassel, 1816), 31, 147–53; Seier and Speitkamp, *Akten*, 104–106.

[43] Friedrich Ludwig von Berlepsch, *Beiträge zu den Hessen-Casselschen Landtagsverhandlungen der Jahre 1815 und 1816* (Erfurt, 1817), 9. The liberal Berlepsch was angered by the statement and announced that he was withdrawing his previous vote for Eschwege.

commission to draft a constitution for Hesse-Kassel. This constitution commission (*Verfassungskommission*) had four members, all nobles (two new nobles and two from the Ritterschaft) who held high government office: the *Landtagskommissar*, Staatsminister Georg von Schmerfeld; Geheimer Regierungsrat Otto von Porbeck; Geheimer Regierungsrat Carl Otto von der Malsburg; and Ferdinand Carl Freiherr von Schenck zu Schweinsberg, president of the supreme court. The commission first met on 6 November 1815 and spent the next two months working on drafts of a constitution.

In an early draft Porbeck, one of the new nobles, proposed eliminating separate estates and replacing them with popular representation (*eine allgemeine Volks-Repräsentation*). Porbeck realized that this would eliminate the knighthood's traditional rights to seats in the Landtag, so he suggested that elections should be set up in such a way as to guarantee that the knighthood would not be excluded. Porbeck also called for the diet to have control over taxation and noted that this would require knowledge of the government's income and expenses.[44]

Porbeck's proposed draft drew sharp criticism from Geheimer Rat von der Malsburg from the Ritterschaft. Malsburg expressed his concern that eliminating the separate estates would cause the Ritterschaft to be mixed together with the mass of the people. Malsburg argued that the three chambers should remain in existence but the third estate, the peasants, should be given the same number of deputies as each of the others.[45]

The other commission member from the Ritterschaft, Freiherr Schenck zu Schweinsberg, took a more liberal stand, arguing in favor of a representative rather than a *ständische* (estate-based) constitution. He opposed Malsburg's idea of simply adding more delegates to the peasants' estate, saying that this would:

> lead to a mixture of old and new, a system both *ständisch* and representative—the constitution would be neither; the privileged estates would believe that their obligations to the rest of the population were eliminated now that it had its own representation; the rest of the population would not believe itself to be adequately represented and would be jealous of and mistrust the privileged estates, believing they were there solely to preserve and expand their privileges against the less privileged estates. . . . The representatives of the country must serve the country as a whole; it is through them that the general will [*Gemeinwille*] is expressed. How can the con-

---

[44] Seier and Speitkamp, *Akten*, 131–35.
[45] Ibid., 135–37.

cepts of general will and privileges be combined when they are actually opposites?[46]

Schenck noted that if the privileged classes needed more guarantees for their privileges, this should be done through an additional assembly made up solely of these groups, separate from the representative assembly. But Schenck's proposal did not include a separate hereditary upper chamber. He favored indirect elections, with nobles and prelates becoming permanent electors in their districts (up to one-third of the total). The other two-thirds of the electors would come from the most prosperous landowners in the district. These rural electors would select a total of twenty delegates, and the diet would also contain five deputies representing the manufacturers and tradesmen in the cities and three deputies representing the intellectual and ecclesiastical elites.[47]

Schenck also called for an increase in the powers and responsibility of the diet. All changes in the laws concerning civil and criminal law, commerce, and taxation should first be approved by the diet. He advocated reforms in the system of taxation (including the elimination of most of the nobility's exemptions), the elimination of all privileged trial status, and the abolition of feudal dues. Finally he called for the separation of the ruler's wealth from that of the state.[48] All in all, this was a very liberal series of proposals for a member of the Ritterschaft to make.

At the end of December 1815 Porbeck and Schmerfeld (the two new nobles) drafted a constitution that eliminated separate representation for each estate: "Each deputy represents all the inhabitants of his district regardless of their estate [*Stand*]." Although the deputies would sit and vote together, with no differences in rank and no special seating for any groups, the proposed composition of the diet still contained many traditional *ständische* elements. The twenty-seven deputies would consist of nine representatives from the prelates and the knights, nine from the towns, and nine from the landowners in the countryside (excluding members of the other two groups).[49]

The two commission members from the Ritterschaft submitted dissenting opinions to the elector. Geheimer Rat von Schenck agreed that the diet should not have separate estates but believed that there should be only two groups represented: landowners and merchants/manufacturers. The rest of the populace, those "who live by the work of their

[46] Ibid., 141.
[47] Ibid., 142–43. See also his memorandum entitled "Die Repräsentation des Landes auf den Landtagen betr.," ibid., 143–44.
[48] Ibid., 145–53.
[49] Ibid., 157–58.

hands," had no strong ties to the state and therefore did not merit political representation. In Schenck's concept the Ritterschaft would be represented in the landowners category, with each district electing one noble and one non-noble landowner.[50]

Geheimer Rat von der Malsburg objected strongly to the elimination of separate estates:

> It seems to me that these changes are due to a misinterpretation of the concept of equality. Absolute equality is impossible. Even political equality is possible only to a limited degree, as long as all citizens do not have the same property rights. . . . As long as there are landlords and peasants, townsmen and countrymen, there will be differences between the classes [*Volks-Classen*], and each has its own particular interests. Therefore each class [*Classe*] must be represented separately, and issues involving its particular rights cannot be subjected to a majority vote without endangering property rights.[51]

Malsburg proposed altering the draft constitution so that the deputies would meet and vote together on matters affecting the whole country but would meet and vote by estate when questions involving the interests of a particular estate were discussed.

When the diet reconvened in February 1816, it received the constitution drafted by Porbeck and Schmerfeld, which was quite progressive for the times. The elector expected the delegates to accept the constitution gratefully, but instead they began to examine it article by article. The nobles, in particular, were upset by the elimination of separate representation. Even the most moderate representative of the nobility, Geheimer Rat Carl von Dalwigk, declared that putting the representatives of different classes together in a single chamber would lead to a "Polish diet." He warned, "What caused the revolution to occur so quickly in France? Without a doubt the fact that all the notables were placed together in a single chamber!"[52] Dalwigk argued that the most logical system of government for Hesse-Kassel would be a diet with two chambers: a chamber of lords (*Herrenbank*) consisting of the royal princes, prelates, and knights and a chamber of deputies for the rest of the population. Realizing that such a two-chamber system was unlikely to be adopted, Dalwigk supported Malsburg's request for separate deliberation by estate in matters concerning individual privileges. Dalwigk

---

[50] Ibid., 169–73.
[51] Ibid., 174; StAM 73, Acc. 1900/33, L-73, Nr. 34.
[52] Seier and Speitkamp, *Akten*, 196.

justified his desire to preserve the rights of the nobility by stating that "these rights are needed to protect the nobility's material existence, to enhance the splendor of the monarchy, and to help the nobility fulfill its essential role as a mediator between the monarchy and the subjects."[53]

The rest of the delegates from the nobility joined with Dalwigk in backing Malsburg's proposal for voting by estate in matters of privilege, and this change to the draft of the constitution was approved by the other two chambers on 4 March 1816.[54] The nobles suggested a number of other important changes in the draft: first, the Landtag should meet at least once every three years (instead of every six), and when it was not in session, a standing committee of three deputies should meet monthly to supervise the treasury and the interests of the country; second, if the monarch dissolved the diet, he must convene it again in the same year; third, government ministers should have definite areas of responsibility; and finally, the government should institute a secret ballot and freedom of the press.[55]

The noble delegates had thus demonstrated their support of some important political reforms aimed at strengthening the power of the diet (as long as the nobility did not lose its separate representation). Nobles also played a leading role in the estates' opposition to the elector's demand for increases in taxes, stating that he first needed to reveal the state's budget to the diet in order to prove that there was a deficit requiring more revenue.[56] But the nobility's willingness to support reforms ended when the subject of equal taxation arose. The most conservative noble deputies, Rau and Eschwege, favored retaining as many of the old tax exemptions as possible, and even the more moderate Geheimer Rat von Dalwigk, who began his speech on taxes by stating, "making the nobility's taxes equal to those of other taxpayers is appropriate for the spirit of the times and the general will of the people," called for the nobility to pay only one-half of the normal land tax because noble estates were burdened by the feudal system.[57]

During the debates in April 1816 the nobility even returned to the question of its lost rights and privileges, which had been one of the main

[53] Ibid., 200. For more information on Dalwigk see *ADB*, 4: 714; Hartwig Brandt, *Landständische Repräsentation im deutschen Vormärz: Politisches Denken im Einflußfeld des monarchischen Prinzips* (Neuwied and Berlin, 1968), 112–13.

[54] The debates on the draft constitution in the first estate from 26–29 February, 1816, are contained in StAM 73, Acc. 1898/6, Nr. 287.

[55] StAM 73, Acc. 1898/6, Nr. 285.

[56] See Dalwigk's speech of 24 March 1816, StAM 73, 1900/33, L-73, Nr. 98.

[57] StAM 73, Acc. 1900/33, L-73, Nr. 197, Votum v. Dalwigk, 23 April 1816; Lichtner, *Landesherr und Stände*, 197–202.

concerns during the previous year's debates. Carl von Eschwege made a detailed list of all the privileges enjoyed by the Ritterschaft prior to 1806 and spoke of the "present oppressed situation" in which the nobility had been thrown together with the lowest classes and stripped of the privileges that had distinguished it as a special elite. As in 1815, Eschwege called for the restoration of the traditional privileges of the nobility.[58] Dalwigk was more willing to consider reforms. He even called for an end to the feudal system binding the nobility to the state, as it was "no longer in harmony with the present times." In place of fiefs Dalwigk called for noble estates to become *Fideikommisse* that would be inherited only by the eldest son, thereby maintaining the nobility as the "indispensable mediator [*Mittelstand*] between the ruler and the people."[59] Dalwigk was also willing to compromise on the issue of seigneurial justice. Although he was not willing to see it abolished completely, he did agree that small, isolated areas of noble jurisdiction should be consolidated or turned over to the state. Only one other noble, the former Teutonic Order official Ernst von Baumbach, supported Dalwigk's moderate approach, so when the prelates and knights presented their "Protest concerning the Privileges of the Hessian Ritterschaft" to the diet on 25 April 1816, they did not compromise on their demand for the restoration of the pre-1806 privileges.[60]

The nobility did show more flexibility when peasant services were discussed. Members of the knighthood had long recognized the drawbacks of compulsory peasant services, and in the diet of 1797 the Ritterschaft had already supported the commutation of services into cash payments. So when the delegates from the peasantry called for the end of compulsory services in April 1816, the response of the noble delegates was favorable. Carl von Eschwege, who drafted the response of the prelates and knights, stated that the commutation of peasant services would be "advantageous for both landlord and peasant, especially because the latter performs services only halfheartedly." Eschwege called for landlords to be given proper compensation for the loss of services through either annual cash payments, transfer of some of the peasants' landholdings, or a lump-sum cash payment. As for peasant quitrents and tithes, Eschwege argued against their commutation, stating that peasants were better able to make such payments in kind than in cash.[61]

---

[58] Lichtner, *Landesherr und Stände*, 200–201; StAM 73, Acc. 1900/33, L-73, Nr. 212.

[59] StAM 73, Acc. 1900/33, L-73, Nr. 211, Promemoria, die Reclamation der Rechte der Ritterschaft betreffend, 8 April 1816.

[60] *Kurhessische Landtagsverhandlungen vom Jahre 1816* (Kassel, 1816), abt. 4, 111–28.

[61] Ibid., 139–44 Deputy von Rau generally supported Eschwege's remarks but declared

Joint action by the peasants and nobles to reform compulsory labor services did not prove possible in the short time remaining to the diet before its dissolution on 10 May 1816. Elector William I took this step because he had grown tired of the diet's lack of progress toward a constitution and was disturbed by the delegates' demand for the separation of his personal wealth from that of the state. The diet had thus failed to achieve its goal of a constitution for Hesse-Kassel, and this failure was due in part to the inflexibility of the delegates of the Ritterschaft. Even in the diet's final memorandum to the elector criticizing the decision to dissolve the diet, the nobles, along with the towns, continued to demand the restoration of their traditional privileges.[62] In their summary of the activities of the Landtag of 1815–16, the government's observers (Georg von Schmerfeld and Johannes Hassenpflug) noted, "To an observer the steps taken by the Ritterschaft were quite remarkable. It concentrated all its efforts on regaining the exemptions and privileges enjoyed up to the year 1806, and it resisted the addition of the peasants to the diet, although the consequence of this seems to have been greater moderation."[63]

After the dissolution of the diet, political life became quiet in Hesse-Kassel for the remaining years of William I's rule. In 1818 the elector briefly considered issuing a constitution of his own choosing without consulting the estates but finally decided to drop the idea. The following year Geheimer Rat von Dalwigk, the most liberal of the noble deputies at the diet of 1815–16, published an anonymous attack on the elector for not granting a constitution,[64] but the book, which was published outside Hesse-Kassel, had little impact on Dalwigk's fellow nobles or Hessian political life in general.

The political climate became more heated after William II became elector in 1821. The new ruler's controversial personal life and disregard of traditional privileges soon caused relations between the monarchy and the Ritterschaft to deteriorate sharply. One of his first acts as elector was to name his mistress, Emilie Ortlöpp—the daughter of a Berlin goldsmith—the Countess Reichenbach, a move that displeased many

---

that peasant dues and services could be eliminated only if the entire feudal system were abolished at the same time. StAM 73, Acc. 1900/33, L-73, Nr. 224, 29 April 1816.

[62] *Landtags-Verhandlungen 1816*, Abt. 4, 204–8.

[63] Seier and Speitkamp, *Akten*, 249. For a recent evaluation of the diet of 1815–16 see Winfried Speitkamp, *Restauration als Transformation: Untersuchungen zur kurhessischen Verfassungsgeschichte 1813–1830* (Darmstadt and Marburg, 1986).

[64] *Etwas über Rechte der Landstände, und Warum hat Kurhessen keine Constitution? Wissenschaftlich geprüft von einem ehemaligen Deputirten zur Ständeversammlung* (Wiesbaden, 1819).

members of old noble families, who were not even allowed to use the title *baron*. Royal mistresses were nothing new in Hesse-Kassel, but the countess soon became very unpopular because of the way in which she used her domination of the elector to gain influence over major political decisions and government appointments. She also laid claim to social preeminence in the capital, and members of the royal court and high officials were required to pay calls upon her rather than the electress, who no longer resided in Kassel. Many nobles refused to associate with the Countess Reichenbach, and a virtual court-in-exile began to form around the electress and the crown prince, who remained loyal to his mother.[65]

The Countess Reichenbach was not the only source of tension between the Ritterschaft and the monarchy. Many knights were unhappy because William II refused repeated requests to convene the estates, even though it was traditional for the diet to meet after a new ruler succeeded to the throne.[66] But the most important source of conflict was the elector's attack upon the knighthood's traditional control over the Stift Kaufungen.

In a decree issued on 24 April 1822 the elector declared that the incomes of the Stift Kaufungen would no longer be used solely for the benefit of the Hessian Ritterschaft. Instead the Stift would also have to support the widows and daughters of holders of the Order of the Golden Lion and the Military Service Order. In addition the decree stated that in the future knights would occupy only two of the three directorships of the Stift Kaufungen; the third post would be filled by a member of one of the orders.[67]

The knights were shocked by this infringement of rights that had been exclusively theirs since the sixteenth century, and the five *Stroms-deputierten* (regional representatives) began collecting the opinions of the membership. Most knights favored drawing up a petition to the elector, although some complained of the uselessness of such petitions and said the matter should be taken to the courts.[68]

While the Ritterschaft was still debating what action to take, the elector and his chief adviser, Geheimer Kabinettsrat Carl Rivalier, came to the conclusion that the nobility was plotting against the monarchy. William ordered Police Director Friedrich Pfeiffer to be on the alert for any meetings of the Ritterschaft and "to take immediate steps to hinder any

---

[65] For more information about William II and the Countess Reichenbach see Losch, *Geschichte des Kurfürstentums*, 129–30; Wippermann, *Kurhessen seit dem Freiheitskriege*, 153, 199.

[66] Wippermann, *Kurhessen seit dem Freiheitskriege*, 155.

[67] *Sammlung von Gesetzen*, 3 (1822): 14–15.

[68] StAM 340 v. Eschwege, Nr. 22.

217

such meetings."[69] Local police officials were ordered to report all political activities by knights, and a police lieutenant was sent to Marburg to make patrols in the countryside and also to keep an eye on towns in neighboring states, in case nobles decided to hold a meeting outside the country.[70]

The elector's fears were groundless, for no large-scale assemblies of knights took place. Instead a petition was circulated at the end of June 1822, and this petition, signed by the three directors of the Stift Kaufungen and sixty-six other knights, was presented to the elector. Although the petition was worded very respectfully, it did ask the elector to cancel his decree, and he reacted angrily. On 28 July he ordered the police director to investigate all signers of the petition, and he also asked the justice ministry about the possibility of taking legal action against the signers, particularly those who were government officials. The justice ministry's reply was not very satisfying to the elector, for it stated that subjects traditionally had the right to present petitions to the monarch, even ones directed against royal decrees. The ministry also noted that it would not be fair to single out the civil servants and treat them differently from the other signers.[71]

The elector had to be content with a sharply worded rejection of the Ritterschaft's petition. In addition he wrote letters to three high-ranking officials who had signed the petition, expressing his displeasure at their actions and warning them not to anger him in the future.[72]

Although some knights had talked of taking the matter to the courts or even protesting to the diet of the German Confederation in Frankfurt, the majority did not wish to push the matter further, and the controversy gradually died down. But the knighthood's opposition to the elector had been strengthened. In June 1823 the elector struck at this opposition by banning four noble officers from the capital, including two members of the Ritterschaft and Joseph Maria von Radowitz, who then left Hesse to begin a dazzling career in Prussia.[73]

Less than two weeks after the banishment of the four officers, the

[69] StAM 24a (Polizeidirektion), Nr. 53, Geh. Rat. Prot., 29 May 1822.

[70] Ibid., Ober-Polizei-Direktor to Polizei Direktion Oberhessen, 2 June 1822. For the reports of the local police officials see also StAM 24c, Nr. 48.

[71] StAM 16, Rep. X, Kl. 16, Nr. 33, Vorstellung der hessischen Ritterschaft gegen die Verordnung vom 24. April 1822.

[72] Ibid. The three officials were Regierungspräsident Ferdinand von Schenck zu Schweinsberg, Staatsminister Friedrich von Witzleben, and Lieutenant General Wilhelm von Urff. Witzleben and Urff immediately apologized, saying they had not realized that their actions were improper.

[73] Emil Ritter, *Radowitz: Ein katholischer Staatsmann in Preussen* (Cologne, 1948), 23–24.

elector received an anonymous letter threatening his and the Countess Reichenbach's lives. Despite a large-scale investigation and the offer of a huge reward, the author of the letter and the members of this alleged conspiracy (the *Rächerbund*—Revenge Society) were never found, but even nobles came under suspicion. The countess's gray eminence at court, Geheimer Kabinettsrat Carl Rivalier, demanded an investigation of the four exiled officers, their relatives, and other members of the nobility.[74]

William II further alienated the knights in 1825 when he not only ennobled Rivalier but also named him a member of the Hessian Ritterschaft. This act was a clear violation of the traditional methods of gaining membership in the knighthood, for Rivalier lacked virtually all of the necessary requirements: noble ancestry, ownership of a noble estate, and the approval of the existing membership (which was unlikely to be granted since Rivalier had shown himself to be no friend of the Ritterschaft during the past three years). A further insult to the knighthood was the new name given to Rivalier. The elector added *von Meysenbug* (a distinguished family that had become extinct just fifteen years earlier) to Rivalier's name. The knights realized that protests would be fruitless, but they never accepted Rivalier as a member.[75]

The elector again rode roughshod over the rights of the Ritterschaft in May 1830, when he ennobled Ferdinand Ortlöpp and, as with Rivalier, named him a member of the Hessian Ritterschaft. Ortlöpp received the name *Heyer von Rosenfeld* (an extinct noble family). Like Rivalier, Ortlöpp lacked noble ancestry, a noble estate, and the approval of the Ritterschaft. Ortlöpp's ennoblement angered the knighthood even more than Rivalier's, for the latter had at least been a high-ranking civil servant. Ortlöpp's main claim to fame was that he was the brother of the Countess Reichenbach. Most nobles realized that, as in the past, protest was futile, but they hoped that when the crown prince eventually came to power, he would repeal his father's numerous infringements of their rights.[76]

As a result of William II's many affronts to the nobility, the traditional ties between the monarchy and the knighthood had been greatly weakened by 1830. One angry noble, Wilhelm von Baumbach-Sontra, wrote:

[74] Losch, *Geschichte des Kurfürstentums*, 133–34; Wippermann, *Kurhessen seit dem Freiheitskriege*, 169.

[75] ARSK, Rep. VI, Gef. 12–14, Nr. 31.

[76] For knights' angry reaction to the order to admit Ortlöpp into the Ritterschaft see ibid., Nr. 34.

Monarchs should recognize what a vital source of support they have in the nobility of their countries, they should bear in mind that only the nobility would be willing to support them against an uprising of the populace, and they should take to heart the tragic examples of Charles I of England and Louis XVI of France. But no, monarchs are rushing to their destruction. They trample upon the only individuals who remain loyal and support the monarchy against demagogic intrigues. The nobility is truly foolish for remaining loyal to a prince who rewards loyalty with such ingratitude.[77]

William II's failure to maintain good relations with the nobility was to have important consequences in the fall of 1830, after widespread unrest in both the cities and the countryside forced him to convene the estates for the first time since 1816. The delegates elected by the nobility were not willing to support the monarchy blindly; in fact most were moderate liberals prepared to work together with the bourgeoisie against the unpopular elector to achieve reforms.

The new Landtag of 1830 was somewhat larger than in the past. The traditional two estates of prelates/knights and towns were joined by the third estate of peasants, as in 1815, and all three estates had been enlarged by the inclusion of delegates from territories outside the old provinces of Upper and Lower Hesse. The first estate thus consisted of seven traditional members (a director of the Stift Kaufungen, a representative of the university, and five deputies from the Hessian Ritterschaft) plus three newcomers: one deputy each from the Schaumburg Ritterschaft, the former imperial knights in Fulda, and the *Standesherren*. In addition, the *Erbmarschall* remained president of the Landtag, as was traditional.[78]

The Ritterschaft sent a highly qualified group of delegates to this crucial Landtag. All six knights (including Obervorsteher Friedrich von Trott zu Solz representing the Stift Kaufungen) were university graduates. Three of them were members of the bureaucracy, while the other three were estate owners.[79]

Unlike 1815 the delegates from the nobility did not devote most of their energies to attempting to regain lost rights and privileges. Although Obervorsteher von Trott did present a list of the Ritterschaft's grievances against the government two days after the opening of the

[77] StAM 340 v. Baumbach-Kirchheim, Nr. 12, undated memorandum (late 1820s or 1830).
[78] Friedrich Goessel, *Geschichte des Landtags von 1830* (Kassel, 1837), 75–77; Wippermann, *Kurhessen seit dem Freiheitskriege*, 204–6.
[79] The five delegates elected by the knighthood were Carl Sigismund Freiherr Waitz von Eschen, Wilhelm von Baumbach-Nentershausen, Ludwig von Milchling zu Schönstadt, Ludwig von Baumbach-Ropperhausen, and Carl von Eschwege.

Landtag, noble delegates realized that the prevailing atmosphere in Hesse-Kassel made reforms unavoidable. Most probably agreed with the sentiments expressed by Wilhelm von Buttlar to one of the deputies from the knighthood shortly before the Landtag opened: "The present moment certainly must be used wisely. It is much better for us to act with honor for the benefit of all by giving up obsolete things voluntarily rather than have them taken from us by force."[80]

The primary task facing the Landtag was to give Hesse-Kassel a constitution, but the actual work of drafting the constitution was carried out by a committee of seven delegates elected by the Landtag. The most important member of this constitution committee was its chairman, Sylvester Jordan, professor of law at the University of Marburg, and his liberal views played a significant role in determining the final outlook of the constitution. Two of the other six members of the committee were knights (Baumbach-Ropperhausen and Waitz), but they were moderates, perhaps less liberal than Jordan and some of the other committee members but still willing to work to bring about needed reforms.[81]

The final draft of the constitution was a compromise resulting from negotiations first within the committee, then in the Landtag itself, and finally between the Landtag and the government. Jordan and the more radical delegates had not achieved all of their goals, but overall the constitution was quite liberal for its day.[82]

The constitution established a one-chamber legislature, and the delegates from the nobility did not object even though the constitutions of most other similar-sized German states provided for two chambers, with a hereditary upper chamber of nobles.[83] The Landtag was no longer divided into separate estates, although many traditional elements

[80] StAM 340 v. Eschwege, Nr. 22, Buttlar to Deputy Carl von Eschwege, 2 October 1830.

[81] For a recent evaluation of Jordan's influence on the Hessian constitution of 1831 see Hellmut Seier, *Sylvester Jordan und die kurhessische Verfassung von 1831* (Marburg, 1981), 15–16; idem., "Zur Entstehung und Bedeutung der kurhessischen Verfassung von 1831," in *Der Verfassungsstaat als Bürge des Rechtfriedens*, ed. Walter Heinemeyer (Marburg, 1982), 21–26; Otto Müller, *Biographische Umrisse der Mitglieder der deutschen konstituierenden National-versammlung* (Frankfurt, 1849), 25; Werner Kaiser, *Sylvester Jordan: Seine Staatsauffassung und sein Einfluss auf die kurhessische Verfassungsurkunde vom 5. Januar 1831* (Dresden, 1936), 61, 64–65.

[82] For a detailed evaluation of the provisions of the constitution see Seier, *Sylvester Jordan*, 17–18.

[83] Jordan had opposed a two-house legislature because of the small size and economic weakness of the Hessian nobility. Even some nobles did not believe that two chambers were practical (see for example Treusch von Buttlar's letter to Wilhelm von Baumbach-Sontra on 3 October 1830, in which he states, "In my opinion 2 chambers are not suitable for Hesse because the state is too small"). StAM 340 v. Baumbach-Kirchheim, Paket 102.

221

were retained, giving the new constitution a strong degree of continuity. As in the past, the nobility was guaranteed a fixed number of delegates, and this number was actually higher than before. Thus the ten noble delegates in the 1830 Landtag would in the future be joined by four more *Standesherren*, the heads of two cadet lines of the royal family, and a representative of the landed nobility of the province of Hanau, bringing the total number of noble deputies to seventeen.

The nobility was thus very well represented in the Landtag (and tremendously overrepresented in terms of its size in relation to the total population), but actually the nobility's political power had been greatly reduced. The Landtag no longer voted by estate but by head, and the nobility was now strongly outnumbered because the number of non-noble delegates had also increased substantially (to sixteen delegates from the towns and sixteen from the peasantry).

In the course of the Landtag's debates on its future composition, an attempt was made to change the basis of representation to emphasize landownership more. On 17 December the *Vermittlungsausschuß*, a committee formed to mediate between the constitution committee and the government's representative at the Landtag, proposed to reduce the number of noble delegates to twelve (four princes, two *Standesherren*, the *Erbmarschall*, an *Obervorsteher*, two Hessian knights, one Schaumburg knight, and one former imperial knight). In addition there would be a delegate from the university and five delegates from the towns. This proposal then added two new categories: eight delegates drawn from the manufacturers, wholesale merchants, bankers, artists, and intellectuals of Hesse-Kassel and—the largest single group of delegates—twenty-four landowners who paid at least twenty-four talers per year in land taxes.[84]

This proposal has been seen by some observers as an attempt by the nobility to gain even more seats as a result of its dominant position among large landowners.[85] But only two of the seven members of the mediation committee were nobles (Baumbach-Ropperhausen and Trott), and the proposal was sharply criticized by many of the other noble delegates, who claimed that the rights of the *Standesherren* and the Hessian Ritterschaft were being violated.[86]

---

[84] StAM 73, Acc. 1900/33, V-1, Fasc. III, Fol. 108, 17 December 1830.

[85] Friedrich Murhard, *Die kurhessische Verfassungs-Urkunde, erläutert und beleuchtet nach Maßgabe ihrer einzelnen Paragraphen: Ein Handbuch für Landstände, Geschäftsmänner, konstitutionelle Staatsbeamte und Staatsbürger*, 2 vols. (Kassel, 1835) 2: 195–96; Bullik, *Staat und Gesellschaft*, 116–17.

[86] StAM 340 v. Eschwege, Nr. 22, draft of a protest by a Standesherr and several knights, 17 December 1830.

The delegates from the towns were also unhappy with the commit-tee's proposal, which would give them only five representatives instead of sixteen, and it is therefore not surprising that on 22 December 1830 the Landtag rejected the proposal and adopted instead the original rec-ommendation of the constitution committee.[87] Not all delegates were happy with the continued representation of the nobility,[88] but the final formula was one that satisfied both the government and the majority of the Landtag delegates by combining elements of both continuity and change.

Although noble delegates did not attempt to regain privileges lost dur-ing the Westphalian period (in contrast to the efforts made at the Land-tag of 1815–16), Kammerherr Carl von Eschwege, the most conservative of the Ritterschaft's deputies, did try to persuade the Landtag at least to give landlords compensation for their losses. In return Eschwege pro-posed ending all tax exemptions, stating, "in the future there should only be one kind of tax on land for all parts of the country." Eschwege coupled his proposal for a single tax on land with a maximum limit on land taxes, to be written into the constitution. He argued, "Hesse is an agrarian country, and the preservation and improvement of the condi-tion of all landowners must be its first priority. If landowners are pros-perous, then artisans and merchants will be too, and the needs of the largest class of subjects, the day laborers, will therefore also be taken care of."[89] Eschwege's limit on taxation was rejected, but the final ver-sion of the constitution did reflect some of his views. Article 148 called for the enactment of a law providing for "equal taxation with the assur-ance of a proper compensation for previous lawfully held tax exemp-tions."[90]

Several of the more liberal noble deputies were also active in pushing for change during the debates. Ludwig von Baumbach-Ropperhausen, along with Jordan and several other deputies, attempted to give Hesse-Kassel's Jews more freedom, but the Landtag as a whole refused to grant any new rights to the Jews.[91] The final draft merely stated, "The already existing rights of the Jews should stand under the protection of the con-stitution." The question of political rights for Jews was again raised by

[87] StAM 73, Acc. 1900/33, V-1, Fasc. III, Fol. 111.

[88] On 24 December 1830 Mayor Johannes Auffarth, representing the cities of the Werra district, declared, "the continued representation of the Hessian Ritterschaft or of noble estate owners lacks sufficient legal basis, is not proportional, and does not correspond to the intentions of the people." Ibid., Fol. 123–24.

[89] StAM 73, Acc. 1900/33, V-1, Fasc. III, Fol. 87–89, 12 December 1830.

[90] Ibid. The previous draft of the article had made no mention of compensation.

[91] StAM 73, Acc. 1900/33, V-1, Fasc. III, Fol. 103–105, 15 December 1830.

a noble during the debate on the election law in January 1831, but Kammerherr Borries von Hammerstein's attempt to help the Jews was also rejected.[92]

Overall the nobility's role in the crucial Landtag of 1830–31 had been progressive. Some conservative observers from other German states were shocked that Hessian nobles had not been loyal supporters of the government against the middle class. On 4 January 1831 the Prussian ambassador in Kassel, Ludwig von Hänlein, reported to his king, "Unfortunately democratic principles dominate everything here, including the constitution, and the nobility is under tremendous pressure. Worst of all, even some members of the knighthood have spoken in favor of such demagogy."[93]

The nobility's liberalism had arisen in part from its alienation from the monarchy since 1821. In addition, the nobility was not inclined to see the bourgeoisie as its enemy, for many of the noble delegates had close ties to the bourgeoisie through education, profession, or even marriage. Cooperation between the nobility and the bourgeoisie was made easier by the moderation of the bourgeoisie, which did not push its demands too far for fear of alienating both the government and the delegates from the nobility. The bourgeoisie and the nobility also shared a common fear of the lower classes. One concrete example of this came early in 1831, when Friedrich von Trott zu Solz reported on the contents of a petition to the Landtag by the artisans and citizens of Marburg calling for (in Trott's words) "the overthrow of all lawful and moral order and the destruction of God's and man's laws." Trott noted that this pamphlet had had a "very negative effect upon the lower classes" and moved that the individuals who had written and distributed this pamphlet be investigated and punished.[94] The Landtag quickly passed Trott's motion. The spirit of the times had also helped shape the attitudes of the noble delegates. Even the highly conservative Carl von Eschwege reported at the end of the Landtag in a letter to his constituents, "The overall well-being of the fatherland was my overriding concern, and it seemed inadvisable to deal with individual privileges at a time whose tendency is well known by every perceptive observer."[95] Eschwege expressed satisfaction with the results of the Landtag and pointed out a number of aspects of the constitution favorable to the nobility. One of the nobles from his district replied, "I never would have thought that the results of the Landtag would turn out so favorably for

---

[92] StAM 73, Acc. 1900/33, L-73, Fol. 238, 10 January 1831.
[93] Cited in Bullik, *Staat und Gesellschaft*, 76.
[94] StAM 73, Acc. 1898/6, Nr. 293, 7 January 1831.
[95] 340 v. Eschwege, Nr. 11, Eschwege to knights of Werra district, 15 March 1831.

us, for the majority of Hesse's inhabitants, as is the case all over, have feelings so strongly against the poor nobility that they are comparable only to the feelings against the Jews."[96]

The good relations that existed between the delegates from the nobility and the other members of the Landtag were clearly demonstrated by the elections to committees. In December 1830, when the assembly selected a committee to mediate between the constitution committee and the government's representatives, nobles were quite well represented. Two of the delegates were selected by the constitution committee, which chose Sylvester Jordan and Ludwig von Baumbach-Ropperhausen, and the Landtag as a whole elected the other four members, including Friedrich von Trott. A second noble, Kammerrat Wilhelm von Baumbach-Nentershausen, tied in the balloting for the fourth seat but lost when the final decision was made by lot.[97]

An even greater demonstration of the general lack of friction between the nobles and the rest of the delegates came at the end of the Landtag's session, when the delegates elected a five-man standing committee to represent the Landtag until the next one was elected. Although the nobility constituted a minority of the delegates overall, three of the five committee members elected were nobles.[98]

Liberal nobles played an important role not only in the legislature but also in the government itself. Faced with continued outbursts of popular unrest in the fall of 1830, the elector found it necessary to appoint the popular head of the provincial government in Marburg, Ferdinand von Schenck zu Schweinsberg (a knight who had served on the constitution commission of 1816), as his new justice minister. Schenck's appointment was designed not only to help restore order but also to conciliate the liberals in the Landtag.[99]

By the beginning of January 1831 the final version of the constitution had been completed and approved by the elector. William thought that the populace would now be satisfied and thus would leave him free to do as he wished. He therefore began to restructure the cabinet, bringing in conservatives and favorites of the Countess Reichenbach, with Carl Ri-

[96] Ibid., Carl von Berlepsch to Eschwege, 22 March 1831.

[97] Hellmut Gembries, *Verfassungsgeschichtliche Studien zur Recht auf Bildung im deutschen Vormärz: Liberale Staatslehre und parlamentarische Diskussion in Kurhessen* (Darmstadt and Marburg, 1978), 133–34.

[98] The three nobles were Trott, Baumbach-Ropperhausen, and Waitz. The other two deputies were Jordan and Mayor Bernhard Eberhard.

[99] Wippermann, *Kurhessen seit dem Freiheitskriege*, 208; Seier, "Entstehung und Bedeutung," 29. For a brief biography of Schenck see Franz, "Ferdinand Freiherr Schenck," in Schnack, *Lebensbilder*, 4: 331–37.

valier von Meysenbug, the new foreign minister, designated to play the leading role. Shortly thereafter the countess returned from exile, and the combination of her return to Kassel (raising fears that she would again dominate the government) and the reactionary character of the new government caused widespread rioting to break out in Kassel on 9 January 1831. The elector had not counted on such opposition, and he backed down, sending the countess away again and restructuring the cabinet to make it acceptable to the Landtag. The dominant figure in the new cabinet was Schenck.[100]

The anti-Reichenbach riots once again united all classes of society against the monarchy, as all feared the return of the countess. Although most of the demonstrators came from the lower classes, some observers believed that the riots had been instigated by the upper classes, particularly the nobility. The military commandant in Kassel, Colonel von Lossberg, reported hearing that "ladies of the highest standing had gone around to the artisans' shops and had stirred up the apprentices not to tolerate the return of the countess."[101] Ten years later an article in the *Leipziger Allgemeine Zeitung* stated that "the brief agitation of a portion of the lower classes of the populace in January 1831 against the Countess Reichenbach was the artificial product of the machinations of an aristocratic clique."[102]

In March 1831 the elector left the capital to join his mistress in Hanau, never to return. Six months later he turned over the government to his son Frederick William without actually abdicating. Thereafter Frederick William bore the title Crown Prince and Co-Ruler until he officially became the elector following his father's death in 1847. One of William II's last official acts in 1831 was to fire the liberal minister Ferdinand von Schenck zu Schweinsberg.

Frederick William's assumption of power did not at first lead to an improvement in relations between the monarchy and the Ritterschaft, for he did not immediately revoke his father's infringements of traditional noble privileges. The issue of the Stift Kaufungen's financial support for individuals outside the Ritterschaft continued to disturb the knighthood, and the new ruler soon began taking additional actions offensive to the knights. Immediately after gaining power he named his morganatic wife (a divorcée) and their three children the Countess and Counts

[100] Seier, "Entstehung und Bedeutung," 47–49; Wippermann, *Kurhessen seit dem Freiheitskriege*, 216–19.

[101] Lossberg to General Müldner von Mülnheim, 9 January 1831, in W. Rogge-Ludwig, *Karl Müldner von Mülnheim: General-Lieutenant und General-Adjutant des Kurfürsten Wilhelm II von Hessen* (Kassel, 1885), 55.

[102] Article of 29 July 1841, quoted in Rogge-Ludwig, *Müldner von Mülnheim*, 70–71.

of Schaumburg and then began trying to get them accepted into the knighthood. He even managed to alienate the knights while making a concession to them. Thus in the fall of 1832 he gave the Ritterschaft back its control over the third directorship of the Stift Kaufungen (taken away by his father in 1822), but soon afterward he ignored the knights' selection for the new post (Captain Ludwig von Baumbach-Kirchheim, later to become one of the leading Hessian liberals), saying the knights had failed to act before the expiration of the traditional six-week deadline. He then made his own choice, the highly conservative Kammerherr Carl von Eschwege. The Ritterschaft refused to accept his selection, and relations with the monarchy were once again at a low point.[103]

For the next two years the monarch and the Ritterschaft held negotiations to settle their many differences. During this period the Ritterschaft drew up a series of statutes designed to codify its remaining privileges and set forth clear procedures for the election of its officials and the admittance of new members, in order to avoid future difficulties with the monarchy. The two sides finally concluded a comprehensive

---

[103] Prior to 1835 the manner in which vacant directorships were filled had often led to controversy. Traditionally when a director died, the other two met to pick a new candidate, whose name was then submitted to the monarch for approval. But in the 1820s, after the elector took one of the directorships away from the knighthood, the choice lay in the hands of only one individual. A similar situation had briefly existed between 1814 and 1816, when the elector had delayed filling a vacant directorship in order to save the Stift Kaufungen money while it was recovering from the depredations of the Westphalian period. To deal with the question of filling a vacancy under these circumstances, William I had decreed that the remaining director should consult with the *Erbmarschall* and the five regional deputies before making his selection. William II did not revive this decree in 1822, and thereafter the selection of a new director by the sole remaining director became controversial. In 1824 after the death of Obervorsteher Wilhelm Friedrich von Trott zu Solz, one of the deputies (Carl von Eschwege) began campaigning for the vacancy and gathered the support of a number of knights. Eschwege argued that the selection of a new director should be made by the entire knighthood, noting, "experience has often taught us that favoritism toward relatives or individuals with other personal ties rather than abilities and service generally determines the filling of vacant directorships." Despite Eschwege's support within the knighthood, the remaining director, Wilhelm Lebrecht von Baumbach-Kirchheim, simply made his own choice without consulting anyone and selected his niece Friederike's husband, Friedrich von Trott, son of the deceased director. The same thing happened the following year after Baumbach died. Eschwege again applied for the vacancy and pushed for the involvement of more knights in the selection process, but Obervorsteher von Trott, after consulting only one of the regional deputies, chose Arnold von Baumbach-Gemünden, who had also applied for the post. It is thus ironic that Eschwege, who had long campaigned for more democracy in the selection of directors, became the center of controversy in 1832 when the elector named him to be director instead of the choice of the *Erbmarschall* and the other four regional deputies. StAM 340 v. Eschwege, Nr. 14, Zur Wahl des Carl Ludwig Ernst von Eschwege zu Reichensachsen zum Obervorsteher, 1824–1834; StAM 16, Rep. X, Kl. 16, Nr. 13, 15, 16.

agreement in April 1835. The monarch agreed to accept the Ritter-schaft's statutes and repeal the ordinance of 1822 changing the statues of the Stift Kaufungen. In return the knighthood promised to continue giving financial support to those widows and daughters of the holders of the royal orders who were already recipients, to drop its objections to the elector's appointment of Eschwege as the third director, and to admit the Counts of Schaumburg (the elector's morganatic offspring) into its membership.[104]

After this agreement was reached, relations generally improved, although in 1837 Frederick William again antagonized the knighthood. Two years earlier he had ennobled the sons of his wife's first marriage (which had ended in divorce), but in October 1837 he changed their name to von Scholley, a family of the Hessian Ritterschaft that was not yet extinct, although the last male in the family had recently died. The elector attempted to get the Ritterschaft to accept them as members, but the knighthood objected strenuously to their lack of noble birth, to their controversial family background, and to the misappropriation of the proud von Scholley name (particularly while some members of this family were still alive). Thanks to the new statutes, which he had personally approved, Frederick William had to back down, but he expressed his displeasure by firing Foreign Minister Friedrich von Trott, who was also a leading official of the Ritterschaft.[105]

During this period of quarrels with the regent, the nobility continued to select primarily moderate liberals as its representatives, and several of these nobles held leading positions in the Landtag. Thus in 1831 Friedrich von Trott served as president of the assembly until he resigned to become justice minister early in 1832, he was succeeded as president for the remaining months of the Landtagsession by Moritz von Baumbach-Kirchheim. The next session (1833) was also presided over by a member of the Ritterschaft (Moritz's brother Ludwig von Baumbach), and Moritz again served as president for the 1839–41 and 1842–44 sessions. In 1847 Friedrich von Trott again became president, but after the unrest of March 1848 he was replaced by the more liberal Ludwig von Baumbach-Kirchheim.[106]

The moderate and liberal leanings of many of the deputies from the

---

[104] StAM 16, Rep X, Kl. 16, Nr. 16; 300 Abt. 11, C7, Nr. 2, Ritterschaft; 340 v. Eschwege, Nr. 14, 18. The statutes were never ratified in their entirety by the Hessian diet. See StAM 73, Acc. 1900/33, R 28, Akten, die Statuten der althessischen Ritterschaft betr., 1837/38.

[105] Philipp Losch, *Letzte deutsche Kurfürst*, 59–60.

[106] Philipp Losch, *Die Abgeordneten der kurhessischen Ständeversammlungen von 1830 bis 1866* (Marburg, 1909), 5–7.

nobility proved very important in the first Landtag elected according to the provisions of the new constitution. This Landtag, which began meeting in April 1831, had the task of drafting concrete legislation to carry out the provisions of the constitution. The delegates from the nobility were not united in their political outlook and included several liberals, as can be seen in the following contemporary analysis by a liberal Kassel newspaper:

> Although it cannot be denied that generally the noble delegates completely gave in to the influence of the court in advancing the interests of their class while encroaching upon the rights of the people, there were some honorable men who did not pursue this course. Among them we must number the estimable president of the chamber, Herr von Baumbach, whose almost unanimous election as president and as member of the standing committee demonstrated the universal trust placed in him. The deputies v. d. Malsburg, v. Heidewolff, v. Trott (captain) and several others were men who, even if not completely free of the prejudices of their class, still followed their humanitarian convictions. . . . Limitation of the rights of the people and expansion of those of the government, along with extension of the nobility's privileges, were the main goals of the deputies v. Eschwege, v. Landsberg, v. Hammerstein, and v. Geyso. The latter two individuals were remarkable only for their sentiments, they were not competent enough to gain any influence in the chamber; Deputy v. Landsberg did not lack intellectual gifts but rather speaking ability; he was not capable of speaking two coherent sentences, and his attempt to read a written speech in the opening session was rejected by the chamber; Deputy v. Eschwege, a man of considerable ability and also great knowledge, at least in the areas of his previous sphere of activity, was thus the only leader of this group.[107]

The most important issue discussed during the Landtag of 1831–32 was the proposed redemption law, which called for the abolition of a number of feudal dues and services. None of the delegates from the nobility opposed this measure; the main concern of both liberal and conservative nobles was to obtain the most favorable terms possible for noble landlords. Waitz and Eschwege argued that peasants should not have the exclusive right to initiate the process of redemption but that land-

---

[107] *Der Verfassungsfreund: Eine Zeitschrift für Staats- und Volksleben*, 12 September 1832, p. 619. The author of this article left no doubt where his own sympathies lay when he stated (p. 623) that the deputies of the bourgeoisie showed "the most intelligence, the greatest independence of judgment, and true intellectual superiority."

lords should also be able to request it.[108] This attempt to improve the position of landlords proved unsuccessful, and afterward noble deputies concentrated on defeating efforts to reduce the amount of compensation for landlords proposed in the original draft of the law—twenty times the annual value of the dues and services. On 15 December 1831 Elias Fuchs, representing the peasants of Schaumburg, moved that the amount of compensation be lowered to only eighteen times the annual value. In reply Wilhelm von Baumbach-Nentershausen argued, "It will not be difficult for individual peasants to raise such small redemption sums, and in such cases it will not make much difference to them whether they must pay eighteen or twenty times the annual value. But for the landlord, who deals with a large number of peasants, the difference of 2 percent is much more important, because he must do without it for all incoming redemption payments."[109] Baumbach also pointed out that many estates were owned by bourgeois, not nobles; furthermore, churches, charitable foundations, and above all the state were important recipients of feudal dues, too. Baumbach was supported by the vice-president of the Landtag, Moritz von Baumbach-Kirchheim (president in 1832), who noted that nothing less than twenty times would be fair. Borries von Hammerstein went even further and proposed changing the amount to twenty-five times, but the other nobles concentrated their efforts on retaining the original amount. Not surprisingly, no nobles supported Fuchs's motion to lower the amount of compensation (only thirteen delegates voted in favor). Hammerstein's motion also proved unsuccessful (no vote totals were given).[110]

The final vote on the law was taken on 5 April 1832, and there was very little opposition. The result of the secret ballot was thirty-seven to three in favor of the bill, so most, if not all, of the noble delegates must have supported it.[111]

When their own interests were not involved, even the most conservative noble deputies could support progressive measures. Thus when the Landtag debated improving secondary education, Carl von Eschwege argued that the proposed legislation should be expanded to include primary schools because the Gymnasia could not become more effective if local schools were not improved.[112]

The moderation and harmony that existed in Hessian politics in the first year after the enactment of the constitution came to an end after the

[108] *LTV*, 7 November 1831, 885–86; 24 November 1831, 989.
[109] *LTV*, 15 December 1831, 1118–21.
[110] Ibid., 1124–29.
[111] *LTV*, 5 April 1832, 1760.
[112] *LTV*, 24 November 1831, 982–83.

new ruler appointed Ludwig Hassenpflug justice and interior minister in 1832. Following the Hambach Festival and similar meetings inside Hesse, Hassenpflug began charting a reactionary course that soon led to a confrontation with the liberal-dominated Landtag. Hassenpflug was a skilled politician who used the provisions of the constitution to defeat the liberals' attacks. Thus their attempt to indict him before the supreme court for violations of the constitution was foiled by his swift dissolution of the Landtag in July 1832. He also began working to make the composition of the Landtag more favorable by enforcing an article of the constitution that required civil servants to receive official permission before sitting in the legislature. In this manner he was able to prevent Sylvester Jordan, Moritz von Baumbach-Kirchheim, and other liberal civil servants from participating in the next legislature. Hassenpflug's enforcement of this provision of the constitution significantly altered the political makeup of the nobility's delegation, for most of the liberal delegates from the nobility were civil servants. Hassenpflug also succeeded in adding several new deputies who were supporters of the government when he persuaded two of the royal princes to allow themselves to be represented by individuals he had selected. In return the princes received a higher appanage. The two new deputies were both conservative nobles: Colonel Ferdinand von Eschwege and Wilhelm Freiherr von Verschuer.[113]

The most prominent liberal noble remaining in the legislature, former army officer Ludwig von Baumbach-Kirchheim, served briefly as president in 1833 before resigning to protest against Hassenpflug's actions.[114] Most of the other noble deputies were now conservatives, and they scored a major success in 1834 when they succeeded in preventing noble estate owners from being placed under the jurisdiction of local villages by the new *Gemeinde Ordnung* (a law regulating local government).[115]

Liberal nobles again began to play a more active role in the assembly after Hassenpflug resigned from office in 1837, following a quarrel with the regent. Once again liberal civil servants could sit in the Landtag, for the new government stopped trying to exclude them. Among these civil servants was Moritz von Baumbach-Kirchheim. In 1834 Hassenpflug

---

[113] Seier, "Entstehung und Bedeutung," 53–54; Wippermann, *Kurhessen seit dem Freiheitskriege*, 284–86, 289–93.

[114] Wippermann, *Kurhessen seit dem Freiheitskriege*, 288.

[115] The original draft of the law exempted only the upper nobility and former imperial knights from the jurisdiction of local villages, but the Hessian and Schaumburg knighthoods succeeded in gaining exemption as well. For knights' protests against being made members of villages see *LTV*, 6 April 1832, 1793, 1797; 1 October 1833, Anlage 171c.

had removed him from the supreme court and had also placed him far from the center of political activity by appointing him director of the superior court in the distant city of Rinteln (in the exclave Schaumburg). With Hassenpflug gone, the citizens of the Schaumburg towns elected Baumbach as their representative to the legislature in 1839, and he soon became its president.[116]

Both liberal and conservative nobles joined to push for a major reform that had been promised by the redemption law but not yet enacted—the abolition of the entire feudal system. Many nobles had become convinced of the need to end their feudal ties to the state because the redemption laws had created considerable difficulties or even financial losses for nobles whose estates were held as fiefs. In particular landlords resented not being able to gain access to redemption payments being held by the *Landeskreditkasse* because the former peasant dues or services were part of a fief.[117]

The government's continued lack of support for a bill to end the feudal system caused the Landtag deputies from the Ritterschaft to write to the regent in 1843 requesting the introduction of such a bill in the legislature.[118] The following year the Landtag as a whole asked the government for a bill to end the feudal system, but this request also met with no response.[119] With the government unwilling to act on ending the feudal system, noble deputies on several occasions sought to eliminate one of its harmful effects—the low rate of interest being paid to landlords whose redemption payments were being held by the *Landeskreditkasse*. In 1843 and again in 1847, nobles' motions to increase the interest rate received the support of the other members of the Landtag, but the government failed to act.[120] Nobles were growing frustrated and angry. At the annual meeting of the Ritterschaft at the Stift Kaufungen in March 1847, the members strongly supported Otto von Trott's proposal to present a list of the knighthood's grievances to the monarch. Trott argued, "the time is right for a noble protest at the highest level because a strongly conservative government will certainly not turn a deaf ear to

---

[116] Ibid., 343–44; *ADB*, 2:155–57. Baumbach's election by a group outside his own constituency (the knighthood) was not an isolated occurence in the nineteenth century. On a number of occasions voters in Hessian towns chose liberal nobles as their representatives. Between 1830 and 1866 eighteen nobles represented constituencies other than the nobility. Losch, *Abgeordnete*.

[117] See above, pp. 89–90. For a good summary of nobles' reasons for wanting an end to the feudal system see Maximilian Freiherr von Ditfurth's letter to the diet on 19 December 1839 in StAM 73, Acc. 1900/33, A-16, Fasc. I.

[118] StAM 340 v. Eschwege, Nr. 18.

[119] StAM 73, Acc. 1900/33, A-16, Landtagsabschied 3 April 1844.

[120] Ibid.; *LTV*, 22 October 1847, 32.

these complaints and thereby alienate the wholehearted support of the conservative elements of the fatherland at a time when the enemies of such policies are preparing for new struggles."[121]

Trott was mistaken; the government failed to act on the Ritterschaft's requests for fewer restrictions upon credit for vassals and easier access for landlords to funds being held by the *Landeskreditkasse*. Thus on the eve of the revolution of 1848, as in 1830, the nobility was alienated from the government, this time for economic reasons rather than questions of privilege and status.

Widespread unrest in March 1848 quickly brought considerable change to both the government and the legislature, with liberal nobles playing an important role in both. On 6 March the conservative ministers resigned, and the following day the elector named a new liberal cabinet with Moritz von Baumbach-Kirchheim holding the key post of justice minister. On 13 March the Landtag reconvened and soon came under new leadership. Friedrich von Trott resigned as president and was replaced by another noble, but one with a strong liberal reputation—Ludwig von Baumbach-Kirchheim. Baumbach's first speech to the Landtag reflected the hopes and fears of the Hessian liberals, both noble and bourgeois:

> Difficult times lie behind us; better times have now arrived. There is now complete harmony between the government and the legislature. The present task of the latter is to work together with the government for the benefit of the country. If the constitution had only become a reality soon after its publication, most of the demands that are currently being voiced would already have been fulfilled. Unfortunately the constitution was for the most part a stillborn child. But we now have the prospect of seeing it come to life and bring its benefits to all groups, thereby ensuring the prosperity of the country. But we also have dangerous enemies; we must support the government so that attacks against individuals and violations of private property no longer occur.[122]

Baumbach's call for reforms as well as protection against the lower classes was supported by the other nobles in the Landtag, for the most conservative nobles stopped attending the debates after the unrest began. Two of these conservative nobles (representing *Standesherren*) were soon stricken from the list of deputies.[123] The *Standesherren* then sent

[121] ARSK, Rep. VI, Gef. 2–3, Nr. 7, 29 March 1847.

[122] *LTV*, 20 March 1848, 10.

[123] Deputies Rudolf von Buttlar and Ludwig von Ochs were stricken from the rolls in April 1848 for failing to attend sessions. Another conservative, Ferdinand Freiherr von

new, more liberal representatives (Moritz von Schenck zu Schweinsberg and Carl Sigismund Freiherr Waitz von Eschen).

The Landtag responded to the unrest in the country with a flurry of reform measures. To placate the peasants, the government quickly drafted a bill ending all vestiges of the feudal system, and the deputies from the nobility did not object. As in 1832, their main concern was to obtain as favorable terms for landlords as possible. An additional reason for noble delegates to support the bill was that it also ended the nobility's feudal ties to the state. Nobles' estates could now become entirely the property of their owners, free of restrictions upon sale or mortgage, and nobles could also gain access to redemption payments being held by the *Landeskreditkasse*.

Despite the nobility's willingness to support reforms in 1848, its continued existence as a privileged political group soon came under attack from both the liberals and a new, more radical group of delegates known as the democrats, who advocated a truly representative government with deputies elected solely on the basis of population. To head off some of this criticism, Moritz von Schenck zu Schweinsberg proposed amending the constitution so that nobles could elect individuals outside their own class as representatives.[124] But pressure continued to grow as petitions arrived in the Landtag calling for changes in the constitution and a new election law to end the special representation of the nobility. On 15 August 1848 the liberal deputy Heinrich Henkel made such a motion, and debate on a new election law began. Otto von Trott zu Solz argued that the Landtag should wait to see what the new national constitution being drafted in Frankfurt would have to say about the political rights of the nobility. But Ludwig von Baumbach-Kirchheim, president of the assembly, declared, "our present situation and the current debates in the national assembly in Frankfurt make separate representation for the knighthood and the nobility seem out of place. There can no longer be any special representation. It is the task of the nobility and of the knighthood to become part of the people and to have the same representatives as the rest of the population." Baumbach's willingness to sacrifice the nobility's representation was not unconditional, for he argued that since Hesse-Kassel did not have a two-chamber system of government, there must be separate representation for large landowners once the representation of the nobility ceased.[125]

Baumbach's desire to avoid a completely representative system and

---

Hutten (representing the nobility of Hanau), had resigned in March. *LTV*, 17 April 1848, 1; Losch, *Abgeordnete*, 30.

[124] *LTV*, 4 July 1848, 5–6.

[125] *LTV*, 15 August 1848, 11–12, 14.

ensure a substantial number of deputies from the propertied classes was shared by many liberals, especially those in the government, and on 21 October 1848 the government presented the Landtag with a proposed election law to eliminate the separate representation of the nobility but replace it with a bloc of sixteen deputies to be selected by the individuals paying the most taxes in their districts. The democrats immediately criticized this proposal as being simply a disguised way of continuing the nobility's representation, but liberals argued that this was not the case, since the new group of electors would number approximately 750 and include both landed and commercial interests, whereas the previous privileged groups from the nobility had included at best one hundred voters.[126]

Many noble deputies were initially cool to this proposal because they wanted to see more weight given to large landowners. Otto von Trott noted that the Frankfurt Parliament would soon "revoke all special political rights for individual classes, which I find in keeping with the times." But Trott stated that he could support the new election law only if it replaced the nobility's representation with representatives of the large landowners. Carl von Eschwege called for the landowners to be separated from the commercial interests and be given sixteen seats to the latter's six.[127]

Eschwege's motion found little support outside the nobility, so Otto von Trott attempted to appeal to the democrats to get them to join with the nobility against the liberals. Noting dissatisfaction from all sides with the government's proposal, Trott pointed out that there was:

a class of the population that, if the government had wanted to act in complete accord with the spirit of the times, should also be represented. I am speaking of all those who pay no taxes at all—the poor, among them the proletariat. Up to now there have been three estates in the diet: nobility, bourgeoisie, and peasantry. Now that the political rights of the nobility are being taken away, only the bourgeoisie and peasants will remain. But it cannot be denied that this third class still exists and that it has recently become very important. I therefore understand the agitation for a new election law and would favor representation for this class of poor individuals who pay no taxes, if in addition the law would establish a perma-

---

[126] *LTV*, 24 October 1848, 8–10. For conflicts in ideology between liberals and democrats in Germany as a whole see Hamerow, *Restoration, Revolution, Reaction*, 60–66; Leonard Krieger, *The German Idea of Freedom: History of a Political Tradition* (Chicago, 1957), 278–329.

[127] *LTV* 24 October 1848, 14–16.

nent basis for a genuine representation of large landholdings along-side the bourgeoisie and peasantry.[128]

No such compromise between the left and the right actually developed in the Landtag, but the two groups remained opponents of the liberals' proposed electoral system. At the end of October the legislative session came to an end with no more progress made on a new election law.

Following elections in November 1848, the new Landtag began its deliberations on 1 December. Ludwig von Baumbach-Kirchheim no longer served as president, for he had become active in politics at the national level. Early in November delegates from a number of political clubs in Hesse had met to form a new liberal party, the *Nationale Partei*, and elected Baumbach as their leader. Baumbach also served as a delegate to the Frankfurt Parliament beginning on 23 November 1848. Here he joined a moderate group of delegates known as the "Augsburger Hof."[129] Baumbach was not the only liberal Hessian noble interested in politics at the national level. In April 1848 Reinhard von Schenk zu Schweinsberg had been an unsuccessful candidate for election to the Frankfurt Parliament. His platform had included the unification of Germany under the leadership of Archduke Johann of Austria, the creation of a constitutional monarchy with responsible ministers, the replacement of standing armies with people's militias, the end of feudal dues and services, and "the abolition of the nobility in its present form."[130]

Ludwig von Baumbach's place as president of the Hessian Landtag was taken by a bourgeois liberal, Johann Schwarzenberg. The delegates resumed debate on the proposed election law, and for a time it looked as if the combined opposition of the nobility and the democrats might be sufficient to defeat the liberals' proposed law. Many nobles continued to push for separate representation for large landowners, and the democrats remained unwilling to support separate representation for wealthy taxpayers. As the radical deputy Carl Winkelblech declared, "If we must have a privileged class in the legislature, then I strongly believe that the nobility should keep its seats. The nobility has already lost its privileges in society, and it is neutral in the coming struggle between the working class and the upper bourgeoisie."[131]

[128] Ibid., 17.

[129] Alfred Tapp, *Hanau im Vormärz und in der Revolution von 1848–1849* (Hanau, 1976), 376; "Ludwig von Baumbach," *Meyers Großes Konversations-Lexikon*, 6th ed. (Leipzig, 1905), 2: 475.

[130] Reinhard von Schenk zu Schweinsberg, "Mein politisches Glaubens-Bekenntnis," 15 April 1848 (pamphlet in StAM library).

[131] *LTV*, 21 December 1848, 26.

On 21 December 1848 a key vote was taken on article 2 of the proposed law, which called for the establishment of sixteen deputies from the wealthiest taxpayers. The article was rejected by a vote of twenty-three to nineteen. Most noble deputies voted against the article, although three representatives of the nobility and two nobles representing other groups sided with the liberals.[132]

The essentially negative coalition of radicals and conservatives against the liberals did not last very long, however. It soon became clear to the delegates from the nobility that their separate representation was doomed, both by the prevailing sentiment in Hesse-Kassel and by the decisions of the Frankfurt Parliament. The nobles also realized that their attempt to achieve separate representation for large landowners had little chance of success. Fearful of the radicals' demands for complete democracy, the conservative noble deputies decided that the liberals' proposed representation for wealthy taxpayers should be supported as the lesser of two evils. Even one of the *Standesherren*, Ferdinand Graf zu Ysenburg-Büdingen, made a strong plea in favor of the proposed law on 24 December 1848. Ysenburg justified his stand by warning that failure to enact the proposed bill would benefit "the party whose goal is to overthrow all existing relationships."[133]

Once the nobles ended their opposition, passage of the electoral law became certain. On 2 February 1849 the diet voted thirty-five to eleven in favor of the bill, giving it the needed two-thirds majority to amend the constitution. Immediately after the vote Wilhelm von Baumbach-Nentershausen made a statement that summarized the reasons that many of the nobles had voted in favor of a bill that ended their right to sit in the diet:

> In the session of 21 December I voted against the proposed election law because I believe that the draft did not provide a sufficient conservative element in the diet and did not ensure that the interests of landowners, which make up the largest portion of the population, would be adequately represented in the future. I still hold the same views but have become convinced that a more satisfactory election law is not attainable. I have therefore voted in favor of the bill.[134]

Soon after the publication of the new election law in April 1849, the Landtag ended its session. When the next Landtag met in July, the dev-

---

[132] Ibid., 34. Nobles favoring the measure were Ferdinand von Rau, Heinrich von Sybel, Maximilian von Ditfurth, Carl von Stiernberg, and Moritz von Schenck zu Schweinsberg.

[133] *LTV*, 22 December 1848, Beilage 17, p. 4.

[134] *LTV*, 2 February 1849, 22.

astating effects of the election law upon the nobility's political power were clearly demonstrated. Only one of the forty-eight delegates was a noble: the liberal Moritz von Schenck zu Schweinsberg, elected by the wealthy taxpayers of the Fulda district.[135]

Along with domestic reforms the Hessian legislature concerned itself with national politics in the spring and summer of 1849. The overwhelming majority of the delegates voted in favor of the selection of the king of Prussia as the new German emperor, but Frederick William IV's refusal to accept the crown ended the Frankfurt Parliament's attempt to unify Germany on a liberal basis. The liberal majority in the Hessian legislature continued to support unification, now in the form of the Prussian-dominated Erfurt Union.[136] But the chances for German unification on any basis were fading, and soon Hesse-Kassel itself became the scene of a major confrontation between Austria and Prussia that ended with the dissolution of the Erfurt Union and the reestablishment of the German Confederation.

The confrontation was caused by a constitutional crisis in Hesse-Kassel that began when Elector Frederick William, who had never been comfortable with the liberal "March Ministry," decided the time had come to return to a reactionary government. Already in August 1849 the elector had accepted the resignation of the entire cabinet, but facing heavy pressure from the legislature and unable to find replacements, he was forced to reinstate the liberal ministers. He refused, however, to reappoint the most liberal noble in the cabinet, Foreign Minister Wilhelm von Schenck zu Schweinsberg. The other liberals in the cabinet did not outlast Schenck by very many months, for in February 1850 the elector felt confident enough to summon Ludwig Hassenpflug back from Prussian service to head a new cabinet to replace the liberals. The era of reaction had begun in Hesse-Kassel.[137]

Almost immediately the new government ran into strong opposition from the liberal legislature. Neither side was willing to compromise, and Hassenpflug dissolved the legislature in June 1850. In the elections that followed, the democrats gained a majority of seats for the first time, narrowly edging out the liberals. The legislature was now even more strongly opposed to Hassenpflug's policies than before the dissolution.

The crisis came to a head at the end of August, when the legislature refused to allow the government to collect taxes. Hassenpflug replied by dissolving the legislature again and ordering the continued collection of

<hr />

[135] Losch, *Abgeordnete*, 49.
[136] Losch, *Geschichte des Kurfürstentums*, 254–57.
[137] Ibid., 258–59.

taxes even without the Landtag's consent. The Landtag's standing committee declared this decree unconstitutional and quickly found support from most members of the Hessian bureaucracy. Financial officials refused to collect taxes, and judges supported the standing committee's contention that the government was acting unconstitutionally. Faced with such widespread opposition, Hassenpflug turned to the army, but here too he was to be disappointed. On 7 September 1850 he declared the country under martial law, but the army's officers soon found themselves facing a severe crisis of conscience when the Hessian supreme court declared Hassenpflug's "September decrees" unconstitutional. The officers felt themselves being ordered to act in violation of their oath to the constitution and sought to end the dilemma by offering their resignations. On 10 October 1850, 241 of the 277 Hessian officers turned in their resignations, including four generals and seven colonels. Although many of the officers who did not turn in their resignations were nobles, the bulk of the nobles serving in the army felt bound by the oath of allegiance to the constitution.[138]

Opposition to the government's reactionary course was also strong among nobles serving in the bureaucracy. Most civil servants in the financial and judicial departments, noble and non-noble alike, had refused to obey the government's order to collect taxes illegally. Many of these "revolutionaries" (to use the government's term) lost their positions in 1850 and were placed on inactive lists at one-quarter of their previous salaries (*Wartegeld*). Among these civil servants were Oberzolldirektor Friedrich von Schmerfeld and Obergerichtsrat Moritz von Schenck zu Schweinsberg. But other noble civil servants did not support the liberals in this crisis, showing that even among nobles in the bureaucracy there was no unanimity of political outlook.[139]

Despite the opposition of Landtag, officer corps, and bureaucracy, Hassenpflug and the elector did not back down in the constitutional crisis of 1850. They appealed for help from the federal diet, which under the leadership of Austria voted to send troops to restore order and suppress the "revolution" in Hesse-Kassel. Prussia initially attempted to oppose the federal intervention but backed down on 29 November 1850,

[138] Reinhard Höhn, *Verfassungskampf und Heereseid: Der Kampf des Bürgertums um das Heer (1815–1850)* (Leipzig, 1938), 200–204. For excerpts from the resignations of the officers, including members of the Ritterschaft, see Eberhard Radbruch, "Offiziere im Konflikt um Gehorsamkeit und Gewissen: Die Haltung des kurhessischen Offizierkorps im Verfassungskonflikt von 1850," *Geschichte in Wissenschaft und Unterricht* 19 (1968): 137–45.

[139] For lists of civil servants and their stands during the constitutional crisis of 1850 see StAM 300, Abt. 11, E 8, Nr. 19, Verzeichnis der revolutionären Staatsdiener 1850; *LTV* 1862/63, Beilage 51; StAM 73, Acc. 1900/33, S-65.

signing the Olmütz agreement with Austria. Hesse-Kassel was now occupied by Bavarian and Austrian troops, and the reaction set in with a vengeance. Many liberal civil servants resigned immediately, and those who did not were soon forced out of office once the government began quartering large numbers of Bavarian soldiers in their homes.[140]

The constitution of 1831 also fell victim to the reaction. It was replaced by a new constitution drawn up by the government without consulting the Landtag and promulgated on 13 April 1852. Although many of the provisions of the old constitution were carried over into the new one, the political system underwent radical change. Not only was the election law of 1849 eliminated, the traditional one-house legislature was replaced by an upper house (*I. Kammer*) consisting of the royal princes; the *Standesherren*; the *Erbmarschall*; eight deputies from the Hessian and Schaumburg knighthoods, former imperial knights, and Hanau nobility; three Protestant church officials and a Catholic bishop; and the vice-chancellor of the university; and a lower house (*II. Kammer*) with sixteen representatives each from the large landowners, towns, and peasantry.[141]

The nobility was once again represented in the legislature, in fact with far more power than in the past, and Hassenpflug therefore expected strong support from the upper chamber. But when the new constitution was presented to the legislature for ratification, the upper house was far more critical than the lower and made a large number of suggestions for improvements designed to give the legislature more power.[142] Despite Hassenpflug's conservatism, he found few strong supporters among the members of the Ritterschaft. Soon after he became the head of the cabinet again, some of his confidants drafted a letter of support for Hassenpflug and circulated it among the members of the Ritterschaft. But as one contemporary noted, "the letter did receive a number of signatures by Hessian knights, but they were accompanied by such coarse remarks against Hassenpflug that the drafters of the letter quickly gave up their endeavor and buried it in silence."[143]

The deputies in the new upper house were hardly liberals. The gov-

[140] Heinrich Gräfe, *Der Verfassungskampf in Kurhessen nach Entstehung, Fortgang und Ende* (Leipzig, 1851), 259–261.

[141] Losch, *Geschichte des Kurfürstentums*, 290–91.

[142] Hans-Georg Rommel, "Der kurhessische Verfassungskonflikt 1859–186: Ein Beitrag zum Problem des bürgerlichen Liberalismus in Deutschland" (Ph.D. diss., University of Marburg, 1950), 9; Ludwig Müller, *Der Kampf um die kurhessische Verfassung* (Marburg, 1895), 36.

[143] Adam Pfaff, *Das Trauerspiel in Hessen: Ein Beitrag zur Geschichte unserer Tage* (Brunswick, 1851), 91–92.

ernment helped ensure this by enforcing the rule that civil servants could not serve in the Landtag without the government's permission. In this manner Hassenpflug was able to remove the noble deputy with the most prominent liberal credentials, Edwin von Bischoffshausen, who had resigned as a superior court judge in 1850, by having him appointed as a *Landrat*. But while the conservative-dominated upper house did not favor a return to the constitution of 1831, the deputies also did not want the legislature to be nothing more than a rubber stamp for the government.[144] During the Landtag of 1852–54 the strongest advocates of changes in the constitution of 1852 to give the legislature more power were Otto von Trott (one of the leading conservatives in the debates of 1848 and 1849) and the upper chamber's president, Obergerichtsrat Ferdinand von Schutzbar genannt Milchling.[145]

The constitutional struggles of 1850 had marked a turning point in the political activities of the nobility. In the 1830s and 1840s the leading noble politicians had been liberals, but after 1850 conservatism became the predominant outlook among nobles who were involved in politics. The defeat of liberalism in 1850 encouraged conservative nobles to become more active politically, and the government's exclusion of liberal civil servants from the legislature enabled these conservatives to dominate the elections of the nobility.

One of the first manifestations of the growing strength and activism of conservatism among Hessian nobles was the formation of the *Bund der Treue mit Gott für Fürst und Vaterland* (generally known as the *Treubund*— Loyalty League) on 6 November 1850. This small group of conservatives elected Rudolf von Buttlar-Elberberg as their president. His brother Julius, a *Landrat* and former supreme court justice Carl von Dehn-Rotfelser were also prominent members.[146]

Conservatism in Hesse-Kassel was often associated with anti-Semitism, and this issue divided the nobility along ideological lines. In the 1830s liberal nobles had actively campaigned for more freedom for Jews, but in the 1840s and 1850s conservative nobles advocated placing restrictions upon Jews. One of the reasons for these proposals was the widespread problem of usury and land speculation by Jews in many

[144] See for example Otto von Trott's speech of 13 August 1853 against any lessening of the Landtag's power over the budget. *LTV*, 13 August 1853, 6. For the nobles' approval of the main feature of the new constitution—the two-house legislature—see StAM 73, Acc. 1905/47, I. Kammer, Rubr. XIV, Nr. 1, Beil. 4.

[145] Although a civil servant, Milchling had received permission from the government to sit in the Landtag because in 1850 he had been one of the few judges to declare Hassenpflug's actions constitutional.

[146] StAM 300, Abt. 11, C 7, Nr. 13. The *Treubund* disbanded in November 1853.

areas of Hesse-Kassel. In November 1847 Rudolf von Buttlar introduced legislation to prevent Jews from speculating in land by making them wait ten years before they could sell property they had purchased. After being studied by a committee, Buttlar's motion was discussed on the floor of the diet in February 1848. To ease criticism that Buttlar's proposal was directed solely against Jews, another noble deputy, Rudolf von Keudell, suggested amending the motion to oppose all usurious trading in land, no matter what the religion of the perpetrator. Buttlar accepted the amendment, and the motion passed.[147]

A much more severe brand of anti-Semitism was demonstrated by Ludwig von Baumbach-Lenderscheid. In 1853 the seventy-four-year-old retired army officer proposed the repeal of the 1833 law that had emancipated the Jews of Hesse-Kassel. Baumbach called for the restoration of special taxes on Jews, limitation of marriages by Jews, the creation of a special fund to encourage and assist Jews in emigrating to America, the prohibition of Jews from holding public office (particularly judgeships), limitation of the number of Jewish lawyers, and measures to prevent Jews from speculating in land. Baumbach closed his motion with a warning, "Even though at present no Jews are representing our Christian people in the diet, we should not feel ourselves too safe from eventual domination by the Jews, for we live in an age in which money dominates everything."[148]

Baumbach's motion was not seriously considered by the upper house, but three years later one of his ideas was taken up by the representative of the Lutheran church. Bishop Julius Martin proposed that only members of recognized Christian churches be allowed to sit in the Landtag. Two nobles, Ludwig Freiherr von Edelsheim and Ferdinand von Schutzbar, opposed this motion, saying it would take away rights granted to the Jews in 1816. But other nobles supported excluding Jews from the diet, and the upper house voted ten to five in favor of Martin's motion (which was later rejected by the lower house).[149]

Two years later, in 1858, the legislature passed a bill with strong anti-Semitic aspects. The new law required local officials to compile lists of all Christians employed by Jews as servants, clerks, journeymen, or apprentices and then report on these individuals' treatment. This measure had resulted from agitation by Ernst von Baumbach-Kirchheim, which

---

[147] *LTV*, 16 November 1847, 4, Beilage 72; 22 February 1848, 3–26.

[148] StAM 73, Acc. 1905/47, I. Kammer, Rubr. XIV, Nr. 4. The author of the anti-Semitic motion, Ludwig von Baumbach-Lenderscheid, should not be confused with Ludwig von Baumbach-Ropperhausen or Ludwig von Baumbach-Kirchheim, who had both advocated more freedom for Hessian Jews, the former in 1830 and the latter in 1848.

[149] *LTV*, I. Kammer, 28 November 1856, 220–32.

seems surprising because he was a supreme court justice and a member of a family with a strong reputation for liberalism in the nineteenth century. His older brothers Moritz and Ludwig were leading liberals, and the latter had actively campaigned in the diet for more freedom for Jews. The letters of the United States consul in Kassel shed some light on Baumbach's motivation. Consul Samuel Rieker was at first baffled by the measure against the Jews, but in May 1858 he reported that he had learned that the decree was "nothing else than the result of private hatred and revenge and the consequence of the denunciation of Mr. Ernest von Baumbach, one of the highest and most influential Electoral-Court-Officers. Mr. von Baumbach lost some time ago a lawsuit against Baron von Rothschild and has been since that very moment filled with so revengeful a hatred against the whole Judaism that he has been at work to bring about that untimely measure of religious espionage."[150]

The main subject of the upper house's debates after its formation in 1852 was not, however, anti-Semitism but revision of the new constitution. When the upper house's proposals for changes were complete on 7 December 1853, Trott moved that the chamber vote on the report as a whole, rather than section by section, in order to prevent the most conservative deputies from delaying or sabotaging parts of it. The motion passed, as did the report itself, whereupon two highly conservative deputies, Rudolf von Buttlar-Elberberg and Otto von der Malsburg-Elmarshausen, protested and then stormed out of the room.[151]

For the next three and one-half years the upper and lower houses labored to revise the government's constitution to make it acceptable to both houses and to the government. By the summer of 1857 the two chambers had agreed upon a draft, but the government did not find all of the alterations acceptable and also proposed changes of its own. As time passed without the establishment of a firm constitution, the lower house grew more restless, in particular due to the efforts of the exiled liberal leader Friedrich Oetker and his journal, the *Hessische Morgenzeitung*. Oetker worked to convince the delegates of the lower house that the compromise constitution approved by both houses was not enough; the only acceptable constitution for Hesse-Kassel was that of 1831, along with the electoral reforms of 1849. Oetker's supporters gained control of the lower house just as the government was finally ready to

---

[150] National Archives of the United States, Record Group T 213, Despatches from United States Consuls in Hesse-Kassel, Germany, Roll 3, Samuel Rieker to Secretary of State Lewis Cass, 26 April 1858, 14 May 1858.

[151] *LTV*, 7 December 1853, 7–8. Along with Ludwig von Baumbach-Lenderscheid they then wrote a letter of protest to the government. StAM 73, Acc. 1905/47, I. Kammer, Rubr. XIV, Nr. 1, 7 December 1853.

accept the new constitution. As a result, in the fall of 1859 the lower house voted to rescind its earlier approval of the constitution. Early in 1860 the delegates from the lower house approved a motion calling for the restoration of the constitution of 1831; the delegates then sent this declaration to the federal diet.[152]

The upper house was stunned by this sudden change of course by the other chamber. In March 1860 the delegates voted unanimously to reject the lower house's contention that no real agreement on a new constitution had been reached.[153] But events soon moved out of the hands of the nobility as Hesse-Kassel entered a new constitutional crisis.

The revised version of the constitution of 1852 received the approval of the federal diet on 24 March 1860 and went into effect on 30 May. The first Landtag elected under the provisions of the new constitution met at the end of November 1860 but proved to be of very short duration. On 8 December the lower house announced that it did not consider itself to be a "legitimate assembly" and therefore could not begin working on the legislature's business. Shortly thereafter the elector dissolved the lower house and held new elections, but Oetker's supporters remained in control. On 1 July 1861 the lower house once again declared itself incapable of acting as a Landtag. In both cases the upper house recessed soon after the lower house was dissolved, but the nobles felt baffled by the actions of the other chamber. On 2 July Obervorsteher Rudolf von Keudell put his views on record shortly before the upper house recessed, never to meet again: "In my opinion the constitution of 1860 exists legally and therefore should at least be seen as the basis for further negotiations. Just which provisions these negotiations should encompass cannot be discussed at present, but I do wish to emphasize that I view the two-house system as a highly beneficial and very necessary institution for the country."[154]

This second Hessian constitutional crisis soon became embroiled in federal politics as Prussia began to champion the cause of the Hessian liberals. By the spring of 1862 the federal diet voted to impose the constitution of 1831 upon Hesse-Kassel, and the elector was forced to bow to this pressure from outside. On 21 June 1862 the constitution of 1831 and the election law of 1849 were restored.[155] Once again the nobility lacked guaranteed representation.

When the new Landtag opened in October 1862, only two nobles were present (both had been elected as representatives of the wealthy

[152] *LTV*, II. Kammer, 18 February 1860; I. Kammer, 28 February 1860, Beilage 103.
[153] *LTV*, 2 March 1860, 921–22; 21 March 1860, 1205–06.
[154] *LTV*. I. Kammer, 2 July 1861, 30.
[155] Losch, *Geschichte des Kurfürstentums*, 312–16.

taxpayers of their districts). Regierungsrat Edwin von Bishoffshausen and Geheimer Rat Wilhelm von Schenck zu Schweinsberg (foreign minister in 1848) were prominent liberals and supporters of Friedrich Oetker, who was also sitting in the Landtag for the first time since 1850. The new Landtag immediately began working on an amendment to the election law, for in restoring the constitution of 1831 and the election law of 1849 the government had insisted that the decisions of the federal diet concerning the rights of the *Standesherren* and imperial knights to political representation be respected. But when the government presented its draft to the legislature, it called for representation not only for these two groups but also for all individuals given the right to seats in the legislature by article 63 of the constitution of 1831, including the *Erbmarschall*, an *Obervorsteher*, eight other members of the lower nobility (Hessian, Schaumburg, and former imperial knights; Hanau nobility), the *Standesherren*, the princes, and the University of Marburg.[156]

The government's proposal caused considerable controversy in the legislature. Most delegates were willing to support representation for the *Standesherren* and imperial knights in order to avoid conflict with the federal diet, but many opposed giving the seats to the Ritterschaft. Both the radical leader Adam Trabert and the liberal leader Oetker made speeches against granting representation to the knighthood, and even the two liberal knights already sitting in the Landtag did not speak out openly in favor of the government's proposal. But many delegates believed that granting some representation to the knighthood was necessary in order to placate the government and prevent it from attacking the election law of 1849 even more, so on 10 April 1863 a majority of delegates voted in favor of a compromise drawn up by the constitution committee eliminating representation for the *Erbmarschall*, *Obervorsteher*, and university, and reducing the number of knights (including the imperial knights) to six. The *Standesherren* and royal princes received one delegate each.[157]

After a summer recess the Landtag reopened on 8 October 1863. The new delegates from the Ritterschaft announced that, along with the government, they considered the election law to be only a provisional measure and expected the knighthood to receive its full rights of representa-

---

[156] The government justified its request by saying that representation solely for the *Standesherren* and imperial knights made no sense, for in that case the two groups of nobles would be alone and isolated. Furthermore, other corporate bodies such as the Ritterschaft also had long-standing rights to seats in the Landtag. *LTV*, 19 March 1863, Beilage 58.

[157] Salomon Hahndorf, *Der kurhessische Landtag von 1862–63* (Kassel, 1863), 17–20. For arguments in favor of the necessity of compromising with the government see *LTV*, 10 April 1863, 25–27.

tion through future legislation.[158] The new version of the election law was very unpopular with the Ritterschaft. Not only was the number of delegates smaller than had been hoped for (based upon the government's original proposal), but the number of voters had been greatly reduced by a provision in the law restricting the right to vote for representatives of the knighthood to those individuals owning land valued at over 1,500 tax guilders (*Steuergulden*); if they were joint owners of an estate, their share had to be that large. Thus many knights had lost their traditional voting rights. The Ritterschaft refused to accept the new law as more than a temporary measure, and many knights would not stand for election or even vote.[159] The knighthood's refusal to come to terms with the new circumstances in the legislature weakened the position of the deputies from the knighthood, and they took virtually no part in the debates during the remaining weeks of the Landtag session and were often absent.

Opposition to the liberal trend in Hessian politics had also led to the formation in November 1862 of the *Hessenverein*, a highly conservative organization that opposed the liberals' desire for unification under Prussian leadership. Among its members were Rudolf von Buttlar-Elberberg (one of the founders of the short-lived *Treubund* of 1850) and seven other members of the Ritterschaft.[160]

In the final three years of Hesse-Kassel's existence, the nobility played a very small role in politics. The delegates from the nobility were now a tiny minority with little influence, and the old ties between the bourgeoisie and the nobility in the 1830s and 1840s had been torn apart. The bourgeoisie had become more radical during the constitutional crises while the nobility had become more conservative because of attacks on its privileges, especially its right to representation in the Landtag. A further gulf between the bourgeois liberals and the nobles was caused by the former's advocacy of German unification and support of Prussia, a position unacceptable to most nobles, who remained Hessian patriots. Not all nobles were staunch conservatives during this period. Those nobles who were elected by the towns or the highest taxpayers were liberals who sided with their fellow liberals from the bourgeoisie rather than with the delegates elected by the nobility.[161]

[158] Statement by Bodo von Trott, *LTV*, 8 October 1863, 5–6.

[159] Losch, *Geschichte*, p. 364. See also the remarks of Karl Oetker in the diet during discussion of a motion to increase the representation of the nobility, *LTV*, 4 April 1865, 37.

[160] Nicholas M. Hope, *The Alternative to German Unification: The Anti-Prussian Party—Frankfurt, Nassau, and the Two Hessen, 1859–1867* (Wiesbaden, 1973), 174, 182, 193, 323–25; StAM 16, Rep. VII, Kl. 12, Nr. 67.

[161] The two most liberal nobles in the diet were Edwin von Bischoffshausen, representing the wealthiest taxpayers of the Werra district in 1862 and the city of Fulda from 1863

At times the nobility's opposition to the liberals in the Landtag led to a surprising combination of nobles and democrats. Although their views were worlds apart, both were united in opposing the goals of the liberals. After the Prussian annexation, the leader of the democrats, Adam Trabert, complimented the stand of the nobility in the Landtag, noting that the nobles "seriously attempted, along with the 'extreme left,' to reduce taxes and, like Trabert and Hüter, disdainfully rejected the thought of working for annexation."[162]

The closest cooperation between the left and the right in the legislature came during the last weeks of Electoral Hesse's independence. When the final showdown between Prussia and Austria began on 14 June 1866, Elector Frederick William and his government supported Austria's call for the members of the German Confederation to mobilize against Prussia. The pro-Prussian liberals in the Landtag strongly opposed siding with Austria, and on 15 June, Edwin von Bischoffshausen moved that the diet "demand that the government should immediately return to its previous position of neutrality, which had been supported by the whole country, and therefore stop the mobilization of the troops."[163] Bischoffshausen's motion was supported by the other liberals, including Wilhelm von Schenck, but the democrats and the delegates from the nobility strongly opposed remaining neutral. Adam Trabert, normally a bitter opponent of the government, stated that it was a "point of honor" for Hesse to support Austria, since Prussia had made a pact with one or more foreign powers against a fellow German state. Other democrats as well as several nobles spoke in favor of Trabert's remarks. Then the liberals began speaking in favor of Bischoffshausen's motion.[164]

In replying to the liberals, the leading noble spokesman, Otto von Trott, noted, "It has been jokingly suggested that the far right and the far left are united here; I have always found this far left to be honorable, one always knows where one stands with them, and in this case I see Herr Trabert as a true Hessian and a true German and believe that under no circumstances does he want to be made into a Prussian, a feeling

through 1866, and Wilhelm von Schenck zu Schweinsberg, who was elected by the wealthiest taxpayers of the principality of Schmalkalden.

[162] Adam Trabert, *Die Todtengräber des kurhessischen Landesrechts: Ein Beitrag zur Zeitgeschichte, insbesondere zur Charakteristik des "national-liberalen" Gothaerthums* (Leipzig, 1868), 81–82. For an analysis of Trabert's politics see Rudolf Stöckl, "Adam Trabert und die demokratisch-republikanische Bestrebungen in Kurhessen, 1848–1868" (Ph.D. diss., University of Marburg, 1958).

[163] *LTV* 15 June 1866, 2–3.

[164] Ibid., 7–12.

which I naturally share with him." Trott criticized Prussia for having signed an alliance with Italy and also having probably reached an agreement with France and said it would be "disgraceful if we do not side with the German power whose destruction is being planned with the cooperation of Germany's archenemies." Trott closed with a strong attack on Bismarck's policies and a prophetic warning to the liberals:

> Frederick the Great has often been called the gravedigger of German unity, but I find that Bismarck is its real gravedigger. You think that the Prussian government may change, that a different one may come to power, but the whole policy of Prussia is that of Emperor Napoleon, it is that which leads to caesarism. If Prussia succeeds in accomplishing what it has set out to do, do not be so naive as to think this is being done for the benefit of liberalism. You will soon see what kind of politics you will have under Bismarck's regime.[165]

The combination of left and right was not enough to defeat the liberal majority, and the diet voted thirty-five to fourteen in favor of Bischoffshausen's motion. All six delegates representing the nobility voted against the motion; only the two liberal nobles elected by other groups (Schenck and Bischoffshausen himself) supported it.[166]

The elector was not swayed by the Landtag's opposition and continued to mobilize in support of Austria. But his military preparations were too little and too late. The next day Prussian troops began to occupy Electoral Hesse. Within a few days the occupation was complete, and the elector had been arrested and taken to Prussia. Austria's defeat at Königgrätz on 3 July 1866 sealed Hesse-Kassel's fate. With the war won, Bismarck decided to annex Austria's allies in northern and central Germany. The annexation of Electoral Hesse was officially proclaimed on 8 October.[167]

The end of the Hessian state was a powerful shock to the members of the Hessian Ritterschaft, and many nobles initially had difficulty adjusting to Prussian rule. But the last two members of the Hessian ruling house had done little to cultivate relations with the Ritterschaft, so most nobles did not become active in movements calling for the restoration of the legitimate dynasty. The leaders of the knighthood also worked to convince the members to adjust to the new circumstances, and the tre-

---

[165] Ibid., 32–33.

[166] Ibid., 39.

[167] For the events during the summer of 1866 see Losch, *Geschichte des Kurfürstentums*, 387–427; Schmitt, "Prussia's Last Fling," 316–47.

mendous outburst of patriotism invoked by the outbreak of war against France in 1870 helped to rally nobles behind the new government.[168]

A few nobles remained unconverted, in particular Otto von der Malsburg-Elmarshausen. He had been especially disturbed by the religious consequences of the Prussian takeover, as the Lutheran church in Hesse came under Prussian control and began undergoing change. Malsburg and other conservative Lutherans broke away and formed a religious movement known as the Hessian Renitence. Later Malsburg and other ultraconservatives entered political life by forming the *Hessische Rechtspartei* in 1890. But the movement was unsuccessful in getting leading Hessian nobles to run as its candidates.[169]

Most Hessian nobles adjusted quickly to the new government, and almost all of those who were politically active joined the German Conservative party. One exception was Ferdinand von Schutzbar, who was a candidate for the Free Conservatives in the 1874 Reichstag elections.[170]

The efforts of Hessian nobles to serve in politics at the national level proved unsuccessful. The only Hessian knight elected to the Reichstag after 1866 was the liberal Wilhelm von Schenck zu Schweinsberg, who sat briefly in the North German Reichstag before his death in 1867. Although he had been an active supporter of unification under Prussian leadership, he did not join the National Liberal party. Instead he was a member of the *Alt-Liberales Zentrum*, a small moderate party composed primarily of nobles (later it became part of the Free Conservative party).[171]

Nobles were more successful politically at the state and local level, thanks to the Prussian government's conservative voting system. In November 1867 four members of the Hessian Ritterschaft were named to the upper house of the Prussian legislature, the *Herrenhaus*, and in the decades that followed several conservative Hessian nobles succeeded in winning seats in the lower house. One of these nobles, Karl Rabe von

---

[168] Kurt Freiherr von Schenk zu Schweinsberg, "Die Althessische Ritterschaft und das Stift Kaufungen in ihrer wechselseitigen Beziehung, nach den erlassenen Vorschriften auszugsweise zusammengestellt und beleuchtet," (typescript, 1920), 23.

[169] Enno Knobel, *Die hessische Rechtspartei: Konservative Opposition gegen das Bismarckreich* (Marburg, 1975), 137, 144, 167.

[170] For the candidacies of Hessian nobles and their lack of success see the election statistics in *Statistik des Deutschen Reiches*, vol. 14 (1875); *Monatshefte zur Statistik des Deutschen Reiches*, June 1879, March 1882, January 1885, April 1887, April 1890; *Vierteljahreshefte zur Statistik des Deutschen Reiches*, 1893, IV; 1898, Ergänzungsheft III; 1899, Ergänzungsheft I; 1903, Heft III, Ergänzungsheft IV; 1907, Ergänzungshefte I, III, IV; *Statistik des Deutschen Reiches*, vol. 250 (1913).

[171] Günther Franz, "Wilhelm Freiherr Schenck zu Schweinsberg (1809–1867): Hessischer Staatsmann," in Schnack, *Lebensbilder*, 4: 345–46.

Pappenheim, became one of the leading members of the Conservative party in Prussia.[172] But the nobles' greatest political strength came at the local level. The newly created *Kommunal-Landtag* for the *Regierungsbezirk* Kassel had essentially the same membership as that called for by the Hessian constitution of 1831, so the Ritterschaft once again had six seats and was joined by the *Erbmarschall*, an *Obervorsteher* of the Stift Kaufungen, and six members of the upper nobility. Noble estate owners were also guaranteed significant representation in local government (the *Kreistage*), so in many respects the political power of the nobility in Hesse-Kassel had been strengthened by the Prussian takeover.[173] This was yet another reason why Hessian nobles quickly accommodated themselves to Prussian rule.

[172] Wilhelm Hopf, "Karl Rabe von Pappenheim (1847–1918): Rittergutsbesitzer und Parlamentarier," in Schnack, *Lebensbilder*, 5: 240–49.

[173] Heinrich Heffter, *Die deutsche Selbstverwaltung im 19. Jahrhundert: Geschichte der Ideen und Institutionen*, 2d ed. (Stuttgart, 1969), 480.

CONCLUSION

By the middle of the nineteenth century many Hessian nobles were deeply upset by the changes that had occurred during the past fifty years. At the annual conference of the delegates of the Ritterschaft in 1847, the main topic of discussion was the nobility's loss of power and influence in recent decades. Obervorsteher Carl von Eschwege drew up a lengthy list of the privileges that had been taken away from the knighthood and decried the nobility's declining influence in the government. Obervorsteher Otto von Trott zu Solz detailed the negative effects of the redemption laws and also complained of the precarious financial situation of many noble estate owners because of government restrictions upon borrowing by vassals.[1]

Nobles attempted to analyze the reasons for the decline in their social and economic position. Some, like Trott, blamed the decline on the influence of liberalism and the "leveling ideas of the French Revolution."[2] But not all knights shared Trott's conservatism. Wilhelm von Schenck zu Schweinsberg, one of the most prominent liberal nobles after 1848, argued in his 1842 proposal for reforming the nobility that the causes for the nobility's poor financial situation lay much farther back in time: the effects of the Thirty Years' War, the loss of positions in knightly orders and in the Catholic church, and the concentration of nobles in military and court service, which resulted in their receiving less education. To Schenck the liberal reforms of the nineteenth century were not the cause of the nobility's difficulties and in fact would prove beneficial to nobles:

> The reasons for the impoverishment of the nobility are often said to lie in representative constitutions and their effects, namely the abolition of peasant dues, heavier taxation, the complete loss of many useful privileges, etc., but the causes must be sought elsewhere. Actually, as this study will show, the above changes, if they are properly understood and exploited by the nobility, can only improve its status and advancement.[3]

[1] ARSK, Rep. VI, Gef. 2–3, Nr. 7. Conferences of 14 June and 19 July 1847.
[2] Ibid.
[3] Schenck, *Über den niederen Adel*, 3–4. Like many prospective reformers of the German nobility, Schenck proposed adopting the English system of nobility (only eldest sons to inherit noble status and estates) along with strict entail of landholdings.

251

Who was right—conservatives like Trott and Eschwege or the liberal Schenck? Was the nobility better off in the second half of the nineteenth century than it had been a century earlier, or had nobles been devastated by the loss of traditional privileges and incomes?

The answer lies somewhere in between, for the nobility had made gains and suffered losses during the nineteenth century. The greatest success story came in the nobles' financial condition. In the mid-eighteenth century many families of the Ritterschaft were seriously indebted and either on the brink of bankruptcy or already involved in bankruptcy proceedings, but just a century later most of these families not only had managed to retain their estates but also had reduced the burden of debts and even purchased additional land. This dramatic improvement in the fortunes of the landed nobility was due in part to the government's timely provision of large, low-interest loans in the late eighteenth century. In Prussia, similar loans were generally granted without restrictions, but the Hessian loans were coupled with strict repayment plans designed to force noble debtors to begin reducing their debts.

Abundant and inexpensive credit was not the only reason for the improved financial position of noble estate owners; in fact, credit became very difficult to obtain during the first half of the nineteenth century. The primary reasons for the increased prosperity of noble landowners must therefore be sought in the account books of noble estates. Were nobles earning more from their landholdings in the nineteenth century than in the eighteenth, or had their landed income been decimated by the loss of feudal dues and services from peasants?

If seigneurial dues and services had been eliminated without compensation, many nobles would have been in serious financial difficulty, for such payments by peasants represented between one-third and two-thirds of the annual income of noble estates. But nobles received twenty times the annual value of peasant dues and services, and this influx of capital proved highly beneficial to the nobility during the nineteenth century. Thanks to the redemption payments, nobles were able to reduce debts and also increase revenues by purchasing additional land or government bonds. A few nobles even used the payments to finance the establishment or expansion of estate-related industries. Although the annual income from investment of redemption payments did not always match the face value of the peasant dues and services they had replaced, nobles were now spared the expenses and difficulties in collecting dues and services from the many peasants who were either unwilling or unable to fulfill their obligations.

The greatest improvement in nobles' financial standing resulted not from the redemption payments but from the rise in income from nobles' demesne holdings. Despite increased burdens from taxation after the loss of traditional fiscal privileges, noble estates yielded far more income in the nineteenth century than in the eighteenth, even without the income from peasant dues and services. Rents rose substantially during the nineteenth century, and income from forests soared as the result of higher wood prices and greater yields brought about by more scientific methods of forestry.

The dramatic rise in profits from landed estates during the nineteenth century greatly assisted nobles in retaining and expanding their landholdings. But even before landed incomes rose substantially, there had been considerable stability in the nobility's landownership. The attitude of Hessian nobles toward their estates played an important role in the preservation of the nobility's landholdings. Knights rarely alienated an estate voluntarily unless it had not been in the family very long. As a result, the families of the Ritterschaft retained most of their ancient estates throughout the nineteenth and early twentieth centuries.

The knighthood was aided in its attempt to preserve its landholdings by its highly flexible inheritance system. Since all male heirs became joint owners of a family's holdings, estates were not burdened with debts resulting from the need to compensate younger sons. Furthermore, the unrestricted marriage policy of the knights tended to prevent families from dying out in the male line very quickly, because there was always a male cousin somewhere who could inherit an estate and keep it in the family. Centuries of identification of a family with a particular estate (which was often part of the surname of the family) reinforced the close ties of nobles to their estates.

Landownership was not the only area in which the Hessian nobility succeeded in surviving the reforms of the nineteenth century, for the nobility also retained substantial influence as a service aristocracy. Nobles' traditional preference for careers in government service remained unchanged in the nineteenth century, and nobles continued to enjoy strong representation in most areas of government service.

The nobility's dominant position in the Hessian army remained unbroken in the nineteenth century. Even in the 1860s nobles still occupied over one-half of the officer positions. More significantly, by 1866 all of the highest-ranking officers (colonels and generals) were nobles, and nobles monopolized the officer positions in the most glamorous branch of service—the cavalry—and the prestigious guards regiments.

The bureaucracy was less of a success story for the nobility. Increased competition from the bourgeoisie for available positions and the increase in the overall size of the bureaucracy led to a gradual decline in the percentage of government offices held by nobles. But the numbers of nobles serving in government remained steady, and by the mid-nineteenth century there were very few new nobles in government, so the number of civil servants from older noble families was actually increasing. Nobles remained strongly represented at the highest levels of government (ministers and directors). And in the two other areas of government service—forestry and the court—nobles remained the leading influence.

Nobles also played an important role in Hessian political life until the mid-nineteenth century. Still the dominant political force at the diet of 1815–16, the nobility saw its power wane in later decades owing to the effects of the revolutions of 1830 and 1848. Nobles remained influential in the legislature during the 1830s and 1840s, often occupying leading offices, because they were willing to work together with the bourgeoisie to carry out needed reforms. But the spirit of harmony between the two elites began to fade after 1850 as the nobility became more conservative because of threats to its remaining privileges, while the bourgeoisie became more radical in its demand for reforms. By the 1860s the bourgeoisie had won the constitutional conflict and completely dominated the legislature. The nobility's political power had become insignificant.

Although politically very weak by the 1860s, the nobility had remained a powerful social and economic force in the Electorate of Hesse-Kassel, but what happened to the nobles after the Prussian takeover in 1866? Could the patriotic Hessian nobles adapt to the new order? The answer is yes, for Prussian rule soon brought many favorable developments for the nobility.

The easiest transition to Prussian rule was made by noble army officers, because almost the entire Hessian officer corps was taken over into Prussian service. Hessian nobles had no difficulty adapting to the "militarization" of Prussian society, for they already had a strong tradition of military service with approximately one-half of all noblemen becoming officers even before the Prussian annexation. The Prussian reserve officer system also came to Hesse-Kassel after 1866, so most nobles serving in the bureaucracy in the late nineteenth century held commissions as reserve officers.[4]

Nobles in the bureaucracy initially suffered a number of setbacks. Many nobles had served in the foreign ministry and therefore lost their jobs after the Prussian takeover. Members of the administrative, judicial, and financial branches of government were incorporated into the

[4] An 1898 list of *Landräte* for the *Regierungsbezirk* Kassel reveals that ten out of the thirteen noble *Landräte* under the age of fifty were reserve officers and one other was a former officer. Two of the five bourgeois *Landräte* under fifty were also reserve officers, and another two were former officers. StAM 165, I, Nr. 7382.

new provincial bureaucracy of the *Regierungsbezirk* Kassel, but their potential for advancement was much more limited because they could no longer hope to advance to the rank of minister. Even the leading provincial positions were at first filled with non-Hessian officials to ensure the loyalty of the bureaucracy to Prussia. However, Hesse-Kassel was soon fully integrated into the Prussian state and the new German Empire, and Hessian nobles again began to occupy positions in the diplomatic service and also advanced to high-ranking offices in the Prussian bureaucracy by the end of the century.[5] Furthermore, the Prussian preference for landed nobles in the office of *Landrat* directly benefited Hessian nobles. In 1865 only six of the twenty-one Hessian *Landräte* were nobles, but by 1900 sixteen of the twenty-two *Landräte* in *Regierungsbezirk* Kassel came from the nobility.

Noble landowners also benefited from Prussian rule. After 1866 a number of Prussian laws were applied to Hesse, leading to reforms that had been advocated by estate owners but not implemented by the elector and his government. Under the new Prussian laws landowners were able to abolish peasants' rights in nobles' forests and also begin the process of rationalizing agriculture by dividing common lands and making both peasant and noble landholdings more compact by trading parcels of land.

As large landowners, members of the Hessian Ritterschaft played a leading role in the agrarian movements that swept Germany in the late nineteenth century. Bodo von Trott zu Solz directed the spread of the Raiffeisen movement in Hesse, which established credit unions to provide low-interest loans to small farmers. Many other knights were also active supporters of this concept in the 1880s.[6] Hessian nobles also participated in the Agrarian League. A member of the von Stockhausen family was the league's director of the provinces Hesse and Saxony in 1914.[7]

The leading role played by nobles in such agrarian movements showed that the nobility was still an important local elite in Hesse in the late nineteenth century. Traditional habits of deference to the nobility by peasants remained strong, and the old sources of tension between landlord and peasant had been removed by the reforms of 1832 and

---

[5] Gustav von Schenk zu Schweinsberg served as an ambassador, and August von Trott zu Solz was *Oberpräsident* of Hesse and later Brandenburg before becoming Prussian minister of culture in 1909. Preradovich, *Führungsschichten*, 94, 96, 120.

[6] Karl von Baumbach, "Bodo von Trott zu Solz," in Schnack, *Lebensbilder*, 2: 375–80.

[7] Hans-Jürgen Puhle, *Agrarische Interessenpolitik und preußischer Konservatismus im wilhelminischen Reich, 1893–1914*, 2d ed. (Bonn–Bad Godesberg, 1975), 313.

1848. The nobility also retained considerable influence in local politics, thanks to Prussian laws that guaranteed substantial representation to nobles in local government.

All in all, the Hessian nobility had survived the turmoil of the nineteenth century quite well. Despite erosion of their influence in some areas, the nobles were still a leading elite under the Hessian government, and the Prussian takeover actually improved the position of the nobility even more. So at the end of the nineteenth century, the Hessian nobility remained a strong regional elite due to its landholdings, service to the state, and local political influence.

Why had the nobility been so successful at retaining so much political, social, and economic power? Much of the credit should go to the nobles themselves for their efforts to adapt to changing circumstances. Nobles worked to increase their educational level to remain competitive for government offices, they sought new methods to improve the productivity of their landholdings, and they demonstrated considerable political flexibility during the times of major reforms. On the other hand, nobles' conservatism also played an important role in the nobility's survival as a landed elite. Nobles refused to part with their family estates and continued to emphasize land as the most important form of wealth for noble families.

The Hessian nobility's survival was made easier by the nature of the region and its governments. Hesse-Kassel underwent less urbanization and industrialization than most other German states during the nineteenth century, so the nobility did not face strong competition from a vigorous economic bourgeoisie. The Hessian state also played an important role in assisting the nobility. Although Hessian rulers (with the possible exception of Frederick II) did not follow a policy of favoring nobles, many royal actions such as the provision of low-interest loans greatly benefited the nobility. The conservative nature of the Hessian rulers also assisted the nobility in maintaining its landed wealth, for the retention of traditional feudal ties ensured considerable stability in noble landownership. After the end of the feudal system in 1848, most nobles imitated the restrictions of fiefs by establishing strict entails for their estates. Such *Fideikommisse* were abolished in the twentieth century, but the continued attachment of the Hessian nobility to the land has enabled most of the surviving families of the Ritterschaft to retain their estates to the present day. Finally, the change in governments in 1866 proved to be beneficial to the nobility, for the Prussian government was much more pro-noble than its Hessian predecessor.

Although Prussian annexation had brought many benefits to the Hessian Ritterschaft, some of the members grew concerned that the ties that had bound the knighthood together would gradually fade now that Hesse-Kassel had ceased to exist. In May 1878 a number of concerned knights met to discuss ways to revitalize the knighthood, and Obervorsteher Bodo von Trott zu Solz suggested that they form an association to advance the interests of the knighthood.[8] On 21 August 1880 this organization—the *Verein der Althessischen Ritterschaft*—formally came into existence, and it still exists today, helping to maintain the interests and common ties of the Hessian Ritterschaft.

[8] Schenk, "Althessische Ritterschaft," 23–25.

257

APPENDIX A
FAMILIES IN THE HESSIAN RITTERSCHAFT DURING THE EIGHTEENTH AND NINETEENTH CENTURIES

von Amelunxen (admitted 1842)
von Baumbach
von Berlepsch
von Biedenfeld
von Bischoffshausen
von Bodenhausen
von Boyneburg
von Boyneburg genannt
   Hohenstein (extinct 1792)
von Buchenau
von Bürgeln
von Buttlar
von Calenberg (extinct 1813)
von Canstein (readmitted 1776)
von Capellan (extinct 1779)
von Cornberg (admitted 1777)
von Dalwigk
von Dernbach (extinct 1748)
von Dersch (extinct 1777)
von Diede zum Fürstenstein
   (extinct 1807)
von Döring (extinct 1791)
von Dörnberg
von Eschwege
von Falkenberg (extinct 1733)
von Fleckenbühl genannt Bürgel
   (extinct 1796)
von und zu Gilsa
Fürsten von Hanau (admitted
   1835)
von Hesberg (admitted 1820)
von Heydwolff (admitted 1741)
von Hundelshausen

von Keudell
von Knoblauch
von Lindau (admitted 1760,
   extinct 1831)
von Linsingen (extinct 1721)
von Löwenstein
von Lüder zu Loshausen (extinct
   1760)
von der Malsburg
von Merlau (extinct 1748)
von Meysenbug (extinct 1810)
von Milchling zu Schönstadt
von Osterhausen (admitted 1830)
von Pappenheim
von Radenhausen (extinct 1786)
von Rau zu Holzhausen
von Riedesel zu Eisenbach
von Rolshausen (extinct 1710)
von Romrod
von und zu Schachten
von Schenck zu Schweinsberg
von Schlieffen (admitted 1781)
von Scholley (extinct in male line
   1829)
von Schutzbar genannt
   Milchling
von Schwertzell
von Stein zu Barchfeld
von Stockhausen
Treusch von Buttlar
von Trott zu Solz
von Uffeln (extinct 1729)
von Urff

von Verschuer (admitted 1820)
von Viermünden (extinct 1744)
von Völkershausen (extinct 1706)
Waitz von Eschen (admitted 1804)
von Wallenstein (extinct 1745)
von Wehrda genannt Noding (extinct 1822)
von Wildungen (extinct 1822)
von Winter (extinct 1783)
von Witzleben (admitted 1819)
Wolff von Gudenberg

APPENDIX B
ENNOBLEMENT OF HESSIANS

(All individuals added *von* to their names unless otherwise noted)

APPENDIX B

Ennobled by the Rulers of Hesse-Kassel

William I (Landgrave William IX 1785–1803, Elector 1803–21)

1814   Geheimer Kriegsrat Karl Friedrich Buderus (as "Buderus von
         Carlshausen")
         Oberappellationsrat Bernhard Heinrich Goeddaeus (had been
         ennobled by King Jerome of Westphalia in 1812)
1816   Geheimer Kriegsrat Richard Lorentz
1817   Staff Captain Wilhelm Steuber
         Staatsminister Georg Schmerfeld (had been ennobled by King
         Jerome of Westphalia in 1812)
1818   Captain Heinrich Reinhard Hoelke (as "Hoelke von
         Sturmfeder")
         Captain Georg Johann Rost (as "Rost von Ritterholm")
         First Lieutenant Burkhardt Wilhelm Rüppel (as "Rüppel von
         Helmschwerdt")

William II (Elector 1821–31, then Co-Regent with his son until 1847)

1821   Caroline Wilhelmine Ortlöpp (as "Gräfin Reichenbach")
1823   Wilhelm Reiss (as "von Lindenfels")
1825   Major Karl Friedrich Wilkens (as "Wilkens von Hohenau")
         Ambassador Geheimer Kabinettsrat Louis Carl Rivalier (as
         "Rivalier von Meysenbug")
1827   General Johann Baptist Lingg (as "Lingg von Linggenfeld")
1828   Archive Director Christoph Rommel (had been ennobled in
         Russia in 1810)
1829   Roger Victor Biela (as "von Aldenburg")
1830   Oberpostdirektor Ferdinand Karl Ortlöpp (as "Heyer von
         Rosenfeld")
         Colonel Carl Müldner (as "Müldner von Mülnheim"), Elector's
         Adjutant

*Frederick William (Crown Prince and Co-Regent, 1831–47; Elector
1847–66)*

1831   Gertrude Lehmann, née Falkenstein (as "Gräfin Schaumburg")
1832   Geheimer Rat Georg Franz Rieß (as "Rieß von
         Scheurnschloss"), Ambassador
1835   Otto and Eduard Lehmann (as "von Hertingshausen")

1836 Obergerichtsrat Jacob Arnold Dehn-Rotfelser
1838 Captain Georg Wilhelm Andrée (as "von Hohenfels"), Elector's
     Adjutant
1844 Wilhelm Dehn-Rotfelser
     Otto Christian Dehn-Rotfelser
     Christian Heinrich Dehn-Rotfelser

APPENDIX C
TABLE OF RANKS

During the eighteenth century the government's table of ranks gradually became shorter and less complicated. The *Rangordnung* of 1710 with its list of twenty-one different ranks was followed in 1762 by a table consisting of only twelve categories. Finally, an 1803 ordinance established a table with only eight different ranks, and this system remained in effect for the rest of Hesse-Kassel's existence, although individual offices sometimes changed in rank.

During the nineteenth century most changes in the table of ranks were minor, so the versions of 1821, 1834, and 1854 are very similar. Table C.1 lists the major offices of the army, bureaucracy, forestry service, and court by rank to facilitate comparisons among different branches of government. This table is based upon the *Rangordnung* of 1834.

TABLE C.1.
1834 Table of Ranks

	Army	Bureaucracy	Forestry Service	Court
1.	General-Lieutenants General-Majors	Wirkliche Staats-Minister Präsidenten der höheren Kollegien	— —	Oberkammerherr —
2.	Obersten	Direktoren der höheren Kollegien	Landforstmeister	Hofmarschall; Ober-Hof-Chargen
3.	Oberst-Lieutenants	Ober-Appellations-Räthe; Geheime Kriegs-, Justiz- Regierungs-, Legations- und Oberfinanz-Räthe	Hofjägermeister	Kammerherren
4.	Majors	Regierungs-, Oberfinanz-, Obergerichts-, Legations- und Ober-Berg-Räthe	Oberforstmeister	—
5.	Capitains; Rittmeister	Hof-, Kriegs-, Justiz- und Finanz-Räthe; Landräthe	Forstmeister; Forstinspektoren	Kammerjunker
6.	Lieutenants	Assessoren; Justizbeamte	Forst-, Jagdjunker	Hofjunker
7.	—	Sekretäre der höheren Behörden	—	—
8.	—	Kreissekretäre	Oberförster	—

NOTE: Position titles are spelled as found in the table of ranks printed in the 1835 *Staatshandbuch*.

APPENDIX D
FERTILITY STATISTICS AND COMPARISONS

Age-specific marital fertility rates are very useful measures of fertility, but because they include so many different numbers, they are not easy to use in comparing the fertility of different population groups. Fortunately, age-specific fertility rates can be used to calculate several measures of fertility that are much easier to use for comparisons. The total marital fertility rate after age twenty (TMF 20+) is simply the total of the age-specific marital fertility rates of women aged twenty and above (multiplied by five because these rates were originally calculated for five-year age intervals). The resultant figure is thus the average number of children per married woman, including marriages of both completed and incomplete fertility. Since family limitation generally involves stopping childbearing after a certain size family has been achieved, it is also useful to calculate the total marital fertility rate after age thirty (TMF 30+) and then compare this to the overall fertility rate expressed in the TMF 20+. If family limitation is not being practiced, the TMF 30+ ranges between 45 and 53 percent of the TMF 20+.[1] Lower percentages of births after age thirty indicate the presence of family limitation. The age-specific marital fertility rates of the Hessian Ritterschaft were presented graphically in figure 3.1, but to ease comparison with future studies, the exact figures are given in table D.1. These rates were used to calculate additional measures of fertility (TMF 20+ and TMF 30+), which can be seen in the comparative table D.2 below.

TABLE D.1. Age-Specific Marital Fertility (Births per Year)

Year Married	Age of Wife						
	15–19	20–24	25–29	30–34	35–39	40–44	45–49
1650–99	0.450	0.505	0.484	0.403	0.312	0.142	0.024
1700–49	0.444	0.512	0.429	0.384	0.294	0.072	0.008
1750–99	0.547	0.452	0.427	0.370	0.285	0.132	0.006
1800–49	0.408	0.416	0.350	0.256	0.170	0.083	0.002
1850–79	0.345	0.411	0.309	0.202	0.108	0.045	0.002

[1] John Knodel, "From Natural Fertility to Family Limitation: the Onset of Fertility in a Sample of German Villages," *Demography* 4 (1979): 502–4.

One additional measure of fertility is the Coale-Trussell Index of Fertility Control (m). This index is calculated by comparing a particular population's age pattern of marital fertility to that of a group of populations known to have practiced little or no birth control. The index m will equal zero if a population's fertility pattern is identical to the "standard"

TABLE D.2.
Fertility Control among European Elites

	1600–49	1650–99	1700–49	1750–99	1800–49	1850–99
nevan Bourgeoisie[a]						
TMF 20+/TMF 30+	9.4/4.4	6.5/2.1	4.8/1.5	4.9/1.5	3.8/1.1	4.1/1.1
MF 30+ as % of TMF 20+	46.4	31.7	30.6	30.4	28.0	27.8
Coale-Trussell index	0.24	1.15	0.85	1.02	1.55	1.33
ilanese Patriciate[a]						
TMF 20+/TMF 30+	—	—	8.1/3.2[c]	5.5/2.0	5.7/2.2	4.0/1.4
MF 30+ as % of TMF 20+	—	—	39.7	36.1	38.2	34.3
Coale-Trussell index	—	—	0.63	0.96	0.62	0.91
orentine Patriciate[a]						
TMF 20+/TMF 30+	—	6.9/2.5[d]	6.0/1.9	5.4/1.2	—	—
MF 30+ as % of TMF 20+	—	36.7	31.2	21.6	—	—
Coale-Trussell index	—	1.08	1.22	2.24	—	—
ench Dukes and Peers[b]						
TMF 20+/TMF 30+	—	5.1/1.7	2.4/0.4[e]	—	—	—
MF 30+ as % of TMF 20+	—	33.8	18.1	—	—	—
Coale-Trussell index	—	1.34	2.01	—	—	—
ssian Ritterschaft[b]						
TMF 20+/TMF 30+	—	9.4/4.4	8.5/3.8	8.4/4.0	6.4/2.6	5.4/1.8[f]
MF 30+ as % of TMF 20+	—	47.1	44.6	47.4	40.0	33.1
Coale-Trussell index	—	0.19	0.56	0.16	0.45	0.88

SOURCES: Henry, *Anciennes familles genevoises*, 76; Massimo Livi-Bacci, *A History of Italian Fertility during Last Two Centuries* (Princeton, 1977), 46; R. Burr Litchfield, "Demographic Characteristics of Florentine trician Families, Sixteenth to Nineteenth Centuries," *The Journal of Economic History* 29 (1969): 200; Levy d Henry, "Ducs et pairs," 817. I would like to thank Professor John Knodel at the Population Studies nter of the University of Michigan for supplying the Coale-Trussell indices of these groups.
[a] Years listed are those of the husband's birth.
[b] Years listed are those of the marriage.
[c] Data is from the period "pre-1750."
[d] Data is from the years 1600–1699.
[e] Data is from the years 1700–1799.
[f] Data is from the years 1850–79.

natural fertility schedule. Higher m values reflect increasing levels of fertility control (although slight departures from zero are not necessarily indicators of family limitation), with modern populations in which contraception is common having m values of well over 1.0.[2] Both the Coale-Trussell index and the total marital fertility rates above ages twenty and thirty are used in table D.2 to compare the Hessian Ritterschaft to other European elites whose fertility rates are known. All of these other groups began limiting the size of families significantly earlier than the Hessian Ritterschaft and also practiced a higher degree of fertility control.

[2] Etienne van de Walle and John Knodel, "Europe's Fertility Transition: New Evidence and Lessons for Today's Developing World," *Population Bulletin* 34 (1980): 14–15.

APPENDIX E
HESSIAN WEIGHTS, MEASURES, AND MONEY

The weights and measures of eighteenth-century Hesse-Kassel could easily be the subject of an entire book, because the units of measurement often varied from province to province or even from village to village. This appendix therefore covers only measures used in the preceding chapters.[1]

The main measure of weight was the pound (*Pfund*), which came in two varieties. The "heavy" pound used in Kassel and Lower Hesse weighed 484 grams, while the "light" pound found in Marburg and Upper Hesse weighed 468 grams. Neither of these Hessian pounds should be confused with the English pound, which equals 454 grams.

The measurement of grain was much more complicated. In Kassel grain was measured in *Viertel* (quarters). One Kassel *Viertel* was divided into 16 *Metzen* and was the equivalent of 160 liters or 4.5 bushels. A number of other areas in Lower Hesse, including Gudensberg, Sontra, and Witzenhausen, used a *Viertel* or *Malter* that was larger than that of Kassel and equaled 18⅔ Kassel *Metzen* or 180 liters (5.1 bushels). The areas around Fritzlar and Fulda used yet another *Viertel*, equal to 170 liters (4.8 bushels). In contrast, Marburg and Upper Hesse used a system containing *Malter*, which were divided into 16 *Mesten*. One Marburg *Malter* equaled 415 liters (11.8 bushels) or 2.6 Kassel *Viertel*.

Distance was measured in "shoes" (*Schuhe*) of 28 centimeters each, *Elle* of 57 centimeters, and *Meilen*, which were approximately 9.2 kilometers. "Shoes" were used in calculating amounts of cut wood. A *Klafter* was a quantity of wood 6 *Schuhe* long, 5 *Schuhe* wide, and 5 *Schuhe* high, or 150 cubic *Schuhe*. This equals 3.5 cubic meters, so a *Klafter* of wood was slightly smaller than an English cord (128 cubic feet or 3.6 cubic meters).

Several unusual items often appear in estate records. Two are terms for quantities: the *Mandel* (fifteen items) and the *Schock* (sixty items), while the *Maß* was a measurement of beer equal to 2.2 liters.

Land was measured in *Kasseler Acker*, which equaled 0.238 hectares or 0.589 U.S. acres. *Acker* were subdivided into 150 square *Ruten*.

---

[1] For additional information on Hessian weights and measures and also on the changes in value of Hessian currency in the seventeenth and eighteenth centuries see George Thomas Fox, "Studies in the Rural History of Upper Hesse, 1650–1830" (Ph.D. diss., Vanderbilt University, 1976), 388–405.

The primary monetary unit of Hesse-Kassel was the *Reichstaler*, which in the eighteenth century was divided into 32 *Albus*, each equal to 12 *Heller*. However, in Upper Hesse, Hanau, and Fulda the currency of Frankfurt, the florin or guilder (*Gulden*), played a very large role. The *Gulden* was worth two-thirds of a *Reichstaler* (21 *Albus*, 4 *Heller*). The term *Gulden* was also incorporated into a monetary unit that existed only for accounting purposes, the *Steuergulden* (equal to 27 Kassel *Albus*).

In the nineteenth century the subdivisions of the *Reichstaler* were changed from *Albus* to *Silbergroschen*, each of which was worth 12 *Heller*. After the creation of the German Empire in 1871, the *Reichsmark* became the official currency, and all Hessian salaries and prices were converted to this system at the rate of 3 marks per taler.

SOURCES AND BIBLIOGRAPHY

ARCHIVAL SOURCES

Staatsarchiv Marburg

Hauptabteilung I: Urkunden
  X. Deposita
    5. Familien
  XII. Landtagsabschiede
Hauptabteilung II: Akten
  Bestand 5, Hessischer Geheim Rat
  Bestand 7, Hessische Hofbehörden
    a. Oberhofsmarschallamt
  Bestand 9, Ministerium des Kurfürstlichen Hauses und der
    auswärtigen Angelegenheiten
  Bestand 11, Militärkabinett
  Bestand 12, Kriegsministerium
  Bestand 16, Ministerium des Innern
  Bestand 17, Regierung Kassel
    c. Lehensrepositur
    d. Familienrepositur
  Bestand 19, Regierung Marburg
  Bestand 24, Polizeidirektion
  Bestand 28, Landwirtschaft
  Bestand 30, Statistische Kommission
  Bestand 31, Kredit- und Depositenverwaltung
    h. Landeskreditkasse
  Bestand 41, Finanzministerium
  Bestand 45, Oberfinanzkammer
    b. Kommission für die Ablösungen
  Bestand 49, Obersteuerkollegium
  Bestand 63, Landständische Kommission
  Bestand 73, Landstände
  Bestand 150, Oberpräsidium der Provinz Hessen-Nassau
  Bestand 165, Preußische Regierung Kassel, Abteilung des Innern
  Bestand 180, Landratsämter
  Bestand 225, Landeskreditkasse
  Bestand 250, Justizminister

Bestand 261, Oberappellationsgericht
Bestand 270, Obergericht Kassel
Bestand 300, Hessen-Rumpenheim, Abteilung 11, Geheimes
    Kabinett
Bestand 304, Stift Kaufungen
Bestand 305, Universität Marburg
Bestand 340, Familienarchive und Nachlässe
Hauptabteilung III: Amtsbücher
    1. Rechnungen
    3. Kataster
Hauptabteilung VI: Sammlungen
    1. Handschriften
        M1, Landau
        M24, Schenck zu Schweinsberg
        M45a, Deutsche Adelsgenossenschaft
    10. Zeitungen

Staatsarchiv Darmstadt

Bestand E12, Adel

Archiv des Ritterschaftlichen Stiftes Kaufungen, 3504 Oberkaufungen

Repositur VI, Ritterschaft

Archiv der Familie von der Malsburg-Elmarshausen, 3549 Wolfhagen 1

Archiv der Freiherrlichen Familie von Dörnberg, Haus Breitenbach, 6440 Bebra 1

National Archives of the United States
    Record Group T 213, Despatches from United States Consuls in
    Hesse-Kassel, Germany

OTHER PRIMARY SOURCES

"Die Ablösungsgesetze und andere Gesetze zur Erfüllung der Forderungen des Liberalismus." *Deutsche Vierteljahrsschrift* (1854): 186–220.
Albrecht, Heinrich, ed. *Borken 1777*. Hessische Ortsbeschreibungen, vol. 4. Marburg, 1962.
Allgemeine deutsche Biographie. 56 vols. Leipzig, 1875–1912.

Baumbach-Nassenerfurth, Karl von. *Stammtafeln der althessischen Ritterschaft aus neueren Zeit.* Rudolstadt, 1932.

Berlepsch, Friedrich Ludwig von. *Beiträge zu den Hessen-Casselschen Landtagsverhandlungen der Jahre 1815 und 1816.* Erfurt, 1817.

Beurkundete Darstellung der Kurhessischen Landtagsverhandlungen mit Blicken auf die Vergangenheit, Gegenwart und Zukunft. Kassel, 1816.

Buttlar-Elberberg, Rudolf von. *Stammbuch der althessischen Ritterschaft, enthaltend die Stammtafeln der im ehemaligen Kurfürstenthum Hessen ansässigen, zur althessischen Ritterschaft gehörigen Geschlechter.* Wolfhagen, 1888.

[Dalwigk, Carl von.] *Etwas über Rechte der Landstände, und Warum hat Kurhessen keine Constitution? Wissenschaftlich geprüft von einem ehemaligen Deputirten zur Ständeversammlung.* Wiesbaden, 1819.

Deutsches Adelsarchiv. *Genealogisches Handbuch des Adels.* 87 vols. to date. Limburg, 1951–.

Dörnberg, Alexander Freiherr von. Interview with author. Hausen, 16 June 1979.

Dörnberg, Siegfried Freiherr von. *Stammtafeln der althessischen Ritterschaft.* Bad Hersfeld, 1958.

Ebel, Wilhelm, ed. *Die Matrikel der Georg August-Universität zu Göttingen, 1837–1900.* Hildesheim, 1974.

Erler, Georg, ed. *Die jüngere Matrikel der Universität Leipzig, 1559–1809.* 3 vols. Leipzig, 1909.

Frank, Karl F. von, ed. *Standeserhebungen und Gnadenakte für das deutsche Reich und die österreichischen Erblande bis 1806.* Schloß Senftenegg, Austria, 1967–74.

Goessel, Friedrich. *Geschichte des Landtags von 1830.* Kassel, 1837.

Gothaisches genealogisches Taschenbuch der briefadeligen Häuser. 34 vols. Gotha, 1907–42.

Gothaisches genealogisches Taschenbuch der freiherrlichen Häuser. 92 vols. Gotha, 1848–1942.

Gothaisches genealogisches Taschenbuch der gräflichen Häuser. 115 vols. Gotha, 1825–1942.

Gothaisches genealogisches Taschenbuch der uradeligen Häuser. 41 vols. Gotha, 1900–1942.

Gräfe, Heinrich. *Der Verfassungskampf in Kurhessen nach Entstehung, Fortgang und Ende.* Leipzig, 1851.

Gritzner, Maximilian, ed. *Standes-Erhebungen und Gnadenakte deutscher Landesfürsten während der letzten drei Jahrhunderte.* Görlitz, 1881.

Habicht, Max Eberhard, ed. *Suchbuch für die Marburger Universitäts–Matrikel von 1653–1830.* Darmstadt, 1927.

Hahndorf, Salomon. *Der kurhessische Landtag von 1862–63.* Kassel, 1863.

Handbuch des Grundbesitzes im deutschen Reiche. Vol. 11, Part 1, *Regierungs-bezirk Kassel.* Berlin, 1895.

Heathcote, Ralph. *Letters of a Young Diplomatist and Soldier during the Time of Napoleon, Giving an Account of the Dispute between the Emperor and the Elector of Hesse.* London, 1907.

Hesse-Kassel. *Hessen-Casselischer Staats- und Adreß Calender.* Kassel, 1764–1866.

————. *Sammlung fürstlich hessischer Landes-Ordnungen, nebst dahin gehöri-gen Erläuterungs- und anderen Rescripten, Abschieden, gemeinen Beschei-den und dergleichen, 1337–1806.* 8 vols. Kassel, 1767–1816.

————. *Sammlung von Gesetzen, Verordnungen, Ausschreiben und sonstigen allgemeinen Verfügungen für die kurhessischen Staaten, 1813–1866.* 18 vols. Kassel, 1813–66.

————. *Verhandlungen des kurhessischen Landtages.* Kassel, 1831–66.

————. Statistische Kommission. "Die Bevölkerung Kurhessens und deren Bewegung." *Zeitschrift für hessische Geschichte* 8 (1860): 328–76.

Hildebrand, Bruno. *Statistische Mittheilungen über die volkswirtschaftlichen Zustände Kurhessens.* Berlin, 1853.

Hintzelmann, Paul, ed. *Die Matrikel der Universität Heidelberg.* Vols. 4–7. Heidelberg, 1916.

Höch, Karl, ed. *Schwebda 1750.* Hessische Ortsbeschreibungen, vol. 10. Marburg, 1971.

Hofmeister, Jakob. *Hessische Erinnerungen: Aus den Papieren eines verstor-benen kurhessischen Offiziers.* Kassel, 1882.

Kneschke, Ernst Heinrich. *Neues allgemeines deutsches Adelslexikon.* 9 vols. Leipzig, 1859–70.

Kopp, Ulrich Friedrich, and Wittich, Carl Friedrich. *Handbuch zur Kenntnis der Hessen-Casselschen Landes-Verfassung und Rechte.* 7 vols. Kassel, 1796–1808.

Kössler, Franz, ed. *Register zu den Matrikeln und Inscriptionsbüchern der Universität Giessen, WS 1807/8–WS 1850.* Giessen, 1976.

Kurhessische Landtagsverhandlungen vom Jahre 1816. Kassel, 1816.

"Kurzgefaßte Beschreibung des hochfürstlich hessischen Kadettenkorps zu Kassel." *Hessische Beiträge zur Gelehrsamkeit und Kunst* 2 (1787): 373–89.

Landau, Georg. *Beschreibung des Kurfürstentums Hessen.* Kassel, 1842.

Ledderhose, Conrad Wilhelm. *Kleine Schriften.* 5 vols. Marburg, 1787–89; Eisenach, 1792–95.

————. *Versuch einer Anleitung zum Hessen-Casselischen Kirchenrecht.* Kas-sel, 1785.

Metz, Ludwig. *Statistische Beschreibung des Regierungsbezirks Kassel.* Kassel, 1871.

Meyers Großes Konversationslexikon. 6th ed. Vol. 2. Leipzig, 1905.

Müller, Otto. *Biographische Umrisse der Mitglieder der deutschen konstituierenden Nationalversammlung.* Frankfurt, 1849.

Murhard, Friedrich. *Die kurhessische Verfassungs-Urkunde, erläutert und beleuchtet nach Maßgabe ihrer einzelnen Paragraphen: Ein Handbuch für Landstände, Geschäftsmänner, konstitutionelle Staatsbeamte und Staatsbürger.* 2 vols. Kassel, 1835.

Niekammers landwirtschaftliche Güter-Adreßbücher. Vol. 6, no. 2, *Regierungsbezirk Kassel.* Leipzig, 1929.

Pfaff, Adam. *Das Trauerspiel in Hessen: Ein Beitrag zur Geschichte unserer Tage.* Brunswick, 1851.

Praetorius, Ottfried, and Knöpp, Friedrich, eds. *Die Matrikel der Universität Giessen: Zweiter Teil, 1708–1807.* Neustadt an der Aisch, 1957.

Prussia. *Königlich preußischer Staatsdienst-Kalender für den Regierungsbezirk Kassel.* Kassel, 1867–1914.

Pütter, Johann Stephen. *Über den Unterschied der Stände, besonders des hohen und niederen Adels in Teutschland.* Göttingen, 1795.

Rauer, K. F. *Hand-Matrikel der in sämtlichen Kreisen des preußischen Staats auf Kreis- und Landtagen vertretenen Rittergüter.* Berlin, 1857.

Reimer, Heinrich. *Historisches Ortslexikon für Kurhessen.* Veröffentlichungen der historischen Kommission für Hessen, vol. 14. Marburg, 1926.

Rügemer, Karl, ed. *Kösener Korps-Listen von 1798 bis 1904.* Starnberg, 1905.

Schenck zu Schweinsberg, Wilhelm von. *Uber den niederen Adel und dessen politischen Stellung in Deutschland.* Stuttgart, 1842.

Schenk zu Schweinsberg, Reinhard von. *Mein politisches Glaubens-Bekenntnis.* 15 April 1848.

Schnack, Ingeborg, ed. *Lebensbilder aus Kurhessen und Waldeck, 1830–1930.* 6 vols. Marburg, 1939–58.

Schutzbar genannt Milchling, Winfried von. *Stammtafeln der althessischen Ritterschaft.* Göttingen, 1977.

Seier, Hellmut and Speitkamp, Winfried, eds. *Akten zur Entstehung und Bedeutung des kurhessischen Verfassungsentwurfs von 1815/16.* Marburg, 1985.

Selle, Götz von, ed. *Die Matrikel der Georg August-Universität zu Göttingen, 1734–1837.* Hildesheim, 1937.

Stockhausen, Heinrich Wilhelm von. "Bruchstücke aus dem Leben von Hans Heinrich von Stockhausen von ihm selbst geordnet." 9 vols. In StAM 340 v. Stockhausen, Nr. 115. (Stockhausen Memoirs).

Strieder, Friedrich Wilhelm; Wachler, L.; Justi, K. W.; and Gerland,

Otto. *Grundlage zu einer hessischen Gelehrten, Schriftsteller und Künstler Geschichte vom 16. Jahrhundert bis auf gegenwärtigen Zeiten.* 21 vols. Kassel, 1781–1863.

Trabert, Adam. *Die Todtengräber des kurhessischen Landesrechts: Ein Beitrag zur Zeitgeschichte, insbesondere zur Charakteristik des "national-liberalen" Gothaerthums.* Leipzig, 1868.

Viebahn, Georg von. *Statistik des zollvereinten und nördlichen Deutschlands.* 3 vols. Berlin, 1858–68.

Wagner, Karl, ed. *Register zur Matrikel der Universität Erlangen.* Munich and Leipzig, 1918.

Westphalia, Kingdom of. *Almanach royal de Westphalie.* Kassel, 1810–13.

Woringer, August, ed. *Die Studenten der Universität zu Rinteln.* Leipzig, 1939.

Secondary Literature

a. Works on Hesse-Kassel

Atwood, Rodney. *The Hessians: Mercenaries from Hessen-Kassel in the American Revolution.* Cambridge, 1980.

Bach, Hugo. "Das kurhessische Heer als militärisches und politisches Machtinstrument, 1803–1866." Ph.D. diss., University of Marburg, 1951.

Bähr, Otto. *Das frühere Kurhessen: Ein Geschichtsbild.* Kassel, 1895.

———. *Der hessische Wald: Eine Darstellung der in dem vormaligen Kurfürstenthum Hessen am Walde bestehenden Rechtsverhältnisse.* Kassel, 1879.

Bätzing, Gerhard. *Pfarrergeschichte des Kirchenkreises Wolfhagen von den Anfängen bis 1968.* Veröffentlichungen der historischen Kommission für Hessen, vol. 33. Marburg, 1975.

Baumbach, Arnold von. "Die bäuerlichen Verhältnisse im Regierungs-Bezirk Kassel." *Schriften des Vereins für Sozialpolitik* 22 (1983): 118–25.

Baumbach, August von. *Geschichte der zur althessischen Ritterschaft gehörenden Familie von Baumbach.* Marburg, 1886.

Baumbach, Karl von. "Geschichte der Familie von Baumbach-Nentershausen vom 18. Jahrhundert bis zur Mitte des 19. Jahrhunderts: Kulturell, sozial und wirtschaftlich." Typescript, 1948.

Baumbach, Reinhold von. *Carl Ludwig Friedrich August von Baumbach: Ein Lebensbild.* Rudolstadt, 1910.

Berding, Helmut. *Napoleonische Herrschafts- und Gesellschaftspolitik im Kö-*

nigreich Westfalen, 1807–1813. Kritische Studien zur Geschichtswissenschaft, vol. 7. Göttingen, 1973.

Berge, Otto. "Beiträge zur Geschichte des Bildungswesens und der Akademien unter Landgraf Friedrich II von Hessen-Kassel (1760–85)." *Hessisches Jahrbuch für Landesgeschichte* 4 (1954): 229–61.

Bödeker, Hans Erich. "Strukturen der Aufklärungsgesellschaft in der Residenzstadt Kassel." In *Mentalitäten und Lebensverhältnisse: Beispiele aus der Sozialgeschichte der Neuzeit; Rudolf Vierhaus zum 60. Geburtstag*. Göttingen, 1982.

Bohmbach, Jürgen. "Die Hungersjahre 1846/47 in Oberhessen, eine Darstellung aus den Akten der Regierung Marburg." *Hessisches Jahrbuch für Landesgeschichte* 23 (1973): 333–65.

Both, Wolf von, and Vogel, Hans. *Landgraf Friedrich II von Hessen-Kassel: Ein Fürst der Zopfzeit*. Munich, 1973.

———. *Landgraf Wilhelm VIII von Hessen-Kassel: Ein Fürst der Rokokozeit*. Munich, 1964.

Brunner, Hugo. *Geschichte der Residenzstadt Cassel*. Kassel, 1913.

———. "Rittergüter und Gutsbezirke im ehemaligen Kurhessen." *Jahrbücher für Nationalökonomie und Statistik* 115 (1920): 50–72.

Bullik, Manfred. *Staat und Gesellschaft im hessischen Vormärz: Wahlrecht, Wahlen und öffentliche Meinung in Kurhessen, 1830–1848*. Neue Wirtschaftsgeschichte, vol. 7. Cologne, 1972.

Dascher, Ottfried. *Das Textilgewerbe in Hessen-Kassel vom 16. bis 19. Jahrhundert*. Veröffentlichungen der Historischen Kommission für Hessen und Waldeck, vol. 28, 1. Marburg, 1968.

Demandt, Karl E. *Geschichte des Landes Hessen*. 2d ed. Kassel, 1972.

———. "Die hessischen Landstände im Zeitalter des Frühabsolutismus." *Hessisches Jahrbuch für Landesgeschichte* 15 (1965): 38–108.

Dörnberg-Hausen, Hugo Freiherr von. *Wilhelm von Dörnberg: Ein Kämpfer für Deutschlands Freiheit*. Marburg, 1936.

Dülfer, Kurt. "Fürst und Verwaltung: Grundzüge der hessischen Verwaltungsgeschichte im 16.–19. Jahrhundert." *Hessisches Jahrbuch für Landesgeschichte* 3 (1953): 150–223.

———. *Die Regierung in Kassel, vornehmlich im 19. und 20. Jahrhundert*. Kassel, 1960.

Fox, George Thomas. "Studies in the Rural History of Upper Hesse, 1650–1830." Ph.D. diss., Vanderbilt University, 1976.

Franz, Eckhardt G. "Vormärz und Revolution in den kurhessischen Landen 'am Werra Strom.'" In *Festschrift zum 60. Geburtstag von K. A. Eckhart*, edited by Otto Perst. Marburg, 1961.

Franz, Günther. "Die Agrarische Bewegung im Jahre 1848." *Hessisches Jahrbuch für Landesgeschichte* 9 (1959): 151–78.

Galera, Karl Siegmar von. *Die Riedesel zu Eisenbach: Geschichte des Geschlechts der Riedesel Freiherren zu Eisenbach, Erbmarschälle zu Hessen.* Vols. 5–6. Neustadt an der Aisch, 1961–65.

Gembries, Hellmut. *Verfassungsgeschichtliche Studien zur Recht auf Bildung im deutschen Vormärz: Liberale Staatslehre und parlamentarische Diskussion in Kurhessen.* Quellen und Forschungen zur hessischen Geschichte, vol. 32. Darmstadt and Marburg, 1978.

Gilsa, C. F. von. *Der Oberstallmeister von Gilsa: Ein Lebensbild aus dem achtzehnten und neunzehnten Jahrhundert.* Berlin, 1862.

Gilsa, Otto Freiherr von und zu. *Studien über die wirtschaftliche Entwicklung des ritterschaftlichen Stiftes Kaufungen, besonders im 18. und 19. Jahrhundert.* Marburg, 1927.

Grotefend, W. "Die Ergänzung des hessischen Offizierkorps zur Zeit Landgraf Friedrichs II." *Hessenland* 14 (1900): 2–4.

Heidelbach, Paul. *Deutsche Dichter und Künstler in Escheberg und die Beziehung der Familie von der Malsburg-Escheberg zu den Familien Tieck und Geibel.* Marburg, 1913.

Heitzer, Heinz. *Insurrektionen zwischen Weser und Elbe: Volksbewegungen gegen die französische Fremdherrschaft im Königreich Westfalen.* Berlin, 1959.

Hildebrand, Margarete. *Die Finanzwirtschaft des Königreichs Westfalen.* Marburg, 1925.

Höffner, Harald. "Kurhessens Ministerialvorstände der Verfassungszeit, 1831–1866." Ph.D. diss., University of Giessen, 1981.

Hope, Nicholas Martin. *The Alternative to German Unification: The Anti-Prussian Party in Frankfurt, Nassau, and the Two Hessen, 1859–1867.* Wiesbaden, 1973.

Hueck, Friedrich. "Geschichte der Familie von Buttlar-Elberberg." Typescript, 1950.

Imhof, Arthur E. "Ländliche Familienstrukturen an einem hessischen Beispiel: Heuchelheim, 1690–1900." In *Sozialgeschichte der Familie in der Neuzeit Europas*, edited by Werner Conze. Stuttgart, 1976.

Ingrao, Charles. "Barbarous Strangers: Hessian State and Society during the American Revolution." *American Historical Review* 87 (1982): 954–76.

——. *The Hessian Mercenary State: Ideas, Institutions, and Reform under Frederick II (1760–1785).* Cambridge, 1987.

Iseler, Johannes. *Die Entwicklung eines öffentlichen politischen Lebens in Kurhessen in der Zeit von 1815–1848.* Berlin, 1913.

Jacob, Bruno. "Die hessische Ritterschaft." *Deutsches Adelsblatt* 52 (1934): 352–55.

Kaiser, Werner. *Sylvester Jordan: Seine Staatsauffassung und sein Einfluss auf die kurhessische Verfassungsurkunde vom 5. Januar 1831.* Dresden, 1936.

Kallweit, Adolf. *Die Freimauererei in Hessen-Kassel: Königliche Kunst durch zwei Jahrhunderte von 1743–1965.* Baden-Baden, 1966.

Klein, Thomas, ed. *Hessen-Nassau (einschließlich Vorgänger-Staaten).* Grundriß zur deutschen Verwaltungsgeschichte, vol. 11. Marburg, 1979.

Knetsch, Carl. "Von der hessischen Ritterschaft." *Hessische Chronik* 9 (1918): 65–75.

Knobel, Enno. *Die hessische Rechtspartei: Konservative Opposition gegen das Bismarckreich.* Marburg, 1975.

Knoblauch, Karl Damian von. *Kurzgefaßte Geschichte der Familie Knoblauch von und zu Hatzbach.* Marburg, 1890.

Kolbe, Wilhelm. *Zur Geschichte der Freimaurerei in Kassel.* Berlin, 1883.

Kühn, Joachim. *Das Ende einer Dynastie: Kurhessische Hofgeschichten von 1821 bis 1866.* Berlin, 1929.

Kuhring, Otto. *Das Schicksal der westfälischen Domänenkäufer in Kurhessen.* Kassel, 1913.

Lerch, Hans. *Hessische Agrargeschichte des 17. und 18. Jahrhunderts.* Hersfeld, 1926.

Lichtner, Adolf. *Landesherr und Stände in Hessen-Cassel, 1797–1821.* Göttingen, 1913.

Losch, Philipp. *Die Abgeordneten der kurhessischen Ständeversammlungen von 1830 bis 1866.* Marburg, 1909.

———. *Geschichte des Kurfürstentums Hessen, 1803 bis 1866.* Marburg, 1922; reprint ed., Kassel, 1972.

———. *Kurfürst Wilhelm I, Landgraf von Hessen: Ein Fürstenbild aus der Zopfzeit.* Marburg, 1923.

———. *Der letzte deutsche Kurfürst: Friedrich Wilhelm I von Hessen.* Marburg, 1937.

Lynker, Karl. *Geschichte der Insurrectionen wider das westfälischen Gouvernement: Beitrag zur Geschichte des deutschen Freiheitskrieges.* Kassel, 1857.

Mahraun, Hans. *Die Gemeinheitsteilungsordnung für den Regierungsbezirk Kassel.* Marburg, 1899.

Malsburg, Otto von der. "Aufzeichnungen aus der Familiengeschichte derer von der Malsburg." Typescript, n.d.

Maurer, Wilhelm. *Aufklärung, Idealismus und Restauration: Studien zur Kirchen- und Geistesgeschichte in besondere Beziehung auf Kurhessen, 1780–1850.* 2 vols. Giessen, 1930.

Metz, Wolfgang. "Das Eindringen des Bürgertums in die hessische Zentralverwaltung." Ph.D. diss., University of Göttingen, 1947.

———. "Zur sozialgeschichte des Beamtentums in der Zentralverwaltung der Landgrafschaft Hessen-Kassel bis zum 18. Jahrhundert." *Zeitschrift des Vereins für hessische Geschichte und Landeskunde* 67 (1956): 138-48.

Möker, Ulrich. "Entwicklungstheorie und geschichtliche Wirtschaft: Makroökonomische Erklärungen wirtschaftlicher Zustände und Entwicklungen der Landgrafschaft Hessen-Kassel vom 16. bis zum 19. Jahrhundert." Ph.D. diss., University of Marburg, 1971.

———. *Nordhessen im Zeitalter der industriellen Revolution*. Neue Wirtschaftsgeschichte, vol. 13. Cologne, 1977.

Müller, Otto. "Studien zur Entstehungsgeschichte der kurhessischen Verfassung vom 5. Januar 1831." *Zeitschrift für Hessische Geschichte* 59/60 (1934): 169-236.

Pappenheim, Gustav Freiherr Rabe von. "Aus der Studienzeit eines hessischen Edelmannes in den Jahren 1767–1770." *Hessenland* 19 (1905): 267–70, 281–84.

Poppe, Karl. *Geschichte des Geschlechtes derer von und zu Schachten*. Göttingen, 1933.

Preser, Carl. "Zur Geschichte der Verkoppelung in Kurhessen." *Hessenland* 9 (1895): 158-59.

Radbruch, Eberhard. "Offiziere im Konflikt um Gehorsamkeit und Gewissen: Die Haltung des kurhessischen Offizierkorps im Verfassungskonflikt von 1850." *Geschichte in Wissenschaft und Unterricht* 19 (1968): 137-45.

Rogge-Ludwig, W. *Karl Müldner von Mülnheim: General-Lieutenant und General-Adjutant des Kurfürsten Wilhelm II von Hessen*. Kassel, 1885.

Rommel, Hans-Georg. "Der kurhessische Verfassungskonflikt 1859–1862: Ein Beitrag zum Problem des bürgerlichen Liberalismus in Deutschland." Ph.D. diss., University of Marburg, 1950.

Rudloff, Hans L. "Beiträge zur Geschichte der Bauernbefreiung und bäuerlichen Grundentlastung in Kurhessen." *Jahrbücher für Nationalökonomie und Statistik* 105 (1915): 802–10.

———. "Die gutsherrlich-bäuerlichen Verhältnisse in Kurhessen." *Schmollers Jahrbuch* 41 (1917): 1233–70.

Rusche, Fritz. "Kurhessen in der bürgerlichen und sozialen Bewegungen der Jahre 1848 und 1849." Ph.D. diss., University of Marburg, 1921.

Sakai, Eihachiro. *Der kurhessische Bauer im 19. Jahrhundert und die Grundlastenablösung*. Hessische Forschungen zur geschichtlichen Landes- und Volkskunde, vol. 7. Melsungen, 1967.

Sauer, Joseph. *Die Finanzgeschäfte der Landgrafen von Hessen-Kassel: Ein Beitrag zur Geschichte des kurhessischen Hausschatzes und zur Entwicklungsgeschichte des Hauses Rothschild*. Fulda, 1930.

Scharlau, Kurt. "Landeskulturgesetzgebung und Landeskulturentwicklung im ehemaligen Kurhessen seit dem 16. Jahrhundert." *Zeitschrift für Agrargeschichte und Agrarsoziologie* 1 (1953): 126-45.

Schenk zu Schweinsberg, Kurt. "Die Althessische Ritterschaft und das Stift Kaufungen in ihrer wechselseitigen Beziehung, nach den erlassenen Vorschriften auszugsweise zusammengestellt und beleuchtet." Typescript, 1920.

Scherer, Carl. "Zur Geschichte des Dörnbergischen Aufstandes im Jahre 1809." *Historische Zeitschrift* 84 (1900): 257–66.

Schleicher, A. "Das kurhessische Landescredit-Institut und seine dreissigjährige Wirksamkeit." *Jahrbücher für Nationalökonomie und Statistik* 1 (1863): 412–37.

Schmitt, Hans A. "Prussia's Last Fling: The Annexation of Hanover, Hesse, Frankfurt, and Nassau, June 15–October 8, 1866." *Central European History* 8 (1975): 316–47.

Schunder, Friedrich. *Die von Löwenstein: Geschichte einer hessischen Familie.* 3 vols. Lübeck, 1955.

Seier, Hellmut. *Sylvester Jordan und die kurhessische Verfassung von 1831.* Marburg, 1981.

———. "Zur Entstehung und Bedeutung der kurhessischen Verfassung von 1831." In *Der Verfassungsstaat als Bürge des Rechtfriedens*, edited by Walter Heinemeyer. Marburg, 1982.

Speitkamp, Winfried. *Restauration als Transformation: Untersuchungen zur kurhessischen Verfassungsgeschichte 1813–1830.* Quellen und Forschungen zur hessischen Geschichte, vol. 67. Darmstadt and Marburg, 1986.

Stahl, Otto. *Denkschrift über Fideikommißrecht und Fideikommißwesen im Gebiet des ehemaligen Kurhessen.* Kassel, 1902.

Stöckl, Rudolf. "Adam Trabert und die demokratisch-republikanische Bestrebungen in Kurhessen, 1848–1868." Ph.D. diss., University of Marburg, 1958.

Strieder, Friedrich Wilhelm. *Grundlage zur Militär-Geschichte des landgräflich-hessischen Corps.* Kassel, 1798.

Tapp, Alfred. *Hanau im Vormärz und in der Revolution von 1848–1849.* Hanau, 1976.

Wagner, Alexander. *Die Waldungen des ehemaligen Kurfürstenthums Hessen.* 2 vols. Hanover, 1886.

Wegner, Karl-Hermann. "Landgraf Friedrich II: Ein Regent der Aufklärung." In *Aufklärung und Klassizismus in Hessen-Kassel unter Landgraf Friedrich II, 1760–1785.* Kassel, 1979.

Wippermann, Carl Wilhelm. *Kurhessen seit dem Freiheitskriege.* Kassel, 1850.

Wolff, Wilhelm. *Die Entwicklung des Unterrichtswesens in Hessen-Kassel vom 8. bis zum 19. Jahrhundert*. Kassel, 1911.

———. *Die Säkularisierung und Verwendung der Stifts- und Klostergüter in Hessen-Kassel unter Philipp dem Großmütigen und Wilhelm IV*. Gotha, 1913.

b. General Literature

Abel, Wilhelm. *Agrarkrisen und Agrarkonjunktur: Eine Geschichte der Land- und Ernährungswirtschaft Mitteleuropas seit dem hohen Mittelalter*. 2d ed. Hamburg, 1966.

———. *Geschichte der deutschen Landwirtschaft vom frühen Mittelalter bis zum 19. Jahrhundert*. 2d ed. Deutsche Agrargeschichte, vol. 2. Stuttgart, 1967.

Bechtolsheim, Hartmann von. *Des Heiligen Römischen Reiches unmittelbarfreie Ritterschaft zu Franken, Ort Steigerwald, im 17. und 18. Jahrhundert: Ein Beitrag zur Verfassungs- und Gesellschaftsgeschichte des reichsunmittelbaren Adels*. 2 vols. Würzburg, 1972.

Berdahl, Robert M. "The Concept of *Stand* as a Reflection of Social Change in Germany before 1848." Paper presented at the ninety-first annual meeting of the American Historical Association, Washington, D.C., 29 December 1976.

———. "Prussian Aristocracy and Conservative Ideology: A Methodological Examination." *Social Science Information* 15 (1976): 583–99.

———. "The *Stände* and the Origins of Conservativism in Prussia." *Eighteenth Century Studies* 6 (1973): 298–321.

Bleek, Wilhelm. *Von der Kameralausbildung zum Juristenprivileg: Studium, Prüfung und Ausbildung der höheren Beamten des allgemeinen Verwaltungsdienstes in Deutschland im 18. und 19. Jahrhundert*. Berlin, 1972.

Blum, Jerome. *The End of the Old Order in Rural Europe*. Princeton, 1978.

Bramsted, Ernest K. *Aristocracy and the Middle Classes in Germany: Social Types in German Literature, 1830–1900*. 2d ed. Chicago, 1964.

Brandt, Hartwig. *Landständische Repräsentation im deutschen Vormärz: Politisches Denken im Einflußfeld des monarchischen Prinzips*. Neuwied and Berlin, 1968.

Brinkmann, Carl. "Die Aristokratie im kapitalistischen Zeitalter." *Grundriss der Sozialökonomik*. 9 (1926): 1–69.

Brunner, Otto. *Adeliges Landleben und europäischer Geist*. Salzburg, 1949.

Büsch, Otto. *Militärsystem und Sozialleben im alten Preussen, 1713–1807: Die Anfänge der sozialen Militarisierung der preussisch-deutschen Gesellschaft*. Veröffentlichungen der Berliner Historischen Kommission, vol. 7. Berlin, 1962.

SOURCES AND BIBLIOGRAPHY

Bush, Michael. *Noble Privilege*. The European Nobility, vol. 1. New York, 1983.

Carsten, F. L. *Princes and Parliaments in Germany: From the Fifteenth to the Eighteenth Centuries*. Oxford, 1959.

Cecil, Lamar. "The Creation of Nobles in Prussia, 1871–1918." *American Historical Review* 75 (1970): 757–95.

———. *The German Diplomatic Service, 1871–1914*. Princeton, 1976.

Conrad, J. "Agrarstatistischen Untersuchungen." *Jahrbücher für Nationalökonomie und Statistik*, 3d ser., 2 (1891): 817–44.

———. "Die Latifundien im preußischen Osten." *Jahrbücher für Nationalökonomie und Statistik*, 2d ser., 16 (1888): 121–70.

Cooper, J. P. "Patterns of Inheritance and Settlement by Great Landowners from the Fifteenth to the Eighteenth Centuries." In *Family and Inheritance: Rural Society in Western Europe*, edited by Jack Goody, Joan Thirsk, and E. P. Thompson. Cambridge, 1976.

Davis, James C. *The Decline of the Venetian Nobility as a Ruling Class*. Baltimore, 1962.

Demeter, Karl. *Das deutsche Offizierkorps in Gesellschaft und Staat, 1650–1945*. 4th ed. Frankfurt, 1965.

Deml, Walter. "Der Adel im Königreich Bayern, 1808–1817." Paper presented to conference "Der Adel im bürgerlichen Zeitalter" at Bad Homburg, Germany, 30 September–2 October 1982.

Dülmen, Richard van. *Der Geheimbund der Illuminaten: Darstellung, Analyse, Dokumentation*. Stuttgart, 1975.

Eckardt, Hans Wilhelm. *Herrschaftliche Jagd, bäuerliche Not und bürgerliche Kritik: Zur Geschichte der fürstlich und adligen Jagdprivilegien, vornehmlich im südwestdeutschen Raum*. Veröffentlichungen des Max-Planck-Instituts für Geschichte, vol. 48. Göttingen, 1976.

Eltz, Erwein H. *Die Modernisierung einer Standesherrschaft: Karl Egon III und das Haus Fürstenberg in den Jahren nach 1848/49*. Sigmaringen, 1980.

Forster, Robert. *The House of Saulx-Tavanes: Versailles and Burgundy, 1700–1830*. Baltimore, 1971.

———. *The Nobility of Toulouse in the Eighteenth Century*. Baltimore, 1960.

———. "Seigneurs and Their Agents." In *Vom Ancien Régime zur Französischen Revolution*, edited by Ernst Hinrichs, Eberhard Schmitt, and Rudolf Vierhaus. Göttingen, 1978.

———, and Litchfield, R. Burr. "Four Nobilities of the Old Regime." *Comparative Studies in Society and History* 7 (1965): 324–32.

Forstmeier, Friedrich, and Meier-Welcker, Hans, eds. *Handbuch zur deutschen Militärgeschichte, 1648–1939*. 9 vols. Munich, 1964–79.

283

Gillis, John. "Aristocracy and Bureaucracy in Nineteenth Century Prussia."*Past and Present* 41 (1968): 105–29.

―――. *The Prussian Bureaucracy in Crisis, 1840 to 1860: Origins of an Administrative Ethos.* Stanford, 1971.

Glas-Hochstettler, Thomas J. "The Imperial Knights in Post-Westphalian Mainz: A Case Study of Corporatism in the Old Reich." *Central European History* 11 (1978): 131–49.

Glaser, Hubert, ed. *Krone und Verfassung: König Max I. Joseph und der neue Staat: Beiträge zur Bayerischen Geschichte und Kunst, 1799–1825.* 2 vols. Munich, 1980.

Gollwitzer, Heinz. *Die Standesherren: Die politische und gesellschaftliche Stellung der Mediatisierten, 1815–1918.* Göttingen, 1964.

Goodwin, Albert, ed. *The European Nobility in the Eighteenth Century: Studies of the Nobilities of the Major European States in the Pre-Reform Era.* London, 1953; reprint ed. New York, 1967.

Görlitz, Walter. *Die Junker: Adel und Bauer im deutschen Osten.* 3d ed. Limburg, 1964.

Hamerow, Theodore S. *Restoration, Revolution, Reaction: Economics and Politics in Germany, 1815–1871.* Princeton, 1958.

Heffter, Heinrich. *Die deutsche Selbstverwaltung im 19. Jahrhundert: Geschichte der Ideen und Institutionen.* 2d ed. Stuttgart, 1969.

Heisch, Günter. *Privilegien und Recht von 1775 bis zur Gegenwart.* Geschichte der Schleswig-Holsteinischen Ritterschaft, vol. 4. Neumünster, 1966.

Hellstern, Dieter. *Der Ritterkanton Neckar-Schwarzwald, 1560–1805: Untersuchungen über die Korporationsverfassung, die Funktionen des Ritterkantons und die Mitgliedsfamilien.* Tübingen, 1971.

Henning, Friedrich-Wilhelm. *Abgaben und Dienste der Bauern im 18. Jahrhundert.* Quellen und Forschungen zur Agrargeschichte, vol. 21. Stuttgart, 1969.

―――. "Die Entwicklung des Grundstücksverkehrs vom ausgehenden 18. Jahrhundert bis gegen Ende des 19. Jahrhunderts." In *Wissenschaft und Kodifikation des Privatrechts im 19. Jahrhundert.* Vol. 3, *Die rechtliche und wirtschaftliche Entwicklung des Grundeigentums und Grundkredits,* edited by Helmut Coing and Walter Wilhelm. Frankfurt, 1976.

―――. "Die Verschuldung der Bodeneigentümer in Norddeutschland im ausgehenden 18. und in den ersten zwei Dritteln des 19. Jahrhunderts." In *Wissenschaft und Kodifikation des Privatrechts im 19. Jahrhundert.* Vol. 3, *Die rechtliche und wirtschaftliche Entwicklung des Grundeigentums und Grundkredits,* edited by Helmut Coing and Walter Wilhelm. Frankfurt, 1976.

Henry, Louis. *Anciennes familles genevoises: Etude demographique, XVIe–XXe siècle*. Paris, 1956.

———. *Manuel de demographie historique*. 2d ed. Paris. 1970.

Hippel, Wolfgang von. *Die Bauerbefreiung im Königreich Württemberg*. 2 vols. Forschungen zur deutschen Sozialgeschichte, vol. 1. Boppard am Rhein, 1977.

Hofmann, Hanns Hubertus. *Adelige Herrschaft und souveräner Staat: Studien über Staat und Gesellschaft in Franken und Bayern im 18. und 19. Jahrhundert*.Studien zur bayerischen Verfassungs- und Sozialgeschichte, vol. 2. Munich, 1962.

Höhn, Reinhard. *Verfassungskampf und Heereseid: Der Kampf des Bürgertums um das Heer*. Leipzig, 1938.

Hollingsworth, T. H. "A Demographic Study of the British Ducal Families." In *Population in History*, edited by D. V. Glass and D.E.C. Eversly. London: Edward Arnold, 1965.

———. "The Demography of the British Peerage." Supplement to *Population Studies* 18 (1964).

Jarausch, Konrad. *Students, Society, and Politics in Imperial Germany: The Rise of Academic Illiberalism*. Princeton, 1982.

Johnson, Hubert C. *Frederick the Great and His Officials*. New Haven, 1975.

Knodel, John. "From Natural Fertility to Family Limitation: The Onset of Fertility Transition in a Sample of German Villages." *Demography* 4 (1979): 493–521.

Köllmann, Wolfgang, ed. *Quellen zur Bevölkerungs-, Sozial- und Wirtschaftsstatistik Deutschlands, 1815–1871*. Vol. 1, *Quellen zur Bevölkerungsstatistik Deutschlands, 1815–1871*. Boppard, 1981.

Kollmer, Gerd. *Die schwäbische Reichsritterschaft zwischen Westfälischen Frieden und Reichsdeputationshauptschluß: Untersuchung zur wirtschaftlichen und sozialen Lage der Reichsritterschaft in den Ritterkantonen Neckar-Schwarzwald und Kocher*. Schriften zur südwestdeutschen Landeskunde, vol. 17. Stuttgart, 1979.

Körber, Gerhard. *Das Kreditwesen des ritterschaftlichen Grundbesitzes in Mecklenburg nach dem Siebenjährigen Kriege bis zur Gründung des ritterschaftlichen Kreditvereins im Jahre 1819*. Schwerin, 1929.

Koselleck, Reinhard. *Preußen zwischen Reform und Revolution: Allgemeines Landrecht, Verwaltung und soziale Bewegung von 1791 bis 1848*. 2d ed. Industrielle Welt, vol. 7. Stuttgart, 1975.

Krieger, Leonard. *The German Idea of Freedom: History of a Political Tradition*. Chicago, 1957.

Lampe, Joachim. *Aristokratie, Hofadel und Staatspatriziat in Kurhannover:*

Die Lebenskreise der höheren Beamten an den kurhannoverischen Zentral- und Hofbehörden, 1714–1760. 2 vols. Göttingen, 1963.

Lévy, Claude, and Henry, Louis. "Ducs et pairs sous l'ancien régime: Caractéristiques demographiques d'une caste." *Population* 15 (1960): 807–27.

Litchfield, R. Burr. "Demographic Characteristics of Florentine Patrician Families, Sixteenth to Nineteenth Centuries." *Journal of Economic History* 29 (1969): 191–205.

Livi-Bacci, Massimo. *A History of Italian Fertility during the Last Two Centuries.* Princeton, 1977.

Loss, Carl Rose. "*Status in Statu*: The Concept of Estate in the Organization of German Political Life." Ph.D. diss., Cornell University, 1970.

Luetge, Friedrich. *Geschichte der deutschen Agrarverfassung.* Deutsche Agrargeschichte, vol. 3. Stuttgart, 1963.

―――. *Die mitteldeutsche Grundherrschaft und ihre Auflösung.* 2d ed. Stuttgart, 1957.

Martiny, Fritz. *Die Adelsfrage in Preußen vor 1806 als politisches und soziales Problem: Erläutert am Beispiele des kurmärkischen Adels.* Stuttgart, 1938.

Meyer, Jean. *La noblesse bretonne au XVIIIe siècle.* 2 vols. Paris, 1966.

―――. *Noblesses et pouvoirs dans l'europe d'ancien régime.* Paris, 1973.

―――. "La noblesse parlementaire bretonne." In *Vom Ancien Regime zur Französischen Revolution*, edited by Ernst Hinrichs, Eberhard Schmitt, and Rudolf Vierhaus. Göttingen, 1978.

McClelland, Charles E. "The Aristocracy and University Reform in Eighteenth-Century Germany." In *Schooling and Society: Studies in the History of Education*, edited by Lawrence Stone. Baltimore, 1976.

―――. *State, Society, and University in Germany, 1700–1914.* Cambridge, 1980.

Mies, Horst. *Die preußische Verwaltung des Regierungsbezirks Marienwerder (1830–1870).* Cologne, 1972.

Mingay, G. E. *English Landed Society in the Eighteenth Century.* London, 1963.

Mitterauer, Michael. "Zur Frage des Heiratsverhaltens im österreichischen Adel." In *Beiträge zur neueren Geschichte Österreichs: Festschrift für Adam Wandruszka*, edited by Heinrich Fichtenau and Erich Zöllner. Vienna, 1974.

Muncy, Lysbeth Walker. *The Junker in the Prussian Administration under William II.* Providence, 1944; reprint ed. New York, 1970.

―――. "The Prussian *Landräte* in the Last Years of the Monarchy: A

Case Study of Pomerania and the Rhineland in 1890–1918." *Central European History* 6 (1973): 299–338.

Nell, Adelheid von. "Die Entwicklung der generativen Strukturen bürgerlicher und bäuerlicher Familien von 1750 bis zur Gegenwart." Ph.D. diss., University of Bochum, 1973.

Neth, Ulrich. *Standesherren und liberalen Bewegung: Der Kampf des württembergischen standesherrlichen Adels um seine Rechtsstellung in der zweiten Hälfte des 19. Jahrhunderts.* Schriften zur südwestdeutschen Landeskunde, vol. 9. Stuttgart, 1970.

Oertzen, Friedrich Wilhelm von. *Junker: Preußischer Adel im Jahrhundert des Liberalismus.* Oldenburg, 1955.

Poten, Bernhard von. *Geschichte des Militär-Erziehungs- und Bildungswesens in den Landen deutscher Zunge.* 5 vols. Monumenta Germaniae Paedagogica. Berlin, 1889–99.

Preradovich, Nikolaus von. *Die Führungsschichten in Österreich und Preußen (1804–1918).* Veröffentlichungen des Instituts für Europäische Geschichte Mainz, vol. 11. Wiesbaden, 1955.

Press, Volker. "Landtage im Alten Reich und im Deutschen Bund: Voraussetzungen ständischer und konstitutioneller Entwicklungen 1750–1830." *Zeitschrift für Württembergische Landesgeschichte* 39 (1980): 100–140.

Puhle, Hans-Jürgen. *Agrarische Interessenpolitik und preußischer Konservatismus im Wilhelminischen Reich, 1893–1914.* 2d ed. Bonn–Bad Godesberg, 1975.

Redlich, Fritz. *Der Unternehmer: Wirtschafts- und sozialgeschichtliche Studien.* Göttingen, 1964.

Reif, Heinz. " 'Erhaltung adligen Stamms und Namens': Adelsfamilie und Statussicherung im Münsterland, 1770–1914." In *Studien zur Geschichte der Familie in Deutschland und Frankreich von 16. bis zum 20. Jahrhundert,* edited by Neithard Bulst, Joseph Goy, and Jochen Hoock. Göttingen, 1981.

———. *Westfälischer Adel, 1770–1860: Vom Herrschaftsstand zur regionalen Elite.* Kritische Studien zur Geschichtswissenschaft, vol. 35. Göttingen, 1979.

Richard, Guy. *Noblesse d'affaires au XVIIIe siècle.* Paris, 1974.

Ritter, Emil. *Radowitz: Ein katholischer Staatsmann in Preussen.* Cologne, 1948.

Rosenberg, Hans. *Bureaucracy, Aristocracy, and Autocracy: The Prussian Experience, 1660–1815.* Cambridge, Mass., 1958.

———. "Die Pseudodemokratisierung der Rittergutsbesitzerklasse." In *Moderne deutsche Sozialgeschichte,* edited by Hans-Ulrich Wehler. Neue Wissenschaftliche Bibliothek, vol. 10. Cologne, 1966.

Rössler, Hellmuth, ed. *Deutscher Adel.* 2 vols. Darmstadt, 1965.

Rumschöttl, Hermann. *Das bayerische Offizierkorps, 1866–1914.* Beiträge zu einer historischen Strukturanalyse Bayerns im Industriezeitalter, vol. 9. Berlin, 1973.

Schärl, Walter. *Die Zusammensetzung der bayerischen Beamtenschaft von 1806 bis 1918.* Kallmünz, 1955.

Schissler, Hanna. *Preußische Agrargesellschaft im Wandel: Wirtschaftliche, gesellschaftliche und politische Transformationsprozesse von 1763 bis 1847.* Kritische Studien zur Geschichtswissenschaft, vol. 33. Göttingen, 1978.

Schultze, Johanna. *Die Auseinandersetzung zwischen Adel und Bürgertum in deutschen Zeitschriften der letzten drei Jahrzehnte des 18. Jahrhunderts (1773–1806).* Berlin, 1925.

Seetzen, U. J. "Ueber dem Handel mit Landgüter." *Annalen der niedersächsischen Landwirtschaft* 3 (1801): 85–101.

Spring, David. *The English Landed Estate in the Nineteenth Century.* Baltimore, 1963.

———, ed. *European Landed Elites in the Nineteenth Century.* Baltimore, 1977.

Stekl, Hannes. *Österreichs Aristokratie im Vormärz: Herrschaftsstil und Lebensformen der Fürstenhäuser Liechtenstein und Schwarzenberg.* Munich, 1973.

Stetten, Wolfgang von. *Die Rechtsstellung der unmittelbaren freien Reichsritterschaft, ihrer Mediatisierung und ihre Stellung in den neuen Landen: Dargestellt am fränkischen Kanton Odenwald.* Forschungen aus Württembergisch Franken, vol. 8. Schwäbisch Hall, 1973.

Stone, Lawrence. *The Crisis of the Aristocracy, 1558–1641.* London, 1965.

———. *The Family, Sex and Marriage in England, 1500–1800.* New York, 1977.

Thompson, F.M.L. *English Landed Society in the Nineteenth Century.* London, 1963.

Toennies, Ferdinand. "Deutscher Adel im 19. Jahrhundert." *Neue Rundschau* 23 (1912): 1041–63.

Treitschke, Heinrich von. *Deutsche Geschichte im neunzehnten Jahrhundert.* 5 vols. Leipzig, 1928.

Trumbach, Randolph. *The Rise of the Egalitarian Family: Aristocratic Kinship and Domestic Relations in Eighteenth-Century England.* Studies in Social Discontinuity. New York, 1978.

Ucke, Arnold. *Die Agrarkrisis in Preußen während der zwanziger Jahren dieses Jahrhunderts.* Halle, 1888.

Van de Walle, Etienne, and Knodel, John. "Europe's Fertility Transition: New Evidence and Lessons for Today's Developing World." *Population Bulletin* 34 (1980): 3–43.

Vierhaus, Rudolf, ed. *Der Adel vor der Revolution*. Göttingen, 1971.

———. "Vom aufgeklärten Absolutismus zum monarchischen Konstitutionalismus: Der deutsche Adel im Spannungsfeld von Revolution, Reform und Restauration (1789–1848)." In *Legitimationskrisen des deutschen Adels, 1200–1900*, edited by Peter Uwe Hohendahl and Paul Michael Lützeler. Stuttgart, 1979.

Weber, Hartmut. *Die Fürsten von Hohenlohe im Vormärz: Politische und soziale Verhaltensweise württembergischer Standesherren in der ersten Hälfte des 19. Jahrhunderts*. Forschungen aus Württembergisch Franken, vol. 11. Schwäbisch Hall, 1977.

Weiss, Eberhard. "Ergebnisse eines Vergleichs der grundherrschaftlichen Strukturen Deutschlands und Frankreichs vom 13. bis zum Ausgang des 18. Jahrhunderts." *Vierteljahrschrift für Sozial- und Wirtschaftsgeschichte* 57 (1970): 1–14.

Weyermann, Moritz. *Zur Geschichte des Immobiliarkreditwesens in Preußen mit besonderer Nutzanwendung auf die Theorie von Bodenverschuldung* Karlsruhe, 1910.

Winkel, Harald. *Die Ablösungskapitalien aus der Bauernbefreiung in West- und Süddeutschland: Höhe und Verwendung bei Standes- und Grundherren*. Quellen und Forschungen zur Agrargeschichte, vol. 19. Stuttgart, 1968.

Wittich, Werner. "Epochen der deutschen Agrargeschichte." *Grundriß der Sozialökonomik* 7 (1922): 1–26.

———. *Die Grundherrschaft in Nordwestdeutschland*. Leipzig, 1896.

Wrigley, E. A. "Family Limitation in Pre-industrial England." *Economic History Review* 19 (1966): 82–109.

Ziekursch, Johannes. *Hundert Jahre schlesischer Agrargeschichte: Vom Hubertusberger Frieden bis zum Abschluß der Bauernbefreiung*. 2d ed. Breslau, 1927.

Zorn, Wolfgang. "Unternehmer und Aristokratie in Deutschland." *Tradition* 8 (1963): 241–54.

INDEX

administration of estates, 57, 103–106; by nobles, 114–15

adoption, 63

Agrarian League, 3, 255

Alix, Jacob, 85n59

allodification, 65, 70. *See also* fiefs

Althaus, Moritz Wilhelm von, 176n72, 261

Amelunxen family, 20

Andrée, Georg Wilhelm, 25, 263

anti-Semitism, 241–43

Apell, Christian Friedrich von, 261

army, Hessian: branches of service, 170; elite regiments; 170; rental to foreign powers, 11–12; size, 11, 203. *See also* officer corps

artisans, 15, 203

Austria: nobility, 38, 40, 42; relations with Hesse-Kassel, 16

Austro-Prussian War, 248

bankruptcy proceedings, 78–79, 81–83, 84. *See also* indebtedness

banks, 79. *See also* Landeskreditkasse

Bardeleben, Friedrich Wilhelm von, 198

Baumbach-Amönau, Carl von (1777–1847), 205

Baumbach-Amönau, Johann von (1748–1804), 178

Baumbach-Amönau, Wilhelm von (1779–1849), 178

Baumbach-Freudenthal family, 34n51, 87

Baumbach-Freudenthal, Carl Friedrich von (1777–1825), 152

Baumbach-Gemünden, Arnold von (1779–1849), 227n103

Baumbach-Gilserhof family, 34n51, 87

Baumbach-Gilserhof, Amalia von (1808–?), 45–46

Baumbach-Gilserhof, Carl von (1773–1848), 46, 148n10

Baumbach-Gilserhof, Friedrich von (1801–70), 46

Baumbach-Kirchheim family, 90, 121

Baumbach-Kirchheim, Ernst von (1804–74), 189, 242–43

Baumbach-Kirchheim, Hermann von (1809–74), 189

Baumbach-Kirchheim, Ludwig von (1799–1883), 227, 228, 231, 233–34, 236, 243

Baumbach-Kirchheim, Moritz von (1789–1871), 184, 228–32, 233, 243

Baumbach-Kirchheim, Wilhelm Lebrecht von (1757–1826), 227n103

Baumbach-Lenderscheid family, 62n47

Baumbach-Lenderscheid, Adolf von (1742–66), 148

Baumbach-Lenderscheid, Carl Friedrich von (1780–1844), 156, 157

Baumbach-Lenderscheid, Caroline von (1782–1814), 206

Baumbach-Lenderscheid, Eduard von (1814–53), 189

Baumbach-Lenderscheid, Ernestine von (1789–1801), 48–49

Baumbach-Lenderscheid, Franz Ludwig von (1753–1817), 157

Baumbach-Lenderscheid, Friederike von (1779–1847), 48–49

Baumbach-Lenderscheid, Ludwig von (1779–1861), 242

Baumbach-Lenderscheid, Sophie von (1750–1809), 206

Baumbach-Lenderscheid, Wilhelm von (1741–1808), 176n73, 177, 179, 201

Baumbach-Nassenerfurth, Carl Ludwig von (1772–1844), 47, 141, 143

Baumbach-Nassenerfurth, Ernst von (1821–70), 154

Baumbach-Nassenerfurth, Henriette von (?–1802), 141

Baumbach-Nassenerfurth, Reinhold von (1822–93), 153–54

Baumbach-Nentershausen family, 87, 90, 139, 141; dues and services to, 116, 120n45, 122, 126; forest income of, 136, 139, 141

Library of Congress Cataloging-in-Publication Data

Pedlow, Gregory W., 1949–
The survival of the Hessian nobility, 1770–1870.

Bibliography: p.   Includes index.
1. Hesse (Germany)—Nobility—History—19th century.
2. Hesse (Germany)—Nobility—Economic conditions.
I. Title.
HT653.G4P44 1988   305.5'223'094341   87–25720
ISBN 0–691–05503–3 (alk. paper)